CliffsNotes®
GRE® General Test with CD-ROM

CliffsNotes®

GRE® General Test
with CD-ROM

A BTPS Testing Project

Contributing Authors

Ed Kohn, M.S.

Barbara Swovelin, M.A.

David A. Kay, M.S.

Karen Elizabeth Lafferty, M.A.

Joy Mondragon-Gilmore, M.S.

Consultants

Ron Podrasky, M.A.

Garth Sundem, M.S.

Angel Acosta, B.A.

WILEY

John Wiley & Sons, Inc.

About the Author

BTPS Testing has presented test preparation workshops at the California State Universities for over 35 years. The faculty at BTPS Testing have authored more than 30 national best-selling test preparation books including CliffsNotes preparation guides for the GMAT, CSET, SAT, CBEST, PPST, RICA and ACT. Each year the authors of this study guide conduct lectures to thousands of students preparing for the GRE and many other graduate-level exams.

Editorial

Acquisitions Editor: Greg Tubach

Project Editor: Christina Stambaugh

Technical Editors: Jane Burstein, David Herzog, Tom Page

Composition

Proofreader: Jacqui Brownstein

John Wiley & Sons, Inc., Composition Services

CliffsNotes® GRE® General Test with CD-ROM

Published by:
John Wiley & Sons, Inc.
111 River Street
Hoboken, NJ 07030-5774
www.wiley.com

Copyright © 2012 John Wiley & Sons, Inc., Hoboken, NJ

Published by John Wiley & Sons, Inc., Hoboken, NJ
Published simultaneously in Canada

Library of Congress Control Number: 2011935812
ISBN: 978-1-118-05760-5 (pbk)
ISBN: 978-1-118-10653-2; 978-1-118-10651-8; 978-1-118-10652-5 (ebk)

Printed in the United States of America
10 9 8 7 6 5 4 3 2 1

For general information on our other products and services or to obtain technical support, please contact our Customer Care Department within the U.S. at (877) 762-2974, outside the U.S. at (317) 572-3993, or fax (317) 572-4002.

John Wiley & Sons, Inc., also publishes its books in a variety of electronic formats and by print-on-demand. Not all content that is available in standard print versions of this book may appear or be packaged in all book formats. If you have purchased a version of this book that did not include media that is referenced by or accompanies a standard print version, you may request this media by visiting http://booksupport.wiley.com. For more information about Wiley products, visit us at www.wiley.com.

This book is dedicated to the memory of

Jerry Bobrow, Ph.D.

Educator and Author

His wisdom, insight, and humor continue to give strength to those who knew him.

Table of Contents

PART II: REVIEW OF EXAM AREAS

PART III: BASIC MATH REVIEW

PART IV: FULL-LENGTH PRACTICE TEST

Preface

In keeping with the fine tradition of CliffsNotes, this guide was developed by leading experts in the field of test preparation and graduate school college entrance preparation. The authors of this text have been successfully teaching thousands of graduate students to prepare for the GRE General Test for many, many years. The material, strategies, and techniques presented in this guide have been researched, tested, and evaluated in GRE preparation classes at leading California universities. BTPS Testing is a leader in the field of graduate test preparation and continues to offer classes at many California State Universities. This test preparation guide uses materials developed for and practiced in these programs.

The GRE General Test measures your ability to use important *critical thinking skills* and *academic knowledge* learned during your undergraduate studies. It is common for many future graduate students to not have utilized some of these skills for many years. *CliffsNotes GRE General Test with CD-ROM* will strengthen your test-taking ability and provide you with important information that looks beyond traditional test-taking strategies. One of our goals is to help you create a personal study plan that increases your ability to become more *accurate and efficient* at mastering the critical thinking processes required on the GRE. Using this book will help you evaluate and analyze your strengths, while providing you valuable instructional information to tackle your weaknesses. The enhanced instructional methods provided in this guide are designed to deepen your understanding of the test format, question types, and practice problems. Most importantly, we hope that the skills and concepts presented will help you become a successful graduate student.

Navigating This Book

This guide is designed to provide you with important information and the tools necessary for a comprehensive and successful preparation. As you work through this book, you will strengthen the critical thinking skills that will boost your learning potential.

For optimal results, try to follow the recommended sequence of topics within each chapter and take detailed notes on the pages of this book to highlight important facts and content information. Each chapter presents subject-matter material in a structured format to enhance your learning. In addition, many of the sample problems are arranged by level of difficulty. Start in sequence with the easy problems first, then work your way up through the difficult problems.

After reading the introductory material, begin with the diagnostic test to assess your strengths and weaknesses. The diagnostic test will help you to pinpoint any areas that may require more concentration and effort. Focus on specific areas to further develop your skills and awareness of GRE test questions. Then continue to work through subsequent chapters, examining the comprehensive analysis and review of each exam area (analytical writing, verbal reasoning, and quantitative reasoning), including question types, step-by-step instructions for solving problems, and up-to-date examples.

Once you have taken the diagnostic test and reviewed the exam areas, this guide provides you with extensive practice, including four full-length model practice tests (one practice test in the book and three additional practice tests on the accompanying CD-ROM). All four practice tests include answers with thorough explanations and sample essay responses. Finally, the last part of this book includes a final checklist on page 413 as a reminder of "things to do" before you take your exam.

How This Book Is Organized

- **Introduction:** A general description of the GRE, test structure, scoring, taking the computer-based GRE, reducing test anxiety, frequently asked questions, and general tips and strategies.
- **Part I – Diagnostic Test:** An introductory diagnostic test acquaints you with GRE question types, evaluates your areas of improvement, and provides you with a baseline starting point.
- **Part II – Review of Exam Areas:** Review chapters focus on the abilities tested in analytical writing, verbal reasoning, and quantitative reasoning, along with basic skills necessary, skills and concepts tested, directions, suggested strategies with samples, and additional tips.

- **Part III – Basic Math Review:** A short, intensive review of the basics of arithmetic, algebra, geometry, data analysis, data interpretation, and word problems. Each review area offers a diagnostic test and illustrated sample problems. Important symbols, terminology, and equivalents are also included.

- **Part IV – Full-Length Practice Test:** One full-length practice test with answers and in-depth explanations. The practice test is followed by analysis worksheets to assist you in evaluating your progress.

- **CD-ROM:** The CD-ROM contains the full-length practice test from the book, plus three additional full-length practice tests with answers and in-depth explanations. PDFs of the Introduction and the review chapters are also included on the CD.

Getting Started

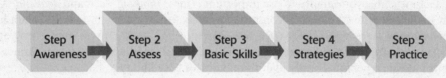

Step 1 – Awareness

Become familiar with the test—the test format, test directions, question types, test material, and scoring—as outlined in the Introduction or by visiting the GRE website at www.ets.org/gre.

Step 2 – Assess Your Strengths and Weaknesses

Take the diagnostic test in Chapter 1 to determine your strengths and weaknesses so that you can develop a study plan unique to your individual needs. "Creating Your Customized Study Plan" on the next page will help you to develop a review plan that is unique to your personal goals.

Step 3 – Basic Skills and Question Types

Review the basic skills required for each measure of the GRE and become familiar with the question types outlined in "Part II: Review of Exam Areas."

- **Analytical Writing (pages 49–69)** measures your ability to think critically, reason, and analyze issues and arguments, then to convincingly articulate and support complex ideas in a well-written essay. There are two writing tasks that appear on the exam—analysis of an issue and analysis of an argument.

- **Verbal Reasoning (pages 71–120)** tests your ability to assess, comprehend, and identify relationships in written material, words, and concepts. Question types include reading comprehension, text completion, and sentence equivalence and may appear as multiple-choice questions (select one answer), multiple-choice questions (select one or more answers), or select-in-passage (select a sentence in the reading passage that answers the question).

- **Quantitative Reasoning (pages 121–202)** tests your knowledge and application of basic math skills and concepts, and tests your ability to reason and solve problems in arithmetic, algebra, geometry, data analysis, data interpretation, and word problems. Many problems are drawn from real-life-scenarios. Questions may appear as quantitative comparison, multiple-choice (select one answer), multiple-choice (select one or more answers), or numeric entry (fill in the blank). Chapter 5, "Math Skills Review," is a comprehensive math review with practice exercises that will help you sharpen your Quantitative Reasoning skills.

Step 4 – Learn Strategies and Techniques

Study the strategies outlined in the Introduction (pages 1–13) and decide which strategy works best for you. Remember that if it takes you longer to recall a strategy than to solve the problem, it's probably not a good strategy for you to adopt. The goal in offering strategies is for you to be able to work easily, quickly, and efficiently. Remember not to get stuck on any one question. Taking time to answer the most difficult question on the test correctly but losing valuable test time will not get you the score you deserve. Most importantly, remember to answer every question, even if you answer with only an educated guess.

Step 5 – Practice, Practice, Practice

Practice is the key to your success on the GRE. In addition to the sample practice problems in chapters 2–4, there is one full-length practice test starting on page 363. The accompanying CD-ROM includes the practice test from this book, plus three additional practice tests to help you benefit from a "computer-based practice experience." Be sure to practice in the format of the actual test as often as possible. To get a realistic sense of the actual test, take the online practice test using the GRE® PowerPrep™ II software published by ETS. This online simulated practice test is available for free at www.ets.org/gre.

Creating Your Customized Study Plan

There are as many "best" ways to study for the GRE as there are people who take the test. Understanding your unique learning style and applying this understanding to a customized study plan will aid in your success on the GRE. Simply, the goal of preparation is to either increase your overall score as much as possible or to increase scores that are specifically relevant to specific graduate school admission requirements. For example, you might need a 750 in the math section to get into a top Ph.D. program in Computer Science, whereas a much lower score on this section might be just fine if you're pursuing a Ph.D. in Comparative History. Before you can begin your preparation, start with exploring desired graduate programs to gather information and set your intended goals. Know the scores that you need for success *before* preparing your unique plan.

Start your preparation for the GRE with an *action plan* that recognizes your test-taking strengths and weaknesses, and that you can personally develop and execute. There are many pathways to learning with different learning styles. This is why we have included hundreds of sample and practice problems with step-by-step explanations, particularly in the math review, that are designed to enhance your learning abilities. While creating your customized study plan it is recommended that you:

- Assess your strengths and weaknesses
- Start with a general plan and move to a specific plan
- Be time wise

Assess Your Strengths and Weaknesses

The universal first step is to assess where you're at right now. By beginning with the diagnostic test in Chapter 1, you will better understand the areas in which you need to improve. Then compare your results with the scores you would like to have. The areas that require the most growth are the areas on which you will want to focus the majority of your limited study time. Starting with a look at the growth you need is also a good way to estimate how much overall time you will need to devote to studying. Then set goals for your study time and be willing to frequently adapt and revise your goals as you evaluate your progress. If time is of the essence, consider at least working through a range of sample questions to get a sense of your starting point.

Start General and Move to a Specific Plan

Even if you've defined the areas that need work, increasing your scores may still not be as simple as studying for a set time each day (though that's a good start!). Again, you know yourself best. Most people find it useful to start by training with general principles and skills that are widely applicable to many problems, and progressing to the memorization of important facts and concepts. For example, you should start your *general* math review with basic arithmetic (fractions, percents, decimals, etc.), and then move to a *specific* plan to tackle certain types of basic arithmetic problems (mixed fractions, converting percents to decimals, etc.). Again, start general and move to more specific problems and concepts. As you progress in your preparation, moving from a general plan to a specific plan, you will notice that you may frequently revise and modify your plan to adapt to newly learned concepts.

Be Time Wise

Your study plan will depend on the total amount of time until the test date. If the test is tomorrow, focus on understanding procedure and instructions (and gathering necessary identification and a map to the test site). If the test is four months from now, you can start with training skills and expect that an understanding of test procedures will materialize as you work your way methodically through this guide. If you have the time, don't forget to check your progress along the way. Every time you take a practice test, you might need to revise how you prioritize your study time—just remember to keep your graduate school goals in mind!

Introduction: An Overview of the GRE General Test

The Graduate Record Exam - GRE General Test is a standardized exam that is commonly required as part of the graduate and graduate business school admissions application process. The weighted degree of importance for graduate admission varies widely by most academic departments within colleges and universities. In general, graduate departments use GRE test results to predict academic performance and to assess your readiness for graduate-level academic coursework. The GRE requires that you critically identify, evaluate, and apply your general abilities in three subject areas: analytical writing, verbal reasoning, and quantitative reasoning. The test emphasizes question-types that highlight your learned skills to think critically and respond to real-life situation questions in graduate school.

Effective preparation for the GRE begins with strategic learning, so you should begin your preparation immediately by contacting the university admissions office for more information about specific minimum score requirements and admission deadlines.

Test Structure

Structure of the GRE General Test		
Content	**Question Type**	**Number of Questions**
Analytical Writing Assessment	Analyze an Issue Task Analyze an Argument Task	1 Analyze an Issue task 1 Analyze an Argument task **Time: 2 writing tasks (30 minutes per task, timed separately) = 60 minutes**
Verbal Reasoning	Reading Comprehension Text Completion Sentence Equivalence (questions intermingled)	2 Verbal Reasoning sections (20 questions each) Total Verbal Reasoning = 40 questions **Time: 2 verbal sections (30 minutes per section) = 60 minutes**
Quantitative Reasoning	Quantitative Comparison Multiple-Choice (one answer) Multiple-Choice (one or more answers) Numeric Entry (fill-in-the-blank) (questions intermingled)	2 Quantitative Reasoning sections (20 questions each) Total Quantitative Reasoning = 40 questions **Time: 2 quantitative sections (35 minutes each section) = 70 minutes**
*Unscored Section and Research Section	Verbal Reasoning or Quantitative Reasoning (unidentified and identified unscored questions)	Varies between 30 to 35 minutes
Total Questions		**80 Multiple-choice Questions** **2 Essay Writing Tasks**
Total Testing Time		**Approximately 3 hours and 45 minutes**

There is a one-minute optional break between each section of the GRE, and following the third section, there is an optional 10-minute recess.

Note: Structure, scoring, and the order of sections is subject to change. Visit www.ets.org/gre for updated exam information.

Experimental Section

The GRE has experimental questions that make up an *unscored* section of the exam. These experimental questions may appear in any order after the Analytical Writing section, but *will not count* toward your GRE score. The experimental questions are multiple-choice questions that will either be verbal or quantitative questions. Experimental questions are designed for research to test future GRE questions, and can be written to a format in any of the abovementioned question-types. Be sure to answer all questions on the test; don't spend valuable time trying to guess which questions are experimental. It is too difficult to differentiate experimental questions from scored questions. Just answer all questions and move along as quickly as possible.

Scoring

Scores on your GRE will be reported for three separate measures. Verbal Reasoning and Quantitative Reasoning measures are scored for multiple-choice and numeric entry questions, and the Analytical Writing measure is scored for two essays. Your score is based on three factors:

- The number of questions answered
- The number of questions answered correctly
- The difficulty of the questions answered

Scaled Scores		
Measure	**Type of Questions**	**Scaled Score**
Verbal Reasoning	Multiple-Choice	130–170
Quantitative Reasoning	Multiple-Choice	130–170
Analytical Writing	Analyzing an Issue Essay Analyzing an Argument Essay	Score 0–6 averaged by two readers Score 0–6 averaged by two readers The two final scores on each essay are totaled and averaged, then rounded up to the nearest half-point to report one score 0–6.

Multiple-Choice Scoring Measures: Verbal Reasoning and Quantitative Reasoning

In the **multiple-choice section,** verbal and quantitative questions are *section-level adaptive*. Your performance on the first section of the measure determines the level of difficulty for the second section. The computer will adjust the questions so that all questions contribute equally to the final score for that measure. Sound confusing? Just remember that the questions are completely random (easy, moderate, and difficult) on the first set of 20 questions of each measure. This means that your first set of 20 questions in the verbal section will determine the second set of verbal questions, and the first set of 20 questions in the quantitative section will determine the second set of quantitative questions. Your final score is based upon the number of questions you answer correctly, so just try to do your best to achieve your best possible overall results. Keep in mind that if you are faced with a question that requires multiple answers such as "indicate one or more answers," you must indicate <u>all</u> possible answers to receive credit for a correct response. There is no partial credit.

Each measure, verbal or quantitative, computes a *raw score* that is based upon the number of questions you answer correctly. The raw score is equated and converted into a *scaled score* from 130 to 170 with 1-point increments for each measure. The "equating" process takes into account different test editions and disparities among different tests. The scaled score also helps to determine your percentile rank that many graduate programs use to compare your score results with those of other applicants. The *average score is 150* on each measure of the GRE, meaning that 50 percent of students scored above and 50 percent of students scored below this score. There is no penalty for an incorrect answer. This means that unanswered questions do not count for or against your score. Remember that scores are only based upon the number of questions you answer correctly. Since there is *no penalty for guessing,* it is in your best interest to take an educated guess on each question.

Analytical Writing Scoring Measure: Analyzing an Issue and Analyzing an Argument

In the **analytical writing section,** two different essays are scored holistically and each essay receives a score from two separate readers that range from 0 to 6 (zero for a blank paper) based on the rubric that follows. To be scored holistically means that readers look at the *overall quality* of each essay. If there is discrepancy of more than one point in the assigned scores from the two readers, a third reader will read and evaluate your essay. The two essay tasks are analyzing an issue and analyzing an argument. After the readers assign a score for each essay, the two essay scores are added together, averaged, and then rounded up to the nearest half-point to produce a single final score that represents both essay responses. The general scoring guidelines in the following table provide you with a brief analysis of criteria for your Analytical Writing essay score. For more information about Analytical Writing scoring criteria, read Chapter 2, "Analytical Writing Assessment." On the Analytical Writing section, the overall mean score is approximately between 4.0 and 4.5.

Analytical Writing Scoring Guide

Analysis of an Issue Task	Analysis of an Argument Task
Score 6 – Convincing and Persuasive Analysis You will receive a score of 6 if the response ❏ demonstrates the ability to reason and put together evidence to present a clear and insightful position that responds directly to the task ❏ provides well-developed and persuasive reasons and/or examples ❏ presents an organized, focused analysis that uses transitions to connect ideas ❏ uses well-chosen vocabulary and varied sentence types to convey meaning ❏ demonstrates correct usage of the conventions of standard written English	**Score 6 – Insightful Analysis** You will receive a score of 6 if the response ❏ identifies specific aspects of the argument relevant to the task and examines them in an insightful way ❏ develops evidence with the ideas coherently and connects them using clear transitions ❏ provides relevant and thorough support from the argument ❏ uses well-chosen vocabulary and varied sentence types to convey complex ideas ❏ demonstrates correct usage of the conventions of standard written English
Score 5 – Thoughtful and Well-Developed Analysis You will receive a score of 5 if the response ❏ presents a clear, well-thought out position that responds directly to the task ❏ provides reasonable and logical reasons and/or examples ❏ presents an organized, focused analysis that connects ideas ❏ uses appropriate vocabulary and sentence variety to convey meaning ❏ demonstrates correct usage of the conventions of standard written English	**Score 5 – Thoughtful Analysis** You will receive a score of 5 if the response ❏ identifies the aspects of the argument relevant to the specific question and examines them in a generally thoughtful way ❏ develops logical and organized ideas and connects them with transitions ❏ provides mostly relevant and complete support from the argument ❏ uses appropriate vocabulary and sentence variety to convey ideas ❏ demonstrates correct usage of the conventions of standard written English

(continued)

Analysis of an Issue Task	Analysis of an Argument Task
Score 4 – Competent Analysis You will receive a score of 4 if the response ❏ presents a complete and reasonable clear position that responds to the task ❏ provides appropriate reasons and/or examples ❏ presents an organized, focused analysis ❏ uses language to convey meaning with adequate clarity ❏ demonstrates general control of the conventions of standard written English, but with some minor errors	**Score 4 – Competent and Generally Acceptable** You will receive a score of 4 if the response ❏ identifies relevant aspects of the argument but also addresses some unrelated points ❏ develops the ideas clearly but may not connect them with transitions ❏ provides some support from the argument but with uneven development ❏ uses language to convey ideas in a generally clear way ❏ demonstrates general control of the conventions of standard written English, but with some minor errors
Score 3 – Flawed Analysis You will receive a score of 3 if the response ❏ shows limited competence, and may be vague or limited in responding to the specific prompt ❏ uses weak or irrelevant reasons and/or examples for support ❏ lacks focus or is poorly organized ❏ has language problems that interfere with communication ❏ demonstrates major errors or frequent minor errors with the conventions of standard written English	**Score 3 – Flawed Analysis** You will receive a score of 3 if the response ❏ shows some competence in examining the issue, but is generally flawed and does not identify most of the relevant aspects of the argument ❏ discusses unrelated points or presents poor reasoning ❏ develops the ideas in a limited or less logical way ❏ provides support that is less relevant to the argument ❏ uses language in an unclear way ❏ demonstrates major errors or frequent minor errors with the conventions of standard written English that interfere with communication
Score 2 – Weak Analysis You will receive a score of 2 if the response ❏ has a significant weakness in responding to the task and does not develop a clear position ❏ provides limited reasons and/or examples for support ❏ lacks focus and is poorly organized ❏ demonstrates limited language skills that impede communication ❏ contains serious errors with the conventions of standard written English	**Score 2 – Inadequate Analysis** You will receive a score of 2 if the response ❏ fails to respond to the directions for the task and/or shows weakness in examining the issue. ❏ does not identify the relevant aspects of the argument but instead presents the writer's own opinion on the issue ❏ does not follow the specific directions for the task ❏ fails to develop ideas or organizes them illogically ❏ provides little to no support ❏ uses language in a way that interferes with communication ❏ contains serious errors in conventions that make meaning unclear
Score 1 – Deficient Analysis You will receive a score of 1 if the response ❏ presents little understanding of the task or issue ❏ provides little or no evidence or support ❏ has severe language problems that prevent communication ❏ contains serious errors with the conventions of standard written English	**Score 1 – Deficient Analysis** You will receive a score of 1 if the response ❏ reveals basic problems in analytical writing ❏ shows little or no understanding of the argument ❏ is short and disorganized ❏ uses language in a way that prevents understanding ❏ contains serious, frequent errors in conventions that lead to incoherence
Score of 0 – Off-Topic These essays are often off-topic, do not respond to the writing task, are written in a foreign language, simply copy the issue statement, or consist of random keystrokes or are left blank.	

Essay Originality

ETS uses a software program that enables GRE readers to detect if your essays are original work, or if the written assignments have been taken from other sources. If there is similar text that has appeared on other GRE essays, or in published works without cited references, it is likely that your essays will be in jeopardy of not reflecting "independent intellectual" thinking. The GRE measures your own personal, independent thinking so it is important for you to compose essays that clearly express your original thoughts, ideas, and perspectives, not those of others. If you write an essay that has been taken from another source, ETS may cancel your scores, and you may be required to take the entire test again.

Taking the Computer-Based GRE

The GRE General Test is offered by computer in the United States, Canada, and many other countries. Paper-based testing is offered only in areas of the world where computer-based testing is not available. If you live outside the United States, check the official GRE website at www.ets.org/gre to see if computer-based or paper-based testing is used in your area.

The computer-based GRE is "section-level adaptive." This suggests that rather than presenting a preordained set of questions to every test-taker, the computer will adjust the question difficulty based on your performance on the first section of each measure. For example, the Verbal Reasoning measure consists of two sections with 20 questions in each section. After you answer the first 20 questions, the computer will adapt the second set of 20 questions based upon your performance from the first 20 questions. Within each of the two sections, all questions contribute equally to the final score.

Because the GRE is a computer-based test, once you have worked through the review chapters of this book, it is important to practice test questions that simulate the actual computer-based exam. This is why we have provided you with computer-based practice on the accompanying CD-ROM.

Advantages of Computer-Based Testing

- Numerous test dates are available because appointments can be scheduled year-round throughout each week.
- Your scores are available immediately for the multiple-choice (verbal and quantitative reasoning measures).
- Answers recorded electronically can reduce the chance of human error in posing written responses.
- Computer-friendly functions— navigate freely within a section after you have viewed each question once (moving forward and backward); use an on-screen calculator for quantitative reasoning and quickly transferring your results to the answer box; highlight passages within reading comprehension (verbal reasoning); mark questions to tag and return to later; change your answers at any time; and edit material (cut, paste, undo) on your analytical writing essays.

Computer Screen Layout

The following example is for informational purposes only and does not reflect the exact reproduction of the official GRE computer screen. Visit www.ets.org/gre to take the official online practice test and view computer screen specifications.

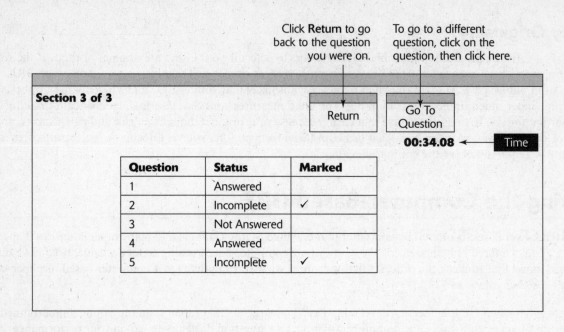

Click **Return** to go
back to the question
you were on.

To go to a different
question, click on the
question, then click here.

Section 3 of 3

Return

Go To
Question

00:34.08 ◄──── Time

Question	Status	Marked
1	Answered	
2	Incomplete	✓
3	Not Answered	
4	Answered	
5	Incomplete	✓

Using a Calculator on the GRE

A simple four-function **on-screen calculator** (with square root) is available to help you perform simple computations on the Quantitative Reasoning measure. The calculator will look something like this:

Calculator	⊠
	0.

MR MC M+ ( )

7 8 9 ÷ C

4 5 6 × CE

1 2 3 − √

± 1 . + =

Transfer Display

Time-Consuming Problems: Although the calculator will help you save time-consuming handwritten calculations, you must have a basic knowledge of math problem solving to be able to determine if your calculation results make logical sense. The general rule of thumb is that you should only use the on-screen calculator for time-consuming computations (square roots, long division, and problems with several digits). Use your time wisely and quickly determine if a problem appears to be easy to solve mentally. Keep in mind that if you use the on-screen calculator for every math problem, you will never be able to complete the test in the allotted time.

Basic Functions: Using your keyboard and mouse, you will be able to move the image of the on-screen calculator to any location on the screen. The on-screen calculator can perform the basic functions of addition, subtraction, multiplication, division, parentheses, and square roots; it also has a memory location. The on-screen calculator has basic functions keys: a *clear* [C] button to help you clear the display, as well as *memory recall* [MR], *memory clear* [MC], and *memory sum* [M+] buttons.

Order of Operations: The on-screen calculator is programmed to follow the rules of order of operations. This means that you will need to be aware of the correct order of operations to key in your instructions and/or number values (parentheses, exponents/square roots, multiplication/division, and addition/subtraction).

Transfer Display: After you have determined that your calculated results are the best answer choice for the numeric entry questions, you can transfer your results to your answer box with one click. Keep in mind, however, that you will need to transfer calculated results in the correct form that the question asks. For example, some numeric entry questions may require you to round off to a certain decimal place, or some may ask you to covert your answer to a percent, etc. Be sure to adjust your on-screen calculator results before transferring your answer to your answer box.

Practice Before the Exam Date: To help you become familiar with the on-screen calculator, use a calculator similar to the on-screen computerized calculator while practicing sample problems from this book. The TI-108 (Texas Instruments 108) calculator has functions that are similar to the on-screen calculator. Familiarize yourself with the best keystrokes to accomplish certain math tasks as you work through sample problems in this book.

Reducing Test-Taking Anxiety

Research shows that learning is greatly improved by preparing and studying prior to an exam. For many people, however, preparing for a test can cause additional stress and anxiety. High levels of anxiety can interfere with retrieval processes (working memory), learning, and performance. Often, test anxiety can yield scores that may not necessarily reflect your knowledge and potential in graduate school. Anxiety can be related to fears of not achieving intended scores, lack of academic background in math or English, or an inability to be able to solve problems quickly.

Although it is natural to be apprehensive about any test, especially one as comprehensive as the GRE, when apprehension impedes your ability to perform, it's time to look for solutions to reduce your anxiety. Test anxiety can present itself in different forms and at different levels of intensity that can affect behaviors, emotions, and physical responses. Luckily there are effective strategies that will help ensure that you remain as focused as possible to get your best possible GRE results.

Helpful vs. Harmful Anxiety

Let's start with distinguishing what anxiety is, and what it is not. **Helpful anxiety** is part of everyday life and is usually accompanied by a fear of a situation outside yourself—something *externally experienced*. For example, you might have a fear that you won't obtain the score you need to be admitted to graduate school, you might have a fear that a letter of recommendation from a professor might not arrive in time, or you might have a fear that math is not your strength and that you might score poorly on Quantitative Reasoning. These types of anxiety are perfectly normal, and are "temporary" emotional states. When you experience this type of anxiety, a signal is sent to your brain to help push you to focus your level of concentration, inspire you to work harder, motivate you to achieve your learning potential, and most importantly, physically and emotionally energize you so that you will be motivated to tackle your preparation and accomplish your goals.

Harmful anxiety, on the other hand, is an *internally experienced* physiological response that can leave you feeling as if you are losing control over yourself and that "something unexplainable is happening" in a bodily response. Often, there is a feeling of powerlessness that can interfere with your ability to think and study. Harmful anxiety can often be brought on merely by thinking about taking the GRE. In other words, you may experience excessive worry that is out of proportion to the actual situation just by anticipating the day of the exam. Signs of harmful anxiety can include difficulty concentrating, difficulty sleeping, tense muscles, irritability, fatigue, shortness of breath, rapid heart rate, dry mouth, dizziness, hot flashes, nausea, racing thoughts, and mentally "blanking out."

The following steps are intended to provide you with practical tips and strategies to reduce anxiety and increase your test performance.

Practical Tips to Help Reduce Test-Taking Anxiety

1. Reduce External Stressors

There are some simple things you can do to help reduce external stressors and thus reduce test anxiety. For example, regular exercise helps to increase your body's endorphins and can help to reduce stress hormones that are responsible for causing health problems. Plan to exercise in the weeks and days leading up to the test. Get a good night's sleep before the day of the test. Eat a well-balanced meal before the test, but reduce your fluid intake so that you will not need to excuse yourself during the test. Dress for success, and in layers. It sounds silly, but it is easier to take off a layer of clothing, than to be cold during the test. Allow yourself ample time to get to the test site, and make sure you know how to get there! Be sure to bring proper identification.

2. Prepare, Prepare, Prepare

Preparation is an ongoing process. You have already accomplished the first step in reducing anxiety by reviewing material that is designed to inform you about the test. Systematically plan your preparation. Be organized, be conscious of time, and be aware of what works for you personally. It is never too late to develop new test-taking habits. It is unrealistic to expect that you will know the answer to every question on the GRE, but at least you can be aware of the directions, question types, and simple strategies. Familiarize yourself with the test directions in this book ahead of time, and take your time to fully read and understand the instructions before trying to answer questions. Pace yourself during your preparation. Do the practice exercises at a comfortable rate, then attempt to do the practice tests in the allotted time. Try to simulate the same time constraints that are on the actual exam. Remember, knowledge provides empowerment, and the more you prepare, the more empowered you will feel and the less anxious you will be.

Preparing can help you internalize the idea that everything will be alright no matter what the outcome. Specifically, you will learn the pace that allows you to complete the needed sections, without the worry that you will run out of time. Time pressures and the idea that you will not finish are among the most common sources of test anxiety.

3. Relax

Practice relaxation techniques. Different techniques work for different people, and it's worth knowing what works for you *before* you need it. Some successful relaxation techniques include deep breathing, counting, grounding (thinking of a place where you feel calm in nature), or repeating a phrase in your mind that helps you to focus.

4. Get Help

Test anxiety is very real and also fairly common. If you're contemplating graduate school, you can expect tests in your future, and it might be worth getting professional help for your test anxiety sooner rather than later. Your college's counseling center or community mental health centers are good places to find help with test anxiety.

Frequently Asked Questions

Q. **Where do I apply to take the GRE?**

A. The GRE is administered by Educational Testing Service (ETS), www.ets.org/gre, P.O. Box 6000, Princeton, NJ 08541-6000, (609) 771-7670, (800) 473-4373.

Q. **Which test should I take (GRE or GMAT)?**

A. The GRE General Test is a widely recognized standardized test for most graduate school programs. In considering which exam to take, start by calling the academic department where you would like to complete your coursework and check admission requirements. Although the GRE is now accepted by many MBA programs, it is wise to check with the graduate department for specific requirements.

Q. What are the types of GRE tests?

A. There are two types of GRE tests: GRE General Test and GRE Subjects Tests. The GRE General Test is the focus of this book, and is the most commonly required test for graduate school admissions. The subject tests include Biochemistry, Cell and Molecular Biology, Biology, Chemistry, Computer Science, Literature in English, Mathematics, Physics, and Psychology. Contact your prospective graduate schools to see if their application requirements include the GRE General Test, GRE Subject Tests, or both. Again, this book focuses solely on the GRE General Test.

Q. When is the computer-based GRE given?

A. The computer-based GRE is offered at most testing sites year-round. You should schedule your GRE CBT appointment early to get your preferred time, date, and location. Testing center hours may vary.

Q. How do I schedule my GRE exam appointment?

A. Registration is available online at the official GRE website: www.ets.org/gre. You may also call the test center directly at 1-800-GRE-CALL (1-800-473-2255).

Q. What computer skills are required to take the GRE?

A. The GRE requires very limited computer skills, including the use of a mouse, keyboard, and an elementary word processing program. "General Tips and Strategies," on the next page will explain the flexibility you will have as you work through problems in each section. You will be able to move forward and backward within a section to skip questions or change responses. Be sure to take the online practice test at www.ets.org/gre to have the experience of using these computer skills. The word processing program is for the Analytical Writing measure of the test and includes basic functions: insert, delete, cut and paste, and undo (previous action).

Q. How much does it cost to take the GRE?

A. At the time of publication, it costs approximately $160 to register for the GRE test. Additional costs apply for late registration, rescheduling, or changing the test site. You can pay these fees with any major credit card, a money order, or a certified check at the time of registration. Fee reductions are available for those in financial need and can be applied for online at www.ets.org/gre. For updated fee information, visit the GRE website.

Q. When will I receive my scores?

A. You can choose to view your scores for the Quantitative and Verbal Reasoning measures immediately after you finish the exam. Your complete score report will be mailed approximately 10–15 days after the testing date.

Q. What is the process for taking the test?

A. When you arrive at the GRE testing center your identification will be verified and if you were issued an authorization voucher, you should present it at this time. You will copy in writing (not print) a confidentiality statement and will then be allowed to sign the test center log on your way into the testing room. You will not be permitted to bring with you a cell phone, smartphone, or any other personal electronics including a calculator. Scratch paper will be provided. There is an on-screen calculator for your use in the Quantitative Reasoning sections.

The test is approximately 3 hours and 45 minutes. A 10-minute break is permitted after the third section, and you will get a short 1-minute break between the other test sections. If you need additional breaks, the time will be deducted from the time allowed. You should plan to be at the testing site at least 5 hours because you want to arrive early, and you have to allow time for check-in, instructions, etc.

Q. Should I guess on the GRE General Test?

A. Yes. There is no penalty for an incorrect answer and unanswered questions do not count for or against your score. Since there is *no penalty for guessing,* it is in your best interest to take an educated guess on each question. You can move forward and backward within each multiple-choice section, so if you have time at the end of the section, you can always go back to recheck your answers.

Q. For how long is a GRE score valid?

A. A GRE score is valid for five years after the test date.

Q. **What if I took the old version of the GRE prior to August 2011. How do I compare results?**

A. Check the ETS website for a concordance table that will help you decipher and compare the old version test scores of the GRE with the 2011 revised General Test scores. The published table will help you to translate your scores for five years after 2011.

Q. **Where are GRE testing centers located?**

A. There are hundreds of testing centers in North America and other selected cities. Most testing centers are at Prometric Testing Centers inside the offices of Sylvan Learning Centers. There are also some testing centers at colleges and universities. A comprehensive list is available online at www.ets.org/gre.

Q. **What should I bring to the testing center?**

A. Bring a valid photo ID (like a driver's license), information about the schools (school code, name, address) where you would like your scores sent, and your authorization voucher (if you requested one from ETS). Scratch paper will be provided so bring some sharpened pencils in the event that you need them.

Q. **How often may I take the GRE?**

A. You may take the GRE no more than one time per month, or five times in one year.

Q. **Is there a penalty for retaking the GRE?**

A. There is no penalty in terms of score for retaking the GRE test, but your previous test scores will appear in the written results provided to your graduate program. Many graduate schools average all the scores you submit, but it would behoove you to contact the school(s) to which you are applying for individual admission regulations.

Q. **Does the GRE measure knowledge of any specific subject area?**

A. No. The GRE General Test is meant to test reasoning skills and not specific knowledge, though the Quantitative Reasoning section tests general mathematical ability, and the Verbal Reasoning section requires knowledge of vocabulary.

General Tips and Strategies

There is no right or wrong method to answering questions on the computer-based GRE, but approaching the exam with the knowledge of helpful test-taking strategies can give you the edge you may need to complete the exam with greater ease and confidence.

The multiple-choice questions cover a broad range of topics while considering a variety of question types. To be successful on the exam, you need to recall basic facts and major concepts that are important in Quantitative Reasoning and Verbal Reasoning. The facts and concepts on the GRE are often presented in subtle variations of selected answer choices that make it difficult for test-takers to narrow down the correct answer. Additionally, subtle variations in answer choices can distract you from choosing the correct answer.

This section was developed as a guide to introduce general test-taking guidelines, approaches, and strategies that are useful on the GRE, and on many other standardized exams. Although this section is limited to general tips and strategies, specific strategies related to *specific subject area question types* are included in Chapter 3, "Verbal Reasoning," and Chapter 4, "Quantitative Reasoning."

As you practice problems using the strategies outlined in this section, determine if the strategies fit with your individual learning style. What may work for some people, may not work for others. If it takes you longer to recall a strategy than to solve the problem, it's probably not a good strategy for you to adopt. The goal in offering you strategies is for you to be able to work through problems quickly, accurately, and efficiently. And remember, not to get stuck on any one question. Taking time to answer the most difficult question on the test correctly, but losing valuable test time will not get you the score you deserve. More importantly, remember to *answer every question* on the test since there is no penalty for guessing.

Consider the following guidelines when taking the exam:

- **Manage your time wisely.** When you begin the exam, make a mental note of the starting time and keep track of the time indicated on the computer screen. Never spend more than a minute and a half on any one question. Remember there are 40 math questions (70 minutes) and 40 verbal questions (60 minutes). With sufficient practice, you will almost automatically know when a problem is taking you too long.

- **Read each question carefully.** Do not make a hasty assumption that you know the correct answer without reading the whole question and all the possible answers. The hurried test-taker commonly selects an incorrect answer when jumping to a conclusion after reading only one or two of the answer choices. Note that some of the answer choices only show a "part" of the correct answer. You must look at the entire list of answer choices for the complete solution.

  Another common mistake is misreading a question that includes the words *except* and *not*. These types of questions reverse the meaning of the questions and ask for the opposite to be true in order to select the correct answer. It is helpful to write down brief notes on scratch paper to avoid misreading a question (and therefore answering it incorrectly). Simply write down on scratch paper *what* you must answer in the question.

- **Click (or fill in) the correct answer.** Be very careful that your responses match your intended response. When answering questions quickly, it is common to click the wrong answer choice by mistake.

- **Guessing.** In the first 20 questions, it is worth taking the time required (within reason) to do your very best to answer the questions correctly. If time is tight later in the section, it might be worth guessing rather than spending an inordinate amount of time on a question. Keep in mind that the GRE does not penalize you for wrong answers, so you should use the elimination or plus-minus approach below and answer every question.

- **Answer all questions.** To guarantee the highest number of correct answers, you must attempt to answer every question in the multiple-choice sections. Try to push yourself all the way through each section.

General Approaches to the Multiple-Choice Questions

The Elimination Approach

For the computer-based GRE, try to eliminate as many of the answer choices as possible, and then make an educated guess on the remaining answer choices. You may find it helpful to quickly write down the numeric position of the wrong answer choices (with a diagonal line through them) to prevent you from spending too much time mulling over the possible choices. For example, if you know that the answer on the second line (or second position on the list) is incorrect, write down the number two (2) with a diagonal line through it. Keep in mind that the answer choices on the actual computer exam are not numbered or lettered. Simply write down the numbered position where the answer is located. It will just take a few seconds to use this strategy, but many test-takers find it helpful to narrow down the possible answer choices. This will help to keep you from reconsidering impossible answer choices.

The Plus-Minus Approach

Many people who take the GRE don't get their best possible score because they spend too much time on difficult questions, leaving insufficient time to answer the easy questions. The plus-minus approach will help you categorize problems so that you can focus your attention on problems that you are able to answer. Making use of this approach will help you to quickly identify problems that are *solvable, possibly solvable* (+), *and difficult* (−).

Because the GRE is a computer-based test, you must click on the matching oval or square boxes provided to mark the correct answer choice (or in some cases you must select more than one answer). The computer will provide you with a list of "incomplete" or "unanswered" questions at the end of each section, and you will be able to pinpoint which questions are unsolved. The computer-generated list is useful in pointing to unanswered questions, but does not categorize and identify problems that are "possibly solvable" and "difficult." To help you keep track of problems that can be solved, use scratch paper provided by the test proctor on the day of the test. This strategy will help trigger your memory and help you avoid "rethinking" the entire set of answer choices when you review the list of unanswered questions.

Follow these steps:

1. **Identify solvable, possibly solvable, and difficult questions.**
    - **Solvable:** Answer easy questions immediately. This type of question is answered with little or no difficulty, and requires little or minimal thought.
    - **Possibly solvable (+):** You will recognize this type of question because it appears to be solvable but is overly time-consuming. This type of question leaves you feeling, "I can answer this question, but I need more time." A time-consuming question is a question that you estimate will take you more than two minutes to answer. When you face this type of question, mark the question, write a large plus sign ("+") on your scratch paper, and then move on to the next question. Because the GRE computer-based software allows you to skip a question and return to it later, this is an excellent test-taking strategy to help you move quickly through your test. This allows you to answer the "solvable" questions first. At the end of each section of 20 questions, you will be able to view a list of questions that are marked, unanswered, or incomplete. This list should match the list on your scratch paper.
    - **Difficult (–):** The difficult question appears "impossible to solve." When you come to a question that seems impossible to answer, write a large minus sign ("–") on your scratch paper, make a pure guess on your answer sheet and move on to the next question. Don't bother with the "impossible" questions. Rather, spend your time reviewing your work to be sure you didn't make any careless mistakes on the questions you thought were easy to answer. You should come back to review the difficult-type questions only after you have checked your work and have answered the "solvable" and "possibly solvable" questions.

Don't spend too much valuable test-time deciding whether or not a question is solvable. Since you have just over a minute to a minute and a half to answer each question, you must act quickly.

2. **Use a sheet of paper to list those questions that may be solvable but will require more time.** Draw two columns on your scratch paper (or fold your scratch paper in half to delineate columns). Label the top of the first column with a plus symbol (+) and the top of the second column with a minus symbol (–). Because "lettered" or "numbered" answer choices (A, B, C, D, E or 1, 2, 3, 4, 5) are not provided on the actual test (we provide lettered choices in this book), you will need to quickly write down the numbered position of your answer choice. Or if you prefer, you can write down a key word for easy reference.

    Example:
    - ○ The author is dubious about success of the program.
    - ○ The author is skeptical about technological innovations.
    - ○ The author is generally optimistic about positive changes occurring.
    - ○ The author is most concerned that legislation is stalled in congress.
    - ○ The author is perplexed about farmers who do not adopt this technology.

    Your scratch paper should look like this:

    Verbal

+	–
3. 1 or 3	1. 2 or 3, not 4̶
11. 2, not 4̶	6. 5?
15. 3?	14. not 4̶

    Remember that the computerized test allows you to go forward and backward from question to question within a section. For those questions that could not be answered immediately, quickly write down the question number in the most appropriate of the two columns, including any notes to help trigger your memory when you go back to the question.

3. **After you have solved all of the easy problems and the problems in the "+" column, attempt to solve the difficult problems in the "–" column.** For those problems you still cannot answer, pick one numbered position equivalent to answer choices (1, 2, 3, 4, 5, etc.) and use that numbered position on the remaining questions. Spend no more than a few minutes to mark all difficult problems that are left unanswered. Remember, there is no penalty for wrong answers, and statistically your chances are better if you pick one numbered position on the list of choices and use it on all unanswered questions.

4. **You can only work on one section at a time (verbal or quantitative reasoning).** Do not proceed to the next section without answering all questions within your section. DO NOT EXIT THE TEST UNTIL YOU HAVE ANSWERED ALL THE QUESTIONS. Once you exit, you cannot return.

PART I

DIAGNOSTIC TEST

Chapter 1

Diagnostic Test

Section 1: Analytical Writing – Analyze an Issue

Time: 30 minutes

Directions: In this section, you will have 30 minutes to plan and write an essay. The topic will appear as a brief quotation about an issue of general interest. You will be required to analyze and explain your views on the issue. A response to any other issue will receive a score of zero.

Take a few minutes to read the topic and intructions before you write your essay. Make sure that you respond according to the specific instructions and support your position on the issue with reasons and examples drawn from such areas as your reading, experience, observations, and/or academic studies. Use the last five minutes to read over your essay and revise as necessary.

Your response will be evaluated for its overall quality, based on how well you:

- Respond to the specific instructions
- Address the complexities and implications of the issue
- Organize and develop your essay
- Express your ideas with reasons and examples that are relevant
- Use standard written English

Issue Topic

Some people believe that sports figures serve as inspirational role models for youth. Others contend that excellence in sports does not automatically make someone an effective role model.

Write a response in which you distinguish between the two viewpoints on the issue and state which one most closely matches your own position. Be sure to discuss both viewpoints as you explain and support your stance.

IF YOU FINISH BEFORE TIME IS CALLED, CHECK YOUR WORK ON THIS SECTION ONLY. DO NOT WORK ON ANY OTHER SECTION IN THE TEST.

Section 2: Analytical Writing – Analyze an Argument

Time: 30 minutes

Directions: In this section, you will have 30 minutes to plan and write a critique of an argument given in the form of a short passage. A response to any other issue will receive a score of zero.

Take a few minutes to analyze the argument and plan your response before you write your essay. Note that you are NOT being asked to present your own views on the subject. Make sure that you respond according to the specific instructions and support your line of reasoning with relevant examples. Use the last five minutes to read over your essay and revise as necessary.

Your response will be evaluated for its overall quality, based on how well you:

- Respond to the specific instructions
- Identify and analyze the components of the arguement
- Organize and develop your critique
- Support your ideas with reasons and examples that are relevant
- Use standard written English

Argument Topic

The following appeared in a company memorandum.

> Sales of all Hopewell Farms' ice cream products have risen dramatically in the past two months with the introduction of the chocolate-orange and vanilla-mint flavors. To capitalize on growing consumer interest in exciting flavor combinations, Hopewell Farms should introduce a minimum of four new flavors in the coming year. This will result in increased profit for the company and its shareholders.

Write a response in which you examine the assumptions, stated and implied, that are present in the argument. Explain how these assumptions form the basis for the argument and how, if proven false, they would affect its persuasiveness.

IF YOU FINISH BEFORE TIME IS CALLED, CHECK YOUR WORK ON THIS SECTION ONLY. DO NOT WORK ON ANY OTHER SECTION IN THE TEST.

Section 3: Verbal Reasoning

The answer choices for multiple-choice questions on the actual computer version of the GRE are not labeled with letters. Answer choices in this study guide have lettered choices A, B, C, D, E, etc. for clarity. On the actual exam, you will be required to click on ovals or squares to select your answer.

HELPFUL HINT:

○ oval – answer will be a single choice

□ square – answer will be one or more choices

Time: 30 minutes
20 Questions

Directions: For questions 1 to 5, indicate <u>one</u> answer choice.

Question 1 is based on the following reading passage.

In the Sichuan Province of Western China, the slopes of Mt. Emei present a veritable cornucopia of visual beauty. Much of this visual splendor is not of natural origin; rather, it comes from the multitude of Buddhist temples which dot the mountain slopes and make this locale a magnet for pilgrims who travel here from far and wide.

1. Which of the following is an inference that can be properly deduced from this passage?

   Ⓐ Mt. Emei provides a visual panorama of beautiful sights.
   Ⓑ Many people travel to Mt. Emei to enjoy the visual splendor.
   Ⓒ Religious pilgrims to Mt. Emei ignore the visual distractions.
   Ⓓ Mt. Emei is located in Sichuan Province, in Western China.
   Ⓔ Religious pilgrims are drawn to Mt. Emei for the splendor of the temples.

Questions 2 to 5 are based on the following reading passage.

(1) Inside a windowless computer vault somewhere in California, massive mainframe computers relentlessly track millions of heads of lettuce, from the time they are plucked from the earth to the moment your bagged salad is scanned at the grocery checkout counter.

(2) That trail can now be traced in seconds, thanks to tiny high-tech labels, new software programs, and hand-held hardware. (3) These tools make it easier for farmers to locate potential problems—is there a leaky fertilizer bin, an unexpected pathogen in the water, unwashed hands on the factory production line?—and then act quickly to avoid the spread of contaminated food.

(4) This innovative project, and similar efforts being launched across the country, represent a fundamental shift in the way that food is tracked from field to table. (5) The change is slow but steady, as a number of industry leaders and smaller players adopt these tools.

(6) However, many in the farming community have yet to follow suit, and federal food-safety legislation is stalled in Congress. (7) Proponents of this technological transformation say that change is inevitable, given the public outrage over the most recent scandal: contaminated eggs. (8) Perhaps most importantly, this new technology could simplify and streamline our current overly-complex system, thus avoiding the harm to the general public that is regularly caused by unsafe food.

2. Which of the following is the best description of the overall tone of the passage above, in regard to possible improvements in food safety?

   Ⓐ   The author is dubious about success of the program.
   Ⓑ   The author is skeptical about the technological innovations.
   Ⓒ   The author is generally optimistic about positive changes occurring.
   Ⓓ   The author is most concerned that legislation is stalled in Congress.
   Ⓔ   The author is perplexed about farmers who do not adopt this technology.

3. According to the passage, all of the following are potential problems that the new technology may be able to mitigate, EXCEPT:

   Ⓐ   Agricultural workers who may not wash their hands.
   Ⓑ   Water-delivery systems that may become contaminated.
   Ⓒ   Unexpected pathogens that may cause disease in people.
   Ⓓ   Overuse of pesticides or herbicides in the fields as the crops grow.
   Ⓔ   Leaks in nutrient-delivery systems, such as fertilizer bins.

4. Which of the following does the passage identify as the most important potential benefit of this new high-tech agricultural tracking system?

   Ⓐ   The new technology can help simplify and streamline the nation's overly-complex food-safety systems.
   Ⓑ   The new technology can help to track leaks of potentially-damaging substances.
   Ⓒ   The new technology can help to track the personal hygiene of agricultural workers.
   Ⓓ   The new technology can help prevent overwatering and underwatering.
   Ⓔ   The new technology will help the growers be more efficient and more profitable.

5. Select the one sentence in the passage that provides a caveat, an admonition as to why this new program may not progress as quickly as it would otherwise.

Directions: For questions 6 to 11, for each blank, select the word or phrase from the corresponding columns that best completes the text. (Your answer will consist of one, two, or three letters, depending on the number of blanks in each question.)

6. The United States Supreme Court still retains a bit of its _____, because, even though cases are always argued in open court sessions and briefs are available for anyone to read, the real work of the Court transpires in private conferences attended by the nine sitting justices, with not a single other person present.

   Ⓐ   mystery
   Ⓑ   openness
   Ⓒ   naiveté
   Ⓓ   pretension
   Ⓔ   accessibility

7. For decades a silent epidemic has _____ wild bird populations across the U.S., resulting in death or disease for millions, including our iconic bald eagles and endangered California condors, because, in the U.S. today, no bird is safe from lead poisoning.

   Ⓐ   alleviated
   Ⓑ   ameliorated
   Ⓒ   mitigated
   Ⓓ   devastated
   Ⓔ   impeded

8. Samuel Langhorne Clemens, better known as Mark Twain, was the (i) _____ satirist of nineteenth century life. His uncensored autobiography, (ii) _____ for 100 years after his death, was finally published in 2010.

Blank (i)	Blank (ii)
Ⓐ caustic and saccharine	Ⓓ sanctioned
Ⓑ sagacious and insipid	Ⓔ embargoed
Ⓒ astute and witty	Ⓕ countermanded

9. As their numbers dwindled, the (i) _____ of all very large North American animals, the so-called megafauna—the enormous camels and the huge wooly mammoths, the giant armadillos and the truly gigantic bears, the terrifying Saber-toothed cats and the monstrous Dire Wolves—occurred relatively soon after the (ii) _____ and influx of humans, about 13,000 years ago.

Blank (i)	Blank (ii)
Ⓐ heyday	Ⓓ disappearance
Ⓑ disappearance	Ⓔ reemergence
Ⓒ climax	Ⓕ arrival

10. The world-weary eyes of the (i) _____ suddenly began to glow with an inner light as he told his stories from long ago: of the youth riding his bicycle all the way down to Floyd Bennett Field, New York City's first municipal airport, to see the flying machines; of the teenager washing greasy airplanes to (ii) _____ for those oh-so-precious minutes aloft; of the handsome young man in uniform striving (iii) _____ to master the complexities of modern warplanes, and finally of the friends lost, of the oh-so-many friends he lost along the way.

Blank (i)	Blank (ii)	Blank (iii)
Ⓐ callow man	Ⓓ barter	Ⓖ industriously
Ⓑ jejune swain	Ⓔ atone	Ⓗ grudgingly
Ⓒ haggard septuagenarian	Ⓕ redress	Ⓘ superficially

11. Deep in the (i) _____ of the American continent, in the area now called the Basin of Mexico, there arose the great capital of a most powerful city-state, situated, amazingly, on an island in Lake Texcoco. This (ii) _____ was called Tenochtitlan, and it was thoughtfully laid out with a grid of long avenues, crisscrossed by canals, and connected to the mainland at various points by long easily-defensible causeways. In the (iii) _____ of the city stood the Sacred Precinct, the religious center of the vast empire, anchored by the Temple Major, built to unite the sky overhead, the earth walked by man, and the unseen worlds below.

Blank (i)	Blank (ii)	Blank (iii)
Ⓐ verge	Ⓓ burg	Ⓖ foot
Ⓑ interior	Ⓔ metropolis	Ⓗ spine
Ⓒ periphery	Ⓕ necropolis	Ⓘ heart

Directions: For questions 12 to 15, select the <u>two</u> answer choices that, when used to complete the sentence, fit the meaning of the sentence as a whole and produce completed sentences that are alike in meaning.

12. The TV mini-series is about a well-known terrorist, the infamous *Carlos the Jackal,* who was _____ a series of bombings, attacks, and kidnappings in the 1970s.

    A cleared of
    B associated with
    C innocent of
    D accused of
    E deeply regretful about
    F not connected to

13. The deep _____ between rural Indian villages and the glitzy "shining India" of big-city shopping malls, rising economic growth, and luxury cars has widened dramatically in recent years.

    A schism
    B harmony
    C kinship
    D variance
    E community
    F nexus

14. The problem was deadly and it was immediate; the situation was quickly becoming _____: In 1943, so many U.S. bombers were being shot down over Europe that American airplane factories and pilot-training schools simply could not keep up with the losses.

    A lackadaisical
    B disparate
    C desperate
    D dire
    E dishabille
    F unacceptable

15. Researchers looking into the depletion of world's fisheries are testing a new technique in their effort to assess the true overall _____ that individual nations have on the oceans. They are examining not only the type and quantity of fish that are caught by each nation, but now they also factor in the fish *consumption* of the residents of that country, because it is this consumption that drives the overall worldwide demand.

    A benefit
    B amelioration
    C impact
    D aftermath
    E repercussions
    F stewardship

Directions: For questions 16 to 20, select <u>one</u> answer choice unless otherwise instructed.

Question 16 is based on the following reading passage.

The term "metaphysical poetry" refers to the work of a group of British poets in the seventeenth century who explored their ideas in most unusual patterns. They wrote extremely witty poetry using metaphorical conceits, making atypical connections between seemingly dissimilar subjects. For instance, in one famous work by John Donne, "The Flea," the speaker argues that his lover should give in to his advances since they have both been bitten by the same flea and the parasite now shares their joined blood. While the poem's reasoning is remarkably sound, its premise and logical progression are so odd that they require great work on the part of the reader to follow. Ironically, the term "metaphysical poets" was not coined until the late eighteenth century, and then was used as a derogatory term for poetry that was too convoluted, too difficult to decipher. This poetic style fell out of favor until T.S. Eliot initiated a resurgence in the art form in the 1920s. Today these poems are regarded with intellectual awe; one who is willing to put in the effort to read and understand them will be rewarded with insightful surprises.

16. Which of the following can be reasonably inferred from the passage above?

 Ⓐ Metaphysical poets took pride in confusing their audience.
 Ⓑ Metaphysical poetry was not popular for over one hundred years.
 Ⓒ T.S. Eliot exclusively wrote metaphysical poems.
 Ⓓ Metaphysical poetry is too difficult to appeal to the modern audience.
 Ⓔ The metaphysical poets were not famous during their lives.

Questions 17 to 18 are based on the following reading passage.

I can vividly recall the details of a dream which I have had repeatedly since childhood: I am in an open space, I start to run, and then with a jump, I can fly! As I begin to soar above the landscape, gazing at the verdant fields and rivers below, I feel amazement, but not surprise, not alarm. I see no awkward wing, no roaring engine, no hang glider holding me up; it's just me flying, pure and simple and delightful and free.

17. All of the following are appropriate descriptions of the tone of this passage, EXCEPT:

 Ⓐ Unrestrained
 Ⓑ Euphoric
 Ⓒ Unbounded
 Ⓓ Unfettered
 Ⓔ Woebegone

Directions: For question 18, consider each of the choices separately and select <u>all</u> that apply.

18. Consider the following choices, then choose the ones that accurately identify visual imagery which was utilized or implied in this passage:

 Ⓐ Looking down on a landscape from above.
 Ⓑ The sweet song of a flying engine.
 Ⓒ The lack of any visible means of support.

Question 19 is based on the following reading passage.

While traveling around the globe, one cannot help but notice large numbers of children hawking trinkets and cleaning up food shops. However, this is only one segment, perhaps the most visible segment, of the overall pool of the world's child laborers. According to the United Nations, 60% of child-laborers toil unseen in the agricultural sector, working long hours for little or no pay. Also, children working in domestic settings are often prone to abuse, due to their limited contact with the outside world.

19. Which of the following conclusions is the most logical point to which this author is leading his readers?

    Ⓐ Child labor is ubiquitous throughout the world.
    Ⓑ Child labor is used in a wide variety of industries.
    Ⓒ Child labor is essential to the economy of some countries.
    Ⓓ Child labor is pernicious in all settings and it should be eradicated.
    Ⓔ Child labor is a long-term issue that has defied solutions for centuries.

Directions: For question 20, consider each of the choices separately and select <u>all</u> that apply.

Question 20 is based on the following reading passage.

    A philosophical debate has simmered for years over what role, if any, social responsibility should play in corporate management. The contemporary trend of corporations donating a portion of their profits or a portion of a product's purchase price to some worthy charity can actually lead to controversy. Termed "cause-related marketing," this practice has both critics and defenders. The disagreement centers on the corporation's motive. Skeptics view the practice as a company doing good deeds only to enhance its reputation and, thus, to enhance its bottom line and make more money; any actual benefit to society is merely a coincidental side advantage. However, philanthropists believe companies should make charitable donations because it is the humane thing to do, and any additional profit the company may get from its enhanced reputation is simply a nice collateral benefit.

20. What unstated inference(s) are made in the above passage?

    Ⓐ Charities ultimately receive more donations because of cause-related marketing.
    Ⓑ Some see a selfish motive in companies that donate to charity causes.
    Ⓒ Some corporations will continue to make business decisions based on social responsibility.

IF YOU FINISH BEFORE TIME IS CALLED, CHECK YOUR WORK ON THIS SECTION ONLY. DO NOT WORK ON ANY OTHER SECTION IN THE TEST.

Section 4: Quantitative Reasoning

The answer choices for multiple-choice questions on the actual computer version of the GRE are not labeled with letters. Answer choices in this study guide have lettered choices A, B, C, D, E, etc. for clarity. On the actual exam, you will be required to click on ovals or squares to select your answer.

HELPFUL HINT:
⬭ oval – answer will be a single choice
☐ square – answer will be one or more choices

Time: 35 minutes
20 Questions

General Directions: For each question, indicate the best answer, using the directions given.

- All numerical values used are real numbers.
- Figures or diagrams are not necessarily drawn to scale and should not be used to estimate sizes by measurement unless they are data displays (graphs and charts) or coordinates on a coordinate axes. These will always be drawn to scale.
- Lines that appear straight can be assumed to be straight.
- A symbol that appears in repeated quantities represents the same value or object for each quantity.
- On a number line, positive numbers are to the right of zero and increase to the right and negative numbers are to the left of zero and decrease to the left.
- Distances are always either zero or a positive value.

Directions: For questions 1 to 8, compare Quantity A and Quantity B, using additional information centered above the two quantities if such information is given. Select one of the following four answer choices below each question.

Ⓐ   Quantity A is greater.
Ⓑ   Quantity B is greater.
Ⓒ   The two quantities are equal.
Ⓓ   The relationship cannot be determined from the information given.

Question 1 refers to the following information.

$$x^2 + 11x + 24 = (x + m)(x + r)$$

	Quantity A	**Quantity B**
1.	$m + r$	$(m)(r)$

Question 2 refers to the following information.

$$0 < x < 1$$

	Quantity A	**Quantity B**
2.	$\dfrac{1}{x}$	$\sqrt{x}$

Question 3 refers to the following figure.

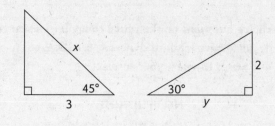

Quantity A	**Quantity B**
3. x	y

Question 4 refers to the following information.

$$(x - 2y)^2 = 16, \; xy = 10$$

Quantity A	**Quantity B**
4. $x^2 + 4y^2$	56

Quantity A	**Quantity B**
5. $(-0.25)^{11}$	$(-0.25)^{13}$

Question 6 refers to the following figure.

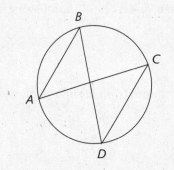

A, B, C, and D are points on the circle

Quantity A	**Quantity B**
6. $\angle ABD$	$\angle DCA$

Question 7 refers to the following information.

$$0 < x < y$$

Quantity A	**Quantity B**
7. percent change from x to y	percent change from y to x

Question 8 refers to the following figure.

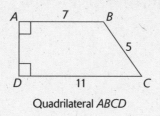

Quadrilateral *ABCD*

Quantity A	**Quantity B**
8. perimeter of *ABCD*	26

Directions: Questions 9 to 20 have several different formats. Unless otherwise directed, indicate a single answer choice. For Numeric Entry questions, follow the instructions below.

Numeric Entry Questions

- Write out your answer choice with numerals.
- Your answer may be an integer, a decimal, or a fraction, and it may be negative.
- If a question asks for a fraction, there will be two boxes—one for the numerator and one for the denominator.
- Equivalent forms of the correct answer, such as 4.5 and 4.50, are all correct. Fractions do not need to be reduced to lowest terms.
- Enter the exact answer unless the question asks you to round your answer.

9. Find the value of $\dfrac{\frac{1}{2}+\frac{5}{6}}{\frac{2}{3}+\frac{3}{4}}$

Ⓐ $\dfrac{8}{17}$

Ⓑ $\dfrac{16}{17}$

Ⓒ $\dfrac{21}{20}$

Ⓓ $\dfrac{17}{16}$

Ⓔ $\dfrac{17}{8}$

10. In the figure below, which of the following could be the value of *x*? Indicate <u>all</u> possible answers.

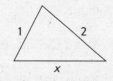

(figure is not drawn to scale)

A 1
B 1.5
C 2
D 2.5
E 3
F 3.5

11. The total amount that Amir has invested for his retirement is $120,000. If he has invested in stocks, bonds, and real estate at a ratio of 7 : 3 : 2, respectively, how much has Amir invested in stocks?

    Ⓐ $10,000
    Ⓑ $20,000
    Ⓒ $30,000
    Ⓓ $70,000
    Ⓔ $84,000

Questions 12 to 14 are based on the following graph.

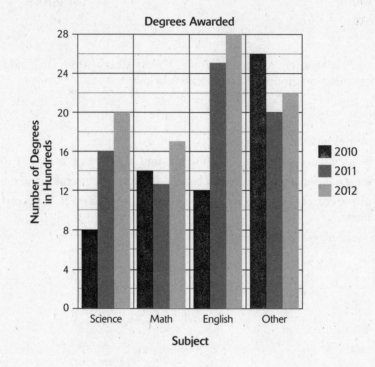

12. Approximately what was the percent change in the number of math degrees awarded from 2010 to 2012? Round your answer to the nearest tenth of a percent.

    [   ] %

13. Which of the following statements must be true about the number of degrees awarded from 2010 to 2011? Indicate all possible answers.

    Ⓐ Both science and math increased in number.
    Ⓑ Both English and math increased in number.
    Ⓒ Both science and English increased in number.
    Ⓓ The combined number of degrees awarded for science, math, and English increased by more than 1,900 degrees.
    Ⓔ The combined "other" category for these two years had less than double as many degrees awarded than the combined number of degrees awarded for math in these two years.

14. In 2010, the number of degrees awarded in English exceeded the number of degrees awarded in science by approximately how many?

Ⓐ 80

Ⓑ 90

Ⓒ 400

Ⓓ 800

Ⓔ 900

15. The letters A, B, C, D, and E are written on separate index cards and arranged in a row, not necessarily in that order. An index card is randomly selected. What is the probability that the index card selected will have the letter A as the first letter on the left and the letter E as the last letter on the right?

Ⓐ $\frac{1}{20}$

Ⓑ $\frac{1}{10}$

Ⓒ $\frac{1}{5}$

Ⓓ $\frac{2}{5}$

Ⓔ $\frac{1}{2}$

16. The average (arithmetic mean) of a set of five numbers is 20. If the average of two of those numbers is 26, what is the average of the other three numbers?

17. If @ is a binary operation such that $x @ y = \dfrac{x^2 - 2xy + y^2}{x^2 - y^2}$ and $x^2 - y^2 \neq 0$, then what is the value of $c @ d$ if $c = 5d$?

Ⓐ $-\frac{3}{2}$

Ⓑ $-\frac{2}{3}$

Ⓒ 1

Ⓓ $\frac{2}{3}$

Ⓔ $\frac{3}{2}$

18. In how many different ways can the letters in the word MODE be ordered?

Ⓐ 4

Ⓑ 10

Ⓒ 24

Ⓓ 216

Ⓔ 256

19. If $6y = -18$, then $y^3 + y =$

   Ⓐ 12

   Ⓑ 6

   Ⓒ −6

   Ⓓ −24

   Ⓔ −30

20. The mean of data set G is how much greater than the median of data set H?

            Data set G : 24, 30, 16, 11, 19

            Data set H : 33, 27, 12, 5, 3

   Ⓐ 1

   Ⓑ 3

   Ⓒ 4

   Ⓓ 7

   Ⓔ 8

IF YOU FINISH BEFORE TIME IS CALLED, CHECK YOUR WORK ON THIS SECTION ONLY. DO NOT WORK ON ANY OTHER SECTION IN THE TEST.

Answer Key

Section 3: Verbal Reasoning

1. E
2. C
3. D
4. A
5. Sentence 6
6. A
7. D
8. C and E
9. B and F
10. C, D, and G
11. B, E, and I
12. B and D
13. A and D
14. C and D
15. C and E
16. B
17. E
18. A and C
19. D
20. A and C

Section 4: Quantitative Reasoning

1. B
2. A
3. A
4. C
5. B
6. C
7. A
8. C
9. B
10. B, C, and D
11. D
12. 21.4
13. C, D, and E
14. D
15. A
16. 16
17. D
18. C
19. E
20. E

Charting and Analyzing Your Test Results

The first step in analyzing your results is to chart your answers. Use the charts on the following pages to identify your strengths and areas of improvement. Complete the process of evaluating your essays and analyzing problems in each area for the diagnostic test. Reevaluate your results as you look for trends in the types of errors (repeated errors), and look for low scores in results in *specific* topic areas. This reexamination and analysis is a tremendous asset to help you maximize your best possible score. The answers and explanations following these charts will provide you clarification to help you solve these types of problems in the future.

Analytical Writing Assessment Worksheets

Analyze your responses using the following charts, and refer to the sample "strong response" on page 35 as a reference guide. Then estimate your score using the Analytical Writing Scoring Guide on pages 3–4 for characteristics of a high scoring essay to rate your essay.

Analysis of an Issue (Essay 1)			
Questions	**Strong Response Score 5 or 6**	**Moderate Response Score 3 or 4**	**Weak Response Score 1 or 2**
1. Does the essay focus on the assigned topic and respond to the specific task?			
2. Does the essay show an understanding of the complexity of the issue?			
3. Does the essay provide well-developed reasons and/or examples?			
4. Does the essay show relevant supporting details?			
5. Is the essay organized and does it use transitions to connect ideas?			
6. Does the essay show a command of standard written English?			

Analysis of an Argument (Essay 2)			
Questions	**Strong Response Score 5 or 6**	**Moderate Response Score 3 or 4**	**Weak Response Score 1 or 2**
1. Does the essay focus on the specific topic and cover all of the tasks?			
2. Does the essay identify and analyze important features of the passage?			
3. Does the essay develop and express your evaluation?			
4. Does the essay support your evaluation with relevant reasons and/or examples?			
5. Is the essay well-organized?			
6. Does the essay show a command of standard written English?			

Multiple-Choice Questions

Verbal Reasoning Worksheet

Types of Questions Missed			
Question Type	Total Possible	Number Correct	Number Incorrect
Reading Comprehension Questions 1 to 5 and Questions 16 to 20	10		
Text Completion Questions 6 to 11	6		
Sentence Equivalence Questions 12 to 15	4		
Totals	**20**		

Quantitative Reasoning Worksheet

Types of Questions Missed			
Content Style Topic	Total Possible	Number Correct	Number Incorrect
Arithmetic Questions 5, 9	2		
Algebra Questions 1, 2, 4, 7, 17, 19	6		
Geometry Questions 3, 6, 8, 10	4		
Data Analysis Questions 16, 18, 20	3		
Word Problems Questions 11, 15	2		
Data Interpretation Questions 12, 13, 14	3		
Totals	**20**		

Analysis Worksheet

One of the most important instructional tools for test preparation is to analyze WHY you answered a problem incorrectly. Using the data gathered from the above worksheets, tally the number of questions that you missed in the table below. As you review the data, you will be able to pinpoint specific areas of concentration. First, review the answer explanations following this worksheet to help you understand how to solve these types of problems. Then, before you take any more practice tests, take advantage of the information gathered in your analysis to help you focus on specific subject areas. The following subject review chapters for Verbal Reasoning and Quantitative Reasoning will introduce you to the GRE question types and fundamental skills necessary in each area to help you accomplish your goals.

Tally Sheet				
Section	Total Incorrect	Possible Explanation: Simple Mistake	Possible Explanation: Misread Problem	Possible Explanation: Lack of Knowledge
Verbal Reasoning 20 Questions Total				
Quantitative Reasoning 20 Questions Total				
Totals				

Answers and Explanations

Section 1: Analytical Writing – Analysis of an Issue

Issue Topic

> Some people believe that sports figures serve as inspirational role models for youth. Others contend that excellence in sports does not automatically make someone an effective role model.

Write a response in which you distinguish between the two viewpoints on the issue and state which one most closely matches your own position. Be sure to discuss both viewpoints as you explain and support your stance.

Strong Sample Response

Who can forget the impact of Jesse Owens winning four gold medals at the 1936 Berlin Olympics, stealing the limelight from Hitler and his racist ideology? Or, consider the boost given to the city of New Orleans when the Saints won the Super Bowl despite the ravages of Hurricane Katrina. These examples highlight how sports serve as models to inspire young people. While not every track and field athlete provides an example of good behavior, sports teach important lessons about perseverance, sportsmanship, and excellence.

This is a strong opening paragraph that clearly states the writer's position and provides examples qualifying that sports figures serve to "inspire young people."

Young people learn lessons best through concrete examples, and sports provide many portrayals of athletes persevering in pursuit of their goals. In interviews, professional athletes often cite the importance of practice and hard work in their success. The basketball great Michael Jordan has often talked about early setbacks, like being cut from his high school team. Despite this tough lesson he worked hard and became who many consider the greatest player of all time. Young people can look to a person like Michael Jordan as a role model for the value of persevering through difficult times. Too frequently youngsters become easily frustrated and give up before reaching their goals. Sports, with the emphasis on championships and record-setting performances, offer opportunities to discuss how to pursue goals and negotiate setbacks.

Each reason for the position is supported by a strong example that illustrates the rationale behind the writer's stance. The second paragraph provides a specific, persuasive example of Michael Jordan "persevering through difficult times."

Another way in which sports can inspire is through the models of good sportsmanship many athletes provide. One inspirational story is of the college softball player who hit a game-winning homerun but due to injury was unable to run the bases and score. Her teammates were unable to help her due to the rules. Although it meant losing the game, the players on the other team supported her as she rounded the bases. To them it was more important to play the game the right way rather than win in a cheapened manner. This example of sportsmanship provides a clear model for young people that illustrates the old saying that it's not whether you win or lose that's important, it's how you play the game.

Each paragraph is focused, while also making smooth transitions from point to point in the writer's chain of logic.

Finally, amazing feats on the field, on the rink, or in the pool can inspire young people to set high goals for themselves. When swimmer Michael Phelps announced that he would try to win seven gold medals, people thought he was overreaching. However, his pursuit and eventual grasp of this lofty goal led to both individual glory and national pride. Of course his later bad behavior involving drugs must be acknowledged, but even then he handled the situation honestly. Young people need to see that even sports figures can make mistakes, but that the way they conduct themselves is what truly matters.

The use of the Michael Phelps example enables the writer to address the opposing view while still maintaining a clear position.

In short, sports can inspire young people in ways that other areas of endeavor cannot. They show athletes striving for goals, working hard, and accepting defeat with grace. Not all athletes are role models, but the ones who are create powerful impressions in the minds of youth.

The conclusion restates the writer's position and provides logical reasons to justify this position, while addressing both points of view.

Moderate Sample Response

Athletes never asked to be role models and many are poor examples to young people. Every week there is a new scandal involving cheating, drug use, or criminal behavior. While some sports figures may inspire, the vast majority are just regular people who happen to have certain physical gifts.

Many people enjoy watching the Olympics, especially the track and field events, but then find out a month later that the gold medalist failed a drug test. Young people get the message that its okay to cheat as long as you don't get caught. Any positive or inspirational message is lost in the news coverage of the scandal. Young people see someone held up as a role model and then the next day that same person is a villain. That's confusing to kids and not helpful in inspiring them to do better.

Then there are the athletes who cheat to get ahead. They may use inside information like stealing signals or plays. This teaches children that it's most important to win at all costs rather than being honest. This is not the kind of role model people want for their children. Of course most athletes are honest and play the game the right way, but the ones who cheat tend to get the most coverage in the press.

There are also problems with players breaking laws and getting in trouble with the police. Sometimes athletes feel like they deserve special treatment and shouldn't have to follow the same rules as everyone else. Just because someone can play golf well or catch a football doesn't mean he should be exempt from the rules everyone else has to obey. It sends a bad message to young people if they see sports figures getting away with bad behavior.

Although some sports figures may inspire young people by providing good examples, its not the case for everyone.

> The writer stakes out a clear position, but shows limited competence in responding to the task.

> The examples provided are adequate and relevant, although they could be developed in more detail. This essay lacks the development of qualifying a position, and does not articulate persuasive reasons why athletes are poor role models.

> The writer does not respond to the prompt asking the writer to address both of the views presented until the very end.

> The organization is clear and logical with some use of transition words to guide the reader. A few minor errors (its, exemt) do not interfere with the response's clarity.

Weak Sample Response

> This essay lacks unity and organization and shows little understanding of analytical writing.

Athletes do a good job being role models for kids. They show how to play the game. Although some also cheat or break rules. Sports figures are good role models because they show good lessons.

Kids can watch the players and base their play on what they do, like when kids imitate a famous batter. They can imitate the player and get better.

Young people can also learn from when players have a bad day or are struggling. They can see how they cope with their problems and use that as a role model. For example, if a basketball player misses a lot of free throws and then practices then that would be a good example.

Not all sports figures are good. Some like Pete Rose cheated and got caught so that is a bad example of a role model. Other cheaters maybe used sterroids or other drugs.

All in all, it's what the young person thinks that's important. Some sports figures are excellent while others are not good examples to follow.

> The overall weak response is vague in presenting and developing a clear position. Although the writer does provide examples, they are not relevant or fully developed.

> The writer does not respond to the issue of athletes acting as role models except in the context of sports and appears to waver in the final paragraph.

> The essay contains many flaws in sentence structure and vocabulary. There are also many fragmented sentences. The essay is poorly organized and lacks a cohesive, clear response to the task.

Section 2: Analytical Writing – Analysis of an Argument

Argument Topic

The following appeared in a company memorandum.

> Sales of all Hopewell Farms' ice cream products have risen dramatically in the past two months with the introduction of the chocolate-orange and vanilla-mint flavors. To capitalize on growing consumer interest in exciting flavor combinations, Hopewell Farms should introduce a minimum of four new flavors in the coming year. This will result in increased profit for the company and its shareholders.

Write a response in which you examine the assumptions, stated and implied, that are present in the argument. Explain how these assumptions form the basis for the argument and how, if proven false, they would affect its persuasiveness.

Strong Sample Response

Consumers do enjoy new tastes in food. Each year new products entice shoppers to try "exciting" new flavors. It appears Hopewell Farms has done well with its two new ice cream flavors, but the company memo recommending the rollout of four new flavors in the next year makes some faulty and dubious assumptions.

The underlying assumption is that the sales data from the last two months is indicative of future performance for new flavors. Although sales have been rising, the memo is unclear on whether the new flavors are contributing the most to the increase. It says that sales of all Hopewell Farms ice cream products have been on the rise. Without specific data on the chocolate-orange and vanilla-mint sales it's an implied assumption that they have contributed the most to the increased sales. It's also unclear whether the trend will continue. For example, if the two months are in the summer it makes sense they would see higher sales in those months and then a dip in the winter.

A further assumption that may not bear out is consumer interest in different and perhaps surprising flavor combinations. Again, since the data on sales does not separate out for the two new flavors it's difficult to tell whether people are embracing them. People may try vanilla-mint and then decide they don't like it. Not all new products drive sales, especially if they distract from the core brand.

It is also likely to cost Hopewell Farms a large amount of money to develop and bring to market four new flavors a year. The research and development may cut into the profits that the memo so confidently predicts. Ingredients for the exciting new flavors may be more costly than plain vanilla, also resulting in lower profits. This plan also assumes that the market will be large enough for their existing products and the new flavors. With limited space in the grocery store freezer, a flavor like cucumber-vanilla may be a hard sell to grocers. If grocers are not willing to add space, the introduction of new flavors could even lower sales for the currently popular Hopewell Farms products.

This response thoroughly addresses the prompt by identifying both stated and implied assumptions and then explaining how they undermine the persuasiveness of the argument.

The essay continues to examine evidence to support the argument.

The concluding paragraph provides additional information to support the argument. The use of effective vocabulary (entice, dubious, indicative), combined with logical transitions, makes for a fluent effect in the writing.

Starting with the first paragraph, notice how each paragraph assesses a particular assumption and the likely ramifications.

This response provides specific evidence to support the argument within each paragraph.

Moderate Sample Response

This paragraph is competent in identifying a major assumption, but does not reach deeper levels of insight.

The essay attempts to connect transitions between the writer's thoughts, but is limited in demonstrating the ability to convey these thoughts in a clear way to provide a sense of unity and cohesiveness.

At first the suggestion in the company memo from Hopewell Farms appears to make a good point about adding more flavors to its line of ice creams. Upon closer reading, however, it is clear that the recommendation relies on several assumptions that could prove false.

A major assumption is that the trend of rising sales in the past two months will continue to hold true. Two months is not a long enough period of time to make accurate predictions about whether new flavors will be popular with consumers. Maybe people buy the ice cream to try it and then decide they don't like it. This could lead to initially high sales that would then fall. This would prove the assumption wrong.

Another assumption is that people will want to continue trying new and unusual flavors. Chocolate-orange doesn't sound too exotic, but what about chocolate-mango? Will Hopewell approve new flavors like watermelon-mint? There may be a limit to what customers are willing to try. If Hopewell Farms invests a lot of money in developing new flavors and they flop then there will not be increased sales or profits. Then that assumption would also be proven false.

Finally, the memo suggests adding four new flavors in the next year. That is going to require a lot of freezer space in the grocery store. What if the stores don't want to give up that much space, or they replace flavors that sell well with the new, "exciting" flavors that people end up not liking. It seems like a big risk with too many possible bad endings.

The opening paragraph identifies and examines the argument's evidence that "could prove false," but tends to be limited and brief. Assumptions must be developed and substantiated more fully to tie into the final conclusion. Providing an introduction with an insightful analysis that supports the writer's ideas would have helped to achieve this goal.

Notice the limited support provided in this paragraph. This leads to an uneven development of the argument. The support, while present, does not fully examine the implications of the argument's assumptions.

This essay contains minimal flaws in mechanical errors.

Weak Sample Response

Notice that the writer only offers an opinion about the topic rather than addressing the writing task.

The argument says to make more new flavors to make more money. This is a bad idea for many reasons.

What if they make strange new flavors peole don't like? Vanilla mint does not sound like a good ice cream flavor. It would be better as a gum or a mint, not as ice cream.

They could make more money by focusing on just the chocolate-ornge, which is much more popular. More people would like and buy. Or it would be better to make a lo-fat or yogurt version because those are popular as well.

Making new flavors could be really expensive and not worth it.

Overall the Hopewell Farms should just stick with the flavors it has and maybe add lo-fat and yogurt.

This weak response suffers from major faults in writing structure, logic, and persuasion. The introductory paragraph is too brief, unconvincing, and presents irrelevant content.

The sketchy paragraphs throughout the essay present little support or explanation. In addition, its short length makes the mechanical errors more evident.

Section 3: Verbal Reasoning

Reading Comprehension

1. **E.** The passage indicates that it is the multitude of temples that makes the locale a magnet for pilgrims. However, the passage does not indicate that the visual splendor is what actually attracts travelers (B), nor does it state that the pilgrims ignore the visual distractions (C). Choice A, which describes the "visual panorama of beautiful sights" on Mt. Emei, is stated in the first sentence of the passage; it is not an inference that can be deduced from the passage. Choice D, identifies a fact that is explicitly stated in the passage; it too is not an inference that can be drawn from the passage.

2. **C.** The most accurate description of the overall tone of this passage is found in choice C; this author appears to be mostly optimistic about progress being made in this industry. On the other hand, there is little to support the idea that this author is "...dubious about success..." or that he is "...skeptical about the technological innovations...," so choices A and B can be eliminated. Finally, while the ideas stated in choices D and E *do* appear in this passage, they are certainly not accurate descriptions of the overall tone.

3. **D.** While choice D, the "overuse of pesticides and herbicides in the fields as the crops grow," does describe a real potential problem in the agricultural community, this particular problem is not mentioned in the passage; therefore, choice D is the correct exception. On the other hand, all of the other answer choices do correctly identify potential problems that are mentioned in the passage and which the new system is designed to mitigate.

4. **A.** Choice A is directly supported in the final sentence, wherein the passage concludes "Perhaps most importantly, this new technology could simplify and streamline our current overly-complex system..." Choices B and C can be found in the passage, but they are not identified as the most important potential benefit. Choices D and E are not mentioned in the passage.

5. **Sentence 6:** The single sentence that most clearly contains a warning, an admonition as to why the new program might not expand and progress as rapidly as it would otherwise is the 6th sentence, which states "However, many in the farming community have yet to follow suit, and federal food-safety legislation is stalled in Congress." Specifically, it criticizes Congress for dragging its heels in food-storage legislation and the farming community for not jumping on the bandwagon and adopting new computer technology in their businesses. All of the other sentences in the passage describe the positive results of using computer software and handheld hardware gear in the farming industry. No other sentence in the passage is critical.

Text Completion

6. **A.** The best word to complete this sentence must somehow include the idea that "the real work of the Court" is done in secret, thus, choice A, *mystery,* is the correct answer. None of the other answer choices include this essential aspect of secrecy.

7. **D.** You should focus on the key phrase "resulting in death or disease," which indicates the correct answer must have a negative connotation. This eliminates choices A, B, and C, because each one has a positive meaning. Choice E is in the right direction; *impeded* is a negative term, but it does not go far enough since impeding something merely slows it down or hinders it. Choice D is correct; *devastated* is the best word to complete this sentence because it means the wild bird population has been ravaged or demolished or depleted.

8. **C and E.** In choice C, the words *astute* and *witty* both describe a successful satirist; the word choices offered in the incorrect choices do not. If the publication of Twain's autobiography was prevented for 100 years, one can correctly say that it was *embargoed* (E), which means to be restricted or held back. *Sanctioned* (D) means to authorize or approve; it is the opposite of what this sentence needs. *Countermanded* (F) means to revoke or cancel something.

9. **B and F.** This question may be more accessible if you focus on the second blank first. It is generally agreed that the first evidence of modern humans in North America dates to about 13,000 years ago; so this is not the time of humans' *disappearance* (D) nor of their *reemergence* (E) but rather, it is the time of their *arrival* (F). Next, knowing that all of these large animals have become extinct since that point in time, it is logical to pair the idea of the *disappearance* (B) of the large animals with the *arrival* (F) of the early humans. Do not be flustered by the fact that the word *disappearance* is an option for blank i and blank ii; remember to find the best word for *each* blank, based on the entire context of the sentence(s).

10. **C, D, and G.** This sentence, which encapsulates an aging man's memories, leads us through his fascination with early airplanes, his early flights, his wartime service, and finally the friends he lost along the way. Choice C fits the first blank perfectly, as the word *haggard* reinforces the phrase "world-weary," while *septuagenarian* (someone aged 70–79) is the appropriate age for the man in the sentence. Choice A is incorrect because the word *callow* describes someone who is immature or inexperienced. Similarly, the word *jejune* in choice B means unsophisticated, and the word *swain* is an archaic term that refers to a young man in love. For the second blank, only the word *barter* (D) fits the context of the sentence; as a teenage boy, he traded his time and labor washing planes for free flights. In the last blank, the word *industriously* (G) completes the vision of a young man "striving…to master the complexities of modern warplanes."

11. **B, E, and I.** In the first blank, being located in the *interior* (B) of the continent fits well with the phrasing "deep in the…Basin of Mexico." The second blank requires a word that includes the idea of a "great capital of a most powerful city-state"; the best choice is *metropolis* (E). The word *necropolis* (F) actually refers to a cemetery, and a *burg* (D) is a town or a smaller city. For the last blank, the word *heart* (I) is the best fit because the Sacred Precinct is located in the center of the city.

Sentence Equivalence

12. **B and D.** The logic of this sentence indicates that a TV mini-series would be produced only about someone who was connected to the bombing, attacks, and kidnappings. Choice A (*cleared of*) may at first sound as if it would fit, but it would require a clarifying word such as "eventually" before the blank. This logic discounts Choice C (*innocent of*) as well. Choice E (*deeply regretful about*) is incorrect for the same reason; it cannot fit properly without another qualifying word or phrase somewhere in the sentence.

13. **A and D.** The elaborate description of "shining India" juxtaposes the simplicity of "rural Indian villages," and then the phrase "widened dramatically" requires that the word used to complete this sentence shows a large difference between the two worlds. No other answer choices connote such a difference.

14. **C and D.** Both *desperate,* which means overwhelmed with urgency, and *dire,* which means potentially disastrous, fit the context of the sentence. Choice F, *unacceptable,* may sound good at first, but it is wrong because the situation in 1943 was *already* "deadly" and "immediate"; therefore, it makes no sense to say that it "was quickly becoming" unacceptable. Choice B, *disparate,* refers to things that are completely unalike. Choice E, *dishabille,* designates a state of being partially undressed, clearly not intended in the meaning of this sentence! This is typical of a word which the test committee might use, believing that some test-takers will be unfamiliar with such a seldom-used word. Choice A, *lackadaisical,* means showing lack of interest and is not appropriate in the context of this sentence.

15. **C and E.** Researchers are interested in learning the "true overall" effect that individual nations have on the oceans of the world and the words *impact* and *repercussions* both fit this meaning perfectly. *Benefit* (A) and *amelioration* (B) are both positive words that do not fit the sentence's meaning. Choices D and F do not make sense in the context of this sentence.

Reading Comprehension

16. **B.** One can infer from this passage that metaphysical poetry was probably unpopular between the late eighteenth century, when the term was coined as a "derogatory term," until the early twentieth century, when T.S. Eliot "initiated a resurgence in the art form," a period of over one hundred years. On the other hand, this passage offers no evidence that the poets *took pride in confusing their audience* (A), nor does it indicate that they were *not famous during their lives* (E). Choice C is inaccurate because of the word *exclusively,* which is too

specific; the passage does not imply T.S. Eliot wrote only metaphysical poetry. Choice D contradicts the passage, which implies that modern audiences do read metaphysical poetry and find it intellectually rewarding.

17. **E.** The correct answer is choice E, because *woebegone* actually means depressed or troubled. All of the other choices accurately reflect the overall positive tone, the feeling of freedom and the lack of restraint.

18. **A and C.** The correct answer must include both choices A and C, because these images do reflect the visual cues in the passage. However, choice B contradicts the passage; the writer enjoys his flying completely free from the roar of an aircraft engine.

19. **D.** A careful reader will notice that the ideas presented in choices A and B *do* actually appear in this passage. However, this particular question asks for the author's yet-to-be-stated *conclusion,* not the facts he has cited thus far. Thus, choice D is the best suggestion for his upcoming conclusion; that is, child labor, by definition, is *pernicious* (hurtful, wicked) and such exploitation should be eradicated. However, the idea that child labor is *essential to the economy of some countries* (C) is not implied in the passage, especially given the passage's negative tone regarding child labor. Choice E is inaccurate because the passage never addresses child labor as a *long-term issue that has defied solutions for centuries*; therefore, it is illogical to think this is the conclusion the author intends.

20. **A and C.** If corporations are making charitable donations, regardless of their motives, one can correctly assume that charities will receive more donations (A). Also, because the passage states that the debate "has simmered for years" and that the trend of corporations' donating to charity continues today, one can also assume this trend will continue (C). Choice B, on the other hand, can be eliminated because the idea is stated in the passage; it is explicit, so it cannot be an unstated assumption underlying the passage.

Section 4: Quantitative Reasoning

1. **B.** Factor the expression $x^2 + 11x + 24$.

$$x^2 + 11x + 24 = (x+m)(x+r)$$
$$(x+3)(x+8) = (x+m)(x+r)$$
$$\text{or}$$
$$(x+8)(x+3) = (x+m)(x+r)$$

Either $m = 3$ and $r = 8$ or $m = 8$ and $r = 3$. In either case, $m + r = 11$ and $(m)(r) = 24$. Quantity B has the greater value.

2. **A.** Experiment with simple numbers and replace x with simple numbers. The given sentence tells us that x is a positive value between 0 and 1. The square root of any positive value between 0 and 1 is another positive value between 0 and 1, but larger than the original value.

For example, suppose $x = \frac{1}{4}$, then $\sqrt{\frac{1}{4}} = \frac{1}{2}$. Notice that $\frac{1}{2}$ is larger than the original value of $\frac{1}{4}$.

Therefore Quantity B is a value between 0 and 1.

$\frac{1}{x}$ means the reciprocal of x. The reciprocal of any positive value between 0 and 1 is another positive value that is greater than 1. For example, suppose $x = \frac{1}{4}$, then $\frac{1}{x} = 4$. Quantity A is a value greater than 1 and Quantity B has a value less than 1.

Therefore Quantity A is greater than Quantity B.

3. **A.** Use the properties of 45-45-90 and 30-60-90 right triangles to determine the lengths of the missing sides x and y. In a 45-45-90 right triangle, the sides opposite the 45° angles are equal in length and the hypotenuse is that length times $\sqrt{2}$. Hence, $x = 3\sqrt{2}$.

In the 30-60-90 right triangle, the side opposite the 30° angle is the short side, the hypotenuse is twice the length of this short side, and the side opposite the 60° angle is the short side times the $\sqrt{3}$. Hence, ratios are $1 : 2 : \sqrt{3}$. Hence, $y = 2\sqrt{3}$.

Now either use the $\sqrt{\ }$ feature on the calculator to compare the values, or rewrite each value as a single number under the square root sign. Using a calculator, $x = 3\sqrt{2} \approx 4.24$ and $y = 2\sqrt{3} \approx 3.46$.

Rewriting each expression as a single number under the square root sign, $x = 3\sqrt{2} = \sqrt{9}\sqrt{2} = \sqrt{18}$ and $y = 2\sqrt{3} = \sqrt{4}\sqrt{3} = \sqrt{12}$. Therefore Quantity A is greater than Quantity B.

4. C. In order to answer this question, you need to solve for Quantity A:

$$(x - 2y)^2 = 16$$
$$(x - 2y)(x - 2y) = 16$$
$$x^2 - 4xy + 4y^2 = 16 \quad \text{(replace } xy \text{ with 10)}$$
$$x^2 - 4(10) + 4y^2 = 16$$
$$x^2 - 40 + 4y^2 = 16 \quad \text{(add 40 to each side of the equation)}$$
$$x^2 + 4y^2 = 56$$

Quantity A has the value 56 and Quantity B has the value 56. Therefore the two quantities are equal.

5. B. Notice that each quantity will have a negative value $\left[(\text{negative})^{\text{odd integer}} = \text{negative}\right]$.

The least negative number has the greater value (for example, –0.3 is greater than –0.4). When a number between 0 and 1 is multiplied by itself repeatedly, the value becomes smaller. Therefore $(0.25)^{11}$ is larger than $(0.25)^{13}$, but making these quantities *negative* makes $(-0.25)^{13}$ less negative than $(-0.25)^{11}$ and therefore the larger value. Therefore Quantity B is greater than Quantity A.

6. C. In a circle, if an angle has its vertex on the circle (called an inscribed angle), its measure is half the degree measure of the arc it intercepts.

That is, $\angle ABD = \frac{1}{2}\left(\overset{\frown}{AD}\right)$ and $\angle DCA = \frac{1}{2}\left(\overset{\frown}{AD}\right)$.

Therefore the two quantities are equal.

7. A. The formula for finding percent change is as follows:

$$\text{percent change} = \frac{\text{amount of change}}{\text{original amount}} \times 100\%$$

Notice that both x and y are positive, and so:

The percent-change from x to $y = \dfrac{|y - x|}{x}$ (before making it a percent value).

The percent-change from y to $x = \dfrac{|x - y|}{y}$ (before making it a percent value).

So now we make the comparison of these two values.

Quantity A	**Quantity B**
$\dfrac{|y - x|}{x}$	$\dfrac{|x - y|}{y}$

Rewrite each fraction with a common denominator of xy.

$$\frac{y|y-x|}{xy} \qquad\qquad \frac{x|x-y|}{xy}$$

Since the denominators are the same, simply compare the numerators.

$$y|y-x| \qquad\qquad x|x-y|$$

Recall that $|y-x|=|x-y|$. So simply compare:

$$y \qquad\qquad\qquad x$$

The original information says that $x < y$ (y is greater than x). Therefore Quantity A is greater than Quantity B.

A different and potentially easier method is to experiment with simple numbers. Suppose x was 1 and y was 2.

Quantity A	**Quantity B**
percent change	percent change
from x to y	from y to x
$\dfrac{|2-1|}{1}\times 100\%$	$\dfrac{|1-2|}{2}\times 100\%$
100%	50%

Therefore Quantity A is greater than Quantity B.

8. **C.** This problem is made easier by drawing in a segment from B perpendicular to CD at E.

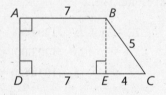

Notice that $DE = AB = 7$ thus $EC = 4$ since $DC = 11$. In order to find AD, find BE, which has the same value as AD. Find BE by using the Pythagorean theorem in right triangle BEC.

$$BE^2 + 4^2 = 5^2$$
$$BE^2 + 16 = 25$$
$$BE^2 = 9$$
$$BE = 3$$

Now the perimeter of the trapezoid = 7 + 5 + 11 + 3 = 26. Therefore the two quantities are equal.

9. B. Step 1: Simplify the numerator and denominator.

$$\frac{\frac{1}{2}+\frac{5}{6}}{\frac{2}{3}+\frac{3}{4}}$$

$$\frac{1}{2}+\frac{5}{6}=\frac{3}{6}+\frac{5}{6}$$

$$=\frac{8}{6}$$

$$=\frac{4}{3}$$

$$\frac{2}{3}+\frac{3}{4}=\frac{8}{12}+\frac{9}{12}$$

$$=\frac{17}{12}$$

Step 2: Remember that dividing by a fraction requires multiplying by its inverse:

$$\frac{4}{3}\div\frac{17}{12}=\frac{4}{\cancel{3}_{1}}\times\frac{\cancel{12}^{4}}{17}$$

$$=\frac{16}{17}$$

10. B, C, and D. The length of any side of any triangle must be greater than the difference between the other two sides, and less than the sum of the other two sides. In this problem, the lengths of two sides are given and thus $x < 2 + 1$ and $x > 2 - 1$. Therefore, $2 - 1 < x < 2 + 1$, which becomes $1 < x < 3$. So, $x > 1$ and $x < 3$.

Only choices 1.5, 2, and 2.5 satisfy these conditions.

11. D. Let $7x$ represent the amount invested in stocks, $3x$ represent the amount invested in bonds, and $2x$ represent the amount invested in real estate. Then,

$$7x + 3x + 2x = 120,000$$
$$12x = 120,000$$
$$x = 10,000$$

The question asked for how much was invested in stocks. We used $7x$ to represent that amount. Therefore,

$$7x = 7(10,000)$$
$$= 70,000$$

12. 21.4 In 2010, the number of math degrees awarded was 1,400. Remember, the number of degrees is in hundreds. In 2012, the number of math degrees awarded was 1,700. So, from 2010 to 2012, there was an increase of 300 degrees. Percent change can be calculated as follows:

$$\text{percent change} = \frac{\text{amount of change}}{\text{starting amount}} \times 100\%$$

Therefore, $\frac{300}{1,400} \times 100\% = 21.42857\%$, which, rounded to the nearest tenth of a percent, becomes 21.4%.

13. C, D, and E. Let's analyze each answer choice:

A. Both science and math increased in number.

From 2010 to 2011, the number of science degrees increased, but the number of math degrees deceased. Therefore, A is not a correct answer.

B. Both English and math increased in number.

From 2010 to 2011 English degrees increased but math did not. Therefore B is not a correct answer.

C. Both science and English increased in number.

From 2010 to 2011 science degrees increased and so did English degrees. Therefore C is a correct answer.

D. The combined number of degrees awarded for science, math, and English increased by more than 1,900 degrees.

The combined number of degrees awarded in 2010 for science, math, and English was 3,400 (800 + 1,400 + 1,200). The combined number of degrees awarded in 2011 for science, math, and English was 5,400 (1,600 + 1,300 + 2,500). The increase in the number of degrees awarded was 2,000 (5,400 − 3,400). This is more than 1,900. Therefore D is a correct answer.

E. The combined "other" category for these two years had less than double as many degrees awarded than the combined number of degrees awarded for math in these two years.

The combined number of degrees for "Other" for these two years is 4,600 (2,600 + 2,000). The combined number of degrees for math for these two years is 2,700 (1,400 + 1,300). 4,600 is less than double the value of 2,700, that is 4,600 < 5,400. Therefore E is a correct answer.

14. D. In 2012, the number of degrees awarded in English was 2,800 and the number of degrees awarded in science was 2,000. Therefore the number of degrees in English exceeded the number of degrees in science by 800 (2,800 − 2,000).

15. A. Since probability $= \dfrac{\text{\# favorable outcomes}}{\text{\# total outcomes}}$, first find the total number of possibilities in which A is on the left and E is on the right. There are a number of ways to do this, the easiest of which is to list the possibilities and then count them: ABCDE, ABDCE, ACBDE, ACDBE, ADBCE, ADCBE for a total of 6 possibilities.

Then find the number of total outcomes. To find the distinct arrangements of x number of distinct things, take $x!$ or "x factorial" or, in this case 5!, $5 \times 4 \times 3 \times 2 \times 1 = 120$.

$$\text{probability} = \frac{\text{\# favorable outcomes}}{\text{\# total outcomes}} = \frac{6}{120} = \frac{1}{20}$$

16. 16 The mean of a set of numbers is found by taking the sum of the numbers and dividing by how many numbers there are. "The average of five numbers is 20" is then translated into

$$\frac{\text{sum of five numbers}}{5} = 20 \quad \left(\text{Multiply each side of the equation by 5}\right)$$

Therefore, the sum of the five numbers is 100. "The average of two of those numbers is 26" is translated into

$$\frac{\text{sum of two numbers}}{2} = 26$$

Therefore, the sum of the two numbers is 52. The remaining three numbers have a sum of 48 (100 − 52 = 48). Therefore the average of these three numbers is then $\dfrac{48}{3} = 16$.

17. D. Use the given definition to represent $c@d$.

$$c@d = \frac{c^2 - 2cd + d^2}{c^2 - d^2}$$

Since $c = 5d$, replace each c with $5d$.

$$c@d = \frac{(5d)^2 - 2(5d)d + d^2}{(5d)^2 - d^2}$$

$$= \frac{25d^2 - 10d^2 + d^2}{25d^2 - d^2}$$

$$= \frac{16d^2}{24d^2}$$

$$= \frac{2}{3}$$

18. C. There are a number of strategies that could be used to solve this problem. First, it wouldn't take long to list the possibilities and then count them (MODE, MOED, MDOE, MDEO, etc.). Second, you could remember that there are as many distinct arrangements of components as "components factorial," in this case 4! or $4 \times 3 \times 2 \times 1 = 24$. Or you can use the counting principal. The first letter could be any of 4 letters, etc.

$$\underset{\text{1st}}{\underline{4}} \quad \underset{\text{2nd}}{\underline{3}} \quad \underset{\text{3rd}}{\underline{2}} \quad \underset{\text{4th}}{\underline{1}} \qquad 4 \times 3 \times 2 \times 1 = 24$$

19. E. If $6y = -18$, then $y = -3$.

$$y^3 + y = (-3)^3 + (-3)$$

$$= -27 - 3$$

$$= -30$$

20. E. *Mean* is synonymous with "average." The mean is found by taking the sum of the values and dividing by the number of values.

The mean of data set G $= \frac{24 + 30 + 16 + 11 + 19}{5} = \frac{100}{5} = 20$.

The *median* is found by arranging the values from least to greatest and taking the middle value. If there is an odd number of values, then one of the data values becomes the middle value. If there is an even number of data values, there are two middle values. In that case, the median is found by taking the mean of these two middle values.

Arrange the values of data set H in order from least to greatest, and find the middle value.

The median of data set H is 12:   3   5   **12**   27   33

The question "The mean of data set G is how much greater than the median of set H?" now becomes "20 is how much greater than 12?" Therefore the answer is 8.

PART II

REVIEW OF EXAM AREAS

Chapter 2

Analytical Writing Assessment

Introduction to Analytical Writing Assessment

Skills and Concepts Tested

The writing tasks of the Analytical Writing portion of the exam are designed to test both your reasoning and writing skills. The Analyze an Issue task requires you to take a stand on an issue and provide support for your position. The Analyze an Argument task asks you to consider an argument and evaluate its persuasiveness. For both tasks you are expected to demonstrate an ability to write using the conventions of standard written English. The entire pool of topics is available on the GRE website, although specific directions for the tasks may vary:

> www.ets.org/gre/revised_general/prepare/analytical_writing/issue/pool
>
> www.ets.org/gre/revised_general/prepare/analytical_writing/argument/pool

Reasoning and Thinking Skills

The two tasks, complement each other. While Analyze an Issue asks you to construct a persuasive argument on the given topic, the Analyze an Argument task requires you to critique a piece of persuasive writing. Both tasks demand that you consider the use of evidence in building an argument and how ideas are organized. You will also need to be clear in defining your position as you consider multiple points of view. You are also expected to respond to the specific directions for each task and focus your essay on the given topic.

Writing Skills Task

For both tasks, the readers are looking at your ability to express ideas clearly in standard written English. Due to the limited period of time allotted for this task (just 30 minutes), infrequent errors in mechanics will not affect your score. It is important, however, to use appropriate vocabulary and a variety of sentence types and lengths. Using transitions will also help guide the reader through the logical development of your ideas.

Computer Word Processor

You will be writing your essay using a very simple word processor within the exam software. The word processor includes basic functions like the typing keyboard, movement arrows, and the Enter key. Since the software does not allow you to use tabs to indicate a new paragraph, you will need to use the Enter key to leave a space between paragraphs. A prompt will appear in a box at the top of the screen and remain there as you prepare, compose, and edit your essay in a separate box below. You will also have functions like cut, paste, and undo. There is no spell-checker or grammar tool. The best way to prepare for use of the word processor is by downloading the free PowerPrep software from ETS. This will allow you to practice with the word processor before the actual exam. The basic word processors available in Windows (Word Pad) and Mac OS (Text Edit) can be used as alternative preparation options.

Directions and Scoring

The two writing tasks make up the first section of the GRE. You will have 30 minutes for each task. For both the Analyze an Issue and Analyze an Argument, you will be given one topic, and you must respond directly to the issue posed or the argument provided. On-screen prompts will indicate the time remaining on the test.

Each essay is scored on a scale from 1 to 6. Two different readers (one human reader and one electronic reader) score each essay and the total score is determined by taking an average of these two scores. For example, if the first reader gives a score of 4 and the second gives a score of 5, the two scores will be averaged to a 4.5. If there is more than a 1-point discrepancy between the two scores, the essay is reviewed by a third human reader who makes the determination to settle the discrepancy. The total score for this section is determined by taking an average of the total scores on both tasks. Official scores are reported in increments of 0.5 and are available approximately 10–14 business days after your exam date.

Analysis of an Issue

Overview of Analysis of an Issue

Time: 30 minutes

This task in the Analytical Writing section asks you to consider a topic of general interest and express your viewpoint about it in an essay. Each statement presents a claim or issue that can be examined from multiple perspectives. Your task is to clearly define your own position and provide examples and support for your viewpoint. You must also consider different viewpoints or situations that might affect your position. You are given one issue statement and must respond to the specific task. There is no "right" or "correct" viewpoint on any issue. Instead, scorers are looking for how well you support your position and respond to the specific instructions for the task.

Each statement will appear with a specific set of directions. You may be asked to:

- state to what extent you agree or disagree with a statement and then consider situations in which the statement may or may not hold true
- state to what extent you agree or disagree with a statement and then consider specific situations in which following its recommendations would or would not provide an advantage
- state to what extent you agree or disagree with a statement and then acknowledge evidence that could be used to challenge your position
- distinguish between two viewpoints and identify the one that most closely aligns with your position on the issue
- state to what extent you agree or disagree with a statement and the evidence on which it is based
- discuss your reasoning for supporting a policy and express the consequences for its adoption

Scoring

Due to the limited time that is allotted for this task (30 minutes), scorers take into consideration that even the highest scoring essay may contain some minor errors. The score from this section is averaged with your score from the Analysis of an Argument task in half-point (0.5) increments.

Score of 6: Convincing and Persuasive

The highest scoring essays present a convincing and articulate analysis. These essays:

- present a clear and insightful position that responds directly to the task
- provide well-developed and persuasive reasons and/or examples
- present an organized, focused analysis that uses transitions to connect ideas
- use well-chosen vocabulary and varied sentence types to skillfully convey meaning
- demonstrate ease with correct usage of the conventions of standard written English

Score of 5: Thoughtful and Well-Developed

These essays present a thoughtful and well-developed analysis. These essays:

- present a clear, considered position that responds directly to the task
- provide reasonable and logical reasons and/or examples
- present an organized, focused analysis that connects ideas
- use appropriate vocabulary and varied sentences to convey meaning
- demonstrate ease with correct usage of the conventions of standard written English

Score of 4: Competent

These essays present a complete and reasonably clear analysis. These essays:

- present a clear position that responds to the task
- provide appropriate reasons and/or examples
- present an organized, focused analysis
- use language to convey meaning with adequate clarity
- demonstrate general control of the conventions of standard written English, but with some minor errors in grammar, spelling, and sentence structure

Score of 3: Flawed

These essays show limited competence in responding to the prompt. These essays:

- may be vague or limited in responding to the specific prompt
- may use weak or irrelevant reasons and/or examples for support
- may lack focus or be poorly organized
- may have language problems that interfere with communication
- may demonstrate major errors or frequent minor errors with the conventions of standard written English

Score of 2: Weak

These essays show serious weakness in responding to the specific directions for the task. These essays:

- may be unclear or very limited in responding to the specific prompt
- may not develop a clear position
- may provide few reasons and/or examples for support
- are lacking focus and are poorly organized
- have serious language problems that impede communication
- have major errors with the conventions of standard written English

Score of 1: Deficient

These essays show major deficiencies in analytical writing. These essays:

- present little understanding of the task or issue
- provide little or no evidence or support
- have severe language problems that prevent communication
- have serious errors with the conventions of standard written English

Score of 0

These essays are often off-topic, do not respond to the writing task, are written in a foreign language, simply copy the issue statement, consist of random keystrokes, or are left blank.

Sample Task 1

Overview

The Issue Task requires that you read and evaluate a statement or claim. The statement will appear with specific directions. Although all of the issue statements are published in the pool of topics available on the GRE website, the specific directions may vary. For that reason it is important to read carefully and respond to the given task. Below is a sample statement with two different sets of directions and sample responses.

Sample Statement

> Everyone should be encouraged to pursue a college education.

Directions for Sample Task 1 (Response 1)

Write a response expressing to what degree you agree or disagree with the statement. Provide explanations for the reasoning behind your position. Be sure to consider situations in which the statement may or may not prove true and explain how this affects your stance.

Directions for Sample Task 1 (Response 2)

Write a response expressing to what degree you agree or disagree with the statement. Be sure to consider and discuss the most persuasive reasons and evidence that could pose a challenge to your opinion.

Analysis of Directions

Both sets of directions ask you to state to what degree you agree or disagree with the recommendation that all students be encouraged to pursue a college education. Your primary job in both cases is to decide on your position. The first task directs you to consider situations in which your position may or may not be valid and how those possibilities influence your viewpoint. The second task asks you to consider alternative viewpoints and to address arguments that would challenge your position. Both tasks are similar but lead to different responses.

Sample Task 1 – Response 1

A High-Scoring Sample Model Essay

Study after study indicates that people holding college diplomas earn significantly more money during their lifetimes than those who only graduate high school. College graduates report not only higher levels of income for themselves but are able to provide better lives for their families, encouraging their children in turn to attend college and better themselves. Higher education is seen as a gateway to happiness and prosperity, lifting people out of ignorance and poverty. It is clear that nearly all people should be encouraged to pursue a college education.

Too often teachers and counselors restrict their advice to attend college to a select few, deeming only some students capable or worthy of a university education. This pre-selection, sometimes based on subconscious beliefs about race, gender, or socio-economic status, limits the range of possibilities for youth who may need a nudge to apply for college. Some Latino teenagers report that teachers don't expect them to attend college or that counselors don't recommend the most rigorous courses for them, assuming that they will not be interested in preparing for college. If all people were encouraged to prepare for and pursue a college education, it would mitigate these subtle forms of prejudice and open the gateway for more students.

There are, of course, situations where students have set out on a different path that does not require a college diploma. Highly motivated students may wish to join the military, attend a specialized institute like for culinary studies, or apprentice themselves in a trade. They may seek out fulfilling careers that do not necessitate a degree from a university. However, all people should be given the option to keep that door open rather than having someone else close it for them.

For most people, a college diploma opens access to work that is meaningful and fulfilling as well as better paid. A generation or two ago, young people could graduate from high school and find good, skilled jobs in manufacturing that would provide for them up to and through retirement. Now the types of work available to those with only a high school diploma are often dirty and dangerous jobs like processing animals in slaughterhouses or ones that pay at the lower end of the scale. Although many workers end up in a field different from the one they studied in college, the skills they learned in problem-solving, reading, and writing transfer across disciplines, making them more nimble in adapting to the workplace. Rather than remaining stuck in a dead-end service job, people who are college-educated have more options available to them.

In the end, all people should be encouraged to attend college and consider the opportunities that will result from having more options.

Sample Task 1 – Response 2

An Average-Scoring Model Essay

Education is the great leveler in American society. With a good education, people can overcome bad situations and raise themselves to new heights. They can raise themselves up both materially and intellectually with the opportunity to pursue a college education. Although some may argue that not all students are cut out to attend college, they must admit that all people deserve a chance to consider that opportunity.

A major factor in encouraging all people to pursue a college education is money. People with college degrees earn significantly more money than those without. Despite the jump in the cost of attending college, it should be considered an investment that will pay off. Tax benefits and write-offs are available for those who pay tuition as well. Of course one might challenge this point by reminding of the people who attend college but find they are ill-suited for university life and drop out. They still incur the costs without the benefit. One consideration is that even preparing for and attempting college-level study gives a person a leg up for other opportunities. The long-term financial advantages of college study outweigh potential drawbacks.

Often these financial considerations are tied to practical ones. In the twenty-first century, many jobs require more education than a high school diploma. Even entry-level positions in finance, business, and management demand skills and content learned through college study. In scientific fields like engineering there are not enough graduates to meet the needs of computer and technology companies so they are forced to look abroad for skilled workers. If all people were encouraged to pursue college study, we might find and nurture the talent we need to meet the demands of biotechnology and engineering research. Some might argue that many high skilled jobs in specialized areas of construction or computer programming do not require a college education. They would be right in this. In these cases apprenticeship or internship would be more appropriate. However, it benefits everyone to be given the option to consider attending college.

It all does come down to providing options and opportunities for all people. Others should not be making the financial and career choices for young people considering their future paths. It is only fair that all people receive encouragement to consider a college education.

Evaluation of Responses

The first response would earn a high score due to its tight focus on the prompt and use of developed examples for support. The writer unwaveringly takes into account situations in which the claim that all people should be encouraged to attend college might not hold true. The vocabulary and sentence structure are varied, and transitions help guide the reader through the essay. The second response is also clear in its stance but without as much development of the position. The transitions are not as smooth and some of the wording is less clear due to more passive voice ("If all people were encouraged..."). The vocabulary is also more casual. Expressions like "not all students are cut out" and "a leg up" are more typical of informal, spoken English than standard written English.

Sample Task 2

Overview

This issue task is based on the claim/reason format. Pay attention to how the directions differ from the previous examples.

Sample Statement

Claim: It is no longer important to remember historical names and dates.

Reason: Information like this is now easily available on the Internet.

Directions for Sample Task 2

Write a response expressing the degree to which you agree or disagree with the claim above and the reason on which that claim is based.

Sample Task 2 Response

An Average-Scoring Model Essay

Some people argue that technology is freeing us from the drugery of having to remember basic facts. We use calculators instead of doing multiplication in our heads and whip out a smartphone to look up facts that generations before would have had drilled in their heads. They argue that people today can look up information on the Internet so there is no need to memorize historical data. In some cases the use of technology to help us recall names and dates from history is a tremendous help, especially for minor details. However, it is important to remember the big names and dates associated with periods in history and to not become too reliant on the Internet.

First, despite the prevalence of smartphones and other mobile technology, the Internet is not always available at a moment's notice. A web-enabled cell phone may not have service in certain areas or a site may be down for maintenance. People who say that it's not important to remember names and dates because you can look them up ignore the fact that access to the Internet is not guaranteed.

Another potential problem with reliance on the Internet is the reliability of information. Many people believe that sites like Wikipedia provide accurate information, not realizing that anyone can edit entries. Without having at least a general sense of historical names and dates, it is difficult to assess whether the information provided appears accurate or not. For example, if you don't know that WWI ended before the 1920s, you might believe an article that discusses the threat of nucleer weapons during the war. You would not have the basic tools to determine the credibility of the information.

A final consideration is that it is simply more efficient to have a working knowledge of the major names and dates from history. If you don't know what search terms to use, it is difficult and time-consuming to find information on the Internet. It's like trying to use the dictionary to find a word you don't know how to spell. Also, in conversation it breaks the flow of discussion if people have to stop every five minutes to look up date. While minor details like the names of vice-presidents may not matter, it is more beneficial to have basic information at ready access in your head. Some dates like the time period of WWII or the terrorist attacks of 9/11 deserve to be remembered, not just looked up in some online database.

Evaluation of Response

This essay presents a clear position on the issue, although it fails to provide deeper insights into why it is important to have a grasp of dates and names from history. The reasons (lack of Internet access, reliability, efficiency) are all logical if not compelling. The use of specific examples and comparisons, such as using a dictionary to spell, helps develop the position more fully. The essay is well-organized by topics, although the flow of ideas in the final paragraph is less focused and coherent. The analysis is not sustained or probed in depth. Vocabulary use is varied, as are the sentence types. There are a few minor typing errors and missing words ("drugery" should be "drudgery" and "nucleer" should be "nuclear"; "look up date" should be "look up a date"). In the last sentence a comma is needed after "dates" and before "deserve," although the meaning remains clear.

Analysis of an Argument

Overview of Analysis of an Argument

Time: 30 minutes

This task in the Analytical Writing section presents a short argument and asks you to evaluate its reasoning. Often the passage is a letter to the editor of a newspaper, company memo, or other short piece that seeks to persuade the reader. All of the arguments are deeply flawed. These flaws include assumptions, missing information, and failure to consider alternative explanations for a given situation. Your task is to identify and analyze the flaws in the argument.

> **Note: You do not take a position on the issue(s) presented. Your task is not to agree or disagree. Instead, explain how the argument could be made more persuasive, what assumptions exist, and which missing information, if supplied, would improve its reasoning.**

Following each argument is a specific task. You may be asked to:

- explain assumptions that the author makes or implies
- suggest evidence needed to evaluate the argument or what evidence would make it more persuasive
- discuss alternative explanations for the situation
- identify questions that would need to be asked and answered

Common Flaws in Arguments

You will begin to see the same flaws in logic repeated as you read argument samples. This list does not contain every flaw, but will give you an idea of what to expect as you read a variety of sample tasks.

1. **extrapolation – applying one instance to every situation**

   Extrapolation flaws take a narrow piece of evidence and then apply it broadly to all cases. For example, the argument may take a study done at one school and try to apply the results to all schools in a state. Because what is true for one school may not apply to others, it is a flaw based on false assumptions.

2. **apples to oranges – making unfounded comparisons**

   These arguments try to compare two situations that are not alike. In this case, the argument may try to compare a small town to a large city, or a private university to a public one. These arguments are flawed because the comparison is not a valid one. The situations are not alike, so the argument is based on false assumptions and usually missing information.

3. **trends – assuming a trend will continue**

   These arguments present a current trend—usually providing numbers or other data—and assume that the trend will remain unchanged. A common example involves prices, say for housing. The argument may assume that home prices will continue to rise and ignore any other factors. These arguments fail to consider alternative explanations.

4. **sole factor – identifying only one variable**

   Most of the arguments for the task involve complex cause-and-effect situations. The sole-factor flaw singles out one reason for a given situation and ignores all others. An argument may cite the increase in the number of police officers as the sole factor for a drop in crime. It may ignore other possible reasons like an improved economy, changes in the weather, and longer prison sentences for offenders. These flaws allow you to discuss other explanations for the cause-and-effect relationship.

5. **weasel words – using deceptive language**

   Many arguments will use deceptive wording to hide missing information. For example, if the number of criminal arrests drops, that may sound good, but has the actual number of crimes decreased? These flaws try to hide missing information that would make the argument less convincing.

Scoring

Because you are writing your essay in a limited time, even the highest scoring essay may contain minor errors. Scorers take this into consideration. Your score for this task is averaged with your score from the Analysis of an Issue task in half-point (0.5) increments.

Score of 6: Insightful

The highest scoring essays present an insightful, well-organized analysis. These essays:

- identify the aspects of the argument relevant to the specific question and examine them in an insightful way
- develop the ideas coherently and connect them using clear transitions
- provide relevant and thorough support from the argument
- use well-chosen vocabulary and varied sentences to convey ideas
- demonstrate correct usage of the conventions of standard written English

Score of 5: Thoughtful

These essays present a thoughtful, organized examination of the issue. These essays:

- identify the aspects of the argument relevant to the specific question and examine them in a generally thoughtful way
- develop the ideas logically and connect them with transitions
- provide mostly relevant and complete support from the argument
- use appropriate vocabulary and sentence variety to convey ideas
- demonstrate correct usage of the conventions of standard written English

Score of 4: Competent

These essays present a competent and generally clear examination of the issue. These essays:

- identify relevant aspects of the argument but also address some unrelated points
- develop the ideas clearly but may not connect them with transitions

- provide some support from the argument but with uneven development
- use language to convey ideas in a generally clear way
- demonstrate mostly correct usage but also have some errors in conventions

Score of 3: Flawed

These essays show some competence in examining the issue but are flawed. These essays:

- do not identify most of the relevant aspects of the argument
- discuss unrelated points or present poor reasoning
- develop the ideas in a limited or less logical way
- provide support that is less relevant to the argument
- use language in an unclear way
- contain either some major or frequent minor errors in conventions that interfere with communication

Score of 2: Weak

These essays either fail to respond to the directions for the task and/or show weakness in examining the issue. These essays may do one or more of the following:

- not identify the relevant aspects of the argument but instead present the writer's own opinion on the issue
- not follow the specific directions for the task
- fail to develop ideas or organize them illogically
- provide little to no support for the argument
- use language in a way that interferes with communication
- contain serious errors in conventions that make meaning unclear

Score of 1: Deficient

These essays reveal basic problems in analytical writing. These essays:

- show little or no understanding of the argument
- are short and disorganized
- use language in a way that prevents understanding
- contain serious, frequent errors in conventions that lead to incoherence

Score of 0

These essays are often off-topic, do not respond to the writing task, are written in a foreign language, simply copy the argument, consist of random keystrokes, or are left blank.

Sample Task 1

Overview

The Argument Task requires that you read and evaluate a short passage. The passage will appear with specific directions. Because the same passages from the pool of topics may appear with different directions, it is important to read the task carefully. Below is a sample argument with two different sets of directions and sample responses.

Sample Argument

The following memo appeared as a recommendation from a traffic planning commission:

> Two months ago, the neighboring town of Beechcroft installed a roundabout at an intersection where many serious accidents had occurred in the past year. A survey of nearby residents reveals that since the installation of the roundabout, motorists have been more careful to respect the speed limit. Also, fewer accidents have been reported. To limit the number of traffic accidents and promote safety, the town of Elmville should consider installing roundabouts at its six most dangerous intersections.

Directions for Sample Task 1 (based on assumptions)

Write a response in which you examine the assumptions, both stated and implied, present in the argument. Explain how these assumptions form the basis for the argument and how, if proven false, they would affect its persuasiveness.

Directions for Sample Task 1 (based on questions)

Write a response that considers which questions would need to be answered about the proposal to determine if it will result in the outcome predicted. Be sure to discuss how answering these questions will help evaluate the recommended proposal.

Analysis of Directions

The first task asks you to identify the assumptions of the argument and then explain how the argument would be undermined if the assumptions prove false. The second task asks you to propose questions that need to be answered. You then must explain how the answers to these questions would help you evaluate the argument's persuasiveness. The tasks are similar in that you must identify the weaknesses in logic and argumentation, but the specific directions lead toward two different responses.

Sample Task 1 – Response 1 (based on assumptions)

A High-Scoring Model Essay

The author of this proposal makes a suggestion about installing roundabouts to decrease traffic accidents but relies on too many faulty assumptions for the argument to be persuasive. These assumptions include information both given and implied by the writer.

The main underlying assumption is a cause-and-effect relationship between the installation of the roundabout in Beechcroft and the claimed reduction in traffic accidents. The author seems to say that the roundabout is the sole factor in reducing accidents. If there were evidence of other factors, say a lowered speed limit in the vicinity or increased police presence, this evidence would undermine the claimed cause-and-effect relationship. Maybe greater enforcement of the speed limit has contributed to the lowered speeds residents are reporting.

Another main assumption is that two months provides sufficient time to judge the effectiveness of the roundabout. Because we do not know the time of year, it is impossible to say whether the lowered speeds and reported decrease in accidents is due to the roundabout or other causes like weather or seasonal traffic due to tourism. The author assumes that two months is long enough to establish a cause-and-effect relationship. If the two months were not representative of the whole year, it would seriously diminish the credibility of the argument.

Finally, even if the above assumptions held true, the argument rests on a final assumption—that what worked for Beechcroft would be successful in Elmville. Beechcroft is described as a neighboring town but no other information is given. We do not know the comparative size of the towns, if they have similar traffic patterns, or if they even share the same problem of accidents at intersections. If the towns do not share enough characteristics, it is not effective to draw comparisons and make assumptions. Although roundabouts may provide a solution, this author relies on too many potentially faulty assumptions to be convincing.

Sample Task 1 – Response 2 (based on questions)

Another High-Scoring Model Essay

The author of this argument suggests that the installation of roundabouts in Elmville will have the same positive effects it did in nearby Beechcroft. While the recommendation raises some interesting points, many questions need to be answered before accepting the proposal.

First, the author would need to answer the question of whether the two towns are similar enough for Elmville to get the same benefits from roundabouts as Beechcroft. For example, do they have the same problems with accidents at intersections? Do they have a similar number of motorists and the same traffic patterns? Are there other factors related to traffic that are alike, such as weather conditions that might contribute to accidents, or the amount of policing in the towns? If it is reasonable to make a fair comparison between the towns, then there remains another set of questions to consider.

The argument states that in the past two months the number of accidents reported has decreased and that residents are seeing motorists respect the speed limit. It is logical to ask if two months is long enough to gather meaningful data. Were the two months typical of a year in Beechcroft, or did they occur during a season where there is less traffic or when a school holiday reduces the number of cars on the road? One could also ask if there is a difference between the number of actual accidents and those that are reported. If not all accidents are reported to police then the recommendation is not as strong. Finally, what did residents mean when they said motorists are respecting the speed limit. Are there real numbers to accompany that statement? More complete answers to these questions would make the recommendation more persuasive.

Even if we can make a reasonable comparison and answer the questions about the data in a satisfactory way, there is still the question of whether the roundabout is the only factor in reducing accidents. Have there been other changes, such as a lowering of the speed limit? Is there now more police presence near the roundabout? If there are too many other contributing factors then it would not be reasonable to move forward with the recommendation to install roundabouts in Elmville.

Evaluation of Responses

Both responses would score well because they answer the specific question posed by the task. The two essays provide smooth transitions, reference the argument consistently, and use effective word choice.

Sample Task 2

Overview

This argument task is based on the set of directions that asks the writer to consider alternative explanations for a given situation. Pay attention to how the two sample responses interpret and respond to the specific task.

Sample Argument

From a memo written by the principal of an elementary school:

> Test scores at Wilson Elementary have dropped three points from last year to this year. Recent studies have shown that completing 10 minutes of homework a night per grade level, for example 30 minutes a night for a third-grader, results in higher test scores for students. Students at Wilson Elementary are currently assigned on average only seven minutes of homework a night per grade level. Clearly, the lack of homework assigned has contributed to the overall decline in student performance. In order to make up this deficit, teachers need to assign 12 minutes of homework per grade level each night.

Directions for Sample Task 2

Write a response in which you consider one or more different explanations that provide an alternative to the one given for the situation. Be sure to examine whether the different explanations fit within the context of the evidence presented.

Sample Task 2 – Response 1

A Low-Scoring Model Essay

According to this argument a ten year old could be assigned almost an hour of homework each night. After a long day at school the last thing a child needs is more time sitting inside. Children today lack time for exercise and play. Assigning more homework will only worsen this problem.

When we were young school ended at 3:00 and then we could play with friends, spend time reading, or simply relax. Today's children are ruthlessly programmed from the time they wake up early until they go to bed. Where is the fun in being a kid if every moment is taken up with school and homework?

Another problem with overwhelming homework loads is the decline in exercise. Childhood obesity is on the rise and a homework policy that limits the time students can spend outside in physical activity is a poorly advised plan. Children need time to run and play, especially those with attention deficit and/or hyperactivity. These students will actually perform worse in school and exhibit behavior problems if they do not have opportunities to unwind after the school day.

Finally, assigning more homework only shifts a greater burden on parents for they are the ones who must supervise at home. Instead of enjoying time with their children, parents will be forced to sit them down at the kitchen table for more study time. This will only result in resentment from both children and their parents. More homework is not the answer.

Sample Task 2 – Response 2

An Average-Scoring Model Essay

The main argument by the principal is that the drop in test scores is directly related to the perceived lack of homework teachers are assigning. The principal's reasoning is flawed because it fails to consider several other, reasonable explanations for the evidence presented.

A first consideration is that a three point drop in test scores may not be a reason for alarm. Without having a basis for comparison or a scale for the test scores, it is plausible that a small dip in scores is not statistically relevant. Test scores vary from year to year for a variety of reasons and could be reasonably accounted for as a natural variance.

The principal also presents the evidence of seven minutes of homework per night average as an accurate figure representing the entire school. With an average, it is possible that some teachers assign much less while others assign much more. Perhaps teachers of very young children, such as kindergarten teachers, are not assigning any homework, which would bring down the overall average. Another reasonable explanation for this number is the difference between what is assigned versus what is completed. Teachers may be assigning what they think will take 10 minutes a night but students are completing work faster and reporting that figure.

Finally, there are many other reasons why test scores might decline. Did a large number of top teachers leave or retire? Losing talented or veteran teachers could contribute to lower student performance. Did class sizes increase? If teachers have to work with larger numbers of students they may not be able to help everyone who needs assistance, which could also lead to a drop in scores. Simply put, the principal's explanation looks at only one explanation rather than considering the many plausible reasons.

Evaluation of Responses

Sample Response 1, although well-written, would likely earn a 2 because it fails to analyze the argument and instead presents the writer's opinion about homework. It does not respond to the task.

Sample Response 2 would score much higher, likely a 4. The writer responds to the task by suggesting several alternative scenarios. The response could be made more logical in organization by moving the two paragraphs on test scores together, but overall it makes a coherent analysis.

The Writing Process Pathway

One of the biggest mistakes a test-taker can make is beginning to write an essay without first taking the time to plan the response. You wouldn't get in the car to go to a new destination without consulting a map or plugging the address into the navigation system. Who knows where you would end up? Likewise, it is important to take the time to organize your ideas before you begin typing your essay. It is also essential to save a few minutes at the end to proofread, check that you have left spaces between paragraphs to indicate breaks, and review the flow of your essay.

Here is a sample Analyze an Argument task and suggested approach:

The following appeared as a recommendation from a city budget committee:

A recent survey of public library patrons found that the majority of visitors are using the branch libraries from 3:00 in the afternoon until 8:00 in the evening. Most of those responding said they would prefer the library hours be extended to 10:00 P.M. during the week. The extension of evening hours can be done by opening the library at 11:00 A.M. rather than the current 9:00 A.M. opening. This will cause the least inconvenience to patrons and allow a better use of library resources.

Write a response in which you consider and suggest the specific evidence necessary to evaluate the argument. Be sure to explain how this evidence would improve or weaken the argument's persuasiveness.

Prewriting

You will have 30 minutes total for each writing task. In the first five you will want to use your scratch paper to brainstorm ideas, organize the logical development of your essay, and map out a strategy. This will also help you manage your time once you begin writing.

Brainstorm

For this argument and set of directions, the first step is brainstorming the types of evidence missing from the recommendation:

- if there is a shortage of library resources
- how many library patrons were surveyed
- how the survey was conducted (handed out to everyone, left at the checkout counter)
- how long the survey was conducted
- who uses the library in the morning (maybe young children, retired people)
- who uses the library in the afternoon (maybe students)
- whether librarians want to work until 10:00 P.M.
- how many people indicated they wanted the library open until 10:00 P.M.
- what activities are scheduled in the morning from 9:00 to 11:00 A.M.

Organize the Brainstorming

The next step is to organize the brainstorming. You will not have time to write an outline. Instead, use numbers to label the points in your brainstorming. In this case, we want to start with the broadest concept and then cluster similar ideas together:

1. if there is a shortage of library resources
2. how many library patrons were surveyed
3. how the survey was conducted (handed out to everyone, left at the checkout counter)
4. how long the survey was conducted for
5. who uses the library in the morning (maybe young children, retired people)
6. who uses the library in the afternoon (maybe students)
7. whether librarians want to work until 10:00 P.M.
8. how many people indicated they wanted the library open until 10:00 P.M.
9. what activities are scheduled in the morning from 9:00 to 11:00 A.M.

Mapping

The final step in prewriting is to map out the strategy. Since the biggest missing piece of evidence is whether there exists a shortage of library resources, it is most logical to begin there (item 1 in list above) and ask about the activities and usage schedule for both the morning and afternoon (items 5, 6, 9). The next set of missing evidence concerns the way in which the survey was conducted (items 2, 3, 4). The final area of evidence centers on the issue of keeping the libraries open until 10:00 (items 7 and 8) and whether there is enough information to support this conclusion.

Writing

The actual writing of the essay should take approximately 20 minutes of the total time. Using the prewriting on your scratch paper for reference, and then focus your attention on developing your ideas in paragraph form with each set of bullet points developed in its own paragraph. For this task explain how the missing evidence would either undermine or strengthen the argument for changing the library hours. Manage your time so that at about 15 minutes you will finish the paragraph on the survey and get ready to make your final set of points about the closing time of 10:00 P.M.

Proofreading

You should use the last three to five minutes to read over your essay and correct errors. You will be able to insert text to add any transitions you have left out and leave spaces between paragraphs using the Enter key. Pay special attention to words you have typed twice or left out. Watch the clock! Once the timer reaches zero you will be unable to make any more changes.

Writing Tips and Strategies

The scoring for the writing tasks emphasizes a few key elements of writing: organization, vocabulary, and sentence variety. Each element can be addressed with a few simple reminders and practiced as you write sample essays in preparation for the exam.

Organization

The first step in logical organization is taking the time to brainstorm and then outline your response. It is best to develop two or three points in depth and aim for paragraphs of three to five sentences in length. For the Analysis of an Issue task, it is recommended that you begin with your strongest point so as to make a solid impression from the outset. You can then prioritize your remaining points to conclude with a strong argument for your position. For the Analysis of an Argument task, it is best to work from general to specific in your development. For example, in responding to a prompt about assumptions, you would begin with the major assumption that underlies the entire argument and then work toward the more specific elements.

Another aspect of organization is providing transitions to guide the reader through your essay. Words and phrases like "first," "initially," and "a primary consideration" indicate the beginning of a chain of logic. Words and phrases like "another," "also," and "in addition" let the reader know you are continuing with the development of your reasoning. To show another point of view, say in a concession, words and phrases such as "although" and "however" are helpful in providing contrast. While these short essays do not require a formal conclusion, a sentence near the end of the final paragraph with the words "finally" or "lastly" let the reader know you are drawing your essay to a close.

Vocabulary

The scorers are looking for effective, appropriate vocabulary that conveys a clear meaning. You should avoid slang, technical jargon, and informal spoken English. For example, in spoken English one might use the expression "on the other hand" while in a written essay "another viewpoint" would be more apt for the task. If you want to use a word but are unsure of spelling, try using your scratch paper to write the word in different ways and determine the correct spelling. If you are still unsure, consider using the word sparingly rather than throughout your response. A single misspelling will not have an impact on your score, whereas multiple errors can have a greater effect.

Sentence Variety

Although scorers will be reading your essay quickly, they will get a sense of your overall style, mainly through sentence variety. Aim to vary the lengths of your sentences to create a rhythm and flow to your writing. Sentences that are all the same length can seem choppy if too short. Conversely, many long and complex sentences will deaden your style. Another way to vary your sentences is by checking the first word of each sentence. Highlight the first word and look for patterns. If each sentence begins with the same word or words (*The, I, This*) this pattern can create monotony for the reader. Try changing the order of ideas in the sentence but beware of obscuring meaning. The primary criterion for scorers is clarity of expression.

Try out these tips by writing practice essays. In the following pages you will find a variety of Analysis of an Issue and Analysis of an Argument topics. You can also find the entire topic pool online at the GRE website (www.ets. org/gre). As you gain more confidence, use a timer to limit yourself to 30 minutes per response. Another strategy is to select topics and complete the prewriting exercises as practice for the reasoning required for the tasks. It is highly recommended you practice typing your essays. The free PowerPrep software available from ETS includes the basic word processor you will use for the actual exam.

Response Scoring Checklists

Use the following checklists to assess your essays. You can either ask someone else to complete the checklist or put your essay aside for a few days and read it again yourself with a fresh eye.

Analysis of an Issue Checklist			
Questions	Completely	Partially	No
1. Does the essay provide a clear position in response to the specific task?			
2. Does the essay use persuasive examples and reasons to support the position?			
3. Is the essay well organized and focused with clear transitions?			
4. Does the essay use effective vocabulary and a variety of sentence types?			
5. Is the essay written using correct English?			

Analysis of an Argument Checklist			
Questions	Completely	Partially	No
1. Does the essay respond directly to the specific directions for the prompt?			
2. Does the essay identify the relevant aspects of the argument and develop an insightful analysis?			
3. Does the essay include support drawn from the argument?			
4. Is the essay well organized with clear transitions?			
5. Is the essay written using correct English and a variety of vocabulary and sentence types?			

Extra Practice Topics

Analysis of an Issue

The ease and prevalence of sharing digital pictures and videos will help ensure that young people act in appropriate ways.

Write a response expressing to what degree you agree or disagree with the statement. Provide explanations for the reasoning behind your position. Be sure to consider situations in which the statement may or may not prove true and explain how this affects your stance.

* * * * *

The goal of all scientific research should be practical, usable information or technologies.

Write a response expressing to what degree you agree or disagree with the statement. Be sure to consider and discuss the most persuasive reasons and evidence that could pose a challenge to your position.

* * * * *

Mature economies, like those in the United States and Europe, would do well to focus on job creation in sectors like management and scientific innovation, rather than encouraging jobs in manufacturing and agriculture.

Write a response asserting to what degree you agree or disagree with the statement's recommendation. Provide explanations for the reasoning behind your position. Be sure to consider specific situations in which following the recommendation would or would not provide an advantage. Tell how these situations affect your point of view.

* * * * *

> It is important for countries to provide quality end-of-life care for all citizens, regardless of cost.

Write a response stating your viewpoint on the recommendation given above. Be sure to explain the reasoning behind your position. In writing your response, consider the possible consequences of adopting the recommendation and explain how they affect your stance.

* * * * *

> Some people believe governments should encourage healthy choices in nutrition and exercise. Others believe that the government has no role to play in the private decisions of its citizens.

Write a response in which you distinguish between the two viewpoints on the issue and state which one most closely matches your own position. Be sure to discuss both viewpoints as you explain and support your stance.

* * * * *

> **Claim:** Nations should promote the planting of genetically modified crops.
>
> **Reason:** These high-yield, insect resistant crops are the answer to worldwide hunger problems.

Write a response expressing the degree to which you agree or disagree with the claim above and the reason on which that claim is based.

* * * * *

> All college graduates should be required to demonstrate proficiency in English and another language.

Write a response asserting to what degree you agree or disagree with the statement's recommendation. Provide explanations for the reasoning behind your position. Be sure to consider specific situations in which following the recommendation would or would not provide an advantage. Tell how these situations affect your point of view.

* * * * *

> A strong work ethic is more important for success than innate talent or ability.

Write a response expressing to what degree you agree or disagree with the statement. Be sure to consider and discuss the most persuasive reasons and evidence that could pose a challenge to your position.

* * * * *

> It is more important to live and act according to principles than to compromise in order to reach a desired end.

Write a response expressing to what degree you agree or disagree with the statement. Provide explanations for the reasoning behind your position. Be sure to consider situations in which the statement may or may not prove true and explain how this affects your stance.

* * * * *

> **Claim:** High-density downtown areas of large cities should ban the use of private vehicles.
>
> **Reason:** The negative results of pollution and congestion outweigh the convenience of private vehicles.

Write a response expressing the degree to which you agree or disagree with the claim above and the reason on which that claim is based.

* * * * *

> Because people will seek out the least expensive options to meet their energy needs, governments should subsidize renewable energy sources to be less costly than fossil fuels.

Write a response stating your viewpoint on the recommendation given above. Be sure to explain the reasoning behind your position. In writing your response, consider the possible consequences of adopting the recommendation and explain how they affect your stance.

* * * * *

> Some people believe that it is essential to maintain a strong public school system. Others contend that it is more important to promote school choice through charter and private schools.

Write a response in which you distinguish between the two viewpoints on the issue and state which one most closely matches your own position. Be sure to discuss both viewpoints as you explain and support your stance.

* * * * *

> When students graduate from high school they should be encouraged to spend a year working or volunteering before starting college.

Write a response expressing to what degree you agree or disagree with the statement. Provide explanations for the reasoning behind your position. Be sure to consider situations in which the statement may or may not prove true and explain how this affects your stance.

* * * * *

> The rapid pace of modern life and use of technology is changing the very ways in which people think.

Write a response expressing to what degree you agree or disagree with the statement. Be sure to consider and discuss the most persuasive reasons and evidence that could pose a challenge to your position.

* * * * *

> Schools should encourage students to take only those courses in which they already have an aptitude or interest.

Write a response asserting to what degree you agree or disagree with the statement's recommendation. Provide explanations for the reasoning behind your stance. Be sure to consider specific situations in which following the recommendation would or would not provide an advantage. Tell how these situations affect your point of view.

Analysis of an Argument

You can practice with each of these arguments using any of the four sets of task directions below:

- Write a response in which you consider and suggest the specific evidence necessary to evaluate the argument. Be sure to explain how this evidence would improve or weaken the argument's persuasiveness.

- Write a response in which you consider one or more different explanations that provide an alternative to the one given for the situation. Be sure to examine whether the different explanations fit within the context of the evidence presented.

- Write a response in which you examine the assumptions, both stated and implied, present in the argument. Explain how these assumptions form the basis for the argument and how, if proven false, they would affect its persuasiveness.

- Write a response that considers which questions would need to be answered about the proposal to determine if it will result in the outcome predicted. Be sure to discuss how answering these questions will help evaluate the recommended proposal.

* * * * *

The following recommendation was made in a memo by the Dean of Academic Affairs:

> Last semester, enrollment in Marcroft University's popular Government in Action course soared, resulting in many students being unable to enroll in the class. Due to the number of student complaints the number of sections of this course should be increased. Adding sections will allow more students to take the course and result in more positive student feedback in college surveys.

* * * * *

The following appeared as a recommendation in a quarterly report:

> Six weeks ago, our flagship restaurant in Los Angeles added sweet potato fries to the menu as an alternative to french fries for patrons ordering burgers and sandwiches. Sales of burgers have increased 10 percent during this time. In order to increase sales of both burgers and sandwiches, our restaurants across the nation should add sweet potato fries to the menu.

* * * * *

The following appeared in a memo to the athletic foundation:

> Enrollment at Crayton University has declined 12 percent over the past three years. This is at the same time that enrollment at local rival Merloy College has risen by the same amount. One significant difference between our two institutions is that Merloy's athletic program includes a football team. Crayton University should consider adding a football, as well as a basketball, program in order to compete with Merloy College for freshman enrollments.

* * * * *

The following appeared in a letter to the editor of the local newspaper:

> The spring migration of red-toed frogs through Palmerville creates traffic jams and other distractions, costing businesses time and money during the three-day period. In neighboring Fryton, the city has created a festival to celebrate the migration, which draws tourists from around the area. A similar festival in Palmerville would be sure to increase tourism and offset current business losses.

* * * * *

The following appeared as a company memo:

> In our latest development of single-family homes, we offered three-, four-, and five-bedroom models while our competitor offered only models with four or five bedrooms. Our development took twice as long to sell out and our customers did not opt for as many upgrades, resulting in a lower profit margin. In order to remain competitive, and offer home buyers the models they prefer, our next development should feature only homes with either four or five bedrooms.

* * * * *

The following recommendation appeared in a budget report:

> A recent series of blind taste tests conducted by Fizzio Bottling Company indicates that customers are not able to tell the difference between soft drinks made with more expensive cane sugar and those made with high fructose corn syrup. However, a majority of survey takers stated a preference for buying soft drinks made with cane sugar. Despite the higher costs, Fizzio should change its recipe to include cane sugar and promote this change in its advertising. This will enable Fizzio to maintain its market share and profits.

* * * * *

The following recommendation appeared in the minutes of the council:

> Last year, the Greater Westfall Youth Council sponsored an arts contest for high school students. Despite an extension of the deadline, only 20 submissions were received, 12 for photography, 5 for drawing, 3 for painting, and none for ceramics. Clearly, there is a lack of interest in the arts among the young people of Westfall. Our committee recommends that the prize monies be reallocated to more popular youth activities.

* * * * *

The following appeared in a letter to the editor of a local newspaper:

> In the past three years, Grantville has become known throughout the county as a culinary center. The many fine restaurants in the downtown area draw both rave reviews and visitors to our town. Only a small number have failed during this time, while an equal number have sought to increase their seating areas to meet demand. In order to support the rising demands of diners, Grantville should begin subsidizing the cost of building permits for new and existing restaurants. This subsidy will be quickly paid for by increased tax revenue.

* * * * *

The following appeared as a recommendation by the director of park services:

> The recent and severe drought in Loopton has meant cutbacks in water usage throughout the city. Some have suggested turning off the large fountain in Graceview Park in order to conserve water. A questionnaire given to visitors at the park on a recent Sunday indicates that a majority do not want to see the city turn off the fountain because it provides a centerpiece for the park. Few people mentioned the grass areas in the park in the questionnaire. Our suggestion is to convert the large grass field adjacent to the fountain into a low-water-use garden with benches. This will allow visitors to continue to enjoy the fountain and the city to conserve water.

* * * * *

The following appeared in a company memo:

> The current lease for our office space is expiring soon. The terms of renewal include both a moderate increase in rent and the addition of fees for parking spaces. Because there is adequate on-street parking within easy walking distance of the building, our office manager will be declining parking spaces in the terms of our new lease. The cost savings will enable us to remain competitive without imposing an undue burden on our workers.

* * * * *

The following appeared in a neighborhood association newsletter:

> This year's holiday lighting display in the neighborhood parks and clubhouse will use only low-output, energy-efficient lights. The energy cost savings will quickly pay for the initial outlay for new light sets and the labor to install them. The new, more efficient lights will provide a more cheerful and cost-effective holiday season for everyone.

* * * * *

The following recommendation appeared in the minutes from a town council meeting:

> The problem of potholes and road erosion continues to plague our town. Fortunately the increase in revenue from property taxes over the past year means that we can finally undertake a program of road improvements. Based on projections of rising tax revenue, we should implement a six-year plan of repaving all roads in the incorporated areas of our town.

* * * * *

The following appeared in a newsletter to parents of a local school district:

> Based on a recent study of a seventh grade class at Mawson Junior High School, the district will be providing compact discs of classical music for all students to listen to as they study at home. The study indicated that when students listened to classical music while reading or working in groups, they performed at a higher level than when working without music. Our aim is for all students to use classical music to improve academic achievement.

* * * * *

The following appeared in an article on linguistics:

> Studies of the Makesh language reveal significant similarities between it and Pakesh, a now extinct language. Because the speakers of Pakesh lived in relative isolation, the most logical explanation is that Makesh-speaking visitors to the region borrowed words and phrases, allowing those pieces of the language to survive while Pakesh as a whole disappeared.

* * * * *

The following appeared in a company memo:

> MegaBo's recent acquisition of Gemstar Organic Dairies means that we can begin to reach local markets using their regional distribution networks. Our popular Jazzberry Yogurt Tubes and flavored milk products will surely be popular with consumers who have had access only to Gemstar's organic yogurts, butter, and milk.

Chapter 3

Verbal Reasoning

Introduction to Verbal Reasoning

The Verbal Reasoning measure of the GRE evaluates the skills you will use in graduate and business school. The focus of this section is assessing your logical reasoning abilities and critical thinking skills while reading, evaluating, and interpreting written material. Verbal reasoning questions are presented and organized in several different formats and by specific *question types:* reading comprehension, text completion, and sentence equivalence. This chapter will review each of these question types and walk you through specific strategies and sample practice problems to help you synthesize the material presented. You are encouraged to pace yourself and become familiar with the question-type models by completing the practice questions outlined in each section of this chapter. At the end of this chapter we have included a list of common prefixes, suffixes, and root words intended to refresh and expand your current working vocabulary. Regardless of the question type, if you can expand your knowledge of word meanings, you can improve your overall performance on the exam.

This chapter provides you essential basic skills consistent with the conventions of standard written English. Carefully review this section, take conscientious notes, and practice diligently. Even if your knowledge of English is strong, you should at least skim through the topic headings to know what to expect on the exam. As you read through this chapter and do the practice questions, you will steadily increase your comfort level with the Verbal Reasoning question types and increase your ability to solve more difficult questions. You will notice improvements in both your accuracy and in your efficiency as you work through this material.

Format

Question Type	Total Number of Questions
Reading comprehension evaluates your comprehension of written material by testing your ability to analyze and draw conclusions from written material, such as reasoning from incomplete data, identifying an author's assumptions or perspective, and understanding multiple levels of meaning. Reading comprehension also assesses your ability to select important points, to distinguish major from minor or irrelevant points, to summarize ideas in the text, and to understand the structure of a passage.	Approximately 20 questions (50%)
Text completion measures your understanding of the meanings of words, sentences, and entire texts, your understanding of the relationships between different words and amongst various concepts, and your understanding of vocabulary within context.	Approximately 12 questions (30%)
Sentence equivalence assesses your vocabulary skills by testing your ability to discriminate word choice using context clues and nuances of language, as well as your ability to think logically while following the flow of ideas and understanding the meaning of the sentence as a whole.	Approximately 8 questions (20%)

You will receive two Verbal Reasoning sections that count toward your score. Each of these sections will be timed at 30 minutes and will have approximately 20 multiple-choice questions. Questions can be presented in any order, but generally reading comprehension questions will appear in two groups within each section.

The GRE is a computer-based *section-level adaptive* test. This means that the computer will adjust the level of difficulty on the second set of twenty questions based on the accuracy of your responses to the first set of twenty questions. Specifically, your performance on the first set of verbal questions determines the difficulty level of the questions in your second set of verbal questions. There may be a difference in the degree of difficulty between your two verbal sections, but within each section all questions have the same point-value.

Overview of Reading Comprehension Questions

Reading comprehension questions are designed to test your ability to read and understand diverse passages that deal with a wide variety of topics and subject matter. Question types will appear in three different formats: select one answer, select one or more answers, and select-in-passage. *Reading comprehension questions account for a half of your total Verbal Reasoning score,* so in order to achieve your best possible score and demonstrate your true abilities, it is essential for you to set time aside to practice your reading skills on a regular basis before you take the exam.

In each of the two twenty-question Verbal Reasoning sections, expect to see approximately five reading passages (or a total of ten reading passages for the entire exam), which will vary in length from one sentence to a few paragraphs. Each passage will be followed by one to four questions based on its content, structure, or style. Most passages will be one paragraph in length.

Skills and Concepts Tested

Reading passages tend to be quite straightforward in style and structure. You are not expected to be familiar with the subject matter of the passage or with its specific content, and you will not be expected to have any prior knowledge of the subject. You will rarely be presented with a convoluted sentence structure or highly-specialized technical jargon. A typical college graduate will have the ability to understand the passages' content and to follow the flow of ideas. The reading passages may discuss such wide-ranging subjects as **social science** (psychology, sociology, history, government, politics), **humanities** (art, music, literary criticism, philosophy), **business** (economics, technology, business law), **science** (biology, medicine, physics, astronomy, botany), and so forth.

The questions test your ability to read prose passages with a critical eye, to correctly understand the author's meaning and purpose, to draw reasonable inferences, and to recognize the importance of certain details in the passage. The specific skills you will need to employ include the following tasks:

- identify and understand the main idea of a passage
- separate the main idea from the supporting ideas and from the specific facts that are cited
- distinguish between what the passage says directly (explicitly) from what it implies indirectly (implicitly)
- draw reasonable conclusions from the information presented in the passage
- understand and delineate the organizational structure of the passage
- identify the intended meaning of individual words and/or phrases in context

Sample Reading Comprehension Question Types

Reading Comprehension (Select One Answer Choice)

The select-one-answer question type requires you to read a passage and answer one to four questions relating to the passage. Each question is followed by five answer choices. Your task is to select the ONE given choice that best answers the question.

> The answer choices for questions on the actual computer-based version of the GRE are not labeled with letters. This book labels each answer choice with a letter choice, A, B, C, D, E, etc. for clarity. These letter labels will not appear on the computer screen when you take the test.

Questions 1 to 3 are based on the following reading passage.

(1) A hailstone does not have an easy life—conditions have to be exactly right for one to even get started. (2) First, you need extremely tall cumulonimbus clouds and they must contain powerful updrafts and downdrafts. (3) Next, the vertical wind blasts must carry water droplets like a high-altitude roller coaster, zipping them up to the frigid cloud tops where they freeze solid, then releasing them to free-fall down into warmer air to collect more moisture, then carrying them back up to freeze another layer. (4) As each hailstone repeats this thrill ride over and over, it grows larger and ever larger, and as the hailstone grows, so too does the danger down below. (5) Every hailstone inevitably meets its end by free-falling to Earth, but the chance of severe damage is limited only to stones that took many rides up and down before their final descent.

Select only <u>one</u> answer choice.

---

1. Which of the following best summarizes the primary subject matter of the passage?

Ⓐ The potential amount of damage that might be caused by hailstones.
Ⓑ The large size of the cumulonimbus clouds required for hailstone formation.
Ⓒ The "life cycle" of hailstones, including their formation, growth, and demise.
Ⓓ The behavior of vertical wind currents in the upper atmosphere.
Ⓔ The large size of the nimbocumulous clouds required for hailstone formation.

With its "life cycle" metaphor, this passage tries to anthropomorphize the hailstones, describing their formation and "demise" as if they are actually alive. The information in several of the other answer choices is mentioned in the passage (choices A, B and D), but these facts are irrelevant to answering this particular question about the primary point of the passage. Choice E is contradicted by the information in the passage; hailstones are made inside *cumulonimbus* clouds, not *nimbocumulous* clouds. The correct answer is **C**.

Reading Comprehension (Select One or More Answer Choices)

The select-one-or-more-answer question type requires you to read a passage and answer a question with three possible answers choices. Your task on this type of reading question is to select ALL of the choices that accurately answer the question. You must be sure to choose all of the correct answers. You will receive no credit for the entire question if you do not select all of the possible correct answers. No partial credit is given for partial answers. To choose your answer(s), simply click on all of the responses that answer the question.

Now let's reconsider the same passage about hailstones, but with a question using this new format.

Consider each of the three choices separately and select <u>all</u> that apply.

---

2. Identify all of the logical reasons why this writer mentions the phrase "roller coaster."

Ⓐ It is a metaphor for the repeated ups and downs the hailstones experience.
Ⓑ It is a means to help the reader visualize and relate to the process of hailstone formation.
Ⓒ The writer mentions that this is the official name for this phenomenon.

Based on the information in this passage, both answers A and B present accurate statements. The author's goal in employing the phrase "roller coaster" is to use something well known that demonstrates the same metaphorical up-and-down path that the hailstones travel. This way, the reader can visualize the phenomenon and better relate to the ideas presented. On the other hand, the author never states that this is the "official" name for the phenomenon; thus, choice C can be eliminated. The correct answers are **A** and **B**.

Reading Comprehension (Select-in-Passage)

The select-in-passage question type is presented in a format that requires you to identify one specific sentence in a passage and "click" on that sentence to highlight your answer. When you click on a sentence, your answer will automatically be recorded. This computer format should save you time and effort.

Select one sentence in the passage.

> **3.** Identify the sentence in which the writer initially introduces the theme of the hailstones having a "life cycle." (Remember that on the computerized test you will simply need to click anywhere on the sentence you choose. In this passage we have numbered the sentences so you can easily identify your choice.)

The correct answer is the opening sentence of the passage, in which this author introduces his overall topic with the lively phrase, "A hailstone does not have an easy life...." The correct answer is **Sentence 1.**

Directions

Each reading comprehension passage will be followed by one or more questions based on the passage's content, structure, or style. The reading passage will appear on one side of the computer screen, and the question with the answer choices will appear on the other side of the computer screen. In the heading above the passage, there is a prompt that verifies the number of questions that pertain to the passage. For example, the phrase "Questions 5 to 7 are based on the following passage" may appear in the heading to remind you which questions need to be answered. In the heading above each question, there is a prompt to remind you which question number you are working on. For example, the phrase "Question 5 of 20," may appear in the heading when you are working on question 5.

After reading the passage, carefully read each question, and choose the best response(s) based only on the information that is directly stated or implied in the passage.

General Strategies

- Concentrate on using your time efficiently and do not allow the reading comprehension passage and questions to slow your pace.
- Use only the information that is directly stated or implied in the passage to answer the questions. Do not apply any outside knowledge that you may have about the subject.
- Read the passages carefully to try to understand the facts, their meaning, their implications, and their logical sequence of progression.
- When you are asked more than one question for any given passage, the passage will remain on the screen so that you can reread or skim it for information at any time.
- Be sure to read all of the answer choices carefully and to eliminate obvious wrong answers as soon as you recognize them.

A Six-Step Approach to Reading Comprehension Questions

Step One: Skim the question.

This strategy will help you identify what to focus on. For instance, does the question ask you to recall specific facts that are presented in the passage? Or do you need to understand the author's position on an issue? Or do you need to draw inferences? By skimming the question first, you will understand the gist of what you're being asked, which in turn will help you to focus as you then read the passage more closely.

Step Two: Read the passage actively.

Keep your mind engaged by concentrating on the passage's content and by thinking critically about its ideas as you read. You will grasp ideas more easily if you concentrate on reading actively. **Active reading** is the interactive reading process of "thinking about thinking." You must read the passage while thinking purposefully (not casually) to keep your mind participating in the reading process. This process helps you to "question" the ideas and the logic behind what is presented in the passage. Consider which key words or phrases you should write down on scratch paper provided by the test administrator to help trigger your memory. This will help you focus on the passage's ideas and avoid distractions during the exam. Another technique is to visualize the passage's main ideas as you read to help your comprehension and retention of these ideas.

Step Three: Paraphrase while you read.

Putting the author's main point(s) into your own words will help you to answer every question that asks about the author's main point(s). Paraphrasing is an essential thinking skill that helps to keep your mind focused on the subject matter and helps you avoid distractions. If you are presented with a multi-paragraph passage, try to both (1) grasp the author's point of view in each individual paragraph and (2) identify the author's overall message.

Practice this skill in preparation for the test by jotting down authors' main ideas in whatever articles you happen to read (magazines, newspapers, scholarly journals, etc.). Read the article, turn the paper over, and then write down what you remember about the author's main point of view. Compare your written response to the article itself. As you practice this technique and hone your skills, you will find that you will become more efficient and more accurate at paraphrasing. If you start practicing this skill on a regular basis about six weeks before the test, by the day of your actual GRE test, you will find that you have become a very efficient and accurate reader.

Step Four: Read the question again carefully after reading the passage.

Be sure that you understand exactly what you are being asked. If you skimmed the question before reading the passage, now is the time to verify and make sure that you have accurately identified what the question is asking. A common mistake is that test-takers read the questions too quickly and end up choosing wrong answer(s).

Step Five: Read all answer choices carefully.

Eliminate the obvious wrong answers as you go by using the elimination strategies on pages 11–13. Always make sure that the answer you choose agrees with the information contained in the passage and that it answers the specific question. In other words, be sure to match your answer to the specific question, with the understanding that if an answer choice does not precisely address what the question requires, it cannot be the correct answer. Use the incorrect answers to help guide you toward the correct answer choice.

Step Six: Revise your answer as necessary.

Remember that the GRE computer software program allows you to return to the question and revise your answer (within each timed section of 20 questions). The GRE permits you to change any answer within a section if you make use of the "mark for review" function. On pages 11–13 of the Introduction, you will find more tips about a "plus-minus" system to help you quickly move through especially difficult questions that you may mark for review and then go back to revise in any time remaining after you have completed easier questions. A word of caution: Be careful not to lose too much valuable testing time if you decide to review your earlier work. Remember, you only have about a minute and a half to work through each question!

Specific "Thinking" Strategies for Reading Comprehension

Identifying the Questions

Test questions on the GRE fall into specific categories. Learning to quickly identify the question category will increase your comfort level and, therefore, increase your competency on the day of the test. When you can quickly identify the type of reading question, you will be better equipped to quickly evaluate exactly what it is that you are being asked. In this way, you will be able to work more efficiently.

Within categories, the exact wording of each of these questions can vary greatly. For example, you may be asked about a passage's logical strengths and weaknesses, the author's assumptions, the passage's structure, vocabulary in the context of the passage, and so forth. That said, in general, the reading comprehension questions on the GRE exam will fall into one of the following three basic categories:

- **Main Idea Questions.** These questions evaluate your ability to understand the author's main point, as well as his or her purpose or meaning. In other words, these questions require you to conceptualize the gist of the passage. Your ability to paraphrase will help you answer these questions, as they basically ask, "Did you get the author's message?"

- **Supporting Idea Questions.** These questions test your ability to distinguish and separate the author's main ideas from the supporting ideas. For example, a question may ask how one sentence functions within a paragraph or how one paragraph relates to the whole passage. These questions require you to break the passage down and examine its component parts.

- **Inferences and Implications.** These "hidden idea" questions require you to read between the lines to understand and identify the ideas that are implied in the passage. The answers to this type of question will not be directly stated in the passage.

Accessing the Accurate Answer

Another effective technique to approach specific reading comprehension questions is to understand what kind of *thinking* is required to access the correct answer. Generally, questions require one of three kinds of thinking: fact-based questions, main idea questions, and hidden idea questions. This classification is NOT specifically related to the difficulty level of the question, but rather it refers to the type of thinking process you utilize to identify the right answer. Now let's explore these three levels of question accessibility.

- **Factual questions** can be correctly answered by referring to the printed passage. In other words, you can always find the answer directly stated somewhere in the passage. When you recognize a factual question, approach this task as if it were a scavenger hunt within the passage. If the question asks you to find a specific bit of information, after you locate it in the passage, simply select the answer choice containing the specific word or phrase that answers the question. Words in the question stem that can help you recognize factual questions include the following: *supplies, states, mentions, considers, claims, provides information about, according to the passage.*

- **Main idea questions** can be answered correctly through the use of accurate paraphrasing. If you paraphrase the gist of the passage correctly, you will be able to answer any main idea questions correctly. When working through this book's practice tests, if you select an incorrect answer for a main idea question, ask yourself how or where you inaccurately paraphrased the passage. To recognize these main idea type questions, look for words and phrases such as the following: *author's strengths or weaknesses; main point; author would agree or disagree with; primary purpose; author's attitude; author believes; author is concerned with; passage can best be described as; author's objective.*

- **Hidden idea questions** require that you read between the lines and draw inferences about information that is not explicitly stated. To answer questions of this type, think about what is NOT stated directly, but rather what is *implied* in the passage. Remember that the credited response (the correct answer) has to be the very BEST response and that whenever you're asked a hidden idea question, you should select the answer choice that is most obvious, most plausible, and most likely to be true. Test-takers sometimes think that the correct answer should be more obscure than it really is—beware of talking yourself out of the correct answer! As with the other question types, you should look for telltale words and phrases to identify hidden idea questions. These words may include the following: *infers, implies, assumes, indicates, suggests, concludes, presumes, not explicitly stated,* and *not directly stated.*

Eliminating Incorrect Answers

Understanding how to quickly eliminate incorrect answer choices will help you save time and increase your accuracy. The test administrators often include answer choices designed to trick the test-taker. If you understand the tricks that are used most frequently, you'll be able to quickly eliminate wrong answers and not be mislead by distracting answers. In this strategy, it helps to think like a test writer, not like a test-taker. In other words, don't fight the test, and try to "go with the flow" of ideas. Once you have eliminated an answer choice, you won't need to waste valuable testing time rereading it. Answer choices can be eliminated for many reasons including the following:

- **Contradictory to the passage.** This type of wrong answer contradicts the information in the passage. If you read the passage carefully and paraphrase its ideas accurately, you won't be tricked into the time-consuming process of having to reread it to find out if a potential answer is consistent with what the author really said. Remember, you should be able to eliminate these wrong answers quickly. Ask yourself, "Is this answer consistent with the passage?" If the answer is no, it is wrong.

- **Irrelevant or not addressed in the passage.** This type of wrong answer either has no supporting evidence in the passage or it provides an answer that is irrelevant to what the question asks. Many readers can be tricked into rereading the passage in hopes of finding these nonexistent ideas. However, readers who are proficient at paraphrasing can quickly eliminate the irrelevant or "never addressed" answer choices because they understand what information is included in the passage. Also remember that if an answer choice does not address the specific question, it is wrong—no matter if it is supported by the passage. Ask yourself, "Does this answer address the question? Does the passage offer evidence to support it?" If no, the answer is wrong and should be eliminated.

- **Unreasonable.** If an answer choice completely contradicts logic and makes you ask, "Where did they get that idea?" it is probably an unreasonable answer choice. You should be able to spot and eliminate unreasonable answer choices quickly. Ask yourself, "Is this a reasonable answer for this question?" If not, you can eliminate it.

- **Too general or too specific for the question.** You must understand the degree of specificity that is required for a correct answer. For instance, if the question asks for the overall point of the passage, you need a general answer, one that encompasses the content of the entire essay. On the other hand, if you're asked about the author's use of a certain word or phrase, the correct answer is likely to be quite specific. Use this awareness to eliminate answer choices that are too narrow or too broad for a specific question. Ask yourself, "Is this answer choice specific (or general) enough for this question?" It will help you judge if it is an appropriately-focused answer for this particular question.

- **Absolutes and Qualifiers.** These words are sometimes easy to miss or ignore when you are reading quickly and focusing mostly on the nouns and verbs. However, these words are often the specific reason an answer choice is wrong. When you spot an absolute or qualifying word, do not assume it makes the answer wrong, but definitely check to make sure it accurately reflects the passage. If it is accurate, the answer might be correct, but if it is inaccurate, the answer is definitely wrong. **Absolutes** include such words as *every, all, everyone, no one, none, never, always, only, must, will* and so forth. **Qualifiers** include such words as *some, few, could, might, may* and so forth. Ask yourself, "Is every absolute word (or qualifier) accurate?" If not, the answer is wrong.

Finally, never forget that every wrong answer is designed to be wrong for a *specific reason,* most commonly one inaccurate word or phrase. Through practice, you can learn to more quickly and accurately spot the exact word or phrase, allowing you to answer reading comprehension questions more quickly and with greater confidence. Remember that each correct answer must not contain a single inaccurate word!

Suggested Strategies with Sample Questions

Now let's get going! We'll examine some sample passages and questions and practice applying the strategies we've discussed thus far.

Strategy: Skim the Question

Skim the question(s) to learn what you should concentrate on as you read the passage. If a question asks for the "author's main point," read the passage while concentrating only on the main point. Practice below—first skim the question and then read for this information in the passage.

Sample Passage A

The tendency for people to connect random events in a way that implies that one *caused* another is simply ludicrous. People forget to use the logical, rational part of their mind as they connect phenomenon like these: quantity of smokers and incidence of heart disease; teacher effectiveness and poor test scores; police use of radar and drivers slowing their speed. A case can be made that any one of these may, perhaps, have caused the other, but it is likely to be a weak argument. These results, including heart disease, poor test scores, and drivers lowering their speeds, can surely be affected by multiple influences, and to simplistically identify a single cause for any of them is illogical. Yet people do it every day. If only people would think more before they jump to conclusions, they might realize how flawed their logic actually is.

---

1. Which of the following most clearly identifies the author's attitude?

   Ⓐ He is concerned that a certain conclusion might not be accurate, because it is based on faulty logic.
   Ⓑ He is confident mankind can be trained to overcome its faulty logic.
   Ⓒ He is cynical about mankind's overall ability to discern cause and effect.
   Ⓓ He is convinced mankind's faulty logic will only get worse in the future.
   Ⓔ He is indifferent to mankind's apparent lack of logical thinking skills.

Since the author's attitude is clearly critical—reflected in words and phrases including "ludicrous," "weak," "illogical," "think more before they jump to conclusions," and "flawed…logic,"—you would want to find an answer choice that reflects this negativity. Thus, for this question, choice C provides the most accurate statement of the author's cynical attitude. The correct answer is C. Notice the key word in each of the wrong answer choices that make it wrong: "concerned" (A), "confident" (B), "convinced" (D), and "indifferent" (E).

Now let's explore this skim-the-question strategy in greater depth, by examining a variety of question types. Take a second to pre-read the question below (the related passage follows the question).

---

2. The author's main criticism of the Romantic poets is clarified in which of the following?

Now read the following passage carefully, and keep in mind the specifics of this main idea question. As you read, be sure to look for *the author's main criticism* of the Romantic poets.

Sample Passage B

The Romantic Age in British literature during the late eighteenth and early nineteenth centuries brought radical changes to poetry. Whereas the poets who came before this time wrote primarily about society and social customs, the Romantic poets wrote about nature and the self. And while the previous poets satirized others in what they saw as a frivolous society, the Romantic poets eschewed society and concentrated only on the self, on what was in their own hearts. Finally, whereas the previous poets had something to say about how to improve mankind, the Romantic poets were only concerned with little more than their own tortured psyches. If the Romantic poets were to look farther than their own backyards, they might have found more important subjects to write about.

As you read carefully, you will find that the author specifically disapproves of the Romantic poets' overly self-centered poetry. This idea is emphasized by the repetition of the word "only," which underscores the concept that these poets concentrated too much on their own concerns. The final sentence, with its disparaging remark that the poets should "look farther than their own backyards" for "more important subjects" confirms the author's criticism.

On the other hand, a different question about this Romantic poets passage might read like this:

> **3.** Which of the following can you reasonably infer the author believes about the *previous poets* versus the Romantic poets?

This question type requires inference, meaning you must read between the lines to deduce what the author would reasonably believe. Notice that you are not being asked to find anything the author stated directly. In fact, choices that restate facts explicitly stated in the passage are incorrect! Instead you must identify an idea or ideas that the author implied. Pre-reading the question is an especially valuable strategy for this question type because it will allow you to nix seemingly attractive answers that simply parrot information from the passage.

Strategy: Practice Paraphrasing

Practice paraphrasing passages to define the author's main point. Read the following passage and then paraphrase the author's main point in your own words.

Sample Passage A

In order to maintain high quality of life while minimizing environmental impact, city planners must carefully balance the needs of different land use groups. For example, development permitted in the most sensitive ecosystems, including wetland and riparian buffer areas, should be limited to access paths and passive recreational uses. Fences and similar improvements that are necessary to protect the wetland or riparian zones should be appropriately restricted to only essential areas of the buffer. Wetland/riparian areas and their associated buffers should be permanently protected from development through the application of an open space easement or other suitable instrument. Developments should be located and designed so as not to contribute to increased sediment loading of the wetland/riparian area or cause disturbances to its fish and wildlife. Exceptions to this policy that advocate development into wetland or riparian areas and their associated buffers should only be considered sparingly, as specified in city management policies.

While not overly-demanding in vocabulary or organization, this passage includes quite specific ideas. An accurate paraphrasing of this passage might read something like this:

> *The passage presents policies that should be used to protect wetlands and riverbank areas, such as restricting human access to paths and limiting activities allowed. Development near these areas should not interfere with fish or wildlife. Exceptions should be few and only allowed after city management policies are consulted.*

Now continue your practice by reading and paraphrasing another passage, one with a different style.

Sample Passage B

Modern life is lived according to the clock. One must either be on time or suffer the consequences. Pity the person who still thinks he can run up to the terminal and board an airplane at the last minute! We have to be on time for the train, for the theater, for the important business meeting. However, many other cultures have a more fluid concept of time, with time and punctuality taking different meanings. Some peoples are not glued to the clock but to the seasons. They live their lives based on when it is time to plant or to harvest. Other cultures relate time to significant events, such as remembering that someone in a village was born after a monumentally large snowfall. Those who live their lives nervously glued to a clock would be well-served to remember that the rest of the world does not necessarily share the same values.

The tone of this passage is much more casual and the ideas flow less formally, in a less list-like fashion, than in the preceding example. A paraphrasing of this passage could read like this:

Time means different things to different people. Modern city life is dictated by the clock, but rural life is ruled more by the seasons and nature. People who live in cities need to remember this.

Let's finish our practice of this strategy by paraphrasing one more passage.

Sample Passage C

"The Great Chain of Being" is a philosophy that is based on the idea that everyone desires order, not chaos—sense, not nonsense—and that everyone wants the world to have some degree of predictability, logic, organization, and harmony. With origins among the ancient Greeks, this philosophy was widely accepted until at least the eighteenth century; thus, it is one of the most long-lasting ideas in the history of Western civilization. Essentially, "The Great Chain of Being" is a hierarchy that organizes *everything* in the known universe. It places God and angels at the top; man belongs directly below the angels, and other animals fall below man; plants are below animals, and minerals (rocks and such) are at the bottom of this hierarchy. Even within these categories, the philosophy further classifies its members by hierarchy. For example, the mighty oak tree was classified higher than mere bramble bushes, and the lion was placed higher than a mouse. The ongoing influence of this philosophy is evidenced in such far-reaching ideas as social order, scientific theory, and literature.

This passage, although fairly straightforward, might pose some paraphrasing challenges due to the large number of ideas it presents. Let's consider one accurate paraphrasing:

"The Great Chain of Being" is a philosophy that Western man believed from the time of the ancient Greeks to at least the eighteenth century. It tries to make sense of the world by placing everything that is known in a hierarchy, like a pyramid, with placement indicating importance. God is at the top, then angels, man below angels, animals below man, plants below animals, and minerals below plants. Further classifications were listed within these categories. Proof that mankind once believed this concept can be seen in many areas of life and intellectual thought.

Strategy: Eliminate Wrong Answer Choices

Let's practice this strategy by applying it to a passage that you've already seen, one that deals with humanity's flawed logic. Remember that the first step is to pre-read the question, before you read this passage. Do that now.

> The best title for this passage is which one of the following?

Sample Passage

The tendency for people to connect random events in a way that implies that one *caused* another is simply ludicrous. People forget to use the logical, rational part of their mind as they connect phenomenon like these: quantity of smokers and incidence of heart disease; teacher effectiveness and poor test scores; police use of radar and drivers slowing their speed. A case can be made that any one of these may, perhaps, have caused the other, but it is likely to be a weak argument. These results, including heart disease, poor test scores, and drivers lowering their speeds, can surely be affected by multiple influences, and to simplistically identify a single cause for any of them is illogical. Yet people do it every day. If only people would think more before they jump to conclusions, they might realize how flawed their logic actually is.

> The best title for this passage is which one of the following?
>
> Ⓐ   Mankind's Flawed Assumption of Cause-and-Effect
> Ⓑ   The Link Between Test Scores and Teacher Effectiveness Revealed
> Ⓒ   Ways to Improve Your Logical Skills
> Ⓓ   A Treatise on Mankind's Logical Abilities
> Ⓔ   Understanding the Difference Between Good Logic and Flawed Logic

To eliminate incorrect answers in a question of this type, a "best title" question, remember that you need to find an answer that is appropriately general; don't choose one that is overly-specific. Choice A fulfills this requirement because it deals directly with the passage's overall content, its main message. You can eliminate choice B because it is too specific. Choices C and E are wrong because the ideas in those choices are not addressed in the passage. Choice D is too global, it presents too large an answer; this short passage can hardly be called a "treatise." The correct answer is **A.**

Strategy: Use the "Thinking" Strategies

Understanding the difference between factual, main idea, and hidden idea questions can help you define what kind of thinking is required to answer a question. Let's reread the passage about humanity's flawed logic one more time and look at the three different levels of questions that may be asked.

Sample Passage

The tendency for people to connect random events in a way that implies that one *caused* another is simply ludicrous. People forget to use the logical, rational part of their mind as they connect phenomenon like these: quantity of smokers and incidence of heart disease; teacher effectiveness and poor test scores; police use of radar and drivers slowing their speed. A case can be made that any one of these may, perhaps, have caused the other, but it is likely to be a weak argument. These results, including heart disease, poor test scores, and drivers lowering their speeds, can surely be affected by multiple influences, and to simplistically identify a single cause for any of them is illogical. Yet people do it every day. If only people would think more before they jump to conclusions, they might realize how flawed their logic actually is.

A sample **factual question** for this passage may be written like this:

> The author makes which of the following claims in the passage?

The word "claims" identifies this question as purely factual. Thus, you should read the passage for its direct meaning; the answer can be found right there in print. In other words, the correct answer will be something the author states directly.

A sample **main idea** question may be written like this:

> Given the author's idea about mankind's ability to think logically, with which one of the following statements would he also agree?

The best way to approach this main idea question is to paraphrase the passage. Once you understand the gist of the author's point, you can then ask yourself with which other ideas the author would also logically agree.

A sample **hidden idea** question may be written like this:

> Given the author's point about mankind's faulty logic, which of the following does the author suggest about mankind's ability to choose a good political leader?

Remember, in hidden idea questions you must read between the lines to understand what the author is suggesting or implying. The correct response will not be anything that is stated directly, nor will it merely be one of the ideas in the passage. You have to do the thinking for yourself to correctly answer a hidden idea question.

Practice Reading Comprehension Questions

Now practice applying these strategies! Utilize the strategies you learned as you read the following passages and answer the questions. Questions are not arranged by difficulty, but the difficulty level of each question and question type will be discussed in the explanations that follow.

For each of the questions 1 to 15, select <u>one</u> answer choice unless otherwise instructed.

Question 1 is based on the following reading passage.

It was not until Leo Tolstoy was 51 years old, a fairly advanced age back in 1879, that he finally began his study of the Bible. But then, in typical style, Tolstoy utterly immersed himself in the subject, dedicating himself to the task of decoding and documenting what he called "the pure teachings of Jesus." He spent three years distilling the four Gospels into just a single volume, his 12-chapter *Life of Jesus,* from which he had purged all doctrine and all scripture. Tolstoy was elated at his achievement; the Russian Orthodox Church, somewhat less so.

1. If all of the information in this passage is true, which of the following statements must also be true?

    Ⓐ Tolstoy considered this one book, the *Life of Jesus,* to be his greatest achievement.
    Ⓑ The Russian Orthodox Church considered Tolstoy's book, his *Life of Jesus,* to be sacrosanct.
    Ⓒ Tolstoy labored for three years to distill all twelve Gospels into a single volume, his 4-chapter *Life of Jesus*.
    Ⓓ Tolstoy's chosen task was to purge the Bible of doctrine and scripture in order to reveal "the pure teachings of Jesus."
    Ⓔ Tolstoy's chosen task was to purge the Bible of doctrine and scripture in order to please the Russian Orthodox Church.

Questions 2 to 4 are based on the following reading passage.

Primitive man originally created simple machines in an effort to make essential but labor-intensive tasks easier. But eventually, as machines became more complex and efficient, they began to actually out-perform their human counterparts. In the initial successes, machines could best humans only at selected, specific tasks; for example, a locomotive could easily out-run a human runner. However, in the early twentieth century, the abilities of machines suddenly expanded, and they were able to outperform humans in a large number of jobs that had formerly been performed only by human workers.

The history of the last 100 years might as well have been written by, and for, a class of intelligent machines. They out-performed human workers on the early assembly lines, and then they evolved into semi-autonomous robots, which today are the world's most efficient industrial workers. Early on, they out-calculated human beings at simple math; now modern supercomputers routinely make billions of decisions per second. Machines used in early exploration were all designed to help their human masters travel to, and survive in, places no man had ever gone before; a good example is a deep-diving bathyscaph submarine. However, by now, some machines have long since discarded their human cargo; unaccompanied robots boldly explore deep oceans and fiery volcanoes, they fearlessly tread on distant planets and they even venture into the trackless depths of intergalactic space.

In the evolution of machines, there is one event that may well be remembered as "One giant leap for machine-kind." That was when machines finally began to beat human champions in endeavors formerly thought to be entirely the province of man. Indeed, many people were surprised when a supercomputer called "Deep Blue" defeated Garry Kasparov, the reigning World Chess Champion, but the populace was stunned at the resounding defeat of two champions, Ken Jennings and Brad Rutter, when a computer named "Watson" was crowned champion of the popular TV trivia-game show *Jeopardy*.

2. Which of the following is an inference that can be logically drawn from this passage about machines?

   Ⓐ Early machines were simple because they were designed to perform basic tasks.
   Ⓑ The ability of machines to perform tasks has increased at a fairly steady rate over time.
   Ⓒ Machines have improved greatly, but it is possible that soon they will reach the point of diminishing returns.
   Ⓓ Machines have demonstrated that they no longer need humans to evolve.
   Ⓔ Machines may have begun as simple tools, but it is likely their abilities will continue to improve in the foreseeable future.

3. Which of the following is the best statement of the main point in the passage's final paragraph?

   Ⓐ Machines' abilities are increasing at an exponential rate.
   Ⓑ The most historic moment in machine evolution occurred when the computer "Deep Blue" defeated Chess Champion Garry Kasparov.
   Ⓒ The abilities of modern machines clearly exceed those of humans, as is demonstrated by machines taking the lead in the field of exploration.
   Ⓓ Humans finally began to take more notice of machines' increasing abilities when machines began defeating human champions at popular games.
   Ⓔ Machines have already improved so very much, that it is likely their abilities will eventually exceed anything we humans can imagine.

For the following question, consider each of the choices separately and then select all that apply.

4. Assuming that the information in the passage is accurate, which of the following statements must also be true?

   Ⓐ Well-designed machines perform many tasks better than humans; many machines are more accurate, more efficient, and more economical.
   Ⓑ Mankind has come to depend on machines to do many jobs that humans cannot or will not perform.
   Ⓒ Machines are always designed to do man's work for him, so any machine that does not perform human-like labor is worthless.

Questions 5 and 6 are based on the following reading passage.

   (1) Ecologists have recently expressed alarm at the potential damage that can result from seeding rare plants out of their normal habitat. (2) When rare plants are placed in the ground in areas outside their native territories, they can disrupt their new environments, hybridize with other related plants, and blur their genetic individuality, or, most alarmingly, might possibly carry pathogens that can devastate other native plants. (3) But how do these rare plants extend their reach beyond their normal domain? (4) Commercial sellers of rare plants, especially those that operate over the Internet, as well as well-meaning citizen conservationists both contribute to the spreading of non-native species. (5) One can easily understand how Internet sales could entice some to buy and plant rare species in nonnative areas. (6) However, one might wonder how citizen conservationists can be contributing to this problem. (7) Researchers claim that these citizen groups sometimes replant species outside their usual habitat, trying to reestablish plants where they used to grow in previous epochs, such as before the last Ice Age. (8) To lessen the problem, researchers suggest more rigorous and uniform regulation of Internet trade in rare plants, plus federal coordination with citizen advocacy groups.

5. Which of the following does the author claim is the most serious potential threat posed by rare plants that are relocated in areas outside their native habitat?

   Ⓐ Rare plants can possibly carry pathogens that can ravage native plants.

   Ⓑ Rare plants might hybridize with other local plants.

   Ⓒ The new environment into which rare plants might be introduced can be irreparably damaged.

   Ⓓ Rare plants can lose their original genetic identity.

   Ⓔ Placing rare plants in environments where they used to live could change the surrounding environment.

6. Select the sentence that signals a transition to explaining a seemingly unusual method by which rare plants can be established in nonnative territories.

Question 7 is based on the following reading passage.

When the process of brewing beer was first mastered several millennia ago, mankind rejoiced. Ever since then, however, brewers have struggled with waste. The beer is great, but what to do with the spent hops, barley, and yeast that are left over from the brewing process? In recent years, brewers have increasingly turned to recycling, both for cost-savings and for environmental reasons. Accordingly, new technology is now offering a win-win solution to this problem in the form of the *Anaerobic Methane Digester©*, which not only extracts energy from brewery waste in the form of methane gas that can be used to power the brewery, but also processes the plant's wastewater.

7. Which of the following is the best statement of the main point of this passage?

   Ⓐ The technical aspects of the beer-making process were well-known to ancient peoples.

   Ⓑ Waste management was a never-ending problem for ancient beer-makers, and this issue continues to bedevil brewers today.

   Ⓒ The brewery waste management problem has been solved through recycling.

   Ⓓ New technology and innovative approaches show that waste management issues can have a win-win solution.

   Ⓔ The new *Anaerobic Methane Digester* is likely to make the brewery more self-sufficient and more profitable.

Questions 8 to 9 are based on the following reading passage.

Whether planning an entire urban cityscape or simply reviewing new building permits, a city planner must always consider a wide array of factors, one of which is the effect of winds on street-level business and pedestrians. Specifically, wind evaluation includes an interesting but little-known phenomena: some man-made structures can significantly affect the wind patterns around them; in fact, some tall buildings and large structures are known to increase ground-level wind in their vicinity. Architects in famously windy cities like Chicago and San Francisco have to pay particular attention to avoiding negative effects from the interaction between their man-made buildings and the local weather.

In all cities, closely spaced groups of similar-sized structures tend to slow the wind velocity near ground level, due to the friction and drag of the structures themselves. However, if one building is much taller than its surroundings, it intercepts overhead winds that would otherwise flow past unimpeded, redirecting them down the vertical face of the building all the way to ground level. Winds that have been so abruptly rerouted can increase in strength and also form vigorous turbulence when they reach ground level. Consequently, such strong downdrafts can be incompatible with many intended uses of nearby ground-level spaces.

Moreover, structural designs that include tall flat surfaces which are perpendicular to strong prevailing winds can create a ground-level environment that is actually hazardous to pedestrians. It is worth noting, however, that structural measures are being developed (most notably, perpendicular side-structures) to help reduce the velocity of the redirected winds to more acceptable levels.

For the following question, consider each of the choices separately and select <u>all</u> that apply.

8. Assuming the information in the passage above is correct, it is logical to infer that which of the following businesses could be negatively affected by winds in poorly planned downtown areas?

   A A street-level café with an open 40-foot indoor-outdoor dining section is located at the entrance to a solitary 30-story building.
   B A rooftop restaurant located in a group of five-story buildings is located immediately next to a single skyscraper, a 45-story office building.
   C A corner newsstand with a 20-foot open counter displaying newspapers, magazines, and candy is located between two blocks, one of which contains high-rise corporate headquarters, the other of which contains a seven-story parking structure.

9. Which of the following facts does the author cite in the discussion of how buildings affect the wind?

   Ⓐ Chicago suburbs are affected negatively by high winds.
   Ⓑ The friction and drag from a group of buildings can increase the wind at street level.
   Ⓒ Structural measures such as perpendicular side-structures can negate the negative effects of downdrafts.
   Ⓓ Pedestrians walking in a city block that has some buildings which are higher than others can be struck by turbulent winds.
   Ⓔ If city planners only approve buildings of the same height, pedestrians will be safe from downdrafts.

Questions 10 and 11 are based on the following reading passage.

When Frank Buckles died in 2011, it seemed that he suddenly became a very popular fellow. This was because, of the millions of American veterans who had returned from World War I, the so-called "War to End All Wars" that began some 97 years earlier, Buckles was the last survivor, the last living link to that long-ago conflict. Thus, it was quite unexpected when a new WWI-related contretemps suddenly arose; it seemed that everyone wanted to honor this man and, indeed, to honor all of the American Veterans of WWI who had passed on before him. However many bickered over the most appropriate way to do it, arguing selfishly over details such as the location for the public viewing of his casket.

For the following question, consider each of the choices separately and select <u>all</u> that apply.

10. Which of the following statements is an accurate inference that can be logically deduced from this passage?

    A Frank Buckles was held in very high esteem during his lifetime.
    B All American veterans of World War I were held in high esteem during their lifetimes.
    C The "contretemps" over how to honor deceased veterans involves issues much larger than just the burial of Frank Buckles.

11. Considering the overall context of the passage, which of the following best delineates the actual intended meaning of the word "popular," as used in the opening sentence?

    Ⓐ Buckles was popular because, in life, everyone wanted to talk to him; he was known for being convivial.
    Ⓑ Buckles was popular because, in life, he was a highly-regarded WWI veteran and he was often interviewed.
    Ⓒ Buckles was popular because people realized his personal memories were unique.
    Ⓓ Buckles was suddenly popular after death, because people truly wanted to honor him individually for his heroic service.
    Ⓔ Buckles was suddenly popular after death because people wanted to reap reflected glory by making a show of honoring him and all WWI veterans.

Question 12 is based on the following reading passage.

In many of Vincent van Gogh's best-known paintings, it is the vibrant strokes of yellow that catch the viewer's eye and linger in the mind. However, in some of the artist's signature works, such as "Starry Night" and his series of sunflower paintings, the formerly-brilliant yellow hues are fading, changing to an unattractive muddy-looking brown, and now an international team of European scientists is struggling to find the cause and, even more important, to ascertain if the process can be reversed. They at least hope to mitigate the damage.

12. Which of the following is an unstated assumption that underlies the author's point in this passage?

   Ⓐ Vincent van Gogh utilized an unusual shade of yellow in his paintings.

   Ⓑ The effect of the yellow hue van Gogh used is to attract the eye and to make the paintings more memorable.

   Ⓒ A number of paintings by Vincent van Gogh, such as "Starry Night" and the sunflower series, are quite well known.

   Ⓓ These paintings by Vincent Van Gogh are treasured by many people and, thus, their restoration is considered to be very important.

   Ⓔ An international team of European scientists struggled for years before they finally discovered the cause of the damage.

Questions 13 to 15 are based on the following reading passage.

A recent biography of the late Mohammad Reza Pahlavi, better known as the last shah of Iran, paints a portrait of this powerful man during the Cold War as an ultimately tragic figure; he was the supreme monarch of a mighty country, but nevertheless, he was brought down by internal forces, most tellingly, by his own character flaws. Moreover, as if completing the pattern of a Greek tragedy, when this man was brought to ruin by his own hubris, overthrown in 1979 and dying in exile in 1980, he was not the only one to suffer. Rather, it is the people of Iran who have suffered ever since; they never achieved the promised open democracy, and they are still oppressed by a government every bit as rigid and autocratic as that of the late shah, only now they are under the flag of an Islamic Republic.

13. An accurate assessment of the author's purpose in writing this piece would emphasize that the passage is

   Ⓐ a diatribe, castigating the former shah of Iran for his harsh treatment of his people.

   Ⓑ a harangue, lecturing that the Iranian people themselves are the ultimate cause of their misfortune.

   Ⓒ a philosophical treatise, arguing that moral relativism explains the schism in Iranian society.

   Ⓓ a nuanced overview, describing the multifaceted tragedy of the shah and placing it into historical context.

   Ⓔ an apologia, defending and justifying the oppressive measures taken by both Iranian regimes.

For the following question, consider each of the choices separately and then select <u>all</u> that apply.

14. Which of the following is an inference that can be logically drawn from this passage?

   Ⓐ Despite the international pressures of the Cold War, Mohammad Reza Pahlavi was ultimately brought down not by external threats, but by interior forces.

   Ⓑ The Iranian people were oppressed by the autocratic rule of the shah, but thanks to the 1979 Islamic Revolution, they now have limited democracy and more personal freedom.

   Ⓒ This is a timeless pattern, wherein a noble man rises to power through sheer force of will, only to be undone by his own flaws, and it is reminiscent of twentieth century Theater of the Absurd.

15. Which of the following is most likely the author's intended meaning when he uses the phrase "internal forces" in the opening sentence?

   Ⓐ The phrase refers to the opposition military forces that arose within the country, which are the "internal forces" that specifically deposed the shah.

   Ⓑ The phrase refers to extremist elements within domestic political opposition, "internal forces" which, ultimately, not even the shah could suppress.

   Ⓒ The phrase refers to the uncontrollable economic forces that were decimating the domestic economy of Iran.

   Ⓓ The phrase alludes to the "internal forces" within the shah himself, to the character flaws and other limitations that eventually doomed him.

   Ⓔ The phrase signals that there were many forces that came together to topple the shah; if some were "internal forces," ipso facto, then some must have been external forces.

Answers and Explanations for Reading Comprehension Practice Questions

1. **D.** This is a hidden idea question because you have to read between the lines to get the answer. It is considered to be of medium difficulty. Based on the information in the passage, there is only one answer choice that absolutely *must* be true and choice D is that answer; the passage entirely supports the idea that Tolstoy labored to reveal "the pure teachings of Jesus." Choice A might at first seem appealing, after all, the passage does state that "Tolstoy was elated at his achievement;" however, this answer is incorrect because it qualifies this as *his greatest achievement,* which simply goes too far. All of the other answer choices can be eliminated using the same tool; your task is to find anything, even just one word that disagrees with the passage. Choice B is disqualified by its improper use of the word *sacrosanct;* the Church certainly did not think Tolstoy's book was sacred. Choice C is disqualified because it improperly swaps the numerical information; there were never *twelve Gospels* nor did Tolstoy produce a *4-chapter* book. Choice E is disqualified because it misstates both Tolstoy's purpose and the reaction of the Church.

2. **E.** This hidden idea question is a quite accessible, easy question. Choice E is an inference that can be logically drawn from the information in this passage. The passage presents the ideas that the first machines were simple tools performing simple tasks, that machines' abilities have grown exponentially, and that their capabilities are still improving in ways that leave humans "stunned." Thus, it is logical to expect that *their abilities will continue to improve* (E). On the other hand, the statement in choice A is definitely not an inference that can be logically drawn from this passage; rather, it merely restates the first sentence of the passage. Choice B actually contradicts the facts; the passage indicates that the ability of machines is increasing at an ever-faster rate. Finally, there is no support in the passage for choice C, the idea of *diminishing returns* in robotic progress, nor is there support for choice D, the idea that *machines…no longer need humans to evolve.*

3. **D.** This question is a main idea question, and thus is most easily solved through paraphrasing—in this case, by accurately paraphrasing the passage's last paragraph. The question is of medium difficulty. In the final paragraph, this author tries to "humanize" the march of machine progress by referencing two events in popular culture, a chess match and a *Jeopardy* championship, wherein a computer bested the human champion(s). This resulted in a much greater appreciation amongst the general public of the ever-evolving abilities of computers, as stated in choice D. The other options are incorrect for a variety of reasons. Choice A might be the main point of the passage as a whole, but it is not the main point of the final paragraph. Choice B presents one individual fact from the final paragraph, not the main point. Choice C actually refers to information in the third paragraph, not the final paragraph. The statement in choice E is a conclusion that one might reach from the passage overall, but it is certainly not the main point of this final paragraph. Therefore, these incorrect answers are irrelevant since they do not answer the specific question.

4. **A and B.** This is a hidden idea question because you must read between the lines to conclude which answer choices logically follow from the passage; it is of medium difficulty. The statements in choice A and choice B both logically follow directly from information in the passage. The idea that machines can perform some tasks more accurately and efficiently than humans (A) underlies the entire argument in the passage. Also, the idea that mankind's dependence on machines is ever-increasing (B) is also discussed in the passage. However, the statement in choice C does not derive from the argument in this passage; in fact, some machines are designed specifically to perform nonhuman labor effectively and are certainly not *worthless*.

5. **A.** The word "claim" shows this to be a fact-based question, which you can answer fairly easily by searching the passage. This question asks you to identify "the most serious potential threat posed by rare plants" being transported and planted in nonnative areas. The passage states that the most alarming aspect of plants being relocated is how they "might...carry pathogens that can devastate other native plants." Choice A restates this idea directly. All of the ideas in the other answer choices are, indeed, stated in this passage; however, they are only mentioned as possible threats from rare plants, and are not identified as "the most serious...threat."

6. **Sentence 6: However, one might wonder how citizen conservationists can be contributing to this problem.** This question asks you to identify the sentence that transitions from one idea to another. This is best described as a main-idea question of medium difficulty. In this passage, the first two sentences introduce the issue of potential dangers from rare plants growing in nonnative territories, and then provide a list the potential threats they pose. The third sentence questions how these plants reach the new areas, and the fourth sentence answers that question by stating that commercial sellers and citizen conservationists both contribute to the problem. One might be misled into thinking that this fourth sentence is the correct answer to the question, but this sentence does not address what the question specifically asks, making it an irrelevant answer choice. The fifth sentence explains the common-sense way that Internet sales can contribute to the problem. Finally, the sixth sentence explicitly answers this question. It begins with the tell-tale transition word "however," noting that a distinctly different or even opposing idea is forthcoming, in this case the idea that well-meaning citizen conservationists contribute to the problem of nonnative species introduction. The seventh sentence further explains this method, and the eighth sentence completes the overall message by providing suggested solutions for this potential problem.

7. **D.** This main-idea question is of medium difficulty. The main idea of this passage is that the long-running problem of brewery waste can now be mitigated through effective and economical technological solutions; thus, choice D is the correct answer for this question. Two of the other choices, A and E, fail to answer this question because, although they cite correct facts from the passage, they do not identify the passage's actual main point; they are irrelevant. For example, choice E posits that the brewery will be *more self-sufficient and more profitable,* which certainly seems to be true, but that fact is not the passage's main point. Choices C and B can be eliminated because they misinterpret facts from the passage: Choice B states that waste-management has been a *never-ending problem,* but it fails to note the possible solution offered by new, improved technology; choice C incorrectly states that the waste-management problem *has been solved through recycling,* which, according to the passage, it has not. Both of these choices are contradictions.

8. **A, B, and C.** This is a hidden idea question and, as such, it requires you to consider all the facts in the passage before you can make an inference about which of the businesses would be negatively affected by poor city planning. However, with the passage's facts firmly in mind, the question itself is on the easy end of the difficulty spectrum. The facts cited in the passage indicate that strong downdrafts incompatible with the intended uses of nearby ground-level spaces result when air is diverted downwards by isolated, tall buildings. This would include the business in choice A, the café, and in choice C, the corner newsstand that has high-rise buildings on one side and a lower parking structure on the other; both businesses are located at street level and, thus, both could be affected by these strong downdrafts. The business in choice B, the rooftop restaurant, is not on the street level, but it is directly adjacent to a 45-story office building; the passage states that solitary taller buildings can redirect winds down toward lower structures. Thus, it is possible that this rooftop restaurant could also be negatively affected and, therefore, all three of the answer choices are accurate.

9. **D.** This is a straightforward factual question, but it still might be considered hard, because it forces you to return to the passage to check the validity of each possible answer. The clue to the correct answer is in the statement, "if one building is much taller than its surroundings, it intercepts…winds…redirecting them down the vertical face of the building…to ground level… [and these] can increase in strength and… turbulence." This verifies that choice D is the correct response, since pedestrians are at ground level and, thus, they could be struck by these increased winds. Choice A is incorrect because it includes the word "suburbs;" while the passage does specify that Chicago is a "famously windy" city, it never mentions suburbs. Choice B is wrong because of the word "increase," which contradicts the facts of the passage; friction and drag can "decrease" the wind at street level below a group of buildings. Choice C is wrong because of the word "negate," which is too strong; rather, the passage states that structural measures can "reduce" the speed of winds at street level. Finally, choice E is also too strong; the passage never assures us that pedestrians "will be safe" if planners approve only buildings of the same height.

10. **C.** This is a hidden idea question, since it asks you to draw an inference. However, it is fairly easy to answer. The opening line of this passage states that it was not until after Frank Buckles' death that "he suddenly became a very popular fellow." This fact specifically contradicts the statement in answer choice A, that *Buckles was held in very high esteem during his lifetime.* This passage includes no discussion of how *all American veterans* were treated during their lifetimes, and so you can also eliminate choice B. Once these two options are eliminated, you can focus your attention on choice C, which must (and in fact turns out to) be true; the root cause of the current fracas or "contretemps" does, indeed, lie in *issues much larger than just…Frank Buckles.* Of these three choices, C is the only inference that can truly be drawn from this passage.

11. **E.** This is a main idea question of medium difficulty. When you consider the overall context of this passage, it becomes clear that the author was being somewhat sarcastic in his use of the word "popular" in the opening sentence; Buckles was "popular" only in the sense that certain people fought bitterly over him, each wanting to get the credit for providing the most "appropriate" and patriotic (and attention-getting) memorial service ever (as in choice E). The other answer choices can be dismissed fairly quickly through effective use of elimination tools. For example, the passage opens with the news that it was not until "…Buckles died…that he suddenly became… popular" so you can eliminate any and all answer choices that refer to him as being popular *in life.* This includes choice A, that he was *convivial,* choice B, that he was *often interviewed,* and choice C, that people were interested in his *unique…personal memories;* none of these issues actually apply, because the sentence states that Buckles was already dead when he became popular. Finally, the statement in choice D, that *people truly wanted to honor him individually,* seems to be in conflict with the overall message of the passage, which was that the brouhaha over his memorial service was rooted in far deeper issues than just the life and death of this one man.

12. **D.** This is a hidden idea question because it asks you to understand an assumption, rather than finding explicitly stated material; you have to read between the lines to choose the correct answer. It is hard. The passage makes the point that top European scientists are trying to preserve these paintings, and so it follows logically that their restoration is considered important (for if not, why go to the effort?). Thus, choice D is an accurate assumption behind this passage. Most of the other choices simply parrot facts from the passage; for example, choice A, *he used an unusual shade of yellow,* choice B, *the yellow hue…is to attract the eye,* and choice C, the *paintings…are quite well-known* are all explicitly stated and thus not assumptions. Choice E contradicts the facts in the passage in its assertion that the scientists have finally discovered the cause, when in fact, the passage states otherwise.

13. **D.** This main idea question is certainly hard. The writer of this passage refers to "paint[ing] a portrait" of an "ultimately tragic figure," which indicates his sensitivity to nuance, and then he expands the narrative to include the tragedy of the Iranian people. Finally he places these events into historical context, by referring back to timeless Greek tragedies. Thus, choice D provides the correct description of the passage's purpose; it is *a nuanced overview, describing the multifaceted tragedy….* Also, if readers note the equable tone of the passage, they will understand that its purpose is not harsh, so it is neither *a harangue* (B) designed to lecture *the Iranian people themselves* nor *a diatribe* (A) designed to castigate the shah. Finally, the two remaining answer choices are not supported by this passage; it is not a philosophical argument for *moral relativism* (C), nor does it attempt to defend or justify the *oppressive measures taken by both…regimes* (E). Both of these answers are irrelevant.

14. **A.** This hidden idea question is a hard question. Choice A presents the only statement that is, indeed, an inference supported by the information in this passage. In spite of the fact that the shah was "the supreme monarch" of a strategically-important "mighty country" during the Cold War, these are not the factors that brought him down. Rather it was the *internal* struggles, that is, uncontrollable forces both within the country and within himself, that ultimately, irrevocably led to his downfall. Each of the other statements contains a true fact, but also a disqualifying idea. Choice B is incorrect because it makes a misstatement about supposed improvements in the daily lives of the Iranian people after the revolution. Choice C begins on a promising note, alluding to the *timeless pattern* that is *reminiscent* of classic works, but then it is undone by an erroneous reference; Theater of the Absurd was not, in fact, mentioned in this passage, and it is too much of a stretch to draw this inference.

15. **D.** This is a hidden idea question of medium difficulty. When this author uses the phrase "internal forces" he immediately follows it with a qualifier, "most tellingly…his own character flaws." Thus, he gives the reader a tip-off that the most important of these "internal forces" were actually internal to the man himself, namely his *character flaws and other limitations,* and so choice D is the accurate answer choice. On the other hand, the passage does not provide support for the idea in choice A, that the shah was deposed by internal *military* forces, nor does it support the idea in choices B and C, that he was brought-down by internal *political* forces or by internal *economic* forces. The idea in choice E is not logically consistent, and it does not agree with the ideas in this passage.

Overview of Text Completion Questions

Text completion questions are designed to test your ability to choose a word or phrase that best completes a sentence or a passage. This portion of the verbal measure will assess how well you understand vocabulary within context and how well you use contextual clues, including grammar and usage, to determine the most logical answer choice(s).

Remember that on the GRE you will have two Verbal Sections that count toward your score, and each section will present twenty questions for you to answer in 30 minutes. Approximately six of each twenty questions will be text completion questions.

Skills and Concepts Tested

This question type tests your skills and understanding of word meanings, context clues, grammar, and usage. To perform well, you need to comprehend the passage and its intent, to think logically, and to understand subtle differences in word choices. Paying close attention to an author's tone and to the nuances of connotation will also help you discern what answer choice best completes the passage. Of course, having a well-rounded college or graduate-level vocabulary will provide invaluable assistance.

Accomplished readers use these skills all the time when they continually interpret, evaluate, and predict as they read. These readers create a picture in their mind and revise that vision as they continue reading while gathering more information. Text completion questions access this ability by removing key words from short passages and asking test-takers to understand what word or phrase would best complete the passage's intent. Adding the missing word or phrases will create a coherent, meaningful passage.

Directions

The directions will tell you to select one entry from the corresponding column of choices for each blank. You will need to fill in all of the blanks in the way that best completes the text.

In each text completion question, you will be presented with a short passage ranging in length from one to five sentences. It will have either one, two, or three blanks you must fill in from the choices provided. When the passage has only one blank, you will have five answer choices from which to choose. When the passage has two or three blanks, you will have just three choices for each blank. In the two- or three-blank questions, you **must choose all** of the correct answers for credit to be given. You will **not be given partial credit** for only selecting a portion of the correct answers.

The answer choices for each blank will be printed vertically in a column and labeled accordingly. For passages with two or three blanks, the first blank will be labeled (i), the second blank will be labeled (ii), and the third blank will be labeled (iii), The three answer choices for the first blank will be in a column labeled Blank (i), the second, Blank (ii), and the third, Blank (iii). You should choose the best word or phrase to fit in each blank independently. In other words, consider the words in each column of choices separately from the other columns. Here is one example:

Blank (i)	**Blank (ii)**	**Blank (iii)**
Ⓐ ostentatious	Ⓓ quotidian	Ⓖ hackneyed
Ⓑ unpretentious	Ⓔ prodigious	Ⓗ forthright
Ⓒ facile	Ⓕ sporadic	Ⓘ clandestine

General Strategies

- Get a sense of the passage's intent by reading it in its entirety. Do not try to choose an answer choice in isolation.
- Before reading answer choices, consider a word or phrase that you might use to complete the passage, and then look for a synonymous answer choice in the appropriate column.
- Be sure you follow the logic of the sentence and the relationship of sentences in multi-sentence passages. Then you can choose answers accordingly to fit that logic.
- Concentrate on finding and understanding the context clues in each sentence; they are included to guide you and to help direct your answer choice, even if you don't know the vocabulary.
- Pay particular attention to transition words that either continue or alter the flow of the passage's ideas.
- Use the positive or negative connotations of words in the passage to help narrow down your answer choices and to eliminate inaccurate ones.
- Mentally insert your answer(s), and then reread the complete passage, making sure the end result is a complete and unified passage.

Transition Words and Phrases That May Be Used to Continue or to Shift a Passage's Idea	
Words that are used to continue similar ideas	**Words that are used to alter or contrast**
and	but
in other words	however
therefore	although
furthermore	instead
in addition	despite
also	regardless
likewise	rather than
moreover	on the other hand
consequently	nevertheless

Suggested Strategies with Sample Questions

Learning how to apply the successful strategies for text completion questions will give you comfort, and practicing will help you build speed for the test. More than one strategy could be used to answer any given passage; however, in the section that follows we will explore how an individual, specific strategy can be applied to a variety of questions.

Strategy 1: Get a sense of the passage's intent by reading it in its entirety. Do not try to choose an answer choice in isolation.

> 1. As farmers across America struggled to reduce operating costs during the recession, more and more decided to (i) _____ the use of automated harvesting machines; some farms have completely changed the type of crops they grow to take advantage of the latest technology, thus reducing their need for seasonal labor and making large numbers of field hands (ii) _____.
>
> | Blank (i) | Blank (ii) |
> |---|---|
> | Ⓐ forego | Ⓓ superfluous |
> | Ⓑ curtail | Ⓔ essential |
> | Ⓒ expand | Ⓕ imperative |

To select the correct answer for the first blank, you must consider this sentence as a whole. A mistake may result from answering the first blank too quickly, by erroneously equating the farmer's goal to "reduce operating costs" with *forgo(ing)* (A) or *curtail(ing)* (B) the use of expensive equipment. The correct answer, on the other hand, is supported by the overall message, that farmers want to "take advantage of the latest technology," so they will *expand* their use of machinery (C). For the second blank, the key is the phrase, "reducing their need for…labor." This indicates that a large labor force is no longer needed, thus, it is now *superfluous* (D); it is certainly not *essential* (E) or *imperative* (F). The correct answers are **C** and **D**.

Strategy 2: Before reading answer choices, consider a word or phrase that you might use to complete the passage and then look for a synonymous answer choice in the appropriate column.

> 2. The _____ smells wafting from behind the kitchen doors were literally mouthwatering; they made the diners involuntarily salivate in anticipation. Apparently the reviewers were not wrong when they awarded this restaurant five stars.
>
> Ⓐ malodorous
> Ⓑ tantalizing
> Ⓒ vacuous
> Ⓓ fetid
> Ⓔ miscellaneous

In this sample, think of possible words you might insert to complete the sentence, such as "delicious" or "aromatic." Similarly, the adjective you chose for the blank needs to be a positive one, since the smells are mouthwatering, the diners are salivating in anticipation, and the restaurant received a five-star rating. Choice B, *tantalizing,* which is synonymous with delicious and aromatic, is the only answer associated with a positive smell. Choices A, *malodorous,* and D, *fetid,* both describe negative smells that would more likely make customers want to leave. Choice C, *vacuous,* means something that lacks substance, and nonexistent smells could not affect the diners at all. Choice E, *miscellaneous,* does not specifically refer to things that smell good, and since it refers to variety and diversity, it connotes too many aromas to be considered enticing. The correct answer is **B.**

Strategy 3: Be sure you follow the logic of the sentence and the relationship of sentences in multi-sentence passages. Then you can choose answers accordingly to fit that logic.

3. When he returned home, the celebrated Olympic champion was initially greeted with (i) _____ for bringing home a gold medal. However, once it was determined he had used a banned performance-enhancing substance, he was stripped of his gold medal, and he became a (ii) _____ for blighting his country's reputation.

Blank (i)	Blank (ii)
(A) derision	(D) martyr
(B) approbation	(E) charlatan
(C) vituperation	(F) pariah

Notice how the flow and logic of this passage shifts between the two sentences. In this passage, the words "initially" and "however" indicate that a change has occurred and, thus, the correct answers must be somewhat opposite in meaning. For the first blank, a positive word is needed to match the connotation of "celebrated," and the word *approbation* (B), meaning praise, meets this requirement. By noting their negative connotations, you can eliminate *derision* (A), which means scorn, and *vituperation* (C), which indicates a verbal attack. The second blank needs a negative connotation, a word that is somewhat opposite in meaning to "praise;" *pariah* (F) is the correct answer, as it means someone who is hated and avoided. The other choices both have the necessary negative connotations, but their denotations are incorrect; a *martyr* (C) is someone who sacrifices himself for a cause, and a *charlatan* (E) is a swindler or con artist, so neither choice is accurate in this sentence. The correct answers are **B** and **F**.

Strategy 4: Concentrate on finding and understanding the context clues in each sentence; they are there to guide you and to help direct your answer choice, even if you don't know the vocabulary.

4. Although saddled with a title that is a bit overly-(i) _____, *US Navy Combat Blimps: Heroic Airships Won the War on Nazi U-Boats,* this valuable new book does, in fact, include a (ii) _____ amount of newly-released information, an abundance of little-known details, and a few previously-(iii) _____ dispatches of World War II.

Blank (i)	Blank (ii)	Blank (iii)
(A) ostentatious	(D) quotidian	(G) hackneyed
(B) unpretentious	(E) prodigious	(H) forthright
(C) facile	(F) sporadic	(I) clandestine

The word to fill the first blank needs to be one that is consistent with the new book's being burdened and "saddled" with a title that is over-the-top; the word *ostentatious* (A) fits this role, as it accurately describes the hyperbole in the book's title. The second blank requires a word that means a large number to fit the concept that the new book is "valuable" with "an abundance of little-known details"; the word *prodigious* (E) means extraordinary in amount and, thus, it fits the context of this sentence. Choice D, *quotidian,* means something that occurs regularly, and choice F, *sporadic,* refers to something that occurs only occasionally or irregularly. Finally, the last blank in this sentence requires a word that is synonymous with the concept of previously-unknown "secrets." The word *clandestine* (I) fits well, because it means secretive or surreptitious. On the other hand, the word *hackneyed* (G) is incorrect because it means something that is banal, trite, and overused. Choice H makes little sense; *forthright* refers to something that is straightforward and frank, so the phrase "previously-forthright dispatches" would equate to saying the dispatches are no longer candid. The correct answers are **A, E,** and **I.**

Strategy 5: Pay particular attention to transition words that either continue or alter the flow of the passage's ideas.

5. In stark contrast to his _____ later in life, as a young, idealistic college student, he campaigned vigorously for every candidate that caught his eye, despite the fact that none of his candidates was ever elected.

    A political indifference
    B opinionated actions
    C intolerant coldness
    D community activism
    E realistic cynicism

In this sentence, notice the transitional phrases that will help you understand the logical flow of the passage. The opening phrase, "in stark contrast," coupled with "despite the fact," shows that you need an answer that will illustrate opposition to the "idealistic college student…[who] campaigned vigorously." The response that best shows this contrasting meaning is *political indifference* (A). Notice how it accurately fits in to the political context of the passage as no other answer choice does. Choice C is inaccurate for two reasons: The phrase "intolerant coldness" does not fit the political context that choice A does, and the word "intolerant" is not necessarily suggested by the passage. Being "idealistic" and "campaign[ing] vigorously" as a youth does not necessarily provide a "stark contrast" to being intolerant "later in life." While choice D does have the hint of political interest with the word *community,* the second word of this pair, *activism,* is the opposite of what this sentence actually needs. Choice E may be equally deceiving because its first word, *realistic,* may appear to be the opposite of "idealistic," but the second word of the pair, *cynicism,* does not accurately fit the flow of the sentence. The correct answer is **A**.

Strategy 6: Use the positive or negative connotations of words in the passage to help narrow down your choices and to eliminate inaccurate answers.

6. Tabloid newspapers are known to publish (i) _____ articles with sensational headlines in order to increase their sales. Many of these stories contain (ii) _____ statements that can end up costing the publishers millions if they are sued for libel.

Blank (i)	Blank (ii)
A exaggerated	D mendacious
B unobtrusive	E irrefutable
C morose	F obsequious

Notice the negative connotations in this passage: It claims that tabloids use "sensational headlines" that can "cost the publishers millions if they are sued for libel." This negative tone indicates the articles that the tabloids publish might not be trustworthy or truthful. Thus, the articles are (A) *exaggerated,* using inflated facts to attract more readers. If the articles were *unobtrusive* (B), which means bland, the tabloid would not be able to generate increased sales. While *morose* (C), which means gloomy, is a negative word, it does not make logical sense here; depressing articles do not increase sales. The second blank requires a word that describes libelous, untruthful statements for which the tabloid could be sued. The correct word that means false or lying is *mendacious* (D). Choice E is inaccurate because *irrefutable* refers to statements that are factually true and have evidence to back them up; it does not have the negative connotation this passage needs. Finally, *obsequious* (F) means to be excessively fawning or eager to please in an insincere fashion. Even if tabloid articles were to be written in an obsequious manner, it is not likely to produce libelous statements. The correct answers are **A** and **D**.

Practice Text Completion Questions

Now you can continue to practice on your own! The following questions are roughly grouped into sets of five by their approximate level of difficulty: easy to moderate, average, and above average to difficult. The answers and thorough explanations follow the questions.

Easy to Moderate

1. In Western culture, we are repeatedly told to look beyond the (i) _____ surface-level, and instead to seek true, (ii) _____ beauty.

   Blank (i)
   - Ⓐ superficial
   - Ⓑ technical
   - Ⓒ elemental

   Blank (ii)
   - Ⓓ ephemeral
   - Ⓔ inner
   - Ⓕ transient

2. The heinous crime against the little girl was especially horrific and so, even months later, the trial was highly-publicized and the press clamored for a conviction. But then the jury surprised everyone by voting to _____ the defendant, citing overwhelming evidence supporting his alibi.

   - Ⓐ condemn
   - Ⓑ exile
   - Ⓒ befriend
   - Ⓓ ameliorate
   - Ⓔ exculpate

3. The flamingo's striking pink color originates in pigments that are created in the bird's primary food source, brine shrimp. However, when the flamingo's pink feathers fade, it is able to brighten its colors by rubbing secretions from a gland near its tail on its feathers, _____ to potential mates.

   - Ⓐ increasing its camouflage
   - Ⓑ escalating its flying ability
   - Ⓒ enhancing its attractiveness
   - Ⓓ beginning its return
   - Ⓔ swelling its fragrance

4. Many gyms brag about their immaculate facilities and state-of-the-art exercise equipment; they use these amenities to justify charging outrageous, (i) _____ membership rates. Many new members, inveigled and swayed by the elaborate facilities and equipment, quickly join (ii) _____ but fail to utilize the gym equipment to their full advantage.

   Blank (i)
   - Ⓐ judicious
   - Ⓑ exorbitant
   - Ⓒ nominal

   Blank (ii)
   - Ⓓ on a whim
   - Ⓔ under distress
   - Ⓕ with resignation

5. For a period of about 75 years, every science class was taught that our solar system was a nine-planet system, but in 2006 Pluto was reclassified as a dwarf planet and the credit—or, as judged by the _____ nine-planet zealots, the blame—goes to a formerly little-noticed group, the International Astronomical Union, or IAU.

   Ⓐ   placated
   Ⓑ   mollified
   Ⓒ   assuaged
   Ⓓ   outraged
   Ⓔ   conciliated

Average

6. When visitors enter the small French town of Rennes-le-Chateau, the newcomers are greeted by an official warning sign, "Digging is forbidden," but this _____ does not come as a surprise, as most visitors are already familiar with the peculiar history of this town; they have heard whispered tales of mysterious buried treasures and of the incessant, secretive, nocturnal digging.

   Ⓐ   description
   Ⓑ   proscription
   Ⓒ   prescription
   Ⓓ   prostration
   Ⓔ   accommodation

7. Over 500 planets have (i) _____ been found orbiting far-distant stars, and now deep-space astronomers are striving to locate their "Holy Grail," to (ii) _____ another world similar to our own Earth, another place in the universe with conditions that are just right to (iii) _____ an oasis for the possible emergence of life.

Blank (i)	Blank (ii)	Blank (iii)
Ⓐ unready	Ⓓ espy	Ⓖ proffer
Ⓑ all ready	Ⓔ posit	Ⓗ eschew
Ⓒ previously	Ⓕ pontificate	Ⓘ gainsay

8. When the psychic astrologer predicted the world would end on a specific date, based on the omens of the stars, few would listen. But when unusually strong storms occurred as the day approached, more and more people began to fear disaster was _____.

   Ⓐ   avoidable
   Ⓑ   uncertain
   Ⓒ   insurmountable
   Ⓓ   ineluctable
   Ⓔ   calculated

9. Scientific research is the engine that propels virtually all modern human progress, but such research can be successful only if careful, (i) _____ procedures are followed throughout. Obviously, all these procedures must be planned in advance in a detailed, organized, (ii) _____ plan of action, but once this organizational requirement is met, researchers are met with a veritable (iii) _____ of choices, indeed, the opportunities seem almost endless.

Blank (i)	Blank (ii)	Blank (iii)
Ⓐ meticulous	Ⓓ exclusive	Ⓖ plethora
Ⓑ haphazard	Ⓔ selective	Ⓗ dearth
Ⓒ bombastic	Ⓕ comprehensive	Ⓘ acrimony

10. In the months leading up to the 150th anniversary of the beginning of the Civil War, an enormous quantity of new books on the subject were released, and both professional historians and the general public were surprised and delighted. While these new books unearthed few revelatory events or characters, they explored unexpected angles and provided fresh _____ regarding events that we thought we knew all too well.

Ⓐ interrogations
Ⓑ interpretations
Ⓒ challenges
Ⓓ verisimilitudes
Ⓔ facts

Above Average to Difficult

11. A press release made some amazing assertions about a new product, the Fire X-Cape Safety Vest, even claiming that "it is your antidote to terror, erasing the ever-present fear of a high-rise building (i) _____." The patented Safety Vest is described as a sturdy fabric backpack containing one personnel parachute, designed so the user can avoid the fear of losing his life, trapped helplessly in a (ii) _____. The manufacturer claims that after you purchase the new Safety Vest, when you encounter a terrorist attack, a fire, or any other event that might leave you trapped and/or helpless, you can simply strap on your Fire X-Cape Safety Vest, hook the convenient static-cord to any sturdy object, and leap aggressively out the window, knowing with (iii) _____ that you'll be on the ground in seconds!

Blank (i)	Blank (ii)	Blank (iii)
Ⓐ confabulation	Ⓓ touring inferno	Ⓖ certainty
Ⓑ configuration	Ⓔ towering inferno	Ⓗ uncertainty
Ⓒ conflagration	Ⓕ towering infernal	Ⓘ incredulity

12. Plastics are as (i) _____ as metals, found in numerous products because they are so easily shaped. However, due to the low cost of plastics, there is little (ii) _____ to recycle used items. Thus, most plastics end up in landfills and are (iii) _____ to the environment.

Blank (i)	Blank (ii)	Blank (iii)
Ⓐ important	Ⓓ innovation	Ⓖ propitious
Ⓑ imposing	Ⓔ justification	Ⓗ deleterious
Ⓒ ubiquitous	Ⓕ incentive	Ⓘ salubrious

13. On June 30, 1914, Igor Sikorsky became the stuff of legend when he successfully completed an astonishing long distance flight in his revolutionary new flying machine, the unprecedented *Il'ya Muromets*. This gargantuan 4-engine biplane, a marvel of its day, was emblematic of the (i) _____ of Imperial Russia at the (ii) _____. The *Muromets'* appointments bespoke luxury, yet her aerodynamics were of the most primitive order. She boasted unprecedented size and payload, yet she was severely underpowered.

Blank (i)	Blank (ii)
Ⓐ opulence and contradictions	Ⓓ nadir of its desperation and hope
Ⓑ complacency and turmoil	Ⓔ birth of its sublimity and ascendancy
Ⓒ splendor and torment	Ⓕ zenith of its power and glory

14. In the annals of Major League Baseball, there have been 53 instances when a player has had a hitting streak in 30 or more consecutive games, that is, he got at least one base hit in every single game. The most (i) _____ of these hitting streaks was by Joe DiMaggio, who successfully made a base hit in 56 consecutive games in 1941, a record that has never been (ii) _____ over these many decades.

Blank (i)	Blank (ii)
Ⓐ prosaic	Ⓓ conquered
Ⓑ quotidian	Ⓔ squandered
Ⓒ astonishing	Ⓕ sustained

15. The astronomer seemed thrilled to announce the discovery of a distant galaxy that is so (i) _____ far away from Earth that it could be the oldest object ever observed in the universe. Furthermore, some scientists are even more (ii) _____ by what they didn't see; the far-distant galaxy is apparently solitary, surrounded by a vast emptiness that is far larger than ever seen before.

Blank (i)	Blank (ii)
Ⓐ exceptionally	Ⓓ intransigent
Ⓑ inconsiderably	Ⓔ intractable
Ⓒ impossibly	Ⓕ intrigued

Answers and Explanations for Text Completion Practice Questions

Easy to Moderate

1. **A and E.** The main point of the sentence is that true beauty is not to be found in surface-level observations, but rather, it is found at a deeper level. Thus, the best word choices to complete this sentence are *superficial* (A) and *inner* (E) because they correctly identify this dichotomy. The other two choices for the first blank simply do not fit the meaning of the sentence. The inaccurate choices for the second blank, *ephemeral* (D) and *transient* (F), are synonyms that refer to something that does not last long, something that is fleeting and temporary.

2. **E.** To determine the correct answer this passage, look for its intent and follow its logic. Since the jury cited "overwhelming evidence" to support the defendant's innocence, you can dismiss any answer choices that mandate a punishment; this eliminates choice A, *condemn,* and choice B, *exile.* Next, consider the specific meanings of the answer choices that remain. Choice C, *befriend,* is simply an illogical action for jurors; it means to accept or support. Choice D, *ameliorate,* is positive-sounding, but its specific meaning is to make something better, or to repair damage, and would be more applicable to the *situation* than to the *defendant.* Finally, choice E presents the accurate word, *exculpate,* which means to absolve or to acquit, which precisely describes the jury's verdict in this case.

3. **C.** For this sentence, consider the intent of the passage as a whole. It describes the flamingo's "striking pink color" and explains how the bird can maintain that color even when its feathers fade. Because the passage deals with the flamingo's appearance regarding "potential mates," it makes sense to choose the answer that explains why the bird's appearance is important: it *enhances its attractiveness* (C). Choice A, *increasing its camouflage,* does not make sense, as the flamingo's "striking pink color" cannot possibly camouflage the bird. The remaining answer choices do not fulfill the passage's intent, as they do not address the bird's appearance at all.

4. **B and D.** In this passage, consider sample words you could insert in the first blank such as "overpriced" or "expensive" that fulfill the concept of gyms having to justify their "outrageous" membership prices for state-of-the-art equipment. Choice B, *exorbitant,* fits that concept. The remaining answer choices do not convey this idea; the word *judicious* (A) means reasonable and the term *nominal* (C) means a small amount. For the second blank, consider a phrase that explains why people join the gym. The word "inveigled" refers to being persuaded to do something you might not otherwise do, but even if this word is unfamiliar to you, the word "swayed" that follows it gives you context to work with. The main idea of this passage is that people are often all-too-quickly persuaded or charmed by "elaborate facilities and equipment" to join gyms when they otherwise wouldn't. Thus, the best answer choice is (D), to join *on a whim.* Choice (E), to join *under distress,* is not implied in the passage; nothing suggests the patrons are in pain or agony. Choice (F), to join *with resignation,* makes little sense. To be resigned to something means one passively accepts it, which does not fit the context of signing up for gym membership.

5. **D.** In this overly-complex sentence, clues to the answer can be found in the context directly adjacent to the blank, in this case, the words that immediately follow it. Begin with the word "blame," and note the negative connotation. Next, connect it to the word "zealots," indicating those who passionately support an idea. Then scan the answer choices to find a strong negative word and you can't miss the correct answer; these unhappy zealots who blame the IAU would, indeed, be *outraged* (D) by their decision. All of the other answer choices lack this essential element, a strong negative emotional reaction; in fact, all of these inaccurate words indicate the contrary, a reaction that is soothing, appeasing, calming.

Average

6. **B.** The key to answering this question is to recognize the significance of the word "forbidden," which indicates that the correct word must somehow include the meaning "refusing to allow." In this case, the best word is *proscription* (B), which literally means something that is forbidden, prohibited by authorities. Two of the other answer choices contradict this meaning. While many people first think of a *prescription* (C) as a written order for a medicine, another definition of this word is something that you *must* do; obviously it does not fit in this sentence. *Accommodation* (E) can mean to adjust or adapt to something, but not to forbid it, so it too does not fit in this sentence. The other two answer choices are simply off-topic; a *description* (A) is a written or spoken representation of something and *prostration* (D) means submission or exhaustion.

7. **C, D, and G.** This sentence explicitly states that "planets have...been found," so the first blank needs an adverb that fits the verb tense and, thus, *previously* (C), is the logical choice. The phrase *all ready* (B) is incorrect, because it means to be completely prepared (as opposed to the related word "already"). For the second blank, choice D, *espy,* is correct because it means to catch sight of something, and that is precisely the scientists' desire; they want to spot or discover another world similar to Earth that might offer, or as stated for the third blank, a world that might *proffer* (G) the conditions necessary for life. The final two choices are off-topic: *eschew* (H) means to shun or avoid something and *gainsay* (I) means to contradict something; their meanings do not fit in this sentence at all.

8. **D.** Using context clues in this passage will help you get a feel for its intent; the main idea is that disaster is unavoidable or eminent. The words *avoidable* (A), *uncertain* (B), and *calculated* (E) make no sense in this passage; they all mean the opposite of what you need in the blank. That leaves you with two viable choices: *insurmountable* (C) and *ineluctable* (D). Both of these words have the same prefix, *in-* which means "not," and the same suffix, *-able,* so it is the word roots that will help you. Something that is *surmountable* is capable of being overcome; one can conquer it. Therefore, something that is *insurmountable* cannot be conquered; this meaning is not the best fit with this context. On the other hand, something that is *ineluctable* cannot be evaded; it is unavoidable and thus choice D provides the best word to complete this passage.

9. **A, F, and G.** For this passage, pay attention to its intent by reading it in its entirety. It establishes that scientific research demands "careful" procedures and "detailed" planning, but that success can yield "endless" results. The correct answer choices all must include this positive connotation and also each one must exactly fit into the context. For the first blank, the only answer choice that works with the word "careful" is *meticulous* (A), as it is synonymous with perfectionist. Neither of the other choices fits correctly in context; *haphazard* (B) means to act without a plan and *bombastic* (C) refers to pompous speech. The best word to accurately complete the second blank is *comprehensive* (F) because a plan that is too *exclusive* (D) or too *selective* (E) would not be sufficiently all-encompassing. The third blank requires a word that mirrors "opportunities [that] seem almost endless," and the correct word is *plethora* (G), which refers to an overabundance of something. The word *dearth* (H), on the contrary, refers to a scarcity, and the word *acrimony* (I) is off-topic, as it means animosity.

10. **B.** The main idea of this passage is that, although most facts about the Civil War are fairly well known, these valuable new books provided their readers a fresh analysis, a new perspective, or as it is called in this case, they provided new *interpretations* (B). However, these new books did not provide new *facts* (E) or *verisimilitudes* (which are truths) as in choice D. The passage has no indication that the new books brought out new *challenges* (C). Finally, these new books certainly did not provide fresh *interrogations* (A), as this term actually refers to a cross-examination or series of questions.

Above Average to Difficult

11. **C, E, and G.** The main thrust of this passage is to quote an advertisement promoting the Fire X-Cape Safety Vest. But if people might question why they would ever actually need such a product, the advertiser mentions many times in the passage the danger of being caught in a high-rise building fire, also known as a *conflagration* (C). Next, to choose the correct phrase for the second blank, you only need to read carefully. A *towering inferno* (E) is the only choice that fits the meaning of the sentence. Notice the close-but-inaccurate words *touring* in choice D and *infernal* (which means wicked or hell-like) in choice F. To complete the final blank, the clear implication is that, if consumers use this product correctly, they can be certain they will reach the ground in seconds. Both of the incorrect answer choices, *uncertainty* (H) and *incredulity* (I), actually have the opposite meaning of this idea of *certainty* (G).

12. **C, F, and H.** To identify all three correct responses in this passage, pay close attention to the logical flow, the signal words that give you context, and the transition words that move the ideas forward. The first blank must mean that plastics are as common as metals because they are also "found in numerous products." The word *ubiquitous* (C) means something that seems to be everywhere and, thus, it is a perfect fit. Choice A is wrong in its concept; plastics may be as *important* as metals, but that does not precisely relate to the idea of being "found in numerous products." Choice B, *imposing,* means something that is excessively large and majestic; it does not fit the passage's context. For the second blank, notice that the key phrase "however, due to the low cost" sets up the concept that plastics are inexpensive, so there is little *incentive* (F) to recycle them. Choices D and E do not relate to this concept of cost and therefore they do not make sense in this second sentence. Finally, the choices for the third blank present the most unusual words in this passage. Notice how the transition word "thus" leads you to continue the logic of the previous sentence, which established that it is plastics' low cost that reduces the incentive to recycle them. Therefore, it logically follows that plastics ultimately end up in landfills where they eventually harm the environment. The negative word that best completes this sentence is choice H, *deleterious,* meaning unsafe or damaging. The two other choices are both positive words and therefore they cannot be accurate; choice G, *propitious,* refers to something favorable, and choice I, *salubrious,* refers to something that promotes good health.

13. **A and F.** Analyzing and understanding the context of the entire passage is necessary to identify the correct responses. Notice the contrasts embedded in the third and fourth sentences; the gigantic biplane had "luxury," and "unprecedented size and payload," yet her aerodynamics were "primitive" and she was "severely underpowered." Therefore, choice A, *opulence and contradictions,* is the best fit for the first blank. To accurately fill in the second blank, you must continue your analysis of the context. This new flying machine is so magnificent that it could not have been built by a nation at the *nadir of its desperation,* so choice D is eliminated as being too negative. Finally, if you compare the two more positive-sounding choices, you will notice that the accurate answer, F, refers to a nation that is mature, one that is already at the *zenith of its power,* not to a nation that is just at the *birth of its sublimity* (E).

14. **C and D.** The context of this passage indicates that the correct word for the first blank must include the idea of something out of the ordinary because this is, after all, a description of the longest hitting streak in all of baseball history. The correct word-choice is *astonishing* (C), which indicates something amazing and astounding. The other two choices, *prosaic* (A) and *quotidian* (B), are incorrect because they refer to something that is commonplace, ordinary. Analysis of the context also leads to the second correct answer; DiMaggio's record is still the longest ever, it has never been bested, or, in this case, it has never been *conquered* (D). Choice F contradicts the passage, because the phrase the "record has never been" *sustained* would indicate that the record has not lasted this long (which it has). Finally, the word in choice E, *squandered,* does not work at all; this record could not be frittered away, as *squandered* implies.

15. **A and F.** One method of tackling this question is to focus more on the overall message and intent and avoid getting lost in the details. The main ideas are that the newly-discovered galaxy is very far away and that it is all alone; also, the connotation is positive, upbeat, as the scientists are "thrilled." For the first blank, the correct word must denote the idea of something very far away; in this case, the best word is choice A, *exceptionally,* because this galaxy's extreme distance is an exception to the rule. The other answer choices are either contrary to the passage, as in choice B (*inconsiderably* means slightly), or they go off on a tangent, as in choice C, *impossibly.* For the second blank, a positive-sounding word is required, which eliminates choices D and E (*intransient* and *intractable;* both indicate someone who is stubborn or obstinate). The correct answer is choice F, *intrigued,* because the scientists are even more attracted to or fascinated by the vast emptiness than by the distant galaxy itself.

Overview of Sentence Equivalence Questions

Sentence equivalence questions are similar in structure to the text completion questions with one blank. In both cases, you will be presented with a sentence containing a single blank space. However, a major difference exists in the structure of the answer choices. Remember that in text completion questions you must choose just one answer from the five possible choices to complete the sentence, but in the sentence equivalence questions, you will be presented with six answer choices and you must choose two answers that both logically complete the sentence. In other words, you must select *two answer choices,* and each one must complete the sentence equally well.

You are not necessarily looking for synonyms among these answer choices; rather, your task is to find the two answers that, when inserted independently, will complete the thought and logic of the sentence. You will earn credit only when you correctly choose both correct answers; no partial credit will be given if you select only one of the two correct choices.

As you will recall, there are two Verbal Reasoning sections that count toward your verbal score on the GRE. Each section contains twenty questions, and you will have 30 minutes to complete each section. You should expect that approximately four of your twenty questions will be sentence equivalence questions on each section. Thus you can expect a total of approximately eight sentence equivalence questions on the Verbal Reasoning measure.

Skills and Concepts Tested

The skills measured in this section include your vocabulary skills, your ability to discriminate using context clues and nuances of language, and your ability to think logically while following the flow of ideas in a sentence.

Similar in structure to text completion questions, sentence equivalence questions ask you to decide how a sentence can best be completed, but to answer sentence equivalence questions you need to focus more on the meaning of the sentence as a whole. In other words, concentrate on the ideas throughout the entire sentence as whole, not just on the ideas in isolated phrases near the blank.

Directions

You will be given one sentence with a single blank in it. Below the sentence you will find six answer choices. The directions will tell you to choose the two answers that equally complete the sentence with similar meaning.

Always keep in mind that you must find two answer choices, each of which fits the sentence. You will only receive credit when you accurately choose both correct answer choices. While the two choices may be synonymous, this is not always the case, so do not fixate on finding two synonyms in the answer choices. The correct answer choices will never be antonyms, but that does not mean they must be direct synonyms. Just be sure that each word you select completes the sentence accurately and produces a similar meaning. The accurate answer choices will always be the correct part of speech needed for the sentence, so do not spend any time trying to rule out answers based on parts of speech.

General Strategies

- Just like the strategy for text completion questions, you should first try to think of sample words that you might use to logically complete the sentence by using the sentence's meaning, structure, and context clues. Then compare these words to the given answer choices; doing so should help you eliminate some choices.

- Get an overall impression of the sentence and the type of idea that is required to make it a complete and logical statement. Specifically useful is defining whether it should have a positive or negative connotation.

- Watch for significant words and phrases in the sentence to help you discern the overall meaning and the kind of word you need to insert.

- Apply your awareness of positive and negative connotations, plus your knowledge of transition and signal words. See page 91 in the text completion section of this chapter for a table of common transition words.

- When confronted with words that are new or unusual, use your knowledge of common word roots and prefixes to help break the new words down into their component parts. A list of common prefixes and roots can be found starting on page 111.

- Do not assume that the two correct answer choices will always be direct synonyms. But do make sure your two choices **each** complete the sentence coherently.

- Be sure to reread the sentence using each answer you select, making sure each word independently completes the idea.

Successful Strategies for Building Your Vocabulary

- **Read, read, read.** The experts all agree that this is the number one vocabulary-building strategy! People who read voluminously almost always know more words than people who do not. It is useful to read material from many different sources: magazines, newspapers, Internet sites, books, journals, and so forth. It is also useful to read material in a wide variety of subject areas, such as science and nature, history, literature, literary criticism, biography and autobiography, politics, and so on. This will ensure that you are exposed to many ideas, from many sources, written in many different styles. Eventually, you will notice improvements in both your vocabulary skills and your general knowledge.

- **Make a personal list of new words.** While you read, take note of words with which you are unfamiliar and also notice familiar words that are used in unusual ways. You should not try to list *every* new word you see; rather, concentrate on new words that you encounter frequently. Use your common sense to decide which words should make it onto your list. Use context clues to try to discern the words' meanings; pay attention to the sentence structure and look for other words that offer meaning clues. Then, when you look up the dictionary definition of your new words, pay attention to the nuances and take note of any synonymous words.

- **Use the new words yourself.** Integrate your new words into your personal vocabulary by using them in your own writing and spoken language. Make sure that you are using the correct part of speech and are pronouncing the word accurately. This disciplined practice will help you to "own" these new words and increase your vocabulary.

- **Examine synonyms for your new words.** Because this particular GRE question-type deals with synonymous terms, look up all the related words for your new words. This will also expose you to many additional new words. Be sure to use more than one source; many excellent thesauruses can be found online and in libraries.

- **Know word stems.** By learning commonly used word stems you will be able to decipher the meaning of unfamiliar vocabulary on the GRE. Most words can be broken down into base words, and by knowing this, you can skillfully make an educated guess about the word's actual meaning. To help you develop this skill, use the table of commonly used prefixes, suffixes, and roots on pages 111–120.

Suggested Strategies with Sample Questions

Learning how to apply these strategies for sentence equivalence will give you comfort, and practicing will help build speed for the test. Of course, more than one strategy could be used to answer any given question; however, in the section that follows we will explore how an individual, specific strategy can be applied to various questions.

Strategy 1: Think of words that you might use to logically complete the sentence, using the sentence's meaning, structure, and context clues; then compare these words to the given answer choices.

1. In order to continue _____ good morale amongst the crew, the ship's commander provided extra rations and movies on Friday nights.

   A   assembling
   B   sustaining
   C   bolstering
   D   evolving
   E   abstaining
   F   pampering

If you were to think of sample words you could use in this sentence, you might come up with words like "fostering," "establishing," "providing," and "maintaining." Notice the phrase following the blank, "good morale," which must make sense paired with the verb you choose for the blank. Of these answer choices, the two best words are *sustaining* (B), which means to support or supply, and *bolstering* (C), which means to add to or uphold something. Both fit well with this context of building up the morale of the ship's crew. The remaining verb choices do not logically fit in. *Assembling* (A) means to put the parts of something together, like assembling a bicycle; it is not appropriate to speak of "putting together" the crew's attitude. The same can be said about choice (D), *evolving;* this refers to things that are changing, which does not make sense in this context. *Abstaining* (E) means to voluntarily hold back from doing an action, and *pampering* (F) means to treat one with over-indulgence; none of these remaining choices accurately completes the sentence's message. The correct answers are **B** and **C**.

Strategy 2: Get an overall impression of the sentence and the type of idea that is needed to make it a complete and logical statement.

2. Without asking for other workers' ideas, the company's office manager often made _____ decisions that discouraged input from other employees.

   A   unilateral
   B   democratic
   C   arbitrary
   D   despotic
   E   oppressive
   F   irrational

It is important to note that the office manager in this sentence is viewed as making decisions without consulting others. The stated idea is that the office manager's behavior discourages input from other employees, and the conclusion, therefore, is that he or she acts too independently. Thus, the correct answers need to describe one-sided decisions like this office manager makes; the best two responses are *unilateral* (A), which means an action that is taken by one side only, and *arbitrary* (C), which indicates a decision that is made capriciously, without contemplation. Both words fit well and each one completes the idea of the whole sentence. On the other hand, choices D *(despotic)* and E *(oppressive)*, which might initially strike you as potential answers, are actually too strong, too negative for the ideas presented in this sentence. The mere fact that the office manager did not ask for other's ideas does not necessarily make the manager *despotic* (D) or *oppressive* (E). Choice F *(irrational)* does not fit the idea of discouraging input from other employees. Finally, choice B *(democratic)* is the opposite of the idea this sentence needs; this office manager is certainly not being democratic. The correct answers are **A** and **C**.

Strategy 3: Watch for significant words and phrases in the sentence to help you discern the overall meaning and the kind of word you need to insert.

3. Some politicians are repeatedly criticized for their _____ responses to reporters' questions; apparently, getting a brief, direct answer from them is seemingly impossible.

    A   oblique
    B   forthright
    C   frank
    D   slanted
    E   circumlocutory
    F   tenebrous

This sentence offers many clues in its phrasing that can help direct you to the correct responses. Some politicians have a reputation for not giving direct answers to questions; it seems they prefer being long-winded and talking in circles, so it makes sense that they will be "repeatedly criticized" for these evasions. Also notice that you need to select responses that denote the opposite of a "brief, direct answer." The two best answers here are, therefore, (A) *oblique,* which can refer to speech that is not straightforward, and (E) *circumlocutory,* which refers to speech that is wordy and verbose and sounds like talking in circles. All of the other answer choices are either antonyms of what is needed for this sentence, or they do not fit into this context. Both *forthright* (B) and *frank* (C) mean to be straightforward and truthfully candid. *Slanted* (D) may at first sound like a viable choice, because politicians may, indeed, be criticized for distorting information to suit their purposes, but *slanted* does not necessarily mean being overly verbose; a politician can give a response that is "brief" and "direct," but that is still *slanted* to fit his views. Finally, *tenebrous* (F) is simply off-topic; it means something that is dark and gloomy. The correct answers are **A** and **E**.

Strategy 4: Apply your awareness of positive and negative connotations, and take special note of transition and signal words.

4. When the Federal Transportation Department proposed building an interstate highway directly across a Civil War battle site, many observers decried the government's insensitivity to such _____ ground.

    A   unsanctified
    B   sacrilegious
    C   irreligious
    D   sacrosanct
    E   vulnerable
    F   hallowed

In this sentence, notice the negative tone of words such as "decried" and "insensitivity." Additionally, the very concept of building a highway over the "hallowed ground" of a Civil War battle site simply reeks of inconsideration. The site is surely revered by many people who believe it should never be desecrated with highway construction. You can use these negative connotations to find opposing positive words to fit in the blank, words that aptly describe the ground upon which a battle was fought. The best choices here are the words *sacrosanct* (D) and *hallowed* (F). Both are positive words, and both mean sacred and revered; they are appropriate to describe the site where soldiers fought and where many died. The other answer choices are all negative words: *unsanctified* (A) means something that is cursed or damned; *sacrilegious* (B) and *irreligious* (C) both refer to something that is specifically not religious; *vulnerable* (E) means something unprotected, something open to attack. The correct answers are **D** and **F.**

Strategy 5: When confronted with new or unusual words, use your knowledge of common word roots and prefixes to help break the word down into its parts.

5. The criminal defendant fidgeted nervously in the witness chair as the prosecutor read his long felony rap sheet and then accused him of being a lifelong _____.

   A   philanthropist
   B   philanderer
   C   benefactor
   D   mischief-maker
   E   miscreant
   F   malefactor

The key is to notice the apprehensive tone of this sentence, which is established by emotional phrases, such as "fidgeted nervously" and "accused him." This tone indicates the answers must have a negative connotation. Next, use your knowledge of prefixes to identify and eliminate positive-sounding words, such as *philanthropist* (A) and *benefactor* (C), which both indicate someone helpful. Choice B, *philanderer,* also has the prefix "phil-" which refers to a love of something, but a philanderer is actually a rakish ladies' man who has several love affairs. While not necessarily ethical, philandering is not technically a crime. Notice that all the negative-sounding words begin with the prefix *mis-* or *mal-*, which specifically indicates something is bad, wrong, or evil. The first of these is *mischief-maker* (D), but this term is far too weak a condemnation for this defendant. Finally, it is apparent that the correct answers are choice E, *miscreant,* meaning someone who is evil, immoral, corrupt, and choice F, *malefactor,* a criminal, a culprit, a villain. Remember that it was your attention to prefixes that narrowed the field of potential answer choices to a more manageable number. The correct answers are **E** and **F.**

Practice Sentence Equivalence Questions

Now you can continue to practice on your own! The following questions are roughly grouped into sets by their approximate level of difficulty: easy to moderate, average, and above average to difficult. The answers and thorough explanations follow the questions.

Easy to Moderate

1. After China placed an embargo on the rare earth minerals used in electronics, the _____ of the dwindling supply sent prices skyrocketing.

   A   accrual
   B   amplitude
   C   paucity
   D   scantiness
   E   plethora
   F   surfeit

2. The uncompromising teacher's _____ tardy policy could not be circumvented easily.

   A   amenable
   B   rigorous
   C   flaccid
   D   stringent
   E   responsible
   F   methodical

3. The _____ and unassuming boy usually sat quietly at the back of the classroom, so his peers were astonished and delighted when he was selected to sing the lead role in the school musical.

   A   garrulous
   B   self-deprecating
   C   lethargic
   D   introverted
   E   reticent
   F   vociferous

4. Friedrich Gauss displayed his mathematical _____ at an early age, even as early as primary school, where he demonstrated his exceptional ability by creating a method of rapidly adding and totaling large sequences of numbers.

   A   affinity
   B   aptitude
   C   prowess
   D   incompetence
   E   impotence
   F   pulchritude

5. The _____ of the untouched Sierra Nevada Mountains that was beautifully captured by Ansel Adams in his nature photography inspired many to join the environmental movement.

   A   adulteration
   B   acrimony
   C   eminence
   D   fortitude
   E   magnificence
   F   sublimity

Average

6. Although the supporting character in the stage play was _____ in nature, when he did utter a brief line of dialog, his words spoke volumes, providing insightful commentary about the other characters.

   A   aloof
   B   taciturn
   C   talkative
   D   loquacious
   E   social
   F   affable

7. The great novelists Virginia Woolf and James Joyce are considered to be the first authors to develop the literary style known as stream of consciousness, a literary technique that reveals the random flow of a character's ideas, the twists and turns and _____ of a character's inner thoughts.

- A pretentions
- B stratagems
- C idiosyncrasies
- D prejudices
- E betrayals
- F peculiarities

8. Marine colonels serving as boot camp trainers are often portrayed as _____ in movies in which they try to turn urban hoodlums into disciplined soldiers through threats and harsh punishments.

- A impertinent
- B simpatico
- C blasé
- D diffident
- E truculent
- F belligerent

9. When the Impressionist art movement first began to take root in Paris with a series of independent art exhibitions, art critics were initially _____ by the unconventional appearance of the paintings, but they soon came to appreciate the new style.

- A elated
- B stunned
- C gratified
- D encumbered
- E enlightened
- F disconcerted

10. As retail gasoline prices across the country continued their inexorable climb to never-before-seen levels, many commentators and politicians _____ their followers to join mass protests, targeted at whatever "threat" they chose to castigate.

- A tricked
- B beguiled
- C connived
- D duped
- E entreated
- F exhorted

Above Average to Difficult

11. The chief engineer was a crusty old-school Navy man, but he had an uncanny knack, the ability to glance at the seemingly-inscrutable electrical diagrams in the original blueprints and immediately _____ a solution: thus, he was the go-to guy for all obscure repair projects.

- A apprehend
- B scrutinize
- C underestimate
- D bifurcate
- E envisage
- F misconstrue

12. After he moved to the New World and made a fortune, the former butler, who had been ridiculed by his employer, affected an air of superiority and became insufferably _____.

    Ⓐ histrionic
    Ⓑ pretentious
    Ⓒ bombastic
    Ⓓ magnanimous
    Ⓔ unassuming
    Ⓕ munificent

13. The award-winning author's inopportune remarks about his profession being mundane, "merely work, devoid of inspiration" cast his normally admirable accomplishments in a(n) _____ light, and his literary reputation suffered.

    Ⓐ ingenious
    Ⓑ innovative
    Ⓒ celestial
    Ⓓ pedestrian
    Ⓔ banal
    Ⓕ lionized

14. In a crude act of censorship, supposedly to make the movie acceptable for general audiences, the script was _____ of any objectionable phrases.

    Ⓐ expurgated
    Ⓑ preserved
    Ⓒ sterilized
    Ⓓ sanctified
    Ⓔ salvaged
    Ⓕ bowdlerized

15. Although the young aviation cadet struggled for weeks to master the unwieldy military trainer, after so many failures he began to fear that, rather than being a valued inspiration, his lifelong dream of flying might instead be a mere _____.

    Ⓐ illustration
    Ⓑ illusion
    Ⓒ crimea
    Ⓓ chimera
    Ⓔ actuality
    Ⓕ quintessence

Answers and Explanations for Sentence Equivalence Practice Questions

Easy to Moderate

1. **C and D.** For this sample, try thinking of words you might use to complete the sentence, and you might come up with such words as "scarcity" or "insufficiency." Also notice the sequence of cause and effect in this sentence. After China placed an embargo, the supply diminished, resulting in a subsequent price increase. The correct answers must be words that describe a lack of supply. The only two answer choices that fit the bill are *paucity* (C), which describes an inadequate supply, and *scantiness* (D), which emphasizes a limited quantity. The incorrect choices *accrual* (A), *amplitude* (B), *plethora* (E), and *surfeit* (F) all indicate

a supply that is either growing or that is in excess. These words do not match with the "dwindling supply," which indicates a decrease in quantity.

2. **B and D.** To successfully complete this sentence, look at its overall meaning. The teacher is "uncompromising," so his or her tardiness policy is inflexible—it is *rigorous* and *stringent,* choices B and D, respectively. The other answer choices do not complete the sentence appropriately—*amenable* (A) means to be agreeable and cooperative, while *flaccid* (C) refers to something that is limp and loose, not something rigid. Finally, the words *responsible* (E) and *methodical* (F) simply do not make sense in this context; they do not describe the idea of a policy that is uncompromising.

3. **D and E.** To find the correct words for this sentence, examine the significant words that will help you discern its overall meaning. The clue words in this sentence are "unassuming" and "quietly," which have the opposite meaning of two of the answer choices *garrulous* and *vociferous,* so you can eliminate choices A and F. Next, the denotation of the word lethargic, which means weary and fatigued, does not make sense in this context, so you can eliminate choice C. Finally, there is no evidence to suggest that the boy is critical of himself, or *self-deprecating* (B). Thus, the accurate answers are choices D and E, *introverted* and *reticent,* both of which refer to a person who is quiet and discreet. Therefore, it also makes sense that his fellow students would be astonished to find he had hidden singing talent.

4. **B and C.** For this sentence, first get an overall impression of the sentence's main idea, and also notice the positive connotations that are needed for the correct answers. You will see that even at an early age, the mathematician Friedrich Gauss demonstrated precocious abilities; thus he displayed mathematical *aptitude* (B) and *prowess* (C), both of which accurately complete the sentence. Choice A, *affinity,* might initially sound like a feasible option, but it means to have a fondness or an alliance; the word does not refer to one's ability (like the correct choices do). The negative meanings in choices D and E do not fit this sentence: *incompetence* (D) means inability or lack of skill; *impotence* (E) indicates weakness. Finally, choice F simply does not make sense in this context, as *pulchritude* refers to physical beauty; this is a good example of a test makers' strategy, selecting a word that you might not know and using it to try to confuse you.

5. **E and F.** For this sentence, look at the overall impression and the positive connotation of its idea. Because Ansel Adams's photography of the "untouched" Sierra Nevada Mountains "inspired" many, it makes sense that the appropriate words must describe the beauty of the natural world. The words in choices A through D do not meet this requirement. Choice A, *adulteration,* means contamination or pollution, the opposite of what is signified by the word "untouched." The other options do not make sense in this context; choice B, *acrimony,* means animosity or contempt; choice C, *eminence,* means distinction or fame; choice D, *fortitude,* means strength in face of adversity. However, notice how accurately the positive connotations of *magnificence* (E) and *sublimity* (F) fit in the context of the sentence's overall meaning.

Average

6. **A and B.** First, try to think of sample words that you could insert into this sentence to accurately complete its meaning, words such as "quiet" or "reserved." Next, identify the two answer choices that best fit into the sentence; these are *aloof* (A) and *taciturn* (B)—both describe someone who is habitually uncommunicative or reserved in speech. All of the remaining answer choices have the opposite meaning, to varying degrees. *Talkative* (C) and *loquacious* (D) are synonyms that refer to someone who is long-winded and wordy. Likewise, the words *social* (E) and *affable* (F) are synonyms, and they both refer to someone who is friendly and easy to talk to.

7. **C and F.** In this sentence, it is necessary to look for words and phrases to help you discern the overall meaning. The sentence provides a definition of stream of consciousness embedded in the phrase, "a literary technique that reveals the random flow of a character's ideas, the twists and turns...of a character's inner thoughts." The answer choices that accurately fit this meaning are *idiosyncrasies* (C) and *peculiarities* (F), which both refer to quirks in a character's distinctive thought patterns. Choice A, *pretentions,* is inaccurate because it refers to behaviors that are designed to give one more importance than one deserves. The word *stratagems* (B) describes actions or schemes that are cleverly designed to deceive; it does not relate to the random thoughts of a character. Choice D, *prejudices,* refers to preconceived opinions and choice E, *betrayals,* refers to some form of disloyalty; neither word fits correctly into this sentence.

8. **E and F.** Use your knowledge of positive and negative connotations to analyze this sentence. The best words must pinpoint the negative characteristics required for Marine trainers who transform thugs into soldiers, because the phrase "threats and harsh punishments" clearly indicates that the answers will have negative connotations associated with them. This immediately eliminates *simpatico* (B) because the trainers probably would not have been portrayed as likeable. Choice C, *blasé*, is also eliminated since if the trainers were indifferent or bored, they would not show interest in their jobs, making them unlikely to make threats or hand out punishments. Choice D, *diffident*, can also be removed because unconfident and timid marines would not be given the task of training recruits. This leaves three possible answer choices: *impertinent* (A), *truculent* (E), and *belligerent* (F). Although *impertinent* (A) may initially seem like a viable option because it does refer to negative behavior; it describes someone who is arrogant and rude and but is not strong enough to fit the context of using "threats and harsh punishments." This leaves only answer choices E, *truculent*, and F, *belligerent*, which both accurately describe the aggressive image of Marine colonels who often yell at and push around new recruits.

9. **B and F.** In this sentence, use your knowledge of positive and negative connotations plus transition words to help you discover the correct answers. Because the art critics eventually developed an appreciation of the new Impressionist style, you need a negative word to convey their initial doubts about accepting its novelty and unconventionality. Choice B, *stunned*, accurately describes their disapproval and negative reaction, so it completes this sentence appropriately, as does choice F, *disconcerted*. On the other hand, the words *elated* (A), *gratified* (C), and *enlightened* (E) all have positive connotations and thus they are not appropriate in this sentence. Finally, critics were not inconvenienced, thus choice D, *encumbered*, is incorrect as well.

10. **E and F.** In this case, examine the overall impression of the sentence to determine what kind of word you need to complete it. In this scenario, the politicians and commentators want their followers to participate in mass protests, so they urge them or plead with them to join in; thus, the best answer choices are *entreated* (E) and *exhorted* (F), both of which mean to beseech or to implore someone to take action. Meanwhile, the other answer choices all include this aspect of a call to action, but they also include a secondary connotation, one of fooling the followers, or tricking them into joining the protests. Therefore, you can discard the overly negative answer choices of *tricked* (A), *beguiled* (B), *connived* (C), and *duped* (D), because they all imply deception.

Above Average to Difficult

11. **A and E.** Since the chief engineer was "the go-to guy" to find "a solution," the correct words must be positive, and they must be indicative of his success in understanding the electrical diagrams. The best answer choices for this question are *apprehend* (A), which means to comprehend something, and *envisage* (E), which means to clearly picture something in your mind. Choice B, *scrutinize*, may seem at first to be a viable choice, but it actually means to examine something closely, whereas the passage states that the chief read the old diagrams at a "glance." Choice F, *misconstrue*, contradicts the main idea in the sentence, because it means to gain the wrong impression about something. Choice D, *bifurcate*, is completely off-topic; it means to split into two branches. Choice C, *underestimate*, does not fit the meaning of the sentence at all.

12. **B and C.** An understanding of the overall impression of this sentence will help you to find the correct answers. The butler had previously worked for an employer who ridiculed him. Then he moved to the New World and made a fortune. After these accomplishments, the former butler began acting superior, and he became insufferable. Therefore, it makes sense that he would be called *pretentious* (B) and *bombastic* (C), both of which indicate a person who is arrogant, self-important, smug, and pompous. Choice (A), *histrionic*, describes someone who is overly dramatic, but it does not mesh with the context of this sentence nearly as well. The remaining choices contradict the ideas in the sentence. Someone who is *magnanimous* (D) is noble and generous in spirit, while someone who is *munificent* (F) is generous, especially with money. Finally, a person who is *unassuming* (E) is modest and humble, which is the opposite of the way the former butler acted.

13. **D and E.** In this sentence, identify the significant words and phrases to help you find the accurate answers. You need to find words that are synonymous with "mundane" and agree with the award-winning author's comment that his writing profession was "merely work, devoid of inspiration." The words *pedestrian* (D) and *banal* (E) both have this connotation; they mean trite, commonplace, and unimaginative. Choices A and B are both antonyms for what is needed, as *ingenious* and *innovative* both mean to be clever and inventive. Choice (C),

celestial, means something that is heavenly and divine, while choice (F), *lionized,* refers to something that is highly-praised and celebrated; neither of these choices fits in with the context of this sentence.

14. **A and F.** To analyze this sentence, examine its overall meaning; the reason "any objectionable phrases" were censored from the movie script was to make to make it "more acceptable" to general audiences. The best answer choices are *expurgated* (A) and *bowdlerized* (F) because they specifically mean to remove potentially offensive phrases and passages from a work of literature; therefore, they fit in perfectly with the sentence's idea. The remaining choices are off the mark. Choices B, *preserved,* and E, *salvaged,* are the opposite of what is needed to complete this sentence; they mean to keep or to save something. The word *sterilized* (C) may at first seem like a viable choice, but when you consider that it means to clean something from possible infection, you realize that it is too far a stretch for this sentence. Finally, choice D is off-topic, as *sanctified* means to give something a religious blessing, to give it holy status.

15. **B and D.** In this sentence, notice the significant words that help you decide the correct answers. In addition to understanding the sentence's overall meaning, look at the key word "rather," which means something is the opposite, so the correct words for the blank must mean the opposite of "a valued inspiration." The best answer choices, therefore, are *illusion* (B) and *chimera* (D), each of which refers to an unattainable dream or a false belief. On the other hand, two of the other answer choices actually contradict the required meaning; choice E, *actuality,* means something concrete and choice F, *quintessence,* refers to the essential core essence of something. Finally, the other two answer choices are off-topic; they are mere distracters: Choice A, *illustration,* merely refers to an image, neither negative nor positive, and choice C, *crimea,* is actually the name of a region of the Ukraine. The test writers choose these distracting answers to see if you can distinguish them from the correct answers that look and sound similar.

Common Prefixes, Suffixes, and Roots

The following table of prefixes, suffixes, and roots is designed to help you increase your ability to understand the meanings of word "parts" that are especially helpful for the sentence equivalence and text completion portions of the GRE. The level of vocabulary on the GRE is often challenging, but as you become familiar with this list you will notice an improvement in your ability to recognize the general meaning of words and arrive at the correct answers.

Common Prefixes		
Prefix	**Meaning**	**Examples**
ab-, a-, abs-	away from	abhor — to withdraw from in fear or disgust abscond — to run away
ad-, a-, ac-, af-, ag-, an-, ap-, ar-, as-, at-	to; toward	adapt — to fit to accede — to agree to
ambi-	both	ambivalent — having two feelings
amphi-	on both sides; around	amphibian — an animal that lives first in the water then adapts to land life amphitheater — a theater with seats all around
ante-	before	antebellum — before the war
anti-	against	antifreeze — a substance added to a liquid to prevent freezing
auto-	self	automobile — a self-propelled vehicle
bi-	two	bifocals — glasses with lenses for two focuses
circum-	around	circumscribe — to draw around; to limit
com-, con-, co-, col-	with; together	combine — to bring together conjoin — to join together co-worker — one who works with

continued

Prefix	Meaning	Examples
contra-, contro-, counter-	against	contradict — to say the opposite counteract — to act against
de-	away from; down; the opposite of	depart — to go away from decline — to turn down deactivate — to make inactive
di-	twice	dioxide — an oxide with two atoms of oxygen in a molecule
dia-	across; through	diagonal — across or through a figure diagnose — to determine what is wrong through knowledge
dis-	apart; not	disperse — to scatter widely dishonest — not honest
dys-	bad; ill	dysfunction — a poor functioning
epi-	upon	epitaph — an inscription upon a tombstone (upon burial)
equi-	equal; equally	equitable — fair
ex-, ej-, ef-	out; from	excavate — to hollow out eject — to throw out effuse — to pour out
extra-	outside; beyond	extraordinary — outside the usual
fore-	before; in front of	foresee — to anticipate
geo-	earth	geology — the study of the earth
homo-	same; equal; alike	homonym — a word with the same pronunciation as another word
hyper-	over; too much	hypertension — unusually high tension
hypo-	under; too little	hypodermic — under the skin
in-, il-, ig-, ir-, im-	not	inactive — not active illegal — not legal ignoble — not noble irreverent — not reverent improbable — not probable
in-, il-, ir-, im-	in; into	inject — to put in illuminate — to light up irradiate — to shine on implant — to fix firmly in
inter-	between; among	interurban — between cities
intra-, intro-	within; inside of	intravenous — directly into a vein introvert — one who looks inside himself
mal-, male-	bad; wrong; ill	malfunction — to fail to function correctly malevolent — wishing harm to others
mis-	wrong; badly	mistreat — to treat badly
mis-, miso-	hatred	misanthrope — one who hates humanity
mono-	one; alone	monologue — a speech by one person
neo-	new	neologism — a new word or a new meaning for an old word
non-	not; the reverse of	nonsense — something that makes no sense
omni-	all; everywhere	omnipresent — present everywhere
pan-	all	pandemic — existing over a whole area
per-	by; through	pervade — to be present throughout
poly-	many	polyglot — speaking or writing several languages

Prefix	Meaning	Examples
post-	after	postwar — after the war
pro-	forward; going ahead of; supporting	proceed — to go forward proboscis — a snout prowar — supporting war
re-	again; back	retell — to tell again retroactive — applying to things that have already taken place
se-	apart	secede — to withdraw
semi-	half; partly	semicircle — half a circle semiliterate — able to read and write a little
sub-	under; less than	submarine — underwater subconscious — beneath the consciousness
super-	over; above	superimpose — to put something greater over something else superstar — a star greater than the others
syn-, sym-, syl-, sys-	with; at the same time	synchronize — to make things agree symmetry — balance on the two sides of a dividing line
tele-	far	telepathy — communication by thought alone
trans-	across	transcontinental — across the continent
un-	not	unhelpful — not helpful

Common Suffixes		
Suffix	Meaning	Examples
-able, -ible, -ble	able to; capable of being	viable — able to live edible — capable of being eaten
-acious, -cious	having the quality of	tenacious — holding firmly
-al	of; like	nocturnal — of the night
-ance, -ancy	the act of; a state of being	performance — the act of performing truancy — the act of being truant
-ant, -ent	one who	occupant — one who occupies respondent — one who responds
-ar, -ary	connected with; concerning	ocular — pertaining to the eye beneficiary — one who receives benefits
-ence	the act, fact, or quality of	existence — the quality of being
-er, -or	one who does	teacher — one who teaches visitor — one who visits
-ful	full of; having qualities of	fearful — full of fear masterful — having the qualities of a master
-fy	to make	deify — to make into a god
-ic, -ac	of; like; pertaining to	cryptic — hidden cardiac — pertaining to the heart
-il, -ile	pertaining to	civil — pertaining to citizens infantile — pertaining to infants
-ion	the act or condition of	correction — the act of correcting
-ism	the philosophy, act, or practice of	patriotism — support of one's country

continued

Suffix	Meaning	Examples
-ist	one who does, makes, or is occupied with	artist — one who is occupied with art
-ity, -ty, -y	the state or character of	unity — the state of being one novelty — the quality of being novel or new
-ive	containing the nature of; giving or leaning toward	pensive — thoughtful
-less	without; lacking	heartless — cruel; without a heart
-logue	a particular kind of speaking or writing	dialogue — a conversation or interchange
-logy	a kind of speaking; a study or science	eulogy — a speech or writing in praise of someone theology — the study of God and related matters
-ment	the act of; the state of	alignment — the act of aligning retirement — the state of being retired
-ness	the quality of	eagerness — the quality of being eager
-ory	having the nature of; a place or thing for	laudatory — showing praise laboratory — a place where work is done
-ous, -ose	full of; having	dangerous — full of danger verbose — wordy
-ship	the art or skill of; the state or quality of being	leadership — the ability to lead
-some	full of; like	troublesome — full of trouble
-tude	the state or quality of	servitude — slavery or bondage
-y	full of; somewhat; somewhat like	musty — having a stale odor chilly — somewhat cold willowy — like a willow

Common Roots		
Root	**Meaning**	**Examples**
acr	sharp; bitter	acrid — sharp, bitter
act, ag	to do; to act	activity — action agent — one who does
acu	sharp; keen	acuity — keenness
alt	high	exalt — to raise or lift up
anim	life; mind	animate — to make alive
ann	year	annual — yearly
anthrop	man; mankind	misanthrope — one who hates people
apt	fit	adapt — to fit to
arch	to rule	patriarch — a father and ruler
aud	to hear	audience — those who hear
bas	low	debase — to make lower
belli	war	bellicose — hostile, warlike
ben, bene	well; good	benevolent — doing or wishing good

Root	Meaning	Examples
bio	life	biology — the study of living things
brev	short	abbreviate — to shorten
cad, cas	to fall	cadence — the fall of the voice in speaking, movement in sound cascade — a small waterfall
cap, capt, cip, cept, ceive, ceit	to take or hold	captive — one who is caught and held receive — to take
cav	hollow	excavate — to hollow out
cede, ceed, cess	to go; to give in	precede — to go before access — a means of giving to
chrom	color	chromatic — having color
chron, chrono	time	synchronize — to make agree in time chronology — the order of events
cid, cis	to cut; to kill	incisive — cutting into, sharp homicide — the killing of a man by another
clin	to lean; to bend	decline — to bend or turn downward
clud, clus, clos, claud, claus	to close; to shut	exclude — to shut out claustrophobia — fear of closed places
cogn, cognit	to know; to learn	cognizant — aware recognition — knowing on sight
cor, cord	heart	accord — agreement
corp, corpor	body	corporal — bodily
cred, credit	to believe	credible — believable
crypt	hidden	cryptic — with hidden meaning
cum	to heap up	cumulative — increasing by additions
cur	to care	accurate — careful and precise
curr, curs, cours	to run	current — the flow of running water
da, date	to give	date — a given time
dem, demo	people	demography — a statistical study of the population
di	day	diary — a daily record
dic, dict	to say	diction — wording; verbal expression indict — to make a formal accusation
doc, doct	to teach	doctrine — something taught
dol	grief; pain	doleful — sorrowful
domin	to rule; to master	dominion — rule; a ruled territory
dorm	to sleep	dormant — sleeping, inactive
duc, duct	to lead	induce — to lead to action aqueduct — a pipe or waterway
dynam	power	dynamite — a powerful explosive
ego	I	egocentric — seeing everything in relation to oneself
eu	good; beautiful	euphonious — having a pleasant sound
fac, fact, fic, fec, fect	to make; to do	facile — easy to do artifact — an object made by man fiction — something that has been made up

continued

Root	Meaning	Examples
fer, ferr	to carry; to bring or bear	refer — to carry to something or somebody else
fid	faith; trust	confide — to tell a trusted person
fin	end; limit	final — coming at the end
fort, force	strong	fortitude — strength enforce — to give strength to
frag, fract	to break	fragment — a part broken from the whole
gen	birth	generate — give birth to
gen, gener	kind; race	general — applying to a whole class or kind gender — classification of words by sex
gnos	to know	agnostic — one who believes people cannot know whether God exists
grad, gress	to step; to go	graduate — to go from one state to another progress — to move forward
graph, gram	writing	graphic — relating to writing telegram — a written message sent over a distance
helio	sun	heliolatry — sun worship
hydro	water	hydrant — a pipe from which one draws water
jac, jact, jec, ject	to throw	trajectory — the path of an object that has been thrown or shot project — to propose; to put forward
junct	to join	junction — a joining
jur	to swear	perjure — to lie under oath
labor	to work	elaborate — worked out carefully
leg, lect	to gather; to choose	legion — a large number gathered together elect — to choose
leg	law	legislate — to make laws
liber	book	library — a book collection
liber	free	liberation — freedom
loc	place	dislocate — to displace
loqu, locut	to talk	loquacious — talkative elocution — style of speaking
luc	light	elucidate — to clarify ("throw light on")
magn	great	magnanimous — of noble mind; generous magnate — an important person
man, mani, manu	hand	manipulate — to work with hands manuscript — a document written by hand
mar	the sea	maritime — having to do with the sea
medi	middle	intermediate — in the middle
meter, metr, mens	to measure	thermometer — an instrument to measure temperature symmetry — similarity of measurement on both sides immense — very large (immeasurable)
micro	very small	microbe — an organism too small to be seen with the naked eye

Root	Meaning	Examples
min, mini	small	minute — very tiny miniature — a small copy of something
mit, mitt, miss	to send	admit — to allow in missile — a projectile
mon, monit	to advise, warn, remind, etc.	monument — a plaque, statue, building, set up to remind one of someone or something premonition — an advance warning
mort, morti	to die	mortal — destined to die moribund — dying
mov, mot, mob	to move	remove — to move away emotion — strong (moving) feelings immobile — not movable
mut	to change	immutable — never changing
nat, nasc	born	prenatal — before birth nascent — coming into being; being born
nav	ship	circumnavigate — to sail around
nocturne	night	nocturnal — taking place at night
nomy	law; arranged order	astronomy — the science of the stars
nov, novus	new	innovation — something new
onym	name	anonymous — without a name
oper	to work	operative — capable of working
pac	peace	pacify — to calm
par	equal	disparate — not alike; distinct
pars, part	part	depart — to go away from
pater, part	father	paternal — fatherly patriarch — a father and a ruler
path, pat, pas	feeling; suffering	empathy — "feeling with" another person patient — suffering without complaint passion — strong emotion
ped, pede, pod	foot	pedestal — the bottom of a statute, column, etc. impede — to hinder podium — a platform on which to stand
pel, puls	to drive	expel — to drive out repulse — to drive back
pend, pens	to hang; to weigh; to pay	pendulous — hanging loosely pensive — thoughtful pension — a payment to a person after a certain age
pet, petit	to seek	impetus — a motive petition — to request
phil, philo	loving	philanthropy — a desire to help mankind philosophy — a love of knowledge
phobia	fear	hydrophobia — fear of water
phon, phone	sound	symphony — harmony of sounds telephone — an instrument for sending sound over a distance

continued

Root	Meaning	Examples
plac	to please	placate — to stop from being angry
polis	city	metropolis — a major city
pon, pos, posit, pose	to place	proponent — a person who makes a suggestion or supports a cause position — to place or put something in a location
port, portat	to carry	porter — one who carries transportation — a means of carrying
psych, psycho	mind	psychology — the science of the mind
quer, quisit	to ask	query — to question inquisition — a questioning
quies	quiet	acquiesce — to agree without protest
radi	ray	irradiate — to shine light on
rap, rapt	to seize	rapine — the act of seizing other's property by force rapture — being seized or carried away by emotion
rid, ris	to laugh	ridiculous — laughable risible — causing laughter
rog, rogate	to ask	prerogative — a prior right interrogate — to question
rupt	to break	disrupt — to break up
sat, satis	enough	satiate — to provide with enough or more than enough satisfy — to meet the needs of
schis, schiz	to cut	schism — a split or division schizophrenia — a mental disorder characterized by a separation of the thoughts and emotions
sci	to know	science — knowledge
scop	to watch; to view	telescope — an instrument for seeing things at a distance
scrib, script	to write	describe — to tell or write about transcript — a written copy
sec, sect	to cut	sectile — cutable with a knife bisect — to cut in two
sed, sess, sid	to sit	sediment — material that settles to the bottom (in liquid) session — a meeting preside — to have authority
sent, sens	to feel; to think	sentiment — feeling sensitive — responding to stimuli
sequ, secu, secut	to follow	sequence — order consecutive — one following another
solv, solut	to loosen	absolve — to free from guilt solution — the method of working out an answer
soph	wise; wisdom	sophisticate — a worldly-wise person
spec, spect, spic	to look; to appear	specimen — an example inspect — to look over perspicacious — having sharp judgment
spir, spirit	to breathe	expire — to exhale; to die spirit — life

Root	Meaning	Examples
sta, stat	to stand	stable — steady stationary — fixed, unmoving
stru, struct	to build	construe — to explain or deduce the meaning structure — a building
suas, suad	to urge	persuasive — having the power to cause something to change dissuade — to change someone's course
sum, sumpt	to take	assume — to take on resumption — taking up again
tact, tang	to touch	tactile — able to be touched or felt intangible — unable to be touched
tempor	time	temporal — lasting only for a time; temporary
ten, tent, tain	to hold	untenable — unable to be held retentive — holding maintain — to keep or keep up
tend, tens	to stretch	extend — to stretch out or draw out tension — tautness
terr	land	territory — a portion of land
the, theo	god	atheist — one who believes there is no God theocracy — rule by God or by persons claiming to represent Him
thermo	heat	thermal — having to do with heat
tract	to draw	attract — to draw
trud, trus	to thrust	protrude — to stick out intrusive — pushing into or upon something
un, uni	one	unanimous — of one opinion uniform — of one form
urb	city	suburb — a district near a city
ut, util	to use; useful	utile — the quality of being useful
vac	empty	vacuum — empty space
ven, vent	to come	convene — to meet together advent — an arrival
ver	true	verify — to prove to be true
verd	green	verdant — green
vert, vers	to turn	avert — to turn away
vi, via	way	deviate — to turn off the prescribed way via — by way of
vid, vis	to see	evident — apparent; obvious invisible — unable to be seen
vinc, vict	to conquer	convince — to overcome the doubts of victory — an overcoming
vit, viv	to live	vital — alive vivacious — lively
voc, voke, vocat	to call	vocal — spoken or uttered aloud invoke — to call on vocation — a calling

continued

Root	Meaning	Examples
void	empty	devoid — without
volv, volut	to roll or turn around	evolve — to develop by stages, to unfold
vol	to fly	volatile — vaporizing quickly

Chapter 4

Quantitative Reasoning

Introduction to Quantitative Reasoning

The Quantitative Reasoning measure of the GRE test is designed to assess fundamental math skills in arithmetic, algebra, geometry, data analysis, word problems, and data interpretation. This chapter will review these fundamental skills presented within specific *question types* that appear on the GRE. The question types (quantitative comparison, multiple-choice with one answer, multiple-choice with one or more answers, and numeric entry) are designed to test your ability to think critically and mathematically and your ability to create mathematical models to solve real-life questions. You are encouraged to pace yourself and become familiar with the question types by completing the practice exercises outlined in each section of this chapter. To enhance individual learning styles, we have organized practice exercises by level of difficulty, starting with easy to moderate questions, then average questions, and finally above average to difficult questions. As you repeat the practice questions, you will be steadily increasing your comfort level with the question types and increasing your ability to solve more difficult questions. Additionally, as you work through specific questions that require further knowledge, take advantage of our comprehensive math review in Chapter 5. Chapter 5 is an excellent resource to walk you through basic concepts and skills to aid in your learning.

The Quantitative Reasoning portion of the exam is comprised of two 20-question sections, each one with a 35-minute time limit. Each question will appear individually on the computer screen or will appear as part of a data interpretation set of questions that are based on facts related to tables, graphs, or other forms of graphic information. During the administration of the exam, you will have the computer capability to skip and/or place a checkmark next to individual questions. You will also be allowed to navigate back and forth within the section you are working in by clicking on the *review* button at the top of your computer screen. Take advantage of this computer flexibility as a test-taking strategy. Within each section, first answer the questions you can quickly solve, and then go back to solve the questions with a checkmark.

Remember that the GRE Quantitative Reasoning measure is a *section-level adaptive* test. This means that the level of difficulty of the questions in the second quantitative section are determined by how well you perform on the first quantitative section of 20 questions. Your overall score is based on a combination of how many questions were answered correctly in combination with their difficulty level.

Quantitative Reasoning General Directions

Consider reviewing the test instructions *before* the day of your test to save you valuable testing time. As you become more familiar with the instructions, you only need to scan the written directions to confirm that no changes have been made to the instructions. The on-screen instructions for the Quantitative Reasoning measure will be similar to the following:

Use the given directions to indicate the best answer for each of the following questions. You can get a more in-depth description of the directions by clicking Help at any time during the test.

- To use the available on-screen calculator, click the icon found at the top of the screen.
- If a question has answer choices with **ovals,** then the correct answer consists of a single choice. If a question has answer choices with **square boxes,** then the correct answer consists of one or more answer choices. Read the directions for each question carefully.
- All numerical values used are real numbers.
- Figures or diagrams are not necessarily drawn to scale and should not be used to estimate sizes by measurement unless they are data displays (graphs and charts) or coordinates on a coordinate axes. These will always be drawn to scale.

- Lines that appear straight can be assumed to be straight.
- A symbol that appears in repeated quantities represents the same value or object for each quantity.
- On a number line, positive numbers are to the right of zero and increase to the right and negative numbers are to the left of zero and decrease to the left.
- Distances are always either zero or a positive value.

Content Style Topics versus Question Types

The diagram below identifies quantitative topics with possible corresponding question types. Notice that there are six different math *content style topics* AND each topic may be matched with any one of the four different *question types.* For example, you may be given an algebra problem that is presented as a quantitative comparison question type, or you may be given an algebra problem that is presented as a multiple-choice question type (select one answer), etc.

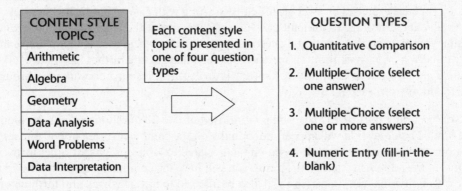

The following table summarizes the possible Quantitative Reasoning content style topics that appear in each question type. Each type of question will be discussed in detail in this chapter.

		QUESTION TYPE			
		Quantitative Comparison	**Multiple-Choice (one answer)**	**Multiple-Choice (one or more answers)**	**Numeric Entry (fill-in)**
CONTENT STYLE TOPIC	**Arithmetic**	X	X	X	X
	Algebra	X	X	X	X
	Geometry	X	X	X	X
	Data Analysis	X	X	X	X
	Word Problems	X	X	X	X
	Data Interpretation	Possible future inclusion	X	X	X

Overview of Quantitative Comparison Question Type

Quantitative comparison questions require that you compare two quantities in two columns. After you compare Quantity A and Quantity B, you must decide which quantity is greater, if the quantities are equal, or if a comparison cannot be determined from the information given.

Skills and Concepts Tested

Quantitative comparison tests your ability to quickly compare two given quantities while applying your knowledge of mathematical insight, approximations, simple calculations, and common sense. This question type tests concepts presented in secondary mathematics classes through first-year algebra and geometry. You will also need to be familiar with statistical concepts that are usually presented as part of a second-year algebra course in high school. There are no concepts tested from trigonometry, calculus or other higher level mathematics courses.

Directions

You will be asked to compare two columns, Quantity A and Quantity B, using information centered above each quantity (if information is provided), and "click" on one of the following ovals to select your answer choice.

Example:

<table>
<tr><th><u>Quantity A</u></th><th><u>Quantity B</u></th></tr>
<tr><td>7×3</td><td>7^3</td></tr>
</table>

   Ⓐ   Quantity A is greater.
   Ⓑ   Quantity B is greater.
   Ⓒ   The two quantities are equal.
   Ⓓ   The relationship cannot be determined from the information given.

REMINDER: The answer choices for questions on the actual computer version of the GRE are not labeled with letters. This book labels each answer choice with a letter choice, A, B, C, D, etc. for clarity. These letter labels will not appear on the computer screen when you take the test.

Common assumptions regarding the use of symbols, diagrams, and numerical values in quantitative comparison include, but are not limited, to the following.

- Information centered above both columns refers to one or both columns.
- All numerical values used are real numbers.
- Figures or diagrams are not necessarily drawn to scale and should not be used to estimate sizes by measurement unless they are data displays (graphs and charts) or coordinates on coordinate axes. These will always be drawn to scale.
- Lines that appear straight can be assumed to be straight.
- Symbols denoting lines and line segments $\left(\text{for example: } \overline{AB} \text{ or } \overrightarrow{AB}\right)$ do not appear on the GRE. The meaning is determined from their context in the question.
- A symbol that appears in both quantities represents the same value or object for each quantity.
- On a number line, positive numbers are to the right of zero and increase to the right, and negative numbers are to the left of zero and decrease to the left.
- Distances are always either zero or a positive value.

Suggested Strategies with Sample Questions

General Strategies for Quantitative Comparison

1. **Practice strategies.** Memorize and practice the four possible answer choices *before* your exam date to save time the day of the test.
2. **Avoid calculations that are not necessary.** When making a comparison, you can often find the answer with limited or partial information. For example, if Quantity A column is greater than 5 and Quantity B column is a less than 5, then there is no reason to perform calculations to determine that Quantity A is greater than Quantity B. This strategy will help you become time efficient.

3. **Narrow your answer choices by eliminating choice D,** "the relationship cannot be determined from the information given." There are four possible answer choices, and if Quantity A and Quantity B are given as *exact values* that can be determined, or in some arithmetic form that can be calculated to an exact value, then the last choice (D), is not a possible answer since the two values *can* be compared.

4. **Select choice D,** "the relationship cannot be determined from the information given," if you are presented with problems that show *different* relationships when substituting values for the unknowns.

5. **Simplify your comparisons.** It is possible to perform certain arithmetic calculations to each quantity or a given relationship in order to simplify the comparisons.

   - If both quantities are known to be positive, then you can square each quantity and the relationship stays the same

   - Add the same amount to each quantity or subtract the same amount from each quantity and the relationship stays the same.

   - Multiply or divide each quantity by the same positive number and the relationship stays the same.

   - Multiply or divide each quantity by the same negative number, but be aware that this reverses the relationship.

Arithmetic Sample Questions

	Quantity A	**Quantity B**
1.	$21 \times 43 \times 56$	$44 \times 21 \times 57$

The answer cannot be D since there are exact values for each quantity. Dividing each side of the comparison by 21 leaves:

43×56	44×57

Since 44 is greater than 43 and 57 is greater than 56, the product of 44 and 57 will be greater than the product of 43 and 56. The comparison could have been made by multiplying out each expression, but that would have used up too much time. The correct answer is **B.** Quantity B has greater value.

	Quantity A	**Quantity B**
2.	$\frac{3}{7} \times \frac{2}{5} \times \frac{5}{8}$	$\frac{2}{5} \times \frac{4}{11} \times \frac{5}{8}$

The answer cannot be D since there are exact values for each quantity.

Each side of the comparison has the expression $\frac{2}{5} \times \frac{5}{8}$. Dividing each side of the comparison by this value leaves:

$\frac{3}{7}$	$\frac{4}{11}$

These fractions can be more easily compared by rewriting them with a common denominator.

$\frac{3}{7}$	$\frac{4}{11}$
$\frac{(3)(11)}{(7)(11)}$	$\frac{(4)(7)}{(11)(7)}$
$\frac{33}{77}$	$\frac{28}{77}$

With both fractions having the same denominator, simply compare the numerators. Since 33 is greater than 28, the fraction $\frac{3}{7}$ is greater than $\frac{4}{11}$. Notice that the common denominator value was not needed, only the result of finding the new numerators. By observation, the new numerators were found by "cross-multiplying" upward as seen in the diagram below.

$$\frac{3}{7} \nwarrow \frac{4}{11} \qquad\qquad\qquad \frac{3}{7} \nearrow \frac{4}{11}$$
$$11 \times 3 = 33 \qquad\qquad\qquad\qquad 7 \times 4 = 28$$

This is a faster method for comparing fraction values. The correct answer is **A.** Quantity A has the greater value.

	__Quantity A__	__Quantity B__
3.	40% of 60	60% of 40

The answer cannot be D since there are exact values for each quantity. No calculations are necessary. After each percent value is rewritten in its decimal form, the arithmetic becomes "multiply 40 times 60 and move the decimal to the left two places." In either case, the result is the same. The correct answer is **C.** The two quantities have equal values.

	__Quantity A__	__Quantity B__
4.	$\sqrt[3]{7^6}$	2^8

The answer cannot be D since there are exact values for each quantity.

$$\sqrt[3]{\underbrace{7 \times 7 \times 7} \times \underbrace{7 \times 7 \times 7}} = 7 \times 7$$
$$= 49$$

As soon as you can see the comparison of 49 with 2^8, stop.

$$2^1 = 2,\ 2^2 = 4,\ 2^3 = 8,\ 2^4 = 16,\ 2^5 = 32,\ 2^6 = 64$$

STOP! Since higher powers of 2 will only give greater values and 2^6 is greater than 49, 2^8 will be greater than 49. The answer is **B.** Quantity B has the greater value.

	__Quantity A__	__Quantity B__
5.	$(0.9)^8$	$(1.01)^4$

The answer cannot be D since there are exact values for each quantity. A fact from arithmetic is that any positive value, less than 1, when multiplied by itself will give a value less than 1 and less than the original value. Any value, greater than 1, when multiplied by itself will give a value greater than 1 and greater than the original value.

For example, $\frac{1}{2} \times \frac{1}{2} = \frac{1}{4}$, which is less than 1 and is also less than $\frac{1}{2}$, and $1\frac{1}{2} \times 1\frac{1}{2} = \frac{3}{2} \times \frac{3}{2} = \frac{9}{4} = 2\frac{1}{4}$, which is greater than 1 and greater than $1\frac{1}{2}$.

Since 0.9 is a value less than 1, multiplying it by itself repeatedly will produce values smaller than 1. Since 1.01 is a value greater than 1, multiplying it by itself repeatedly will produce values greater than 1. Quantity A is less than 1 and Quantity B is greater than 1. The correct answer is **B.** Quantity B has the greater value.

	__Quantity A__	__Quantity B__
6.	$(-10)^{100}$	$(-10)^{101}$

The answer cannot be D since there are exact values for each quantity. A negative number raised to an even exponent will always produce a positive value. A negative number raised to an odd exponent will always produce a negative value. Therefore Quantity A is a positive value and quantity B is a negative value and positive values are always greater than negative values.

The correct answer is **A.** Quantity A has the greater value.

The following information refers to question 7.

$$x \text{ is a prime number between 4 and 10}$$
$$y \text{ is a prime number between 12 and 16}$$

	Quantity A	**Quantity B**
7.	$x + y$	20

The prime numbers between 4 and 10 are 5 and 7. Thus x could be 5 or 7. The only prime number between 12 and 16 is 13. Thus $y = 13$. The possible values for $x + y$ can now be shown in the following chart:

x	y	$x + y$
5	13	18
7	13	20

For the replacement of 5 for x and 13 for y, Quantity B is greater and for the replacement of 7 for x and 13 for y the two quantities have the same value. The correct answer is **D.** The relationship cannot be determined from the given information.

	Quantity A	**Quantity B**
8.	$\frac{1}{3} - \frac{1}{11}$	$\frac{1}{4} - \frac{1}{9}$

Finding common denominators, doing the arithmetic, and then comparing the resulting fractions can occasionally be too time consuming. Making some partial comparisons can sometimes help in recognizing the entire comparisons.

Notice that $\frac{1}{3}$ is greater than $\frac{1}{4}$, and that $\frac{1}{11}$ is less than $\frac{1}{9}$.

Beginning with a larger value then subtracting a smaller value will give a result that is greater than beginning with a smaller value and then subtracting a larger value.

Using simpler numbers can make this clearer: 50 is greater than 40 and 17 is less than 23.

Therefore, $50 - 17$ is greater than $40 - 23$. The correct answer is **A.** Quantity A has the greater value.

Algebra Sample Questions

The following information refers to question 9.

$$a > 0$$
$$b > 0$$
$$c < 0$$

	Quantity A	**Quantity B**
9.	$(3a)(3b)(3c)$	$3abc$

Method 1: Multiplying out Quantity A gives 27*abc*. The comparison is now

27*abc*   3*abc*

Since *a* and *b* are positive, and *c* is negative, then *abc* is a negative value. After dividing each quantity by *abc*, the comparisons get reversed. That is, what appears to be the greater value is in fact the lesser value. The comparison appears now as

27   3

Since the comparisons are reversed, the one that appears to be less becomes the greater value. The correct answer is **B**. Quantity B has the greater value.

Method 2: The above example can be made easier to see if *a*, *b*, and *c* were replaced with simple values. Let *a* = 2, *b* = 1, and *c* = –1. Then 27*abc* becomes 27(2)(1)(–1)= –54 and 3*abc* becomes 3(2)(1)(–1) = –6. Since –6 is a greater value than –54, Quantity B would have the greater value. If you divided each quantity by (2)(1)(–1) or –2, before doing the multiplying, Quantity A would become 27 and Quantity B would become 3. By dividing each quantity by a negative value, the comparison reverses. Thus, because 3 appears to be the lesser value, it in fact becomes the greater value.

The following information refers to question 10.

Quantity A	**Quantity B**
a + *b*	*ab*

10.

If both *a* and *b* were zero, then the two quantities would have equal values of zero. If only one of the two values was zero and the other was not, then Quantity A would not be zero but Quantity B would be zero. Since different relationships result with changing the values of the variables, a relationship cannot be determined. The correct answer is **D**. The relationship cannot be determined from the given information.

The following information refers to question 11.

$$x > y > 0$$

x and *y* are integers

Quantity A	**Quantity B**
$\dfrac{(x+y)^x}{x}$	$\dfrac{(x+y)^y}{y}$

11.

Since *x* and *y* are positive integers, the smallest values they could be is *x* = 2 and *y* = 1. Replace *x* and *y* with these values and make the comparison.

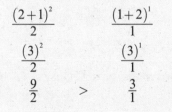

$$\frac{(2+1)^2}{2} \qquad \frac{(1+2)^1}{1}$$

$$\frac{(3)^2}{2} \qquad \frac{(3)^1}{1}$$

$$\frac{9}{2} \quad > \quad \frac{3}{1}$$

Replace x with 3 and y with 2 and you will find again that Quantity A is greater than Quantity B.

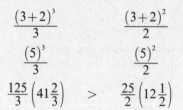

$$\frac{(3+2)^3}{3} \qquad \frac{(3+2)^2}{2}$$
$$\frac{(5)^3}{3} \qquad \frac{(5)^2}{2}$$
$$\frac{125}{3}\left(41\frac{2}{3}\right) \quad > \quad \frac{25}{2}\left(12\frac{1}{2}\right)$$

Changing the values of the variables did not change the comparisons.

The correct answer is **A.** Quantity A has greater value.

The following information refers to question 12.

$$x + 2y = 10$$

Quantity A	**Quantity B**
12. x	0

There are an endless number of values for x and y that can make this sentence true. It is possible that $x = 0$ and $y = 5$. Then Quantity A and Quantity B would have equal values. Another possibility for x and y could be $x = 2$ and $y = 4$. Then Quantity A would be greater than Quantity B. Since replacing the variables with different values changes the relationship, the relationship cannot be determined.

The correct answer is **D.** The relationship cannot be determined from the given information.

The following information refers to question 13.

$$4x + 8y = 24$$

Quantity A	**Quantity B**
13. $x + 2y$	5

This problem seems similar to the previous problem. There are endless numbers of x and y values that can make $4x + 8y = 24$ into a true sentence. At this point, you might consider that the comparison of $x + 2y$ and 5 cannot be determined. However, you must be careful to examine the information provided and compare it to Quantity A. If you compare this information, the expression $4x + 8y$ becomes the expression $x + 2y$ when it is divided by 4. Take the given information and divide each side of the original equation by 4.

$$\begin{aligned} 4x + 8y &= 24 \\ \frac{4x + 8y}{4} &= \frac{24}{4} \\ x + 2y &= 6 \end{aligned}$$

Now Quantity A has the value 6. The correct answer is **A.** Quantity A has greater value.

The following information refers to question 14.

$$3x + 4y = 6$$
$$2x + 4y = 4$$

Quantity A	**Quantity B**
14. $\quad y$	2

Notice that if you were to subtract the lower equation from the upper equation, the variable y is eliminated.

$$3x + 4y = 6$$
$$\underline{-(2x + 4y) = -(4)}$$
$$x = 2$$

Be careful, x, not y, is 2. Now replace x with 2 in either of the original equations and find y.

$$3x + 4y = 6$$
$$3(2) + 4y = 6$$
$$6 + 4y = 6$$
$$4y = 0$$
$$y = 0$$

The correct answer is **B.** Quantity B has the greater value.

The following information refers to question 15.

$$2x - 3y = 5$$
$$3x + 4y = 7$$

Quantity A	**Quantity B**
15. $\quad x + 7y$	2

At first glance, this may appear to be a problem that requires you to solve for x and y so that the values can be substituted into the expression $x + 7y$ in order to compare it with 2. The method for solving this problem is not as simple to solve as the last problem. Look again at the information provided and compare it to Quantity A. If you add the two equations, the variable expression would begin with $5x$. But if you subtract the upper equation from the lower equation, the variable expression would begin with just x. Reverse the order of the equations and subtract.

$$3x + 4y = 7$$
$$\underline{-(2x - 3y) = -(5)} \quad \text{(Recall that to subtract is the same as to add the opposite.)}$$
$$x + 7y = 2$$

Now Quantity A is 2. The correct answer is **C.** The two quantities have equal values.

The following information refers to question 16.

AB passes through $(2,5)$ and $(-3,4)$

CD has equation $x + 4y = 8$

Quantity A	**Quantity B**
16. $\quad$ slope of AB	slope of CD

If the line passes through (x_1, y_1) and (x_2, y_2), then its slope $= \dfrac{y_2 - y_1}{x_2 - x_1}$.

$$\text{Slope of } AB = \frac{4-5}{-3-2} = \frac{-1}{-5} = \frac{1}{5}.$$

To find the slope of a line given its equation, rewrite the equation in the $y = mx + b$ form. The value of m is the slope of the line.

$$x + 4y = 8$$
$$4y = -1x + 8$$
$$y = -\frac{1}{4}x + 2$$

Slope of $CD = -\dfrac{1}{4}$.

Quantity A $= \dfrac{1}{5}$. Quantity B $= -\dfrac{1}{4}$.

Remember: Line segment symbols $\left(\overrightarrow{AB} \text{ and } \overrightarrow{CD} \right)$ will not appear on the GRE. Meaning is determined by the context of the question.

The correct answer is **A.** Quantity A has the greater value.

The following information refers to question 17.

$$x^2 - 5x + 6 = 0$$

	Quantity A	**Quantity B**
17.	x	2

If you were to do a direct replacement of x with 2, you would see that

$$(2)^2 - 5(2) + 6 = 4 - 10 + 6$$
$$= 0$$

This would lead you to believe that the two quantities are equal. But if you were to solve $x^2 - 5x + 6 = 0$ algebraically, you would get two possible replacements for x.

$$x^2 - 5x + 6 = 0$$
$$(x - 2)(x - 3) = 0$$

$$x - 2 = 0 \quad \text{or} \quad x - 3 = 0$$
$$x = 2 \quad \text{or} \quad x = 3$$

Quantity A could be either 2 or 3. The correct answer is **D.** The relationship cannot be determined with the given information.

Geometry Sample Questions

	Quantity A	**Quantity B**
18.	Perimeter of an equilateral triangle with side length of $5x$	Perimeter of a square with side length of $4x$

A sketch might be helpful.

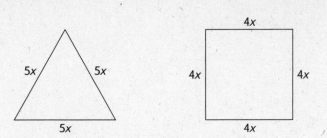

Perimeter means distance around. The distance around the equilateral triangle is $3(5x) = 15x$, and the distance around the square is $4(4x) = 16x$. Since $4x$ and $5x$ represent lengths of sides, x must be a positive number.

Therefore, $15x < 16x$. The correct answer is **B.** Quantity B has greater value.

Quantity A	**Quantity B**
19. Volume of a right circular cylinder with diameter 10 in.	Volume of a right circular cylinder with radius 5 in.

The volume of a right circular cylinder requires knowing its height. Since the height is not provided, no comparisons are possible.

The correct answer is **D.** The relationship cannot be determined with the given information.

The following information refers to question 20.

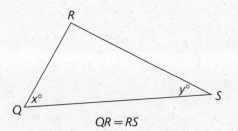

QR = RS

Quantity A	**Quantity B**
20. x	y

At first glance you might think that x is greater than y by appearance, but remember that diagrams are not necessarily drawn to scale. If you use the information provided to mark the triangle, it would appear as a different shape as shown below.

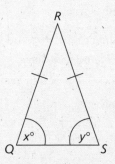

In a triangle, if two of its sides have equal length, then the angles opposite those sides have equal measure. With $QR = RS$, then $x = y$ since x is opposite the side RS and y is opposite the side QR. The correct answer is **C.** The quantities have equal values.

The following information refers to question 21.

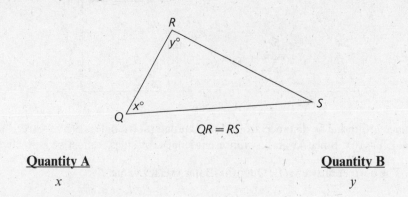

QR = RS

	Quantity A		**Quantity B**
21.	x		y

Although this problem appears to be identical to the last example, take a closer look; the only angle measures that can be compared would be those opposite the sides *QR* and *RS*. Since *y* is not opposite either of these sides, its value cannot be compared to that of *x*.

The correct answer is **D**. The relationship cannot be determined with the given information.

The following information refers to question 22.

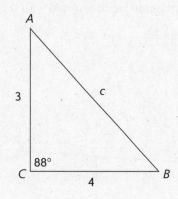

C is the largest angle in $\triangle ABC$

	Quantity A		**Quantity B**
22.	5		c

If the 88° angle was a 90° angle, you could have applied the Pythagorean theorem to find the value of c ($c^2 = a^2 + b^2$). You can still use this concept to solve this problem. If c is the longest side of a triangle, with a and b representing the lengths of the other two sides, then the following is true.

If the largest angle is greater than 90°, then $c^2 > a^2 + b^2$ and vice-versa.

If the largest angle is 90°, then $c^2 = a^2 + b^2$ and vice-versa.

If the largest angle is less than 90°, then $c^2 < a^2 + b^2$ and vice-versa.

In this problem, the largest angle is less than 90°. Therefore,

$$c^2 < 3^2 + 4^2$$
$$c^2 < 9 + 16$$
$$c^2 < 25$$
$$c < 5$$

The correct answer is **A**. Quantity A has greater value.

The following information refers to question 23.

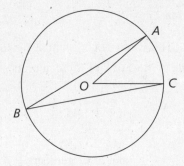

Circle *O* with a radii *OA* and *OC* ; chords *AB* and *BC*
$\angle AOC = 20°$

Quantity A	Quantity B
23. $\quad$ $\angle ABC$	15°

Angle *AOC* is a central angle. A central angle has the same measure as its intercepted arc. Therefore $\overset{\frown}{AC} = 20°$. Angle *ABC* is an inscribed angle. An inscribed angle has as its measure half of its intercepted arc. Therefore angle $ABC = \frac{1}{2}(20°) = 10°$.

The correct answer is **B.** Quantity B has the greater value.

The following information refers to question 24.

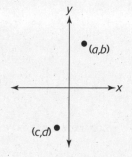

Quantity A	Quantity B
24. $\quad$ $c + d$	$a + b$

Even though the exact values of *a, b, c,* and *d* are not known, you can determine some information to solve this problem. Point *(a,b)* is in quadrant 1. Every point in quadrant 1 has a positive *x*-value and a positive *y*-value, which makes both *a* and *b* positive numbers. The sum of two positive numbers is positive. Point *(c,d)* is in quadrant 3. Every point in quadrant 3 has a negative *x*-value and a negative *y*-value, which makes both *c* and *d* negative numbers. The sum of two negative numbers is negative. Any positive number is always greater than any negative number.

The correct answer is **B.** Quantity B has the greater value.

Data Analysis Sample Questions

The following information refers to question 25.

The average of 12 numbers is 6.
The average of 9 of these numbers is 3.

Quantity A	Quantity B
25. The average of the remaining 3 numbers	14

"The average of 12 numbers is 6" translates into $\dfrac{\text{sum of 12 numbers}}{12} = 6$.

Multiply each side of this equation by 12: sum of 12 numbers = 72.

"The average of 9 numbers is 3" translates into $\dfrac{\text{sum of 9 numbers}}{9} = 3$.

Multiply each side of this equation by 9: sum of 9 numbers = 27.

The remaining three numbers have a sum that is the difference between 72 and 27, or 45. The average of these three numbers is then $\dfrac{45}{3} = 15$. The correct answer is **A.** Quantity A has the greater value.

The following information refers to question 26.

A bag contains 3 blue marbles,
2 red marbles, and 4 green marbles

Quantity A	Quantity B
26. The probability of randomly selecting a red marble.	The probability of randomly selecting two green marbles, one after the other, without replacing the first green marble.

Probability $= \dfrac{\text{number of favorable outcomes}}{\text{number of total outcomes}}$. Since there are 2 red marbles and a total of 9 marbles, the probability of randomly selecting a red marble is $\dfrac{2}{9}$. Therefore, Quantity A $= \dfrac{2}{9}$. Since there are 4 green marbles and a total of 9 marbles, the probability of randomly selecting a green marble on the first selection is $\dfrac{4}{9}$. Since this marble is not being replaced, there will now only be 3 green marbles available and only 8 total marbles remaining. The probability of randomly selecting a green marble for the second selection is $\dfrac{3}{8}$. The probability of randomly selecting a green marble for each selection is now the product of these two probabilities. Therefore, Quantity B $= \dfrac{4}{9} \times \dfrac{3}{8} = \dfrac{\cancel{4}^{1}}{\cancel{9}_{3}} \times \dfrac{\cancel{3}^{1}}{\cancel{8}_{2}} = \dfrac{1}{6}$.

To easily compare the Quantity A with Quantity B, use the common denominator of 18. Quantity A $= \dfrac{2}{9} = \dfrac{4}{18}$, and Quantity B $= \dfrac{1}{6} = \dfrac{3}{18}$. The correct answer is **A.** Quantity A has the greater value.

You can also solve this problem using the "cross multiply" method:

$$\dfrac{2}{9} \diagdown \dfrac{1}{6} \qquad \dfrac{2}{9} \diagup \dfrac{1}{6}$$
$$6 \times 2 = 12 \qquad 9 \times 1 = 9$$
$$12 > 9$$

Use the frequency table below for questions 27 and 28.

Data value	Frequency
3	4
4	1
5	2
8	3

	Quantity A		Quantity B
27.	median		mean

The median of a set of data is the middle value when the values are listed from least to greatest. From the frequency column, we see that there are 10 data values, (4 + 1 + 2 + 3 = 10). The median is then the average (arithmetic mean) between the 5th and 6th scores. From the table we see that the first 4 scores are 3, the 5th score is 4, and the 6th score is 5. The median then is found by finding the sum of 4 and 5 and dividing it by 2. The median $= \frac{4+5}{2} = \frac{9}{2} = 4\frac{1}{2}$.

The mean of a set of data is found by finding the sum of all the data values and dividing by how many data values there are. Using the frequency table, we find the sum of the data as follows:

$$(3)(4) + (4)(1) + (5)(2) + (8)(3) = 12 + 4 + 10 + 24 = 50$$

Since there are 10 data values, the mean $= \frac{50}{10} = 5$. The correct answer is **B**. Quantity B has the greater value.

	Quantity A		Quantity B
28.	mode		standard deviation

The *mode* is simply the number that is most repeated in a set of data values. The mode in the frequency table is 3.

Steps to Calculate Standard Deviation

1. Find the mean of the data set.
2. For each data value, do the following: (data value − mean)^2.
3. Find the sum of all the answers from step 2.
4. Divide the result from step 3 by how many data values there were.
5. Find the square root of the result in step 4.

The mean for this data set is 5.

$(3 - 5)^2 = 4$ This must be done 4 times for a total of 16.

$(4 - 5)^2 = 1$ This is only done once for a total of 1.

$(5 - 5)^2 = 0$ This is done 2 times for a total of 0.

$(8 - 5)^2 = 9$ This must be done 3 times for a total of 27.

The sum of all these results is 44 (16 + 1 + 0 + 27 = 44).

This result divided by the number of data values is 4.4 (44 ÷ 10 = 4.4).

The square root of 4.4 is a value between 2 and 3.

Since the mode of the data set was 3, you need only compare the standard deviation value to 3. Since the square root of 4.4 is known to be less than 3, you do not need to have a more exact approximation for it.

The correct answer is **A.** Quantity A has the greater value.

Word Problem Sample Question

	Quantity A	**Quantity B**
29.	The number of minutes it would take to go 10 miles at 15 miles per hour.	The number of ounces of water needed to dilute 30 ounces of a 70%-acid solution to a 50%-acid solution.

To go 10 miles at 15 miles per hour will take $\dfrac{10 \text{ mi}}{15 \text{ mi/hr}} = \dfrac{2}{3}$ hr.

Quantity A is to be in minutes. $\dfrac{2}{3}$ hr $= \dfrac{2}{3}$ hr $\times \dfrac{60}{1}$ min/hr $= 40$ minutes.

A simple chart might be of assistance for solving the mixture problem. Since you begin with 30 ounces of a solution that is 70% acidic, that means you also begin with 30% of the solution that is nonacidic. The following chart organizes all this information.

Let x = # ounces of water added

Liquid	Starting amount	Liquid added	Final amount
Not acid	0.3(30)	x	0.5(x + 30)
Acid	0.7(30)	0	0.5(x + 30)

Now either the equation $0.3(30) + x = 0.5(x + 30)$ or $0.7(30) + 0 = 0.5(x + 30)$ can be used to find the value of x. Choose the second one since the unknown only appears on one side of the equation.

$$0.7(30) + 0 = 0.5(x + 30) \qquad \text{(distribute the 0.5)}$$
$$21 = 0.5x + 15 \qquad \text{(subtract 15 from each side)}$$
$$6 = 0.5x \qquad \text{(divide each side by 0.5)}$$
$$12 = x$$

Therefore Quantity B is 12. The correct answer is **A.** Quantity A has the greater value.

Data Interpretation Sample Question

The following information refers to question 30.

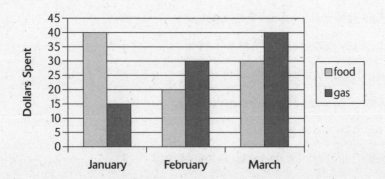

Quantity A	**Quantity B**
30. Percent change in the amount spent on food from January to February	Percent change in the amount spent on gas from February to March

Percent change can be found the following way.

$$\text{percent change} = \frac{\text{amount of change}}{\text{starting amount}} \times 100\%$$

Amount spent for food in January was 40 and in February it was 20.

The percent change becomes $\frac{40-20}{40} \times 100\% = \frac{20}{40} \times 100\% = 50\%$.

Amount spent for gas in February was 30 and in March was 40.

The percent change becomes $\frac{40-30}{30} \times 100\% = \frac{10}{30} \times 100\% = 33\frac{1}{3}\%$.

The correct answer is **A**. Quantity A has the greater value.

Practice Quantitative Comparison Questions

Easy to Moderate

Quantity A	**Quantity B**
1. $a\%$ of b	$b\%$ of a

Quantity A	**Quantity B**
2. $\frac{1}{3} \times \frac{2}{5} \times \frac{11}{13}$	$0.4 \times 0.33 \times 0.125$

The following information refers to question 3.

r and s are consecutive prime numbers

$$r > s$$

Quantity A	**Quantity B**
3. $r - s$	3

The following information refers to question 4.

$$x > 0$$

Quantity A	**Quantity B**
4. $x + \frac{x}{2}$	$x - \frac{x}{2}$

137

The following information refers to question 5.

$$a = b$$
$$a < c$$

Quantity A	**Quantity B**
5. $2a$	$b + c$

The following information refers to question 6.

$$\frac{x+3}{2} = \frac{2x-1}{3}$$

Quantity A	**Quantity B**
6. x	10

The following information refers to question 7.

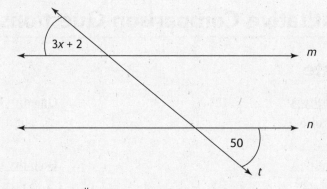

$m \parallel n$, $3x + 2$ and 50 are angle measures

Quantity A	**Quantity B**
7. x	20

The following information refers to question 8.

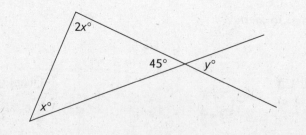

Quantity A	**Quantity B**
8. x	y

The following information refers to question 9.

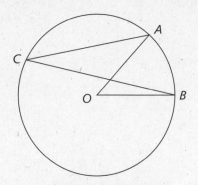

Circle with center at *O*.
Points *A*, *B*, and *C* lie on the circle
$\angle AOB = 46°$.

Quantity A	**Quantity B**
9. $\angle ACB$	25°

The following information refers to question 10.

Data Set Q: $\{2, 2, 4, 6, 8, 3, 4, 7, 9, 8\}$
Data Set R: $\{3, 2, 1, 5, 4, 3, 8, 7, 6, 4\}$

Quantity A	**Quantity B**
10. median of Data Set Q	mean of Data Set R

Quantity A	**Quantity B**
11. The number of ways to put 4 out of 7 books on shelf	The number of ways to put 3 out of 10 books on shelf

The following information refers to question 12.

A container is filled $\frac{3}{5}$ full in 30 minutes.

Quantity A	**Quantity B**
12. The time it would take to fill the remainder of the container at the same rate.	18 minutes

Average

The following information refers to question 13.

$$a > b > 0$$

Quantity A	**Quantity B**
13. Percent change from *a* to *b*	Percent change from *b* to *a*

	Quantity A	Quantity B
14.	The number of prime numbers between 1 and 10	The number of common multiples of 6 and 9 between 1 and 80

The following information refers to question 15.

$$a > 0$$

	Quantity A	Quantity B
15.	$5ab$	$10ab$

The following information refers to question 16.

$$T > x$$
$$y < m$$
$$x < y$$

	Quantity A	Quantity B
16.	$x + y$	$T + m$

The following information refers to question 17.

$$0 < a < b < c < d$$

	Quantity A	Quantity B
17.	$\dfrac{c}{d}$	$\dfrac{b}{a}$

The following information refers to question 18.

$$x^2 - 5x - 24 = 0$$

	Quantity A	Quantity B
18.	10	x

The following information refers to question 19.

Circle Q has a diameter of 5 inches.
Circle R has an area of 36π square inches.

	Quantity A	Quantity B
19.	The ratio of the circumference to diameter in circle Q	The ratio of the circumference to diameter in circle R

The following information refers to question 20.

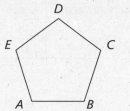

ABCDE is a regular pentagon

Quantity A	**Quantity B**

20. $\angle A$ 100°

The following information refers to question 21.

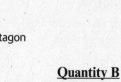

$\angle A = x + 2y;\ \angle B = 3x + y;\ \angle C = 2x + 3y$

Quantity A	**Quantity B**

21. $x + y$ 30

The following information refers to question 22.

Data set	Set size	Median value
A	10	6
B	12	8
C	14	10

Quantity A	**Quantity B**

22. The overall median for the 3 data sets   8

The following information refers to question 23.

The average (arithmetic mean)
of *a*, *b*, *c*, and 6 is 2.

Quantity A	**Quantity B**

23. $\dfrac{a+b+c}{4}$ $\dfrac{1}{2}$

The following information refers to question 24.

Investment	Annual Return	Annual Management Fee
A	6%	0.5%
B	7%	0.4%

	Quantity A	**Quantity B**
24.	Net amount earned in one year of $6,000 in investment A	Net amount earned in one year of $5,000 in investment B

Above Average to Difficult

	<u>**Quantity A**</u>	<u>**Quantity B**</u>
25.	The number of integers between 10 and 200 that are not squares of an integer.	179

The following information refers to question 26.

$$8 \text{ is } x\% \text{ of } 40$$
$$y \text{ is } 30\% \text{ of } 60$$

	<u>**Quantity A**</u>	<u>**Quantity B**</u>
26.	%-change from x to y	%-change from y to x

The following information refers to question 27.

$$x^3y^2 < 0$$
$$x^2y^3 > 0$$

	<u>**Quantity A**</u>	<u>**Quantity B**</u>
27.	$(xy)^3$	0

The following information refers to question 28.

$$x^2 - 4x - 5 = 0$$
$$|y - 3| = 6$$

	<u>**Quantity A**</u>	<u>**Quantity B**</u>
28.	The least value of $x^2 + y^2$	10

The following information refers to question 29.

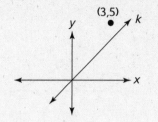

Line *k* passes through the origin as shown.

Quantity A	Quantity B

29.   slope of line *k*   1.7

The following information refers to question 30.

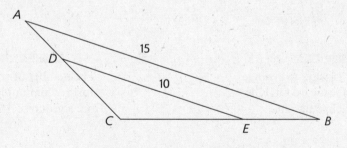

$\angle 1 = 3x + 6$, $\angle 2 = 5x + 5$; $\angle 3 = x^2 + 2$
All angles are measured in degrees

Quantity A	Quantity B

30. $\angle 1$ 30

The following information refers to question 31.

$AD = 2$, $CE = 8$, $CD = x$, $BE = y$
$DE \parallel AB$

Quantity A	Quantity B

31.   *x*   *y*

The following information refers to question 32.

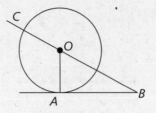

O is the center of the circle.
C lies on the circle.
AB is tangent to the circle at A.
∠CBA = 30°

	Quantity A	**Quantity B**
32.	$\frac{1}{2}\overset{\frown}{AC}$	$\angle AOB$

The following information refers to question 33.

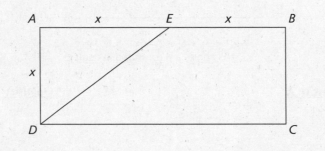

	Quantity A	**Quantity B**
33.	$\dfrac{\text{Area of } DEBC}{\text{Area of rectangle } ABCD}$	$\dfrac{2}{3}$

	Quantity A	**Quantity B**
34.	The number of ways to arrange the letters in the word QUICK using each letter once	The number of ways to form a committee of 2 from a group of 16 people

The following information refers to question 35.

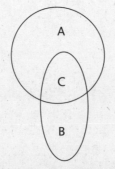

Set A = all integers between 20 and 50
Set B = all prime numbers between 15 and 60

	Quantity A	**Quantity B**
35.	The probability of randomly selecting a value in Set C that is less than 30	$\frac{1}{2}$

	Quantity A	**Quantity B**
36.	The change in speed in miles per hour to go from traveling 60 miles in 90 minutes to traveling 60 miles in 75 minutes	10

Answers and Explanations for Practice Quantitative Comparison Questions

Easy to Moderate

1. **C.** This is best seen if you were to make the "% into the fraction $\frac{1}{100}$. $a\%$ of b becomes $\left(\frac{a}{1} \times \frac{1}{100}\right) \times \frac{b}{1}$. This is the same as $\frac{a}{1} \times \left(\frac{1}{100} \times \frac{b}{1}\right)$, which is the same as saying $b\%$ of a.

2. **A.** Begin by recognizing that $\frac{2}{5}$ and 0.4 have equal values. Divide each side of the comparison by this value. Now you have $\frac{1}{3} \times \frac{11}{13}$ as Quantity A and 0.33×0.125 as Quantity B. Notice that $\frac{1}{3} > 0.33$ and $\frac{11}{13} > 0.125$. Therefore, the product of the larger numbers will have a greater value than the product of the smaller numbers.

3. **D.** There are consecutive prime numbers that have a difference of only 1. The prime numbers 2 and 3 have a difference of 1. There are consecutive prime numbers that have a difference of 2. The prime numbers 5 and 7 have a difference of 2. There are consecutive prime numbers that have a difference of 4. The consecutive prime numbers 7 and 11 have a difference of 4. The difference of r and s could be less than 3 or could be more than 3. Therefore, the relationship cannot be determined with the given information.

4. **A.** First, subtract x from each side of the comparison. Since the value of x is positive, $(x > 0)$, $\frac{x}{2}$ is positive, and $-\frac{x}{2}$ is negative. Quantity A is positive and Quantity B is negative. A positive value is always greater than a negative value.

5. **B.** If $a = b$ and $a < c$, the following substitutions make for a simpler comparison.

Quantity A	**Quantity B**	
$2a$	$b+c$	
$a+a$	$b+c$	(replace $2a$ with $a+a$)

Since $a = b$, replace one of the "a's" on the left side with a "b."

$a+b$	$b+c$

Subtract a "b" from each side of the comparison.

a	c

Since the original information states that $a < c$, Quantity B has the greater value.

6. A. Use the "cross multiply" technique to clear the proportion and solve the resulting equation for x.

$$\frac{x+3}{2} = \frac{2x-1}{3}$$
$$3(x+3) = 2(2x-1)$$
$$3x+9 = 4x-2 \qquad \text{(subtract } 3x \text{ and add 2 to each side of the equation)}$$
$$11 = x$$

Quantity A has the greater value.

7. B. When parallel lines are crossed by a third line, angles in the same relative position have equal measures. When two lines cross one another, angles opposite each other have the same measure. In the diagram provided, place a y in the angle position opposite the angle labeled $3x + 2$.

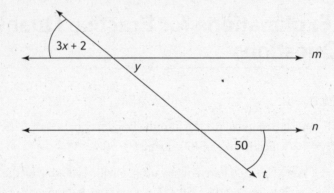

Therefore, $3x + 2 = y$ and $y = 50$. Hence,

$$3x+2 = 50 \qquad \text{(subtract 2 from each side of the equation)}$$
$$3x = 48 \qquad \text{(divide each side of the equation by 3)}$$
$$x = 16$$

Quantity B has the greater value.

8. C. The sum of the angles of a triangle is 180°. When two lines cross each other, the opposite angles have the same measure. Based on the diagram,

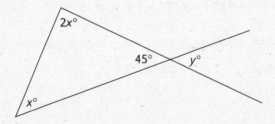

$$x + 2x + 45 = 180 \quad \text{and} \quad y = 45$$
$$3x + 45 = 180 \qquad \text{(subtract 45 from each side of the equation)}$$
$$3x = 135 \qquad \text{(divide each side of the equation by 3)}$$
$$x = 45$$

Therefore the quantities have equal values.

9. B. In a circle, a central angle (an angle with its vertex at the center of the circle) has the same number of degrees as the arc of the circle it intercepts. An inscribed angle (an angle with its vertex on the circle) has half as many degrees as the arc it intercepts. Take a look at the diagram again.

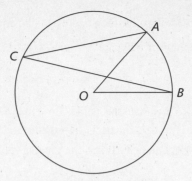

Circle with center at O.
Points A, B, and C lie on the circle.
$\angle AOB = 46°$.

Therefore, $\overset{\frown}{AB} = 46°$ and $\angle ACB = \frac{1}{2}(46°) = 23°$. Quantity B has the greater value.

10. **A.** The median is the middle value when the data values are listed from least to greatest. In each data set, there are 10 values. The median is then the average (arithmetic mean) of the two middle values. List the data values for Data Set Q from least to greatest.

$$\text{Data Set Q: } 2, 2, 3, 4, \underset{\substack{\text{middle} \\ \text{values}}}{\underline{4, 6}}, 7, 8, 8, 9 \quad \text{median} = \frac{4+6}{2} = 5$$

Data set R: The sum of all values in Data Set R is 43. There are 10 values in Data Set R.

The average (arithmetic mean) is the sum of the values divided by the number of values.

That is: $\frac{43}{10} = 4.3$, Quantity B = 4.3 and Quantity A = 5.

Quantity A is the greater value.

11. **A.** To find the number of ways to put 4 of 7 books on a shelf, you can either use the counting principle or the permutations formula. Using the counting principle, there are 7 ways to put the first book on the shelf, then 6 ways to put the second book on the shelf, 5 ways to put the third book on the shelf, and finally 4 ways to put the fourth book on the shelf. That is, there are $7 \times 6 \times 5 \times 4$ ways to put 4 of 7 books on a shelf. In a similar manner, there are $10 \times 9 \times 8$ ways to put 3 of 10 books on a shelf. Either multiply out each expression or look for some shortcut to make the comparison simpler.

$$
\begin{array}{ccl}
7 \times 6 \times 5 \times 4 & 10 \times 9 \times 8 & \text{(Divide each comparison by 5, then by 4)} \\
7 \times 6 & 2 \times 9 \times 2 &
\end{array}
$$

Now Quantity A is 42 and Quantity B is 36. Quantity A has the greater value.

The permutations formula can be used because the order in which the books are put on the shelf can be distinguished from one another. Using the permutations formula $P(n,r) = \frac{n!}{(n-r)!}$ with $n = 7$ and $r = 4$, you get

$$\frac{7!}{(7-4)!} = \frac{7!}{3!} = \frac{7 \times 6 \times 5 \times 4 \times \overset{1}{\cancel{3}} \times \overset{1}{\cancel{2}} \times 1}{\cancel{3} \times \cancel{2} \times 1} = 7 \times 6 \times 5 \times 4$$

Similarly, with $n = 10$ and $r = 3$ you get

$$\frac{10!}{(10-3)!} = \frac{10!}{7!} = \frac{10 \times 9 \times 8 \times \overset{1}{\cancel{7}} \times \overset{1}{\cancel{6}} \times \overset{1}{\cancel{5}} \times \overset{1}{\cancel{4}} \times \overset{1}{\cancel{3}} \times \overset{1}{\cancel{2}} \times 1}{\underset{1}{\cancel{7}} \times \underset{1}{\cancel{6}} \times \underset{1}{\cancel{5}} \times \underset{1}{\cancel{4}} \times \underset{1}{\cancel{3}} \times \underset{1}{\cancel{2}} \times 1} = 10 \times 9 \times 8$$

12. **A.** If a container is filled $\frac{3}{5}$ full in 30 minutes, then each $\frac{1}{5}$ of the container is filled in 10 minutes $\left(\frac{30}{3}=10\right)$. Therefore the remaining $\frac{2}{5}$ of the container will take 20 minutes $(2 \times 10 = 20)$. Quantity A has the greater value.

Average

13. **B.** One method for solving this is to give yourself values for a and b such that $a > b > 0$. Let $a = 2$ and $b = 1$. Then the percent change from a to b is calculated as $\frac{2-1}{2} \times 100\% = 50\%$, and the percent change from b to a is calculated as $\frac{2-1}{1} \times 100\% = 100\%$. Quantity B has the greater value.

14. **C.** The prime numbers between 1 and 10 are 2, 3, 5, and 7. There are 4 of them. The first common multiple of 6 and 9 is 18. Counting by 18s until you get to 80, you have 18, 36, 54, 72. There are 4 of them. Instead of listing the multiples of 18, you could have divided 80 by 18, then seen that it divides into 80 only 4 times, meaning there are only 4 multiples of 18 between 1 and 80. The quantities have equal values.

15. **D.** You can divide each side of the comparison by a and the comparison will not change since a is positive. So now you have $5b$ compared to $10b$. Since you do not know whether b is positive, zero, or negative, the relationship cannot be determined.

16. **B.** Not all information given must be used. The comparisons involve $x + y$ and $T + m$. Find the inequalities that involve these variables and make the inequalities face the same direction.

$$x < T$$
$$y < m$$

Therefore,

$$x + y < T + m$$

Quantity B has the greater value.

17. **B.** Since $c < d$ and they are both positive, the fraction $\frac{c}{d}$ has a positive value less than 1. Similarly, since $a < b$ and they are both positive, the fraction $\frac{b}{a}$ has a positive value greater than 1. Therefore Quantity B has the greater value. Another approach is to replace a, b, c, and d with simple values and then make the comparisons. Let $a = 1$, $b = 2$, $c = 3$, and $d = 4$. Then $\frac{c}{d} = \frac{3}{4}$ and $\frac{b}{a} = \frac{2}{1}$. Quantity B has the greater value.

18. **A.** Factor the quadratic and set each factor equal to zero.

$$x^2 - 5x - 24 = 0$$
$$(x-8)(x+3) = 0$$

$$x - 8 = 0 \quad \text{or} \quad x + 3 = 0$$
$$x = 8 \qquad\qquad x = -3$$

The value 10 is greater than either possible value of x. Quantity A has the greater value.

19. **C.** The ratio of the circumference to the diameter of any circle is always the same. It is the value referred to as π. The quantities have equal values.

20. **A.** The sum of the interior angles of any polygon is found by using the formula $180(n - 2)$, where n represents the number of sides of the polygon. A regular polygon has sides of equal length and angles of equal measure. Find the interior angle sum then divide it by the number of angles to find one of the interior angles of a regular polygon.

A pentagon is a 5-sided polygon. Therefore, $\angle A = \frac{180(5-2)}{5} = \frac{\overset{36}{\cancel{180}}(3)}{\underset{1}{\cancel{5}}} = 108$.

Quantity A has the greater value.

21. **C.** The sum of the angles of a triangle is 180°. Therefore,

$$\angle A + \angle B + \angle C = 180$$
$$(x+2y)+(3x+y)+(2x+3y)=180$$
$$6x+6y=180 \qquad \text{(divide each side of the equation by 6)}$$
$$x+y=30$$

The quantities have equal value.

22. **D.** The fact that the median of set A is 6 and that there are 10 values, points to the average (arithmetic mean) of the 5th and 6th values is 6. Similarly, the average of the 6th and 7th values of set B is 8 and the average of the 7th and 8th values of data set C is 10. All three data sets together will have 36 values. The median for all 3 data sets is then the average of the 18th and 19th values. There is no information as to what those values have to be. Let's consider some extreme possibilities.

1. **Set A** has 10 values that are each 6

   Set B has 12 values that are each 8

   Set C has 14 values that are each 10.

   The combined data sets will have as their 18th and 19th values, the number 8.

   The median for the combined data sets would be 8.

2. **Set A** has its first 6 values the number 6, and each of the remaining values is greater than 100.

   Set B has as its first 7 values the number 8, and each of the remaining values is greater than 100.

   Set C has as its first 8 values the number 10, and each of its remaining values is greater than 100.

   The combined data sets will have as their 18th and 19th values, the number 10.

   The median for the combined data sets would be 10.

The relationship cannot be determined with the information given.

23. **C.** The average of *a, b, c,* and 6 is 2 is translated into the following.

$$\frac{a+b+c+6}{4}=2 \qquad \text{(multiply each side of the equation by 4)}$$
$$a+b+c+6=8 \qquad \text{(subtract 6 from each side of the equation)}$$
$$a+b+c=2$$

Now Quantity A becomes $\frac{2}{4}=\frac{1}{2}$. The quantities have equal values.

24. **C.** The net percentage earned for investment A is 5.5% (6% − 0.5% = 5.5%).

The net earned in one year of $6,000 in investment A is $6,000 × 5.5% = $330.

The net percentage earned for investment B is 6.6% (7% − 0.4% = 6.6%).

The net earned in one year of $5,000 in investment B is $5,000 × 6.6% = $330.

The quantities have equal values.

Above Average to Difficult

25. **B.** First count the number of integers "between 10 and 200." A common mistake is made when you count both 10 or the 200, but the correct answer only includes those numbers "between," not including 10 and 200. The integers between 10 and 200 start with 11 and end with 199. There are 189 integers from 11 to 199 (be sure to add 1 to the subtraction of 199 − 11 since you are counting the number 11). Of these 189 integers, we need to see how many are not squares of an integer. The squares of integers between 10 and 200 are $4^2, 5^2, 6^2, \ldots, 14^2$ ($15^2 > 200$). There are 11 of them (14 − 4 + 1 = 11).

Quantity A then has the value 189 − 11 = 178. Quantity B has the greater value.

26. B. 8 is $x\%$ of 40 can be solved using proportions: $\frac{x}{100} = \frac{8}{40}$, $40x = 800$, $x = 20$.

y is 30% of 60 can be solved using proportions: $\frac{30}{100} = \frac{y}{60}$, $100y = 1{,}800$, $y = 18$.

%-change from x to y is $\frac{20-18}{20} \times 100\% = \frac{\overset{1}{\cancel{2}}}{\underset{10}{\cancel{20}}} \times 100\% = 10\%$.

%-change from y to x is $\frac{20-18}{18} \times 100\% = \frac{\overset{1}{\cancel{2}}}{\underset{9}{\cancel{18}}} \times 100\% = 11\frac{1}{9}\%$.

Quantity B has the greater value.

Note: You did not have to convert to percent. Once you find the fraction values, you can compare them, $\frac{1}{9} > \frac{1}{10}$.

27. B. In order for $x^3y^2 < 0$, x would have to be a negative value, because y^2 can never be negative. In order for $x^2y^3 > 0$, y would have to be a positive value, since x^2 can never be negative. Now, with x a negative value and y a positive value, xy will be a negative number. Any negative number raised to an odd power will have a negative value. Therefore $(xy)^3$ will have to be a negative value. Zero is greater than any negative value. Quantity B has the greater value.

28. C. Solve the quadratic and the absolute value equations.

$$x^2 - 4x - 5 = 0 \qquad\qquad |y - 3| = 6$$
$$(x-5)(x+1) = 0$$
$$y - 3 = -6 \quad \text{or} \quad y - 3 = 6$$
$$x - 5 = 0 \quad \text{or} \quad x + 1 = 0 \qquad y = -3 \quad \text{or} \quad y = 9$$
$$x = 5 \quad \text{or} \quad x = -1$$

In order to get the least value for $x^2 + y^2$, $x = -1$ and $y = -3$.

Then $x^2 + y^2 = 10$. The quantities have equal values.

29. B. Line k will have a slope that is less than the slope of the line that passes through $(0,0)$ and $(3,5)$. Therefore, slope of line $k < \frac{5-0}{3-0}$, or slope of line $k < \frac{5}{3}$.

$\frac{5}{3}$ expressed as a decimal is $1.666\ldots$, which is a value less than 1.7.

Quantity B has the greater value.

30. A. The exterior angle of a triangle has the same measure as the sum of its remote interior angles. Use this to solve for x, replace x with that value in the expression for $\angle 1$, then make the comparison.

$$\angle 3 = \angle 1 + \angle 2$$
$$x^2 + 2 = (3x + 6) + (5x + 5)$$
$$x^2 + 2 = 8x + 11 \qquad\qquad \text{(subtract } 8x \text{ and 11 from each side)}$$
$$x^2 - 8x - 9 = 0$$
$$(x - 9)(x + 1) = 0$$
$$x - 9 = 0 \quad \text{or} \quad x + 1 = 0$$
$$x = 9 \quad \text{or} \quad x = -1$$

If $x = -1$, then $\angle 2 = 5x + 5$ would have a zero value, and that is not possible.

Therefore, the only value for x is 9. Then $\angle 1 = 3(9) + 6 = 33$.

Quantity A has the greater value.

31. C. With $DE \parallel AB$, $\triangle ACB$ will be similar to $\triangle DCE$. Draw the two triangles separately and include the lengths of the sides. With $AD = 2$ and $CD = x$, then $AC = x + 2$. With $BE = y$ and $CE = 8$, then $BC = y + 8$.

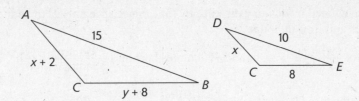

Now you can create proportions to find the values of x and y.

$$\frac{x}{x+2}=\frac{10}{15} \qquad \frac{8}{y+8}=\frac{10}{15} \qquad \text{(cross multiply)}$$
$$15x=10x+20 \qquad 120=10y+80 \qquad \text{(isolate the variable)}$$
$$5x=20 \qquad 40=10y \qquad \text{(divide by 5 for } x \text{, by 10 for } y\text{)}$$
$$x=4 \qquad 4=y$$

The quantities have equal values.

32. **C.** A 90-degree angle is formed where a radius and a tangent meet on a circle.

Therefore, $\angle BAO = 90°$, which makes $\angle AOB = 60°$ since the sum of the angles of a triangle is $180°$. With $\angle AOB = 60°$, then $\angle COA = 120°$ (the two angles form a line). Since $\angle COA$ is a central angle, $\overset{\frown}{AC} = 120°$.

Quantity A is $\frac{1}{2}\overset{\frown}{AC} = \frac{1}{2}(120°) = 60°$. The two quantities have equal values.

33. **A.** Drawing additional lines in the figure can help you see the relationship. Draw a segment from E perpendicular to DC. Call the point of intersection point F. Then draw a segment that connects B to F.

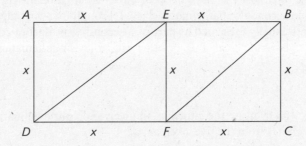

The figure $ABCD$ can now be seen as having four identical triangles within it.

The area of $DEBC$ consists of 3 of these triangles. Therefore, $\frac{\text{area } DEBC}{\text{area } ABCD} = \frac{3}{4}$. Quantity A has the greater value.

34. **C.** The number of ways to arrange the 5 letters in the word QUICK is 5! or the result of multiplying $5 \times 4 \times 3 \times 2 \times 1 = 120$.

The number of ways to select 2 people from a group of 16 people requires the use of the combinations formula. The combinations of n things taken r at a time is given by $C(n,r) = \frac{n!}{(n-r)!r!}$.

$$C(16,2) = \frac{16!}{(16-2)!2!} = \frac{16!}{14!2!} = \frac{16 \times 15 \times \cancel{14!}^{1}}{\cancel{14!}2!} = \frac{\cancelto{8}{16} \times 15}{\cancelto{1}{2} \times 1} = 120.$$

The quantities have equal values.

35. **B.** Set A = {21, 22, 23, ..., 47, 48, 49}. Remember, to be "between" does not include the ends. Set B = {17, 19, 23, 29, 31, 37, 41, 43, 47, 53, 59}. The odd integers left out of this list were either divisible by 3, by 5, or by 7 thus not making it a prime number. Set C has the integers that were in both Set A and in Set B. Set C = {23, 29, 31, 37, 41, 43, 47}. In Set C, there are 7 integers, 2 of which are less than 30. The probability of randomly selecting a value in Set C that is less than 30 is $\frac{2}{7}$, which is less than $\frac{1}{2}$. Quantity B has the greater value.

36. **B.** Speed can be calculated by dividing distance by time. Since speed needs to be in miles per hour, distance needs to be in miles and time in hours.

90 minutes becomes $\dfrac{90 \text{ min}}{60 \text{ min/hr}} = \dfrac{3}{2}$ hr and 75 minutes becomes $\dfrac{75 \text{ min}}{60 \text{ min/hr}} = \dfrac{5}{4}$ hr.

The speed to go 60 miles in 90 minutes becomes $\dfrac{60 \text{ mi}}{\frac{3}{2} \text{ hr}} = \dfrac{\overset{20}{\cancel{60}}}{1} \times \dfrac{2}{\underset{1}{\cancel{3}}} = 40 \text{ mi/hr.}$

The speed to go 60 miles in 75 minutes becomes $\dfrac{60 \text{ mi}}{\frac{5}{4} \text{ hr}} = \dfrac{\overset{12}{\cancel{60}}}{1} \times \dfrac{4}{\underset{1}{\cancel{5}}} = 48 \text{ mi/hr.}$

The change in speed in miles per hour is 8. Quantity B has the greater value.

Overview of Multiple-Choice (Select One Answer Choice) Question Type

The Multiple-Choice (Select One Answer Choice) question type requires you to solve math problems and then choose the single given answer that best answers the question.

Skills and Concepts Tested

Multiple-choice, single-answer questions test your ability to use mathematical insight, approximations, simple calculations, or common sense to choose the one correct or best answer from among a list of five given answers. They test concepts presented in secondary mathematics classes through first-year algebra, and geometry. They also include statistical concepts usually presented as part of a second-year algebra course in high school. There are no concepts tested from trigonometry, calculus, or other higher level mathematics courses.

Directions

Solve each problem in this section by using the information given and your own mathematical calculations. Select the one correct (best) answer choice from the five given answers.

There are some additional assumptions made regarding the use of symbols, diagrams, and numerical values. These assumptions include, but are not limited to, the following.

- All numerical values used are real numbers.
- Figures or diagrams are not necessarily drawn to scale and should not be used to estimate sizes by measurement unless they are data displays (graphs and charts) or coordinates on a coordinate axes. These will always be drawn to scale.
- Lines that appear straight can be assumed to be straight.
- A symbol that appears in repeated quantities represents the same value or object for each quantity.
- On a number line, positive numbers are to the right of zero and increase to the right and negative numbers are to the left of zero and decrease to the left.
- Distances are always either zero or a positive value.

Suggested Strategies with Sample Questions

- The correct answer is in the list provided. If your answer is not in the list, your answer is incorrect.
- In some questions, you are asked which answer choice meets certain requirements. This usually involves examining each answer choice individually. You may notice some relationship among the answer choices that allows you to settle on the correct answer more quickly.

- Working backwards from the answer choices is an accepted method for solution, although it usually takes longer than using logical reasoning to find the correct answer.

- Some questions require approximation. It may be useful to look at the answer choices and see how close together or far apart the answer choices are. This will guide you in determining how close your approximation needs to be to choose the correct answer. Some questions require accurate computations, for others, estimation may be all you need to arrive at the correct answer.

- Use the answer choices to help guide you. For example, whole number answer choices may suggest less accuracy needed in computations than fractions.

Arithmetic Sample Questions

1. If a mixture is $\frac{3}{7}$ alcohol by volume and $\frac{4}{7}$ water by volume, what is the ratio of the volume of alcohol to the volume of water in this mixture?

   Ⓐ $\frac{3}{7}$

   Ⓑ $\frac{4}{7}$

   Ⓒ $\frac{3}{4}$

   Ⓓ $\frac{4}{3}$

   Ⓔ $\frac{7}{4}$

The first bit of information that you should pull out is what you are looking for: "ratio of the volume of alcohol to the volume of water." Rewrite the ratio that you're looking for as $A:W$, and then rewrite it into its working form: $\frac{A}{W}$. Next, pull out the volumes of each; $A = \frac{3}{7}$ and $W = \frac{4}{7}$. Now, you can easily figure out the answer by inspection or substitution: $\frac{A}{W} = \frac{\frac{3}{7}}{\frac{4}{7}} = \frac{3}{7} \cdot \frac{7}{4} = \frac{3}{4}$. The ratio of the volume of alcohol to the volume of water is

3 to 4. The correct answer is **C.** When pulling out information, write out the numbers and/or letters on your scratch paper, putting them into some helpful form and eliminating some of the wording.

Sometimes, combining terms, performing simple operations, or simplifying the problem in some other way will give you insight and make the problem easier to solve.

2. Which of the following is equal to $\frac{1}{5}$ of 0.02 percent?

   Ⓐ 0.4
   Ⓑ 0.04
   Ⓒ 0.004
   Ⓓ 0.0004
   Ⓔ 0.00004

Simplifying this problem first means changing $\frac{1}{5}$ to 0.2.

Next change 0.02 percent to 0.0002 (that is, $0.02 \times 0.01 = 0.0002$).

Now that you have simplified the problem, multiply 0.2×0.0002, which gives 0.00004. The correct answer is **E.** Notice that simplifying can make a problem much easier to solve.

If you immediately recognize the method or proper formula to solve the problem, go ahead and do the work. Work forward.

> 3. Which of the following numbers is between $\frac{1}{3}$ and $\frac{1}{4}$?
>
>   Ⓐ 0.45
>   Ⓑ 0.35
>   Ⓒ 0.29
>   Ⓓ 0.22
>   Ⓔ 0.20

Focus on "between $\frac{1}{3}$ and $\frac{1}{4}$." Since $\frac{1}{3} = 0.333\ldots$ and $\frac{1}{4} = 0.25$, and since 0.29 is the only number between 0.333... and 0.25, the correct answer is **C**. By the way, a quick peek at the answer choices would tip you off that you should work in decimals.

If you don't immediately recognize a method or formula, or if using the method or formula would take a great deal of time, try working backwards from the answer choices. Because the answer choices are usually given in ascending or descending order, almost always start by plugging in choice C first. Then you'll know whether to go up or down on your next try. (Sometimes, you may want to plug in one of the simple answer choices first.)

> 4. What is the greatest common factor of the numbers 18, 24, and 30?
>
>   Ⓐ 2
>   Ⓑ 3
>   Ⓒ 4
>   Ⓓ 6
>   Ⓔ 12

The largest number that divides evenly into 18, 24, and 30 is 6. You could have worked from the answer choices, but here you should start with the largest answer choice, because you are looking for the *greatest* common factor.

The correct answer is **D**.

If you don't immediately recognize a method or formula to use to solve the problem, you may want to try a reasonable approach and then work from the answer choices.

> 5. A corporation triples its annual bonus to 50 of its employees. What percent of the employees' bonus is the increase?
>
>   Ⓐ 50%
>   Ⓑ $66\frac{2}{3}\%$
>   Ⓒ 100%
>   Ⓓ 200%
>   Ⓔ 300%

First, notice that the number 50 does not enter into the solution. It is an unnecessary piece of information. Be careful that you are using only that data that is necessary to solve the problem. Since we are dealing in percentages and not specific amounts, choose an amount that is easy to use. For example, try $100 for the normal annual bonus. If the annual bonus was normally $100, tripled it would be $300. Therefore, the increase is $200. That is $\frac{2}{3}$ of the new bonus of $300. Two-thirds is $66\frac{2}{3}\%$.

The correct answer is **B**.

> If it appears that extensive calculations are going to be necessary to solve a problem, check to see how far apart the answer choices are, and then approximate. The reason for checking the answer choices first is to give you a guide for how freely you can approximate.

6. The value for $(0.889 \times 55) \div 9.97$ to the nearest tenth is

    Ⓐ 0.5
    Ⓑ 4.63
    Ⓒ 4.9
    Ⓓ 7.7
    Ⓔ 49.1

Before starting any computations, take a glance at the answer choices to see how far apart they are. Notice that the only close answers are choices B and C, but B is not possible because it is to the nearest hundredth, not tenth. Now, approximating 0.889 as 1 and approximating 9.97 as 10 leaves the problem in this form $(1 \times 55) \div 10 = 55 \div 10 = 5.5$.

The closest answer choice is **C**; therefore, it is the correct answer. Notice that choices A and E are not reasonable.

Algebra Sample Questions

7. If $x + 6 = 9$, then $3x + 1 =$

    Ⓐ 3
    Ⓑ 9
    Ⓒ 10
    Ⓓ 34
    Ⓔ 46

You should first focus on $3x + 1$, because this is what you are solving for. Solving for x leaves $x = 3$, and then substituting into $3x + 1$ gives $3(3) + 1$, or 10. The most common mistake is to solve for x, which is 3, and *mistakenly choose* A as your answer. But remember, you are solving for $3x + 1$, not just x. You should also notice that most of the other choices would all be possible answers if you made common or simple mistakes. The correct answer is **C**. *Make sure that you are answering the right question.*

8. If $\frac{x}{2} + \frac{3}{4} = 1\frac{1}{4}$, what is the value of x?

    Ⓐ −2
    Ⓑ −1
    Ⓒ 0
    Ⓓ 1
    Ⓔ 2

First, if you know how to solve this type of equation, then:

$$\frac{x}{2} + \frac{3}{4} = 1\frac{1}{4}$$

$$\frac{x}{2} + \frac{3}{4} = \frac{5}{4}$$

$$4\left(\frac{x}{2} + \frac{3}{4}\right) = 4\left(\frac{5}{4}\right)$$

$$2x + 3 = 5$$

$$2x = 2$$

$$x = 1$$

The correct answer is choice **D.**

Remember, you should first focus on "the value of x." If you've forgotten how to solve this kind of equation, work backward by plugging in answer choices. Start with choice C; plug in 0:

$$\frac{0}{2} + \frac{3}{4} \neq 1\frac{1}{4}$$

Because this answer is too small, try choice D, a larger number. Plugging in 1 gives you:

$$\frac{1}{2} + \frac{3}{4} = 1\frac{1}{4}$$

$$\frac{2}{4} + \frac{3}{4} = \frac{5}{4}$$

$$\frac{5}{4} = \frac{5}{4}$$

The answer is true, so **D** is the correct answer. *Working from the answers is a valuable technique.*

Some problems may not ask you to solve for a numerical answer or even an answer including variables. Rather, you may be asked to set up the equation or expression without doing any solving. A quick glance at the answer choices will help you know what is expected.

9. Rick is three times as old as Maria, and Maria is four years older than Leah. If Leah is z years old, what is Rick's age in terms of z?

Ⓐ $3z + 4$

Ⓑ $3z - 12$

Ⓒ $3z + 12$

Ⓓ $\dfrac{(z+4)}{3}$

Ⓔ $\dfrac{(z-4)}{3}$

The correct answer is **C.** We are given Leah's age as z. Each additional piece of information allows us to work toward the desired result:

$$z = \text{Leah's age}$$

$$z + 4 = \text{Maria's age (Maria is four years older than Leah)}$$

$$3(z + 4) = \text{Rick's age (Rick is three times as old as Maria)}$$

$$\text{or } 3z + 12 = \text{Rick's age}$$

In some problems, you may be given special symbols that you are unfamiliar with. Don't let these special symbols alarm you. They typically represent an operation or combination of operations that you are familiar with. Look for the definition of the special symbol or how it is used.

---

10. If $\odot$ is a binary operation such that $a \odot b$ is defined as $\dfrac{a^2 - b^2}{a^2 + b^2}$, then what is the value of $3 \odot 2$?

Ⓐ $-\dfrac{1}{3}$

Ⓑ $\dfrac{1}{13}$

Ⓒ $\dfrac{1}{5}$

Ⓓ $\dfrac{5}{13}$

Ⓔ 1

The correct answer is **D.** Start with the definition: $a \odot b = \dfrac{a^2 - b^2}{a^2 + b^2}$.

Then, simply replace a with 3 and b with 2:

$$a \odot b = \frac{a^2 - b^2}{a^2 + b^2}$$

$$3 \odot 2 = \frac{3^2 - 2^2}{3^2 + 2^2}$$

$$3 \odot 2 = \frac{5}{13}$$

Geometry Sample Questions

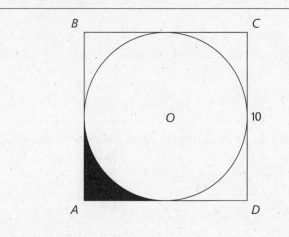

11. Circle O is inscribed in square $ABCD$ as shown above. The area of the shaded region is approximately

Ⓐ 10

Ⓑ 25

Ⓒ 30

Ⓓ 50

Ⓔ 75

Many problems can be solved using multiple methods. This problem can be solved using a more "mathematical" approach or by using a more "logical" approach.

Using the "mathematical" approach:

Calculate the area of the square: $A = s^2 = 10^2 = 100$

Calculate the area of the circle with diameter 10 (radius is 5): $A = \pi r^2 = (3.14)(5^2) \approx 78$

Subtract to find the difference and then divide by 4: $(100 - 78) \div 4 = 22 \div 4 = 5.5$

Clearly, answer choice **A** (10) is the closest and therefore the correct answer.

Using a more "logical" approach:

Divide the figure into fourths.

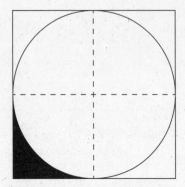

Since the area of each fourth of the square is $100 \div 4$, which is 25, and the shaded area is clearly less than half of that, the correct answer choice must be choice **A** (10).

Sketching diagrams or simple pictures can also be very helpful because the diagram may tip off either a simple solution or a method for solving the problem.

12. What is the maximum number of square pieces of birthday cake of size 4" by 4" that can be cut from a square cake 20" by 20"?

    Ⓐ 5
    Ⓑ 10
    Ⓒ 16
    Ⓓ 20
    Ⓔ 25

Sketching the cake and marking its sides as the following figure shows make this a fairly simple problem.

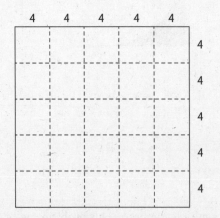

Notice that five pieces of cake will fit along each side; therefore, $5 \times 5 = 25$. The correct answer is **E.** Finding the total area of the cake and dividing it by the area of one of the 4×4 pieces $((20 \times 20) \div 16 = 25)$ would also give you the correct answer of 25, but beware of this method because it may not work if the pieces don't fit evenly into the original area.

13. If point P lies on $\overparen{ON}$ such that $\overparen{OP} = 2\overparen{PN}$ and point Q lies on $\overparen{OP}$ such that $\overparen{OQ} = \overparen{QP}$, what is the relationship of $\overparen{OQ}$ to $\overparen{PN}$?

    Ⓐ $\dfrac{1}{3}$

    Ⓑ $\dfrac{1}{2}$

    Ⓒ $\dfrac{1}{1}$

    Ⓓ $\dfrac{2}{1}$

    Ⓔ $\dfrac{3}{1}$

A sketch that represents the relationship would look like this:

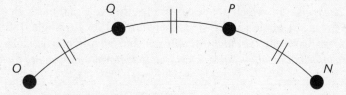

It is evident that from the sketch that $\overparen{OQ} = \overparen{PN}$, so that the ratio (relationship) of $\overparen{OQ}$ to $\overparen{PN}$ is 1 to 1 or $\frac{1}{1}$, which is answer choice C. Or, you could assign values on $\overparen{ON}$ such that $\overparen{OP} = 2\overparen{PN}$, such as: $\overparen{OP}$ equals 2, and $\overparen{PN}$ equals 1. If Q lies on $\overparen{OP}$ such that $\overparen{OQ} = \overparen{QP}$, then $\overparen{OP}$ is divided in half by point Q. So $\overparen{OQ} = 1$, and $\overparen{QP} = 1$. Therefore, the relationship (ratio) of $\overparen{OQ}$ to $\overparen{PN}$ is 1 to 1. The correct answer choice is **C.**

> **Redrawing and marking in diagrams on your scratch paper as you read them can save you valuable time. Marking can also give you insight into how to solve a problem because you will have the complete picture clearly in front of you.**

14. In the triangle below, *CD* is an angle bisector, angle *ACD* is 30°, and angle *ABC* is a right angle. What is the measurement of angle *x* in degrees?

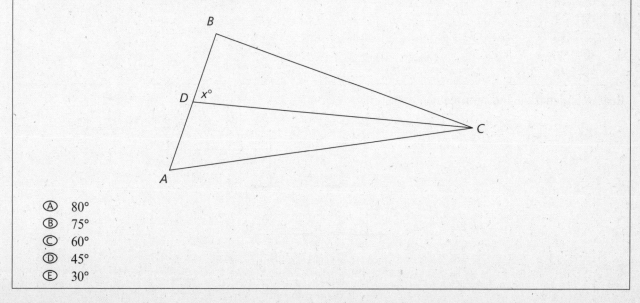

    Ⓐ 80°
    Ⓑ 75°
    Ⓒ 60°
    Ⓓ 45°
    Ⓔ 30°

After redrawing the diagram on your sketch paper, read the problem and mark as follows:

In the previous triangle, *CD* is an angle bisector (*stop and mark in the drawing*), angle *ACD* is 30° (*stop and mark in the drawing*), and angle *ABC* is a right angle (*stop and mark in the drawing*). What is the measurement of angle *x* in degrees? (*Stop and mark in or circle what you're looking for in the drawing.*)

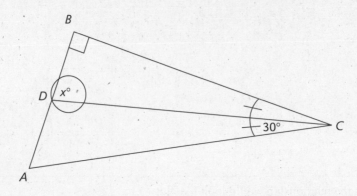

With the drawing marked in, it is evident that, because angle *ACD* is 30°. Angle *BCD* is also 30° because both angles are formed by an *angle bisector*, which divides an angle into two equal parts. Because angle *ABC* is 90° (right angle) and angle *BCD* is 30°, angle *x* is 60° since there are 180° in a triangle; 180 – (90 + 30) = 60. The correct answer choice is **C**. *After redrawing the diagrams on your sketch paper, always mark in the diagrams as you read their descriptions and information about them, including the information you are looking for.*

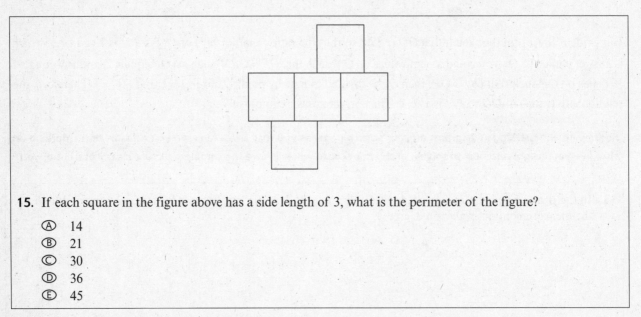

15. If each square in the figure above has a side length of 3, what is the perimeter of the figure?

Ⓐ 14
Ⓑ 21
Ⓒ 30
Ⓓ 36
Ⓔ 45

Redraw and mark in the information given.

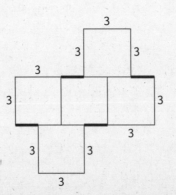

You now have a calculation for the perimeter: 30 *plus* the darkened parts. Now look carefully at the top two darkened parts. The total width of the three central squares is 9. A total of 6 is already accounted for. Thus, the darkened two parts must total to 3.

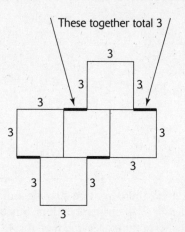

Each darkened part is not necessarily $1\frac{1}{2}$, but together the darkened pair must total to 3. (Notice how the top square may slide over to illustrate the fact.) The same is true for the bottom two darkened parts. They will also add up to 3.

Thus, the total perimeter is 30 + 6 = 36, answer choice **D.**

Be careful to note the difference between perimeter and area. Each square in the figure has an area of 9. Thus the area of the entire figure is 9 times 5 or 45. So, answer choice E represents the area, not the perimeter of the figure.

Data Analysis Sample Questions

16. Given that x is a negative number, y is a positive number, and z is a nonzero number such that $x < z < 2y$, which one of the following <u>must</u> be negative?

   Ⓐ $2x^2 - y^2$
   Ⓑ $x - 2y + z$
   Ⓒ $z - x$
   Ⓓ $x + 2z - y$
   Ⓔ $x + z - y$

Choice A is not correct since, depending on values, this expression could be positive.
If $x = -10$ and $y = 5$, $2x^2 - y^2 = 2(-10)^2 - 5^2 = 175$.

Choice C is not correct since, depending on values, this expression could be positive.
If $z = -2$ and $x = -5$, $z - x = -2 - (-5) = 3$.

Choice D is not correct since, depending on values, this expression could be positive.
If $x = -2$ and $z = 10$ and $y = 12$, $x + 2z - y = (-2) + (2)(10) - 12 = 6$.

Choice E is not correct since, depending on values, this expression could be positive.
If $x = -1$ and $z = 10$ and $y = 7$, $x + z - y = -1 + 10 - 7 = 2$.

Choice **B** is correct, since it must be negative. Examine each part. We know x is negative. Since we are subtracting twice a positive number, that is also negative. Also, since $x < z < 2y$, even if z was positive, it must be less than $2y$, therefore we are subtracting more than we are adding. **Once you find the correct answer, there is no need to continue checking the other answer choices.**

17. There are 120 students in a class. One-third of the students are male, two-fifths of the students are business majors, and one-half of the female students are business majors. If a male student is chosen at random from the class, what is the probability that he will be a business major?

   Ⓐ $\frac{1}{5}$

   Ⓑ $\frac{1}{4}$

   Ⓒ $\frac{1}{3}$

   Ⓓ $\frac{2}{5}$

   Ⓔ $\frac{3}{2}$

Since one-third of the 120 students are male, there must be 40 male and 80 female students. Since two-fifths of the 120 students are business majors, there are 48 business majors. Since one-half of the 80 female students are business majors, there are 40 female business majors, leaving 8 of the 48 business major to be male. Therefore 8 of the 40 male students are business majors, so the probability of selecting a business major from among the male students is $\frac{8}{40} = \frac{1}{5}$. Thus answer choice **A** is correct.

18. There are 12 jelly beans in a bag: 6 red, 3 green, 2 yellow, and 1 orange. What is the probability that 3 randomly selected jelly beans, chosen without replacement, will all be red?

   Ⓐ 0.08
   Ⓑ 0.09
   Ⓒ 0.10
   Ⓓ 0.11
   Ⓔ 0.12

Six of the 12 jelly beans are red. So, the probability that the first one selected is red is $\frac{6}{12}$. Out of the remaining 11 jelly beans, there are 5 red ones. Thus, the probability that the second selection is red given that the first selection was red is $\frac{5}{11}$. Out of the remaining 10 jelly beans, there are 4 red ones. Thus, the probability that the third selection is red given that the first two selections were red is $\frac{4}{10}$. Therefore, to find the probability that all three selections were red would be the product of these three probabilities: $\frac{6}{12} \times \frac{5}{11} \times \frac{4}{10} = \frac{1}{11} \approx 0.09$. Answer choice **B** is correct. **Although there is a more "statistical" method of solving using "combinations," these functions will not be available using the on-screen calculator, so it is better to use methods that use simple arithmetic computations.**

19. How many ways can you select 3 cards from a deck of 6 different cards?

   Ⓐ 2
   Ⓑ 6
   Ⓒ 20
   Ⓓ 30
   Ⓔ 120

The correct answer choice is **C,** 20 ways. A direct approach, although somewhat time consuming, would be to list the 20 ways. Let the 6 different cards be numbered 1, 2, 3, 4, 5, and 6. The 20 ways can now be listed as follows: 123, 124, 125, 126, 134, 135, 136, 145, 146, 156, 234, 235, 236, 245, 246, 256, 345, 346, 356, 456. Notice that all 20 selections have the digits listed in ascending order. When asked for "how many ways" selections can be made, when *order does not matter*, you are finding what is known as a *combination*. If *order does matter*, then you would be finding a *permutation*. To find the combination of *n* things taken *r* at a time, use this formula: $_nC_r = \dfrac{n!}{r!(n-r)!}$. In our case, $_6C_3 = \dfrac{6!}{3!(6-3)!} = \dfrac{6 \times 5 \times 4 \times 3 \times 2 \times 1}{3 \times 2 \times 1 \times 3 \times 2 \times 1} = \dfrac{6 \times 5 \times 4}{3 \times 2 \times 1} = 20$. The permutations formula is $_nP_r = \dfrac{n!}{(n-r)!}$

---

20. Given the following two sets of data:

Set P: {3, 4, 4, 4, 5, 5, 5, 6, 6, 8, 10, 10}

Set Q: {5, 5, 8, 8, 11, 11, 11, 11, 12, 12}

If one number is randomly selected from each set, what is the probability that the sum of the two numbers will be an even number?

Ⓐ   0.43
Ⓑ   0.47
Ⓒ   0.49
Ⓓ   0.53
Ⓔ   0.58

The sum of two numbers are even if they are either both even or both odd. First compute the probability that both selected numbers are even. Then compute the probability that both selected numbers are odd. Then add together the two probabilities. In Set P, 8 of the 12 numbers are even, and in Set Q, 4 of the 10 numbers are even. Therefore, the probability that both selected numbers are even is $\dfrac{8}{12} \times \dfrac{4}{10} = \dfrac{2}{3} \times \dfrac{2}{5} = \dfrac{4}{15}$. In Set P, 4 of the 12 numbers are odd, and in Set Q, 6 of the 10 numbers are odd. Therefore, the probability that both selected numbers are odd is $\dfrac{4}{12} \times \dfrac{6}{10} = \dfrac{1}{3} \times \dfrac{3}{5} = \dfrac{3}{15}$. Adding the two probabilities gives $\dfrac{4}{15} + \dfrac{3}{15} = \dfrac{7}{15} \approx 0.47$. Thus, answer choice **B** is correct.

Number Value	8	6	2	1
Number Quantity	3	4	6	7

21. Given the number distribution described in the table above, by how much does the mean exceed the median?

Ⓐ   0.65
Ⓑ   0.95
Ⓒ   1.15
Ⓓ   1.25
Ⓔ   1.35

Compute the mean and the median, and then subtract to find the difference. There are 20 numbers described in this distribution: 3 eights, 4 sixes, 6 twos, and 7 ones. One method to find the mean (average) would be to add up all 20 numbers and then divide by 20. Another method would add the four products (value × quantity) as follows: $(8 \times 3) + (6 \times 4) + (2 \times 6) + (1 \times 7) = 24 + 24 + 12 + 7 = 67$. Then divide by 20: $67 \div 20 = 3.35$. Next find the median. The median is the middle number when all the numbers are listed in order. Since there are 20 numbers total, the median is the average of the tenth and eleventh numbers. Since both of these numbers are 2, the median is 2. Therefore, the difference between the mean and median is $3.35 - 2 = 1.35$. The correct answer choice is **E.**

Word Problem Sample Questions

---

22. Barney can mow the lawn in 5 hours, and Fred can mow the same lawn in 4 hours. How long will it take them to mow the lawn if they work together?

   Ⓐ   5 hours

   Ⓑ $4\frac{1}{2}$ hours

   Ⓒ   4 hours

   Ⓓ $2\frac{2}{9}$ hours

   Ⓔ   1 hour

Some assumptions must be made in order to properly solve this type of "work" problem. You must assume that each worker (Barney and Fred) works independently and that the speed at which they work is not influenced by the fact that the other worker is also working. Also, assume they work at a constant rate.

Suppose that you are unfamiliar with the type of equation used for this type of problem. Try a "reasonable" approach. Because Fred can mow the lawn in 4 hours by himself, it will take less than 4 hours to mow the lawn if Barney helps him. Therefore, choices A, B, and C are not reasonable. Taking this logical method a little further, suppose that both Barney and Fred could each mow the lawn independently in 4 hours. Then together it would take them 2 hours to mow the lawn. Suppose that Barney and Fred could each mow the lawn independently in 5 hours. Then it would take them $2\frac{1}{2}$ hours to mow the lawn together. Thus, the time required for Barney and Fred to mow the lawn must be between 2 and $2\frac{1}{2}$. Therefore, the correct answer choice is **D**, $2\frac{2}{9}$ hours.

Using a more mathematical approach, the equation for this type of word problem would look like this: $\frac{1}{5}+\frac{1}{4}=\frac{1}{x}$, where the $\frac{1}{5}$ represents the part of the job Barney could do in 1 hour, the $\frac{1}{4}$ represents the part of the job Fred could do in one hour, and the $\frac{1}{x}$ represents the amount of lawn mowed in one hour. An alternative and more useful form on the equation would result by multiplying through by x giving:

$$\frac{x}{5}+\frac{x}{4}=1$$

This second form of the equation is useful if the workers do not work an equal amount of time. The numerator of each fraction on the left represents the time actually worked by each worker to finish the job. The denominator of each fraction on the left represents the time required for the workers to do the job alone. The "1" on the right side of the equation represents finishing "one complete job." Solve this equation as follows:

$$\frac{x}{5}+\frac{x}{4}=1$$
$$4x+5x=20$$
$$9x=20$$
$$x=\frac{20}{9}$$
$$x=2\frac{2}{9}$$

If the problem had presented different information, such as, "Fred was one hour late in starting to work on the job," then he would have worked one hour less than Barney. This would simply mean replacing the x in the first fraction with an "$x + 1$" OR replacing the x in the second fraction with an "$x - 1$". Then solve the equation as before.

23. An employee's annual salary was increased $15,000. If her new annual salary now equals $90,000, what was the percent increase in her salary?

   Ⓐ 15%

   Ⓑ $16\frac{2}{3}\%$

   Ⓒ 20%

   Ⓓ 22%

   Ⓔ 24%

Focus on what you are looking for. In this case, *percent increase*.

$\text{Percent Increase} = \dfrac{\text{Increase}}{\text{Starting Amount}} \times 100\%$. If the employee's annual salary was increased $15,000 to new annual salary of $90,000, then the starting annual salary was $90,000 − $15,000 = $75,000. Therefore,

$$\text{Percent Increase} = \frac{\text{Increase}}{\text{Starting Salary}} \times 100\% = \frac{15,000}{75,000} \times 100\% = 0.20 \times 100\% = 20\%$$

The correct answer choice is **C**.

> "Pulling" information out of the word problem structure can often give you a better look at what you are working with, and therefore, you gain additional insight into the problem. Organize this information on your scratch paper.

24. Five years from now, Ellen will be three times as old as Bryan. Fifteen years from now, Ellen will be twice as old as Bryan. How old is Ellen now?

   Ⓐ 5 years old

   Ⓑ 10 years old

   Ⓒ 15 years old

   Ⓓ 20 years old

   Ⓔ 25 years old

First, consider the more traditional method for solving an age problem. Construct a grid that organizes the variables and information you are given:

	Now	+5	+15
Ellen	E	$E + 5$	$E + 15$
Bryan	B	$B + 5$	$B + 15$

This method involves setting up two equations, one representing the "+5" time frame and the other representing the "+15" time frame, then solving to get the variable for the correct age now.

$$E + 5 = 3(B + 5) \qquad E + 15 = 2(B + 15)$$
$$E + 5 = 3B + 15 \qquad E + 15 = 2B + 30$$
$$E = 3B + 10 \qquad\quad E = 2B + 15$$

Since E is expressed as two different expressions, simply equate and solve for B:

$$3B + 10 = 2B + 15$$
$$3B = 2B + 5$$
$$B = 5$$

Therefore, Bryan is 5 years old now. *Be careful to choose the correct answer.* The question asked for the current age of Ellen, not Bryan. Don't be misled and choose (A), 5 years old, since this is Bryan's age now. Find Ellen's age now by substituting back in either of the previous equations:

$$E = 3B + 10 = 2B + 15$$
$$E = 3(5) + 10 = 2(5) + 15$$
$$E = 25$$

Therefore, answer choice **E** is correct.

If you try to solve for Ellen's age directly, you will probably run into more complex algebraic equations to solve. It is usually best to solve for the smallest value in the table and then adjust your answer.

A more logical approach might be to work from the answer choices to determine the correct answer. Picking different values for Ellen's age now and testing them to see if they work will lead to the correct answer, although it may take longer than simply solving the equations. Also, if this problem were not a multiple-choice problem, but a numeric entry "fill-in" question, you would have to work directly with the equations to determine the correct answer.

Data Interpretation Sample Questions

Questions 25–27 are based on the following data:

Product	Total Unit Sales
V	600
W	1,000
X	800
Y	700
Z	900

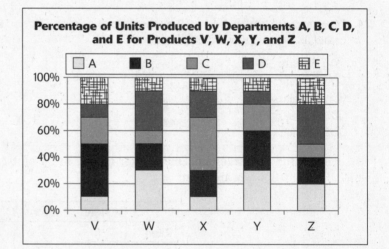

Percentage of Units Produced by Departments A, B, C, D, and E for Products V, W, X, Y, and Z

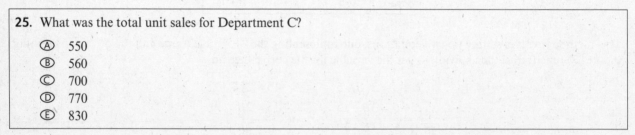

25. What was the total unit sales for Department C?

Ⓐ 550
Ⓑ 560
Ⓒ 700
Ⓓ 770
Ⓔ 830

First calculate the number of units produced by Department C for each of the six Products and add them together:

(20% of 600) + (10% of 1,000) + (40% of 800) + (20% of 700) + (10% of 900) = 120 + 100 + 320 + 140 + 90 = 770. Therefore, answer choice **D** is the correct answer.

26. What percent of the total unit sales for Department D came from Product X?

    Ⓐ   15.4%

    Ⓑ   16.1%

    Ⓒ   17.4%

    Ⓓ   18.6%

    Ⓔ   20.0%

First calculate the number of units produced by Department D for each of the six Products and add them together. Then divide the number of units that came from Product X by that total:

(10% of 600) + (30% of 1,000) + (20% of 800) + (10% of 700) + (30% of 900) = 60 + 300 + 160 + 70 + 270 = 860. Dividing Product X units by the total gives 160 ÷ 860 = 0.186 = 18.6%. Therefore answer choice **D** is the correct answer. Be careful to divide by the correct total, 860, not 800.

27. For Department B, what was the ratio of unit sales for Product V to Product X?

    Ⓐ $\dfrac{2}{3}$

    Ⓑ $\dfrac{1}{1}$

    Ⓒ $\dfrac{3}{2}$

    Ⓓ $\dfrac{2}{1}$

    Ⓔ $\dfrac{5}{2}$

Calculate the number of unit sales of Department B for Products V and X, and divide. $\dfrac{40\% \text{ of } 600}{20\% \text{ of } 800} = \dfrac{240}{160} = \dfrac{3}{2}$.
Thus, answer choice **C** is the correct answer. Do not calculate more than the items you need.

Questions 28–30 are based on the following data:

Distribution by Teacher of 1,440 Mathematics Students				
	% of Students	# of Male Students	% of Male Students Passing Class	% of Female Students Passing Class
Teacher A	20	175	85	75
Teacher B	20	180	70	75
Teacher C	20	150	75	65
Teacher D	25	260	65	80
Teacher E	15	180	55	55

28. Which teacher passed the greatest number of female students?

    Ⓐ   Teacher A

    Ⓑ   Teacher B

    Ⓒ   Teacher C

    Ⓓ   Teacher D

    Ⓔ   Teacher E

We know the percent of female students who were passed by each teacher, but we need to know the number of female students assigned to each teacher. We can calculate this by first finding the total number of students assigned to each teacher and then subtracting the number of male students.

	# of Students	# of Female Students	# of Female Students Passing Class
Teacher A	20% of 1,440 = 288	288 − 175 = 113	75% of 113 = 85
Teacher B	20% of 1,440 = 288	288 − 180 = 108	75% of 108 = 81
Teacher C	20% of 1,440 = 288	288 − 150 = 138	65% of 138 = 90
Teacher D	25% of 1,440 = 360	360 − 260 = 100	80% of 100 = 80
Teacher E	15% of 1,440 = 216	216 − 180 = 36	55% of 36 = 20

We see that Teacher C passed approximately 90 female students, more than any other teacher, thus, answer choice **C** is the correct answer.

---

29. What percent of Teacher C's students were male?

 Ⓐ 43%
 Ⓑ 49%
 Ⓒ 52%
 Ⓓ 56%
 Ⓔ 60%

From the table calculated in the previous problem, we see that there were 288 students assigned to Teacher C, and 150 of the students were male. Therefore, the percent of male students in Teacher C's class is 150 ÷ 288 = 0.52 = 52%. Thus, answer choice **C** is correct.

---

30. Teacher A passed approximately what percent of her students?

 Ⓐ 78%
 Ⓑ 79%
 Ⓒ 80%
 Ⓓ 81%
 Ⓔ 82%

First, we notice that all the answer choices are close together in value. This means, of course, that more accuracy is required in the calculations. To answer this problem, we need to calculate the number of male and female students in Teacher A's class as well as the percent who passed. We know from the tables above that Teacher A passed 85 female students. Since Teacher A passed 85% of the 175 male students in her class, she passed 85% of 175 = 149 male students. Therefore, Teacher A passed 85 female students and 149 male students from the total of 288 students. Thus, (149 + 85) ÷ 288 = 0.8125, which is approximately 81%. So, answer choice **D** is the closest and therefore the correct choice.

We know from the original given information that since 85% of male students and 75% of female students passed Teacher A's class, the overall percentage must be between them. But additionally, since there were more male students in the class than female, the overall percentage would have to be closer to 85% than 75%, or more than 80%. So, if you were running out of time or didn't know how to proceed, your guess would be narrowed down to either choice D or E.

Practice Multiple-Choice (Select One Answer Choice) Questions

Easy to Moderate

1. If $3x = -9$, then $3x^3 - 2x + 4 =$

   Ⓐ −83
   Ⓑ −71
   Ⓒ −47
   Ⓓ −17
   Ⓔ 61

2. In the sequence 8, 9, 12, 17, 24. . . the next number would be

   Ⓐ 29
   Ⓑ 30
   Ⓒ 33
   Ⓓ 35
   Ⓔ 41

3. A third-grade class is composed of 16 girls and 12 boys. There are 2 teacher-aides in the class. The ratio of girls to boys to teacher-aides is

   Ⓐ 16 : 12 : 1
   Ⓑ 8 : 6 : 2
   Ⓒ 8 : 6 : 1
   Ⓓ 8 : 3 : 1
   Ⓔ 4 : 3 : 1

4. If $4a + 2 = 10$, then $8a + 4 =$

   Ⓐ 5
   Ⓑ 16
   Ⓒ 20
   Ⓓ 24
   Ⓔ 28

5. The closest approximation of $\dfrac{69.28 \times 0.004}{0.03}$ is

   Ⓐ 0.092
   Ⓑ 0.92
   Ⓒ 9.2
   Ⓓ 92
   Ⓔ 920

6. In a survey of students that was conducted at a junior high school, 30% of the students said they like broccoli and 15% of the students said they like spinach. If every one of the students who said they like spinach also said they like broccoli, what fraction of the students responding to the survey said they liked at least one of the two vegetables?

   Ⓐ $\dfrac{3}{20}$

   Ⓑ $\dfrac{3}{10}$

   Ⓒ $\dfrac{9}{20}$

   Ⓓ $\dfrac{11}{20}$

   Ⓔ $\dfrac{7}{10}$

7. At checkout in a supermarket, 45% of shoppers ask for a paper bag, 60% pay by credit card, and 10% ask for a paper bag and pay by credit card. What is the probability that a shopper will use a credit card given that they have asked for a paper bag?

   Ⓐ 0.133
   Ⓑ 0.167
   Ⓒ 0.222
   Ⓓ 0.550
   Ⓔ 0.700

8. Teachers at a private college are on a 3-step salary schedule earning $32,000 on step 1, $42,000 on step 2, and $52,000 on step 3. If 60% of the teachers are on step 3, with the remaining teachers split evenly on the other two steps, what is the mean salary of the teachers?

   Ⓐ $44,000
   Ⓑ $45,000
   Ⓒ $46,000
   Ⓓ $46,600
   Ⓔ $46,800

9. Professor Goodnotes has kept records of all the grades he has given to former students. He has given 18% A's, 26% B's, 34% C's, 12% D's, and 10% F's. If a former student did not get a D or F, what is the probability that the student got a B?

   Ⓐ 0.220
   Ⓑ 0.260
   Ⓒ 0.333
   Ⓓ 0.380
   Ⓔ 0.780

Use the following information for questions 10–12.

The following tables represent how male and female students voted on a petition to increase fees to pay for additional security on campus. One newspaper reporter said that more males favored the petition than females. A second reporter said that if you consider daytime and evening students separately, the opposite is true.

	Students	
	Male	Female
Yes	242	159
No	325	274

	Daytime Students	
	Male	Female
Yes	80	135
No	210	260

	Evening Students	
	Male	Female
Yes	162	24
No	115	14

10. What percentage of male students favor the petition?

   Ⓐ 28%
   Ⓑ 37%
   Ⓒ 43%
   Ⓓ 58%
   Ⓔ 67%

11. What percentage of female evening students favor the petition?

   Ⓐ 34%
   Ⓑ 37%
   Ⓒ 40%
   Ⓓ 58%
   Ⓔ 63%

12. What percentage of students are daytime students?

   Ⓐ 32%
   Ⓑ 40%
   Ⓒ 46%
   Ⓓ 54%
   Ⓔ 69%

Average

Use the following information for question 13.

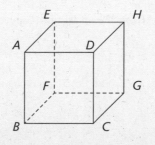

13. In the figure above, *AB* is one edge of a cube. If *AB* equals 5, what is the surface area of the cube?

    Ⓐ 25
    Ⓑ 100
    Ⓒ 125
    Ⓓ 150
    Ⓔ 300

14. Which of the following is the largest?

    Ⓐ half of 30% of 280
    Ⓑ one-third of 70% of 160
    Ⓒ twice 50% of 30
    Ⓓ three times 40% of 40
    Ⓔ 60% of 60

15. If $n! = (1)(2)(3)\cdots(n)$, what is the value of $\dfrac{(6!)(4!)}{(5!)(3!)}$?

    Ⓐ $\dfrac{5}{4}$

    Ⓑ $\dfrac{8}{5}$

    Ⓒ 10

    Ⓓ 24

    Ⓔ 1,152

Use the following information for question 16.

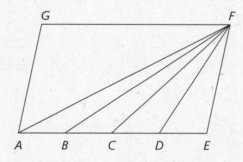

16. In parallelogram *AEFG* above, if *AB* = *BC* = *CD* = *DE*, what is the ratio of the area of triangle *CDF* to the area of triangle *ABF* ?

    Ⓐ 1 : 4
    Ⓑ 1 : 1
    Ⓒ 2 : 1
    Ⓓ 4 : 1
    Ⓔ The ratio cannot be determined from the information given.

Use the following information for questions 17–19.

The following table represents the election results of a ballot proposal:

	Freshman	Sophomore	Junior	Senior
Yes	210	180	110	130
No	165	210	245	140

17. Which of the following orders represents approval percentages from highest to lowest?

   Ⓐ Freshman, Sophomore, Junior, Senior
   Ⓑ Freshman, Senior, Sophomore, Junior
   Ⓒ Senior, Freshman, Junior, Sophomore
   Ⓓ Senior, Sophomore, Freshman, Junior
   Ⓔ Sophomore, Senior, Junior, Freshman

18. What percent of the "yes" votes were sophomores?

   Ⓐ 13%
   Ⓑ 21%
   Ⓒ 29%
   Ⓓ 47%
   Ⓔ 86%

19. Which class had an approval percentage closest to the overall school approval percentage?

   Ⓐ Freshman
   Ⓑ Sophomore
   Ⓒ Junior
   Ⓓ Senior
   Ⓔ Not enough information in the table to determine the answer.

20. The average of 9 numbers is 7, and the average of 7 numbers is 9. What is the average of all 16 numbers?

   Ⓐ 8

   Ⓑ $7\frac{7}{8}$

   Ⓒ $7\frac{1}{2}$

   Ⓓ $7\frac{1}{4}$

   Ⓔ $7\frac{1}{8}$

Use the following information for question 21.

8	1	6
3	5	7
4	9	2

21. The figure above consists of 9 small squares and is called a "magic square" because the total of the numbers added horizontally, vertically, or diagonally are all equal. If the total of the two diagonal rows are subtracted from the total of the three horizontal rows, the result obtained will equal

    Ⓐ   two-thirds a diagonal row
    Ⓑ   three-halves a diagonal row
    Ⓒ   any vertical row
    Ⓓ   double a horizontal row
    Ⓔ   one-half a horizontal row

22. Jane is six years older than Tom, and Tom is five years younger than Phillip. Chris is three years older than Tom. If Jane's age is expressed as J, what is the sum of the ages of Jane, Tom, Phillip, and Chris in terms of J?

    Ⓐ $4J - 10$
    Ⓑ $J - 9$
    Ⓒ $3J - 6$
    Ⓓ $4J + 12$
    Ⓔ $J + 14$

23. If $6x - 3y = 30$ and $4x = 2 - y$, what is the value of $x + y$?

    Ⓐ   2
    Ⓑ   −4
    Ⓒ   −6
    Ⓓ   −8
    Ⓔ   −10

Use the following information for question 24.

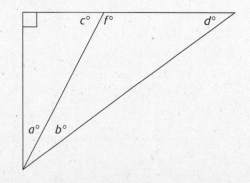

24. In the right triangle above, $c° = 2a°$ and $d° > 2b°$. Which of the following statements must be true?

    Ⓐ $c° > b° + d°$
    Ⓑ   angle a is greater than angle b
    Ⓒ   angle a equals angle b
    Ⓓ   angle b is greater than angle a
    Ⓔ   angle d equals twice angle a

Use the following information for question 25.

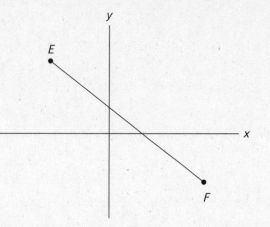

25. If point *E* has coordinates (−3,5) and point *F* has coordinates (6,−7), then the length of *EF* =

Ⓐ 21
Ⓑ 15
Ⓒ 7
Ⓓ 5
Ⓔ 3

26. You are designing a game for a Las Vegas casino. People will buy tickets and then be allowed to select a box that contains a cash prize. Fifty percent of the boxes are empty. Thirty percent contain $5. Fifteen percent contain $20. Four percent contain $50. Three-quarters of one percent contain $100. One-quarter of one percent contain $1,000. What is the expected value of each selection?

Ⓐ $8.50
Ⓑ $8.75
Ⓒ $9.50
Ⓓ $9.75
Ⓔ $10.25

27. If $ab \neq 0$, then $\dfrac{a+8b}{8a} - \dfrac{a+2b}{2a} =$

Ⓐ $-\dfrac{3}{8}$

Ⓑ $\dfrac{-3a-16b}{8a}$

Ⓒ 0

Ⓓ $\dfrac{3a+6b}{8a}$

Ⓔ $\dfrac{10b}{8a}$

28. What is the area of a square in square inches if its perimeter is 10 feet?

Ⓐ 6.25
Ⓑ 25
Ⓒ 400
Ⓓ 900
Ⓔ 1,600

29. If x and y are integers such that $2 < y < 25$ and $5 < x < 13$, then the largest possible value of $\frac{y}{x} + \frac{x}{y}$ is

   Ⓐ $\frac{1}{2}$

   Ⓑ 4

   Ⓒ $4\frac{1}{4}$

   Ⓓ 8

   Ⓔ 10

30. Mary will be y years old x years from now. How old will she be z years from now?

   Ⓐ $y - x + z$

   Ⓑ $y + x + z$

   Ⓒ $y + x - z$

   Ⓓ $y - x - z$

   Ⓔ $x + z - y$

Use the following information for questions 31–33.

Four departments in a company, A, B, C, and D, are responsible for sales of the four different products, W, X, Y, and Z, that the company sells. The stacked bar chart below shows the sales records of units sold by each of the four departments. During the reporting period represented by the chart, the company sold the same number of units of each of the four products.

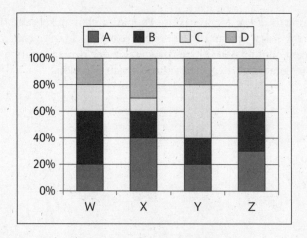

31. Which department sold 25% of all units sold by the company?

   Ⓐ Department A

   Ⓑ Department B

   Ⓒ Department C

   Ⓓ Department D

   Ⓔ Cannot be determined from the information given in the chart.

32. Which departments sold the same number of units?

   Ⓐ Department A and Department B

   Ⓑ Department A and Department C

   Ⓒ Department B and Department C

   Ⓓ Department B and Department D

   Ⓔ Department C and Department D

33. If Department B sold 30 units of product X, how many units of product Z did Department C sell?

   Ⓐ 30

   Ⓑ 35

   Ⓒ 40

   Ⓓ 45

   Ⓔ Cannot be determined from the information given in the chart.

34. As a payment for helping at home, you have been given a choice of either a flat payment of $5, or a chance of randomly drawing a bill from a box. The box contains one $100 bill, two $20 bills, seven $10 bills, ten $5 bills, and thirty $1 bills. Which choice gives you the greatest expected payment?

   Ⓐ Flat payment because the expected value of selecting a bill from the box is less than $5.

   Ⓑ Flat payment because the expected value of selecting a bill from the box is equal to $5 and it is better to have a sure thing.

   Ⓒ Draw from the box because the expected value of selecting a bill from the box is greater than $5.

   Ⓓ Draw from the box because the expected value of selecting a bill from the box is equal to $5, so you have nothing to lose.

   Ⓔ Flat payment because the expected value of selecting from the box cannot be determined.

For questions 35–37, use the information in the following table. The information came from 272 employment applications. Some were handwritten and some were typed. Some contained mistakes and some did not.

	Mistakes	No Mistakes	Total
Typed	38	66	104
Handwritten	122	46	168
Total	160	112	272

35. What is the probability that an application was typed and had no mistakes?

   Ⓐ 0.243

   Ⓑ 0.449

   Ⓒ 0.551

   Ⓓ 0.589

   Ⓔ 0.635

36. What is the probability that an application was typed, given that mistakes were made?

   Ⓐ 0.140

   Ⓑ 0.238

   Ⓒ 0.365

   Ⓓ 0.589

   Ⓔ 0.831

37. What is the probability that an application was handwritten or had mistakes?

   Ⓐ 0.243

   Ⓑ 0.449

   Ⓒ 0.726

   Ⓓ 0.757

   Ⓔ 0.762

38. On a recent administration of a state bar exam, 22% of the test-takers passed the test, 78% of those who passed were first-time test-takers, and 60% of those who failed were first-time test-takers. What percent of first-time test-takers passed the test?

Ⓐ 17%
Ⓑ 27%
Ⓒ 47%
Ⓓ 64%
Ⓔ 73%

39. If m and n are integers and $\sqrt{mn} = 10$, which of the following CANNOT be a value of $m + n$?

Ⓐ 25
Ⓑ 29
Ⓒ 50
Ⓓ 52
Ⓔ 101

Above Average to Difficult

40. How many times does the digit "8" appear in all the integers between 200 and 1,200?

Ⓐ 120
Ⓑ 210
Ⓒ 300
Ⓓ 320
Ⓔ 360

41. If x, y, and z are consecutive negative integers, not necessarily in that order, which of the following may be true?

Ⓐ $x + y > z$
Ⓑ $xy < z$
Ⓒ $z + y = y + x$
Ⓓ $2x = \dfrac{yz}{2}$
Ⓔ $x + y = z$

42. How many pounds of tea worth 93¢ per pound must be mixed with tea worth 75¢ per pound to produce 10 pounds worth 85¢ per pound?

Ⓐ $2\dfrac{2}{9}$

Ⓑ $3\dfrac{1}{2}$

Ⓒ $4\dfrac{4}{9}$

Ⓓ $5\dfrac{5}{9}$

Ⓔ $9\dfrac{1}{2}$

43. If m is an integer such that $-5 < m < 2$, and n is an integer such that $-4 < n < 5$, what is the least possible value for $3m^2 - 2n$?

Ⓐ -85
Ⓑ -75
Ⓒ -10
Ⓓ -8
Ⓔ 0

44. If # is a binary operation such that $a \# b$ is defined as $\dfrac{a^2 + b^2}{a^2 - b^2}$ and $a^2 - b^2 \neq 0$, then what is the value of $a \# b$ if $2a = b$ and $a \neq 0$?

Ⓐ $1\dfrac{1}{3}$

Ⓑ $\dfrac{3}{5}$

Ⓒ $-\dfrac{1}{2}$

Ⓓ $-\dfrac{3}{5}$

Ⓔ $-1\dfrac{2}{3}$

45. The product of x and y is a constant. If the value of x is increased by 50%, by what percentage must the value of y be decreased?

Ⓐ 50%
Ⓑ 40%
Ⓒ $33\dfrac{1}{3}\%$
Ⓓ 25%
Ⓔ 20%

46. The following graph represents the relative frequency of test scores on a recent exam taken by students in a local school.

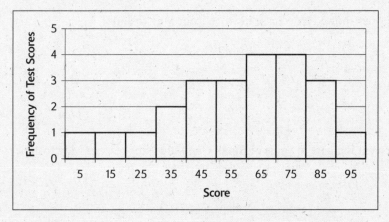

Approximately what percentage of students scored between 50 and 80?

Ⓐ 44%
Ⓑ 46%
Ⓒ 48%
Ⓓ 50%
Ⓔ 52%

47. Tom is filling a bathtub with hot and cold water. Running by itself, the hot water tap would fill the tub in exactly 40 minutes. The cold water tap, running by itself, would fill the tub in exactly 20 minutes. With the plug out, it takes 30 minutes to empty a full tub. Tom accidentally leaves the plug out of the tub. When Tom checks on the tub 16 minutes after turning on the hot and cold water, he finds the tub

Ⓐ empty
Ⓑ one-third full
Ⓒ one-half full
Ⓓ two-thirds full
Ⓔ overflowing

Questions 48–50 use the following data:

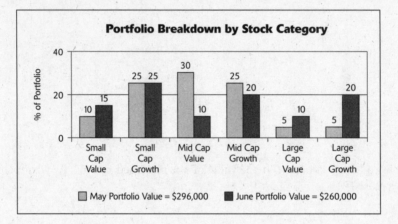

48. By how many dollars did the value of the Growth stocks in the portfolio change from May to June?

Ⓐ $6,200
Ⓑ $8,600
Ⓒ $10,000
Ⓓ $16,600
Ⓔ $24,200

49. How many categories showed a decrease in value from May to June?

Ⓐ 0
Ⓑ 1
Ⓒ 2
Ⓓ 3
Ⓔ 4

50. What was the percent increase in value of Small Cap Value stocks from May to June?

Ⓐ 5%
Ⓑ 9.4%
Ⓒ 24%
Ⓓ 32%
Ⓔ 50%

Answers and Explanations for Practice Multiple-Choice (Select One Answer Choice) Questions

Easy to Moderate

1. **B.** First solving $3x - 9$, $x = -3$. Now plug the value of x into $3x^3 - 2x + 4$:

$$3x^3 - 2x + 4$$
$$3(-3)^3 - 2(-3) + 4$$
$$3(-27) + 6 + 4$$
$$-81 + 10$$
$$-71$$

2. **C.** Start by taking a closer look at the sequence: 8, 9, 12, 17, 24 . . .

$$9 - 8 = 1 \qquad 12 - 9 = 3 \qquad 17 - 12 = 5 \qquad 24 - 17 = 7$$

The difference between successive pairs of numbers increases by 2. Hence, the difference between 24 and the next term must be 9. Therefore, the next term is 33.

3. **C.** Girls to boys to teacher-aides are in proportion 16 to 12 to 2. Ratios should be written in reduced form. Dividing each number by 2 gives a ratio of $8 : 6 : 1$.

4. **C.** One approach to answering this question is solving $4a + 2 = 10$ for a:

$$4a + 2 = 10$$
$$4a = 8$$
$$a = 2$$

Now, substituting 2 for a: $8a + 4 = 8(2) + 4 = 20$.

A faster way to solve this problem is to notice that the quantity $8a + 4$ is twice the size of the quantity $4a + 2$. Therefore the value of $8a + 4$ must be twice the value of $4a + 2$. Thus, the answer must be twice 10, or 20.

5. **C.** This problem is most easily completed by rearranging and approximating as follows: $\dfrac{69.28 \times 0.004}{0.03} = \dfrac{69.28}{1} \times \dfrac{0.004}{0.03} \approx 69 \times 0.13 \approx 9$. Therefore, the only reasonable answer is 9.2.

6. **B.** Since spinach is a subset of broccoli, $P(S \cup B) = P(B) = 0.30 = \dfrac{3}{10}$.

7. **C.** We need to calculate the conditional probability of using a credit card given that they ask for a paper bag. Using a diagram to organize the data will help.

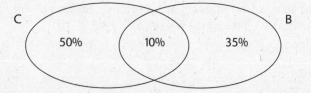

The Paper Bag oval (B) must total to 45% and the Credit Card oval (C) must total 60%. Since you are asked for the probability of Credit given bag, we divide the Credit Card portion of the Bag oval by the total in the Bag oval. Therefore: $P(C \text{ given } B) = \dfrac{0.10}{0.45} = 0.222$. Statistically, this is written as follows:

$$P(C) = 0.6$$
$$P(B) = 0.45$$
$$P(B \text{ and } C) = 0.10$$
$$P(C|B) = \frac{P(B \text{ and } C)}{P(B)} = \frac{0.10}{0.45} = 0.222$$

(The vertical bar between the C and B means "given that.")

8. **C.** The mean (average) salary is the sum of the products of the values of the salaries and their respective probabilities.

$$\text{Mean} = (32,000)(0.2) + (42,000)(0.2) + (52,000)(0.6) = 46,000$$

9. **C.** Eliminate the percentages for the D and F grades. Divide the percentage for the B grade by the sum of the percentages for the A, B, and C grades.

$$P(B) = \frac{0.26}{0.18 + 0.26 + 0.34} = 0.333$$

10. **C.** Totals can be added to each of the charts (see below).

Students		
	Male	**Female**
Yes	242	159
No	325	274
	567	433

Daytime Students		
	Male	**Female**
Yes	80	135
No	210	260
	290	395

Evening Students		
	Male	**Female**
Yes	162	24
No	115	14
	277	38

Divide the "yes" votes by the total. $\frac{242}{567} = 0.427 = 43\%$

11. **E.** Divide the "yes" votes by the total. $\frac{24}{38} = 0.631 = 63\%$

12. **E.** Divide the total number of daytime students by the total number of students.
$\frac{290 + 395}{567 + 433} = \frac{685}{1,000} = 0.685 \approx 69\%$

Average

13. **D.** Since one edge of the cube is 5, all edges equal 5. Therefore, the area of one face of the cube is (5)(5) = 25. Since a cube has 6 equal faces, its surface area will be (6)(25) = 150.

14. **D.** Calculate the value of each:

　　A. (0.5)(0.3)(280) = 42

　　B. (0.33)(0.7)(160) = 36.96

　　C. (2)(0.5)(30) = 30

　　D. (3)(0.4)(40) = 48

　　E. (0.6)(60) = 36

At 48, choice D is the largest.

15. D. $\dfrac{(6!)(4!)}{(5!)(3!)} = \dfrac{(6 \cdot 5 \cdot 4 \cdot 3 \cdot 2 \cdot 1)(4 \cdot 3 \cdot 2 \cdot 1)}{(5 \cdot 4 \cdot 3 \cdot 2 \cdot 1)(3 \cdot 2 \cdot 1)} = \dfrac{(6)(4)}{1} = 24$

16. B. In parallelogram *AEFG*, all the small triangles have the same base and they all meet at *F*, giving them all the same height. The area formula for a triangle is $A = \frac{1}{2}bh$, therefore all the small triangles have equal areas. Therefore, the ratio of the area of triangle *CDF* to the area of triangle *ABF* is 1:1 (choice B).

17. B. To answer this question, add totals to the chart.

	Freshman	Sophomore	Junior	Senior	Total
Yes	210	180	110	130	630
No	165	210	245	140	760
Total	375	390	355	270	1,390

Calculate the "yes" percentage for each class.

Freshman: $\dfrac{210}{375} = 0.560$

Sophomore: $\dfrac{180}{390} = 0.462$

Junior: $\dfrac{110}{355} = 0.310$

Senior: $\dfrac{130}{270} = 0.481$

Ordered from highest to lowest is: Freshman, Senior, Sophomore, Junior (choice B).

18. C. There were 630 "yes" votes and 180 were cast by sophomores. Therefore, divide 180 by 630. $\dfrac{180}{630} = 0.2857 = 29\%$

19. B. The overall approval percentage is $\dfrac{630}{1,390} = 0.453 = 45\%$. Using the results from explanation for question 17, the approval percentage of Sophomores is the closest at 46%.

20. B. If the average of 9 numbers is 7, then the sum of these numbers must be $(9)(7) = 63$. If the average of 7 numbers is 9, then the sum of these numbers must be $(7)(9) = 63$. The sum of all 16 numbers must be $63 + 63$, or 126. Therefore, the average of all 16 numbers must be $\dfrac{126}{16} = \dfrac{63}{8} = 7\dfrac{7}{8}$.

21. C. Since all rows are equal, subtracting 2 rows from 3 rows gives a result of 1 row, either vertical, horizontal, or diagonal.

22. A.

Jane: Jane = *J*

Tom: Since Jane is six years older than Tom, Tom is six years less than Jane, or Tom = $J - 6$

Chris: Since Chris is three years older than Tom, add three to Tom to get Chris's age. Chris = $J - 6 + 3 = J - 3$

Phillip: Tom is five years younger than Phillip, so Phillip is five years older than Tom. So add five to Tom to get Phillip's age. Phillip = $J - 6 + 5 = J - 1$

The sum of their ages is $J + (J - 6) + (J - 3) + (J - 1) = 4J - 10$ (choice A).

23. B. We solve simultaneously:
$$6x - 3y = 30$$
$$4x + y = 2$$

Multiply the bottom equation by 3 and add the two equations together to isolate x.

$$
\begin{array}{r}
6x - 3y = 30 \\
\underline{12x + 3y = 6} \\
18x = 36 \\
x = 2
\end{array}
$$

Substitute $x = 2$ back into one of the original equations, and we find that $y = -6$. Thus, their sum is -4.

24. **B.** In the right triangle, if $c° = 2a°$, then angle $a = 30°$ and angle $c = 60°$, since there are a total of $180°$ in a triangle. Because angle f is supplementary to angle c, angle f must be $120°$. If angle f is $120°$, then there are $60°$ left to be divided between angles d and b. Because $d > 2b$, b must be less than $30°$; therefore, the correct answer is **B**; angle a ($30°$) is greater than angle b (less than $30°$). Notice the way you should have marked the diagram to assist you.

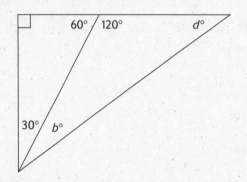

25. **B.** If two points have coordinates (x_1, y_1) and (x_2, y_2), the distance between these points is defined to be $D = \sqrt{(x_2 - x_1)^2 + (y_2 - y_1)^2}$. Since point E has coordinates of $(-3,5)$ and point F has coordinates of $(6,-7)$, the distance between E and F is:

$$
\begin{aligned}
D &= \sqrt{(x_2 - x_1)^2 + (y_2 - y_1)^2} \\
&= \sqrt{(6 - (-3))^2 + ((-7) - 5)^2} \\
&= \sqrt{(9)^2 + (-12)^2} \\
&= \sqrt{225} \\
&= 15
\end{aligned}
$$

26. **D.** The expected value, or mean, is the sum of the products of the values of the boxes and their respective probabilities.

$$E(x) = (0)(0.5) + (5)(0.3) + (20)(0.15) + (50)(0.04) + (100)(0.0075) + (1,000)(0.0025) = 9.75$$

27. **A.** Using $8a$ as a common denominator:

$$\frac{a + 8b}{8a} - \frac{a + 2b}{2a} = \frac{a + 8b}{8a} - \frac{4a + 8b}{8a} = \frac{-3a}{8a} = -\frac{3}{8}$$

28. **D.** Perimeter = 10 feet = $(10)(12)$ inches = 120 inches

Perimeter = $4s$ (where s = length of side)

$4s = 120$, so $s = 30$. Next, find the area:

Area = $s^2 = 30^2 = 900$ square inches

29. **C.** To obtain the largest sum of $\frac{y}{x} + \frac{x}{y}$, make the numerators as large as possible and the denominators as small as possible. So, for $\frac{y}{x}$, y is 24 and x is 6. Therefore, $\frac{y}{x} = \frac{24}{6} = 4$. For $\frac{x}{y}$, x is 6 and y is 24. So, $\frac{x}{y} = \frac{6}{24} = \frac{1}{4}$. Therefore, the largest sum of both fractions is $4 + \frac{1}{4} = 4\frac{1}{4}$. You can also use the opposite extremes of $x = 12$ and $y = 3$ to get the same answer: $\frac{12}{3} + \frac{3}{12}$ is also $4 + \frac{1}{4} = 4\frac{1}{4}$.

30. **A.** Because Mary will be y years old x years from now, she is $y - x$ years old now. Hence, z years from now she will be $y - x + z$ years old.

31. **C.** The total number of units sold is not given, but we know that the number of units sold for each product is the same. For ease of computation, assume that 100 units of each product were sold by the company. This gives a total of 400 units for the four products. The number of units sold by each department can be calculated.

    If the total units sold is 400 then:

    Units sold by Department A: 20% of 100 + 40% of 100 + 20% of 100 + 30% of 100 = 110

    Units sold by Department B: 40% of 100 + 20% of 100 + 20% of 100 + 30% of 100 = 110

    Units sold by Department C: 20% of 100 + 10% of 100 + 40% of 100 + 30% of 100 = 100

    Units sold by Department D: 20% of 100 + 30% of 100 + 20% of 100 + 10% of 100 = 80

    The percentage sold by Department C is 25% of 400.

32. **A.** From the information derived in the previous answer, Department A and Department B both sold the same number of units.

33. **D.** Department B sold 20% of the total units of product X. If this is 30 units, then the total number of units sold of product X must be 150. Since the total number of units sold of each product is the same, 150 units of product Z were sold by the company. Since Department C sold 30% of the units sold of product Z, Department C sold 45 units of product Z.

34. **C.** In order to determine what choice should be made, the average value of a bill chosen from the box must be calculated. There are 50 bills in the box. Add together the products of the various bill values and their respective quantities. Then divide by 50, the total number of bills in the box.

$$\text{Average} = \frac{(100)(1) + (20)(2) + (10)(7) + (5)(10) + (1)(30)}{50} = \frac{290}{50} = 5.80$$

The average bill value is greater than \$5. Notice that this is nothing more than determining the total value of the bills in the box and dividing by the number of bills.

35. **A.** This intersection is read directly from the table. (You will not be required to know the statistical symbolism for intersection.) Out of the total of 272, 66 were typed with no mistakes.

$$P(\text{T} \cap \text{N}) = \frac{66}{272} = 0.243$$

36. **B.** This is a conditional probability. We want to know the probability it was typed given that mistakes were made. This isolates the "mistakes" column. The total for the "mistakes" column is 160. Out of these, 38 were typed. (The vertical bar between the T and M means "given that.")

$$P(\text{T} | \text{M}) = \frac{38}{160} = 0.238$$

37. **D.** This is union of a row and column in the table. Add in any values in either the "handwritten" row or the "mistakes" column. (You will not be required to know the statistical symbolism for union.)

$$P(\text{H} \cup \text{M}) = \frac{38 + 122 + 46}{272} = 0.757$$

38. B. This problem may be solved with the help of either a table or a tree-diagram.

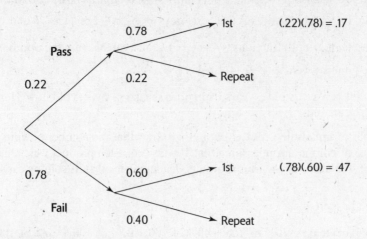

Note that you do not have to write down the probabilities or names on paths you do not use. In this case, the "repeat" values are not used. From the drawing above, the total for the first-time test-takers is $0.17 + 0.47 = 0.64$. Out of this total, 0.17 passed the test. Divide to get the answer.

$$P(P|F) = \frac{0.17}{0.17 + 0.47} = \frac{0.17}{0.64} = 0.27$$

Using a table gives the same information.

	Pass	Fail	Total
First Time	$(0.78)(0.22) = 0.17$	$(0.60)(0.78) = 0.47$	0.64
Repeat	$(0.22)(0.22) = 0.05$	$(0.04)(0.78) = 0.31$	0.36
Totals	0.22	0.78	1.00

Again, it is not necessary to fill in what you do not need.

39. C. Because $\sqrt{mn} = 10$ and $mn = 100$, the possible values for m and n are 1 and 100, 2 and 50, 4 and 25, 5 and 20, and 10 and 10. Because none of these combinations yield a sum of 50, choice C is correct.

Above Average to Difficult

40. C. Although writing out all 1,001 integers from 200 through 1,200 and counting the 8s would certainly work, it clearly is not the best method. One method would be to examine each digit position individually.

Ones digit: 100 groups of 10 with one 8 in each group = 100 8s.

Tens digit: 10 groups of 100 with ten 8s in each group = 100 8s.

Hundreds digit: 1 group of 100 with one hundred 8s = 100 8s.

Therefore, the digit 8 appears 300 times in the integers from 200 to 1,200. The correct answer choice is C.

41. E. Since x, y, and z are consecutive negative integers, try plugging in values to test each choice. For example, x, y, and z could equal -1, -2, and -3 (not necessarily in that order) or, for that matter, -8, -9, and -10. Only choice E may be true, and that will occur if x equals -1, y equals -2, and z equals -3. Choice A is eliminated since the sum of any two consecutive negative integers is less than or equal to the third, not greater than. Choice B is eliminated since the product of any two of the negative integers would be positive, and therefore greater than, not less than, the third. Choice C is eliminated since x and z are of different value. Choice D is eliminated since $2x$ is negative and $\frac{yz}{2}$ must be positive.

42. **D.** The only reasonable answer is $5\frac{5}{9}$, because 85¢ per pound is slightly closer to 93¢ per pound than to 75¢ per pound. Therefore, since the average of 85¢ is closer to 93¢, slightly more than half of the 10 pounds must be valued at 93¢ per pound.

Algebraically, if we let x stand for the quantity in pounds of 93¢ tea, then $10 - x$ can be used to represent the quantity of the 75¢ tea. This leads to the equation

$$0.93x + 0.75(10 - x) = 0.85(10)$$
$$93x + 75(10 - x) = 850$$
$$93x + 750 - 75x = 850$$
$$18x = 100$$
$$x = \frac{100}{18}$$
$$x = 5\frac{5}{9}$$

43. **D.** First examine what you are trying to minimize. The first term, $3m^2$, must be positive or could be zero if m is zero. To minimize the second term, $2n$, n should be as large as possible. Therefore, let $m = 0$ and $n = 4$. Therefore, $3m^2 - 2n = 3(0)^2 - 2(4) = 0 - 8 = -8$.

44. **E.** Since $2a = b$, substitute in the formula:

$$a \# b = \frac{a^2 + b^2}{a^2 - b^2} = \frac{a^2 + (2a)^2}{a^2 - (2a)^2} = \frac{a^2 + 4a^2}{a^2 - 4a^2} = \frac{5a^2}{-3a^2} = \frac{5}{-3} = -1\frac{2}{3}$$

45. **C.** If x is increased by 50%, you can use $\frac{3}{2}x$ to represent it. You must multiply this by $\frac{2}{3}y$ in order to keep the product equal to xy. That is, $\left(\frac{3}{2}x\right)\left(\frac{2}{3}y\right) = xy$. Because $\frac{2}{3}y$ is a $\frac{1}{3}$ reduction from y, choice C is the correct response.

46. **C.** Add up the frequencies for each group of score values. The total is $1 + 1 + 1 + 2 + 3 + 3 + 4 + 4 + 3 + 1 = 23$. The total for the scores from 50 to 80 is $3 + 4 + 4 = 11$. Therefore $\frac{11}{23}$ scores were in this range, or approximately 48%, answer choice C.

47. **D.** This problem involves items that are either working with or against each other. Organizing the information is important. One method involves setting up a set of fractions, each one representing a "worker." In this case, the "workers" worked for 16 minutes. The numerator of each fraction represents the time actually worked while the denominator represents the time required to complete the entire task alone. Since the cold and hot water work together, they get added together. The drain works against, so it is subtracted, as follows:

$$\frac{16}{40} + \frac{16}{20} - \frac{16}{30} = \frac{48}{120} + \frac{96}{120} - \frac{64}{120} = \frac{80}{120} = \frac{2}{3}$$

Thus, the tub will be two-thirds full after 16 minutes.

48. **A.** First, calculate the value of the Growth stocks for the month of May:

$$(0.25 + 0.25 + 0.05)(296,000) = (0.55)(296,000) = 162,800$$

Next calculate the value of the Growth stocks for the month of June:

$$(0.25 + 0.20 + 0.20)(260,000) = (0.65)(260,000) = 169,000$$

Subtract to find the change: $169,000 - 162,800 = 6,200$. Therefore, the value of the growth stocks increased by \$6,200.

49. **D.** Clearly, Mid Cap Value and Mid Cap Growth had a decline. But, even though the percentages are the same for each month for Small Cap Growth, the portfolio value decreased, so did the value of this category. Therefore, 3 categories decreased in value from May to June.

50. **D.** The value of Small Cap Value stocks in May was 10% of 296,000 or 29,600. The value of Small Cap Value stocks in June was 15% of 260,000 or 39,000. Subtract to find the increase: 39,000 − 29,600 = 9,400. So, the percent increase is 9,400 ÷ 29,600, which is approximately 32%.

Overview Multiple-Choice (Select One or More Answer Choices) Question Type

The Multiple-Choice (Select One or More Answer Choices) question type requires you to solve math problems and then choose ALL the answer choices that are correct. If you do not mark all correct answer choices, you will not be given any credit; there is no partial credit.

Skills and Concepts Tested

Multiple-choice questions with one or more correct answers tests your ability to use mathematical insight, approximations, simple calculations, or common sense to choose ALL the correct or possible answers from among a list of several choices. It tests concepts presented in secondary mathematics classes through first-year algebra and geometry. It also includes statistical concepts usually presented as part of a second year algebra course in high school. There are no concepts tested from trigonometry, calculus or other higher level mathematics courses.

Directions

Solve each problem in this section by using the information given and your own mathematical calculations. Select ALL of the correct choices from the list of choices given.

There are some additional assumptions made regarding the use of symbols, diagrams, and numerical values. These assumptions include, but are not limited to, the following.

- All numerical values used are real numbers.
- Figures or diagrams are not necessarily drawn to scale and should not be used to estimate sizes by measurement unless they are data displays (graphs and charts) or coordinates on a coordinate axes. These will always be drawn to scale.
- Lines that appear straight can be assumed to be straight.
- A symbol that appears in repeated quantities represents the same value or object for each quantity.
- On a number line, positive numbers are to the right of zero and increase to the right and negative numbers are to the left of zero and decrease to the left.
- Distances are always either zero or a positive value.

Suggested Strategies with Sample Questions

- One or more of the answer choices is correct. If your answer(s) is/are not in the list, your answer is incorrect.
- In some questions, you are asked which answer choice(s) meets certain requirements. This usually involves examining each answer choice individually. You may notice some relationship among the answer choices that allows you to settle on the correct answer choice(s) more quickly.
- Working backwards from the answer choices is an accepted method for solution, although it usually takes longer than using logical reasoning to find the correct answer(s).

- Some questions require approximation. It may be useful to look at the answer choices and see how close together or far apart the answer choices are. This will guide you in determining how close your approximation needs to be to choose the correct answer(s). Some questions require accurate computations, for others, estimation may be all you need to arrive at the correct answer(s).

- Use the answer choices to help guide you. For example, whole number answer choices may suggest less accuracy needed in computations than fractions.

Arithmetic Sample Question

1. If x and y are integers such that $1 < x < 7$ and $4 < y < 7$, then what is the last (right-most) digit of y^x? Indicate <u>all</u> such digits.

   - [A] 2
   - [B] 3
   - [C] 4
   - [D] 5
   - [E] 6
   - [F] 7

Since $4 < y < 7$, y must be either 5 or 6. Since $1 < x < 7$, x must be either 2, 3, 4, 5, or 6. If we start looking at the powers of 5, such as $5^2 = 25$, $5^3 = 125$, and $5^4 = 625$, we see that all the units digits are 5. Continuing the sequence would continue to result in a number ending in 5. If we start looking at the powers of 6, such as $6^2 = 36$, $6^3 = 216$, and $6^4 = 1,296$, we see that all the units digits are 6. Continuing the sequence would continue to result in a number ending with 6. Therefore, 5 (D) and 6 (E) are correct.

Algebra Sample Question

2. Solve the following system of equations and indicate <u>all</u> possible values of $x + y$.

$$y = 2x^2 - x + 4$$
$$x = \frac{10 - y}{2}$$

   - [A] $8\frac{1}{2}$
   - [B] 10
   - [C] $11\frac{1}{2}$
   - [D] 12
   - [E] $15\frac{1}{2}$
   - [F] 16
   - [G] $16\frac{1}{2}$

One method is to solve both equations for y, equate the two equations, then solve for x. After solving for x, substitute back into one of the equations and solve for y.

$$x = \frac{10 - y}{2} \qquad\qquad -2x + 10 = 2x^2 - x + 4$$
$$2x = 10 - y \qquad\qquad 2x^2 + x - 6 = 0$$
$$y = -2x + 10 \qquad\qquad (2x - 3)(x + 2) = 0$$

Therefore, x could be either -2 or $\frac{3}{2}$. (NOTE: If you don't see how to factor the equation, you could always use the quadratic formula.)

Substitute the values of -2 and $\frac{3}{2}$ back in the first equation to get the corresponding values of y.

$$y = -2x + 10 \qquad\qquad y = -2x + 10$$
$$y = -2(-2) + 10 \qquad\qquad y = -2\left(\frac{3}{2}\right) + 10$$
$$y = 14 \qquad\qquad\qquad y = 7$$

So, the possible values of $x + y$ are $-2 + 14 = 12$ (choice D) and $\frac{3}{2} + 7 = 8\frac{1}{2}$ (choice A).

Geometry Sample Question

3. In right triangle ABC, if $30° \le x° \le 60°$, which of the following could be the value of a? Indicate <u>all</u> such values.

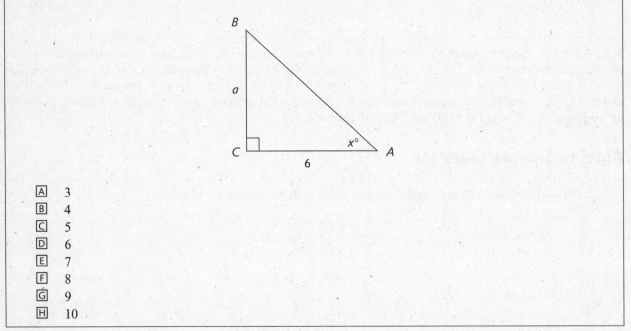

A	3
B	4
C	5
D	6
E	7
F	8
G	9
H	10

Calculate the value of a for the two extremes of the range of $x°$.

If $x = 30°$, then using the 30°-60°-90° ratio relationship $\left(1 : 2 : \sqrt{3}\right)$, the length of side AB is $2a$ and the length of side AC is $a\sqrt{3}$. Since side AC is given as length 6, we have $a\sqrt{3} = 6$, or $a = \dfrac{6}{\sqrt{3}} = \dfrac{6\sqrt{3}}{3} = 2\sqrt{3}$. Similarly, if $x = 60°$, using the 30°-60°-90° ratio relationship $\left(1 : 2 : \sqrt{3}\right)$, the length of side AB is $2 \times 6 = 12$, and the length of side BC is $6\sqrt{3}$. Therefore, $a = 6\sqrt{3}$. These are the two extremes for the value of a. The relationship can be written as $2\sqrt{3} \le a \le 6\sqrt{3}$. What remains to be done is to determine between what pairs of consecutive integers these values are located. If we square $2\sqrt{3}$, we get 12. The square root of 12 is between 3 and 4. If we square $6\sqrt{3}$, we get 108. The square root of 108 is between 10 and 11. Also remember that you have the use of a calculator. Therefore, possible values of a are 4, 5, 6, 7, 8, 9, and 10 (choices B, C, D, E, F, G, and H, respectively).

Data Analysis Sample Question

4. Given the following data set: {2, 2, 3, 3, 3, 4, 6, 7, 7, 7, 7, 8, 10, 12, 12}, which of the following values of x satisfy this relationship: mean < x < median? Indicate all such values.

    A   5.8
    B   6.0
    C   6.2
    D   6.4
    E   6.6
    F   6.8
    G   7.0
    H   7.2

The median of a set of numbers is the middle number when the numbers in the data set are ranked in order. In this case, since there are 15 numbers in the data set, the eighth number, 7, is the median. The mean is the arithmetic average of the numbers in the data set. mean $= \dfrac{\text{sum}}{\text{quantity}} = \dfrac{93}{15} = 6.2$. Therefore, the values between 6.2 and 7.0 satisfy the relationship (choices D, E, and F).

Word Problem Sample Question

5. Liam has 12 pounds of ground coffee valued at $8.50 per pound. Which of the following amounts (listed in pounds) of ground coffee valued at $4.00 per pound, when added, would yield a mixture worth from $5.50 to $6.00 per pound? Indicate all such amounts.

    A   12
    B   15
    C   18
    D   20
    E   22
    F   24

Calculate the amount needed for each of the two extremes. Set up equations in terms of cost.

For the $5.50 per pound coffee:

$$(12)(8.50)+(x)(4.00)=(12+x)(5.50)$$
$$(12)(85)+(x)(40)=(12+x)(55)$$
$$1{,}020+40x=660+55x$$
$$360=15x$$
$$24=x$$

For the $6.00 per pound coffee:

$$(12)(8.50)+(x)(4.00)=(12+x)(6.00)$$
$$(12)(85)+(x)(40)=(12+x)(60)$$
$$1{,}020+40x=720+60x$$
$$300=20x$$
$$15=x$$

So the range of amounts needed to yield coffee worth from $5.50 to $6.00 per pound is from 15 to 24 pounds. So choices B, C, D, E, and F are correct.

Data Interpretation Sample Question

Question 6 is based on the following data:

% of Units Sold								
	Model X			Model Y			Model Z	
Salesperson	Jan	Apr		Jan	Apr		Jan	Apr
A	12	16		16	14		15	15
B	14	14		12	13		14	16
C	16	18		17	10		16	16
D	11	16		16	12		15	10
E	18	14		14	10		10	12
F	14	16		12	14		12	14
G	15	6		13	27		18	17

Total Number of Units Sold			
	Model X	Model Y	Model Z
January	1,600	1,900	2,200
April	1,500	1,700	2,400

6. Which salesperson(s) showed increased sales figures, in units sold, for at least two models from January to April? Indicate all that apply.

   Ⓐ Salesperson A
   Ⓑ Salesperson B
   Ⓒ Salesperson C
   Ⓓ Salesperson D
   Ⓔ Salesperson E
   Ⓕ Salesperson F
   Ⓖ Salesperson G

Salesperson A is a correct choice since Model X sales increased, $(0.12)(1,600) < (0.16)(1,500)$ and Model Z sales increased, $(0.15)(2,200) < (0.15)(2,400)$.

Salesperson C is a correct choice since Model X sales increased, $(0.16)(1,600) < (0.18)(1,500)$ and Model Z sales increased, $(0.16)(2,200) < (0.16)(2,400)$.

Salesperson F is a correct choice since Model X sales increased, $(0.14)(1600) < (0.16)(1,500)$ and Model Y sales increased, $(0.12)(1,900) < (0.14)(1,700)$ and Model Z sales increased, $(0.12)(2,200) < (0.14)(2,400)$.

Salesperson G is a correct choice since Model Y sales increased, $(0.13)(1,900) < (0.27)(1,700)$ and Model Z sales increased, $(0.18)(2,200) < (0.17)(2,400)$.

Salespersons A, C, F and G are correct choices. Salespersons B, D, and E are not correct choices because they had decreased sales figures for at least two models.

Practice Multiple-Choice (Select One or More Answer Choices) Questions

1. Given even integer a and odd integer b such that $1 < a < 13$ and $1 < b < 13$. For all the quotients that are integers, what is the value of $\frac{a}{b}$? Indicate all such values.

   A   1

   B   2

   C   3

   D   4

   E   5

   F   6

2. In 2008, Robbie spent between 20% and 25% of her \$40,400 salary on lodging. In 2009, she spent between 15% and 20% of her \$45,000 salary on lodging. Which of the following could have been the percent change in the amount Robbie spent on lodging from 2008 to 2009? Indicate all such values.

   A   0%

   B   10%

   C   15%

   D   20%

   E   25%

   F   30%

   G   35%

3. Aaron, Bryan, Jamie, Katie, and Logan, each received \$1,200 from their father on their respective birthdays. Aaron saved between $\frac{1}{2}$ and $\frac{7}{8}$ of his gift. Bryan saved between $\frac{1}{3}$ and $\frac{3}{4}$ of his gift. Jamie saved between $\frac{1}{3}$ and $\frac{2}{3}$ of her gift. Katie saved between $\frac{3}{8}$ and $\frac{3}{4}$ of her gift. Logan saved between $\frac{1}{2}$ and $\frac{2}{3}$ of his gift. Which of the following amounts could be the amount that exactly three of them could have saved? Indicate all such amounts.

   A   \$375

   B   \$425

   C   \$500

   D   \$700

   E   \$850

   F   \$950

4. The following chart represents the ages of the guests on board the *Sea Sickness III* while cruising the North Atlantic:

Age Range	# of Guests
10–19	2
20–29	5
30–39	10
40–49	4

Which of the following could be the average age of the guests? Indicate <u>all</u> such values.

- [A] 24
- [B] 26
- [C] 29
- [D] 32
- [E] 35
- [F] 37
- [G] 39

5. Given parallelogram *ABCD* below, if $45° < a < 90°$, which of the following could be the area of the parallelogram? Indicate <u>all</u> such values.

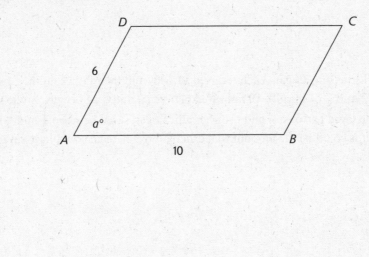

- [A] 30
- [B] 35
- [C] 40
- [D] 45
- [E] 50
- [F] 55
- [G] 60

6. Gavin bought 200 decks of cards for $2.20 per deck. He plans to sell these decks at a swap meet and make a profit of from 15% to 25% per deck. If he sells all 200 decks, all at the same price, which of the following could be the total sales revenue? Indicate <u>all</u> such values.

- [A] $500
- [B] $520
- [C] $540
- [D] $560
- [E] $580
- [F] $600

Answers and Explanations for Multiple-Choice (Select One or More Answer Choices) Questions

1. **B and D.** Since a is an even integer, its possible values are 2, 4, 6, 8, 10, and 12. Since b is an odd integer, its possible values are 3, 5, 7, 9, and 11. In order for the quotient $\frac{a}{b}$ to be an integer, the numerator, a, must contain a factor that is odd. The only possible combination of values that yield an integer quotient are: $\frac{6}{3} = 2$, $\frac{10}{5} = 2$, and $\frac{12}{3} = 4$ (choices B and D, respectively).

2. **A, B, C, D, E, and F.** First determine the four lodging amounts in question:

    20% of 40,400 = 0.20 × 40,400 = 8,080

    25% of 40,400 = 0.25 × 40,400 = 10,100

    15% of 45,000 = 0.15 × 45,000 = 6,750

    20% of 45,000 = 0.20 × 45,000 = 9,000

    Since the two ranges overlap, the minimum change could be $0.00 or 0%. To determine the maximum change, consider the two extremes:

    $8,080 \rightarrow 9,000$ $\qquad$ % change $= \dfrac{\text{change}}{\text{starting value}} \times 100\% = \dfrac{920}{8,080} \times 100\% \approx 0.114 \times 100\% = 11.4\%$

    $10,100 \rightarrow 6,750$ $\qquad$ % change $= \dfrac{\text{change}}{\text{starting value}} \times 100\% = \dfrac{3,350}{10,100} \times 100\% \approx 0.332 \times 100\% = 33.2\%$

    Therefore, the percent change could range from 0% thru 33.2% (choices A through F).

3. **C and E.** First compute the range of amounts that each could have saved:

    Aaron: $\frac{1}{2}$ to $\frac{7}{8}$ is 600 thru 1,050

    Bryan: $\frac{1}{3}$ to $\frac{3}{4}$ is $400 thru $900

    Jamie: $\frac{1}{3}$ to $\frac{2}{3}$ is $400 thru $800

    Katie: $\frac{3}{8}$ to $\frac{3}{4}$ is $450 thru $900

    Logan: $\frac{1}{2}$ to $\frac{2}{3}$ is $600 thru $800

    $375 is not a correct choice since no one could have saved this amount.

    $425 is not a correct choice since it could have been saved by only two: Bryan and Jamie.

    $500 is a correct choice since it could have been saved by exactly three: Bryan, Jamie and Katie.

    $700 is not a correct choice since it could have been saved by all five.

    $850 is a correct choice since it could have been saved by exactly three: Aaron, Bryan and Katie.

    $950 is not a correct choice since it could only be saved by one: Aaron.

4. **C, D, and E.** To calculate the possible average age, first consider the youngest the guests could be, and calculate their average age. Then consider the oldest the guests could be and calculate the average age. In each case, find the sum of the products of the age and number of guests. Then divide by the total number of guests, which is 21 guests.

$$\text{Youngest: } \frac{(10\times2)+(20\times5)+(30\times10)+(40\times4)}{21}\approx27.6$$

$$\text{Oldest: } \frac{(19\times2)+(29\times5)+(39\times10)+(49\times4)}{21}\approx36.6$$

Therefore, the correct answer choices are 29, 32, and 35 (choices C, D, and E, respectively).

5. **D, E, and F.** If $a = 90°$, then the height would be 6, since the parallelogram would be a rectangle. But, $a < 90°$, so the height is almost 6. Therefore the area would be just under 60.

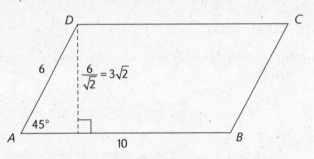

If $a = 45°$, then the height would be $3\sqrt{2}$. (Recall that in the 45-45-90 right triangle, the relationship is $1:1:\sqrt{2}$ and if the hypotenuse is 6, the height would be $\frac{6}{\sqrt{2}} = 3\sqrt{2}$.) But, $a > 45°$, so the height is a little more than $3\sqrt{2}$. Therefore the area would be a little more than $10 \times 3\sqrt{2} = 30\sqrt{2}$. We can determine between which two given choices $30\sqrt{2}$ lies by squaring it along with the answer choices. Squaring $30\sqrt{2}$ gives 1,800. Since squaring 40 gives 1,600 and squaring 45 gives 2,025, $30\sqrt{2}$ must be greater than 40 and less than 45.

Using a calculator, $30\sqrt{2} \approx 42.4$. Therefore the correct answer choices are 45, 50, and 55 (choices D, E, and F, respectively).

6. **B and C.** If all 200 decks were sold at a price yielding a 15% profit, the price per deck would be (1.15)($2.20) = $2.53. Total revenue would be (200)($2.53) = $506. If sold at a price yielding a 25% profit, the price per deck would be (1.25)($2.20) = $2.75. Total revenue would be (200)($2.75) = $550. The two answer choices yielding a revenue between $506 and $550 are choice B, $520, and choice C, $540.

Overview Numeric Entry (Fill-in) Question Type

The numeric entry (fill-in) question type requires you to solve math problems with numeric answers and fill in the blank space with correct answer based on the guidelines given in the problem.

Skills and Concepts Tested

Fill-in questions test your ability to use mathematical insight, approximations, simple calculations, or common sense to calculate a numeric response. They test concepts presented in secondary mathematics classes through first-year algebra, and geometry. It also includes statistical concepts usually presented as part of a second-year algebra course in high school. There are no concepts tested from trigonometry, calculus, or other higher level mathematics courses.

Directions

Solve each problem by using the information given and your own mathematical calculations. Arrive at a numeric response based on the specifications given in the problem. Use the mouse to click in the rectangular answer area, then type in your answer. Answers may also be transferred from the on-screen calculator.

There are some additional assumptions made regarding the use of symbols, diagrams, and numerical values. These assumptions include, but are not limited to, the following.

- All numerical values used are real numbers.
- Figures or diagrams are not necessarily drawn to scale and should not be used to estimate sizes by measurement unless they are data displays (graphs and charts) or coordinates on a coordinate axes. These will always be drawn to scale.
- Lines that appear straight can be assumed to be straight.
- A symbol that appears in repeated quantities represents the same value or object for each quantity.
- On a number line, positive numbers are to the right of zero and increase to the right and negative numbers are to the left of zero and decrease to the left.
- Distances are always either zero or a positive value.

Suggested Strategies with Sample Questions

- Calculate the answer using the requirements of the problem.
- If answering a question using a decimal response, do not forget to include the decimal point, if required. For example, if the answer is "23", then answers such as "23", "23." or "23.0" are all correct. If the answer is "5.2", then answers such as "5.2", "5.20" or "05.2" are all correct.
- If answering a question using a common fraction response, place the numerator in the upper box and the denominator in the lower box. Fractional answers do not have to be reduced. For example, if an answer is "three-fourths," then the answer could be entered as $\frac{3}{4}$, $\frac{9}{12}$, or even $\frac{-6}{-8}$.
- Information will be given in the question if an answer is required to be in reduced form.
- Rectangular answer boxes indicate that a fill-in answer is required.

Arithmetic Sample Question

1. If the pattern established in the first five fractions in the following list continues, what is the next fraction in the list?

$$\frac{2}{3}, \quad \frac{3}{5}, \quad \frac{5}{9}, \quad \frac{8}{15}, \quad \frac{12}{23}, \quad \frac{\square}{\square}$$

Look for patterns in numerators and denominators. In this case, the numerators increase, first by 1, then by 2, then by 3, and then by 4. If this pattern continues, the next numerator would increase by 5. The denominators increase, first by 2, then by 4, then by 6, and then by 8. If this pattern continues, the next denominator would increase by 10. This yields an answer of $\frac{17}{33}$.

Algebra Sample Question

2. What is the slope of the line that is perpendicular to the line that passes through the points whose coordinates are (4,6) and (–2,3)?

$$\frac{\square}{\square}$$

To find the slope of the line that passes through the two given coordinates, use the slope formula: $m = \dfrac{(y_2 - y_1)}{(x_2 - x_1)} = \dfrac{(3-6)}{(-2-4)} = \dfrac{-3}{-6} = \dfrac{1}{2}$. The line in question is perpendicular to this line and therefore has a slope that is the negative reciprocal of $\frac{1}{2}$, or $-\frac{2}{1}$. This should be entered as $\dfrac{-2}{1}$ or $\dfrac{2}{-1}$.

Geometry Sample Question

3. A triangle has vertices with coordinates of (7,8), (1,0), and (7,0). Excluding units, what is the ratio of the perimeter to the area of the triangle?

$$\frac{\square}{\square}$$

To answer this problem, a figure should be drawn to help determine the length of each side of the triangle and the shape of the triangle.

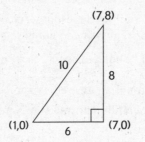

From the placements of the coordinates, the resulting triangle is a right triangle. The horizontal side of the triangle has a length of 6, the vertical side has a length of 8. Using the Pythagorean theorem, the third side has length of 10. The perimeter of the triangle is the sum of the three sides: 6 + 8 + 10 = 24. The area is equal to $\frac{1}{2}(8)(6) = 24$. Therefore, the ratio of the perimeter to the area would be $\frac{24}{24}$. Unless otherwise stated, this would be a satisfactory response. Reducing is not necessary, but acceptable. If reduced, the ratio would be $\frac{1}{1}$.

Data Analysis Sample Question

4. The average of 6 numbers is 8. If three additional numbers are combined with these 6 numbers, the average of the 9 numbers increases to 11. What is the average of the 3 additional numbers?

$$\boxed{}$$

If the average of 6 numbers is 8, their total must be $6 \times 8 = 48$. After the 3 additional numbers are combined the total must be $9 \times 11 = 99$. This is an increase of $99 - 48 = 51$. Therefore, these three additional numbers sum to 51. Thus, their average is $\frac{51}{3} = 17$. So, the correct answer is 17.

Word Problem Sample Question

5. Six years from now, San will be twice as old as Tina. Three years ago, San was three times as old as Tina. How old, in years, is San now?

A chart can be useful in solving an age problem. Placing the variable in the smallest valued box simplifies the computation. Fill in what you know using the fact that three years ago, San was three times as old as Tina.

	Three Years Ago	Now	In Six Years
San	$3x$	$3x + 3$	$3x + 9$
Tina	x	$x + 3$	$x + 9$

Now, set up an equation using the relationship established for the right hand column.

The first sentence said "Six years from now, San will be twice as old as Tina." This is now translated as follows:

$$3x + 9 = 2(x + 9)$$
$$3x + 9 = 2x + 18$$
$$x = 9$$

Use the value of x to determine San's age now: $3x + 3 = 3(9) + 3 = 30$.

The correct answer is 30.

Data Interpretation Sample Question

For question 6, refer to the following data:

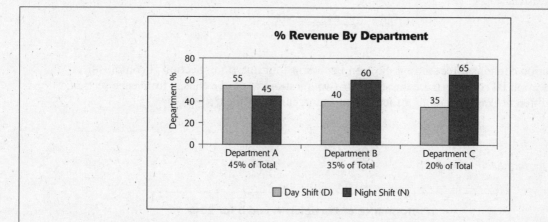

6. Three departments, A, B, and C, each have a day shift (D) and a night shift (N). If Department A's total revenue, day shift and night shift combined, was $3,600, then the combined revenues of the night shifts of the three departments surpassed the combined revenues of the day shifts of the three departments by how many dollars?

Since Department A's total revenue was \$3,600, and this was 45% of the total revenue of the three departments, the total revenue of the three departments was $\frac{\$3,600}{0.45} = \$8,000$. To obtain the overall percent for the combined night shifts, multiply the percentages for each department by the percentage of its night shift and add together: $(0.45)(0.45) + (0.35)(0.60) = (0.20)(0.65) = 0.5425$. Multiply this number by the total revenue of \$8,000: $(\$8,000)(0.5425) = \$4,340$. This is the revenue for the combined night shifts. Subtracting from \$8,000, gives \$3,660 for the combined day shifts. Subtracting gives the difference of \$680. The correct answer is 680.

Practice Numeric Entry (Fill-in) Questions

1. The ratio of the surface areas of cube X to cube Y is 4 to 9. If the volume of cube X is 24 cubic units, what is the volume, in cubic units, of cube Y?

2. What is the sum of the positive integer divisors that are greater than one that 96 and 80 have in common?

3. What is the sum of the coordinates of the intersection of the lines given by:

$$3x - 4y = 6$$
$$4x - 3y = 1$$

4. Gina's salary went through the following 5 consecutive monthly percent changes: +10%, –8%, –6%, +15% and +7%. Compared to her starting salary, rounded to the nearest tenth of one percent, what was the percent increase in salary?

[   ]%

5. An examination contains three sections. Section I contains four questions. Section II contains five questions. Section III contains three questions. If two questions are to be chosen from each section, how many different exam variations, order unimportant, can be formed?

For question 6, refer to the following data:

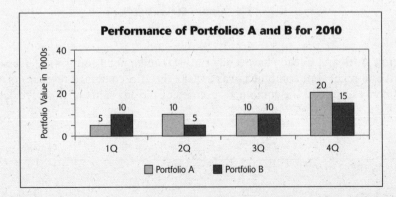

6. Rounded to the nearest tenth of one percent, what was the percent change in value of the combined portfolios from the 2nd to the 4th quarters?

$$\boxed{}\%$$

Answers and Explanations for Practice Numeric Entry (Fill-in) Questions

1. **81** For cubes, and other similar geometric solids, the ratio of their surface areas is the square of the ratio of their linear measures (length, width, radius, etc.). So the ratio of their linear measures would be the square root of the ratio of their surface areas. In this case, $\sqrt{\frac{4}{9}} = \frac{2}{3}$. The ratio of their volumes would be the cube of the ratio of their linear measures, or $\left(\frac{2}{3}\right)^3 = \frac{8}{27}$. Since the volume of cube X is 24, which is 8 times 3, the volume of cube Y must be 27 times 3, or 81.

2. **30** One approach is to list the divisors for each number:

    96: 2, 3, 4, 6, 8, 12, 16, 24, 32, 48, 96

    80: 2, 4, 5, 8, 10, 16, 20, 40, 80

    The common divisors are: 2, 4, 8, and 16. Their sum is 30.

    Another approach would be to factor each number to determine the common factors:

    $96 = 2 \times 2 \times 2 \times 2 \times 2 \times 3$

    $80 = 2 \times 2 \times 2 \times 2 \times 5$

    The common factors are 2, 2, 2, and 2. Therefore, the common divisors must be 2, 4, 8, and 16. This also gives the sum of 30.

3. **−5** Multiplying the top equation by −3 and the bottom equation by 4 gives:

    $$-9x + 12y = -18$$
    $$16x - 12y = 4$$

    Adding the two equations and solving for x gives:

    $$7x = -14$$
    $$x = -2$$

    Solving for y using either equation gives

    $$3x - 4y = 6$$
    $$3(-2) - 4y = 6$$
    $$-6 - 4y = 6$$
    $$-4y = 12$$
    $$y = -3$$

    Therefore the sum of the coordinates, x and y, is −5.

4. **17.1%** Note that you cannot just add the percent changes together. Percent increases and decreases must be accounted for. The result after a 10% increase can be found quickly by multiplying the original by $(100\% + 10\%)$ or 110% or 1.10. An 8% decrease can be found quickly by multiplying by $(100\% - 8\%)$ or 92% or 0.92. Using these shortcuts, we can determine the final result by doing the following successive multiplications: $(1.10)(0.92)(0.94)(1.15)(1.07) = 1.17055$. This indicates an increase of 0.17055 over the original value. Therefore, rounded to the nearest tenth of one percent the percent increase is 17.1%.

5. **180** Although you can use the combinations formula to determine the number of ways the questions can be chosen, simple lists are probably faster. There are 6 ways to choose 2 from a list of 4: 1-2, 1-3, 1-4, 2-3, 2-4, and 3-4. There are 10 ways to choose 2 from a list of 5: 1-2, 1-3, 1-4, 1-5, 2-3, 2-4, 2-5, 3-4, 3-5, and 4-5. There are 3 ways to choose 2 from a list of 3: 1-2, 1-3, 2-3. Multiply to arrive at the total number of different examinations: $6 \times 10 \times 3 = 180$. Had you used the combinations formula to find the different combinations and multiplied those values together, the work would have looked like the following.

$$(_4C_2)(_5C_2)(_3C_2) = \left(\frac{4!}{2!2!}\right)\left(\frac{5!}{2!3!}\right)\left(\frac{3!}{2!1!}\right) = \left(\frac{(4)(3)}{(2)(1)}\right)\left(\frac{(5)(4)}{(2)(1)}\right)\left(\frac{(3)(2)}{(2)(1)}\right) = (6)(10)(3) = 180$$

6. **133.3%** In the 2nd Quarter, the total value of the two portfolios was 15,000. In the 4th Quarter, the total value of the two portfolios was 35,000. The increase in value was 20,000. Therefore,

$$\% \text{ increase} = \frac{\text{increase}}{\text{starting amount}} \times 100\% = \frac{20,000}{15,000} \times 100\% = 133.3\%.$$

PART III

BASIC MATH REVIEW

Chapter 5

Math Skills Review

This chapter is designed to provide you with a comprehensive basic math review and walk you through fundamental math skills and concepts that are important for your success on the GRE. Math concepts include topics in arithmetic, algebra, geometry, data analysis, word problems, and data interpretation. As you review this chapter, continue to assess your strengths and evaluate areas in which you feel you may need improvement. Even if your cumulative knowledge of math is strong, you should at least skim through the topic headings to help trigger your memory of forgotten math concepts.

The first part of this chapter begins with an *overview* section that contains commonly encountered math symbols and terminology. The next part of the chapter consists of a thorough review of six math topic areas. Each topic area includes a *diagnostic test* to help you assess your knowledge of that topic and a *review section* that provides you with illustrated examples, explanations, and clarifications about solving basic math problems. After you have taken the diagnostic test and systematically reviewed the explanations with examples in a topic area, you will be ready to practice what you have learned with the *practice exercises* provided at the end of each topic area subject.

Pace yourself as you work through each topic area, and remember that the Quantitative Reasoning section of the GRE measures your ability to use your *cumulative knowledge* of mathematics and your ability to *reason quantitatively.* Try to focus your attention on one math concept at a time (i.e., finish the arithmetic diagnostic and arithmetic review before you begin the algebra diagnostic and algebra review, etc.).

The Six Math Review Topic Areas					
Arithmetic (pages 211–248)	**Algebra (pages 248–288)**	**Geometry (pages 288–326)**	**Data Analysis (pages 326–336)**	**Word Problems (pages 337–346)**	**Data Interpretation (pages 347–359)**
❏ Arithmetic diagnostic test	❏ Algebra diagnostic test	❏ Geometry diagnostic test	❏ Data analysis diagnostic test	❏ Word problems diagnostic test	❏ Data interpretation diagnostic test
❏ Sets of numbers	❏ Set notations	❏ Lines, segments, rays, and angles	❏ Methods for counting	❏ Motion problems	❏ Circle or pie graphs
❏ Divisibility rules	❏ Variables	❏ Polygons and their angles	❏ Permutations	❏ Work problems	❏ Bar graphs
❏ Grouping symbols	❏ Solving linear equations in one or two variables	❏ Triangles	❏ Combinations	❏ Mixture problems	❏ Line graphs
❏ Order of operations	❏ Solving linear inequalities in one variable	❏ Quadrilaterals	❏ Probability	❏ Age problems	❏ Venn diagrams
❏ Integers	❏ Polynomials	❏ Circles	❏ Basic statistics	❏ Integers problems	❏ Charts and tables
❏ Fractions	❏ Algebraic fractions	❏ Perimeter, circumference, and area of plane figures	❏ Frequency table and measure of central tendency		
❏ Factors	❏ Solving quadratic equations in one variable	❏ Surface area, volume, and diagonal lengths of 3-dimensional figures	❏ Five steps to calculate the standard deviation		
❏ Decimals	❏ Coordinate geometry	❏ Congruence and similarity			
❏ Ratios and proportions	❏ Functions and function notation				
❏ Percents					
❏ Exponents					
❏ Square Roots					

Overview

This overview section contains basic references that you will refer to again and again during your GRE math preparation. These fundamental facts and formulas were compiled so that you can easily have important basic math concepts at your fingertips. As you review different math topics, keep in mind that these basic references will help you solve math problems so that you don't spend valuable time trying to search math information and formulas. The math overview includes the following: common math symbols, vocabulary related to sets of numbers, common math conventions and terminology, geometric formulas (perimeter, area, and volume), important fraction-decimal-percent equivalents, and measurement equivalents (English and metric systems).

Common Math Symbols

$x = 5$	x is equal to 5
$x \neq 5$	x is not equal to 5
$x \approx 5$	x is approximately equal to 5
$x \leq 5$	x is less than or equal to 5
$x < 5$	x is less than to 5
$x \geq 5$	x is greater than or equal to 5
$x > 5$	x is greater than to 5
$|x|$	the absolute value of x
$\sqrt{x}$	the nonnegative square root of x when $x \geq 0$
$-\sqrt{x}$	the nonpositive square root of x when $x \geq 0$
$n!$	the product of the positive integers 1, 2, 3, ..., n
$0!$	is defined to have the value of 1
$k \parallel p$	line k is parallel to line p
$k \perp p$	line k is perpendicular to line p

Numbers Vocabulary

Natural numbers	{1, 2, 3, 4, ...} The counting numbers.
Whole numbers	{0, 1, 2, 3, 4, ...} The counting numbers and zero.
Integers	{0, ±1, ±2, ±3, ±4, ...} The whole numbers and their opposites.
Positive integers	{1, 2, 3, 4, ...} The natural numbers.
Nonnegative integers	{0, 1, 2, 3, 4, ...} The whole numbers.
Negative integers	{−1, −2, −3, −4, ...} The opposites of the natural numbers.
Nonpositive integers	{0, −1, −2, −3, −4, ...} The opposites of the whole numbers.
Rational numbers	Any value that can be expressed as $\frac{p}{q}$, where p is any integer and q is any nonzero integer. In decimal form, it either terminates or has a block of repeating digits. For example, $\frac{3}{4} = 0.75$, $\frac{1}{12} = 0.8333... = 0.8\overline{3}$
Irrational numbers	Any value that exists that cannot be expressed as $\frac{p}{q}$, where p is any integer and q is any nonzero integer. In decimal form, it neither terminates nor has any block of repeating digits. For example, $\sqrt{2}$, π.
Real numbers	All the rational numbers and irrational numbers.
Prime numbers	Any integer, greater than 1, that only has 1 and itself as divisors. The first 10 prime numbers are 2, 3, 5, 7, 11, 13, 17, 19, 23, 29.

Composite numbers	Any integer greater than 1, that is not prime. The first 10 composite numbers are 4, 6, 8, 9, 10, 12, 14, 15, 16, 18.
Even integers	$\{0, \pm2, \pm4, \pm6, \ldots\}$ Integers that are perfectly divisible by 2.
Odd integers	$\{\pm1, \pm3, \pm5, \pm7, \ldots\}$ Integers that are not perfectly divisible by 2.
Squares	$\{(\pm1)^2, (\pm2)^2, (\pm3)^2, (\pm4)^2, \ldots\} = \{1, 4, 9, 16, \ldots\}$ The squares of the nonzero integers.
Cubes	$\{(\pm1)^3, (\pm2)^3, (\pm3)^3, (\pm4)^3, \ldots\} = \{\pm1, \pm8, \pm27, \pm64, \ldots\}$ The cubes of the nonzero integers.

Common Mathematical Conventions and Terminology

All numbers used on the GRE are **real numbers.** Imaginary values such as $\sqrt{-1}$ are not considered. Values that have no value, real or imaginary, such as $\frac{8}{0}$, $\frac{0}{0}$, 0^0, are not considered.

Exponents can be positive, negative, or zero. For example, $5^2 = 5 \times 5 = 25$, $5^{-2} = \frac{1}{5^2} = \frac{1}{25}$, and $5^0 = 1$.

When **function notation** is used on the test, it will be standard function notation. For example, $f(x) = 2x$ and $g(x) = x + 3\sqrt{x}$. Replacements for the variable are assumed to be all real numbers except for those that produce values not allowed. For the function called f, $f(x) = 2x$, all real numbers can be used for replacements. For the function called g, $g(x) = x + 3\sqrt{x}$, only nonnegative replacements are allowed for the variable. The composition of the two functions, g with f, is shown by $g(f(x))$, which requires you to evaluate $f(x)$ first, and then bring its value to the g function. For example, using the f and g functions described above, $g(f(50))$ has you first find $f(50)$. Since $f(x) = 2x$, then $f(50) = 2 \times 50 = 100$. Now use this value to replace the variables in the g function. Since $g(x) = x + 3\sqrt{x}$, then $g(100) = 100 + 3\sqrt{100} = 100 + 3(10) = 130$. Hence, $g(f(50)) = 130$.

Geometric Figures on the GRE

- Lines are assumed to be straight and extend indefinitely in opposite directions.
- Triangles will have interior angle sums of 180 degrees.
- Angle measures will be assumed to be positive and less than or equal to 360 degrees.
- All closed geometrical figures are assumed to be convex.
- The area of a figure refers to the region enclosed by the figure.
- The perimeter of a figure, or circumference in the case of circles, refers to the distance around the figure.
- If A and B refer to points on a figure, AB will refer to the segment joining A and B or the distance between A and B. For example: Symbols $\overleftrightarrow{AB}$ and $\overline{AB}$ denoting lines and line segments will NOT appear on the GRE. Rather, AB will appear instead. (You can determine which is being used through context.)
- Since figures are not necessarily drawn to scale, do not assume quantities such as lengths, angle measurements, areas, or perimeters based on appearance.

The diagram below will illustrate some things that can and cannot be assumed from a figure.

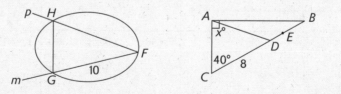

In geometric figures on the GRE, you _can assume_:

- ABD, ACD, ABC, and FGH are triangles.
- D lies between C and E on segment BC, E lies between D and B on segment BD
- $CD = 8$
- $BC > 8$

- Angle C has a measure of 40 degrees
- Angle CAB has a measure of 90 degrees (indicated by the small square symbol at A)
- x has a measure less than 90 degrees
- The area of triangle ABC is greater than the area of triangle ABD
- F, G, and H lie on the closed curve.
- H and F lie on line p, F and G lie on line m.
- Lines p and m intersect at F
- $FG = 10$
- The area of the closed curve region is greater than the area of triangle FGH

In geometric figures on the GRE, you _cannot assume_:

- $BD < 8$
- Angle $BAD < x$ degrees
- Area of triangle $ABD <$ area triangle ACD
- Angles FGH, FHG, and HFG are each less than 90 degrees
- Line HG is parallel to line AC
- Area of the region between FH and the closed curve > area of the region between GH and the closed curve

Important Geometric Formulas

The table below is a reference with formulas of basic shapes: perimeter, area, and volume. The Pythagorean theorem follows the table to illustrate how the lengths of the sides of a right triangle relate to one another.

Shape	Illustration	Perimeter	Area
Square	a	$P = 4a$	$A = a^2$
Rectangle	h b	$P = 2b + 2h$ or $P = 2(b + h)$	$A = bh$
Parallelogram	a h b	$P = 2a + 2b$ or $P = 2(a + b)$	$A = bh$
Triangle	x y h b	$P = x + y + b$	$A = \dfrac{bh}{2}$ or $A = \dfrac{1}{2}bh$
Rhombus	a h	$P = 4a$	$A = ah$
Trapezoid	b_1 x h y b_2	$P = b_1 + b_2 + x + y$	$A = \dfrac{h(b_1 + b_2)}{2}$ or $A = \dfrac{1}{2}h(b_1 + b_2)$

Shape	Illustration	Perimeter	Area
Circle		$C = \pi d$ or $C = 2\pi r$	$A = \pi r^2$

Shape	Illustration	Surface Area	Volume
Cube		$SA = 6a^2$	$V = a^3$
Rectangular Prism		$SA = 2(lw + lh + wh)$ or $SA = $ (Perimeter of base)h + 2(Area of base)	$V = lwh$ or $V = $ (Area of base)h
Prisms in general		$SA = $ (Perimeter of base)h + 2(Area of base)	$V = $ (Area of base)h
Cylinder		$SA = $ (Perimeter of base, or Circumference)h + 2(Area of base) or $SA = 2\pi rh + 2\pi r^2$ or $SA = 2\pi r(h + r)$	$V = $ (Area of base)h or $V = \pi r^2 h$
Sphere		$SA = 4\pi r^2$	$V = \dfrac{4}{3}\pi r^3$

Pythagorean Theorem

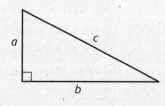

Pythagorean theorem: The sum of the squares of the legs of a right triangle equals the square of the hypotenuse ($a^2 + b^2 = c^2$).

Fraction-Decimal-Percent Equivalents

A time-saving tip is to try to memorize some of the following equivalents before you take the GRE to eliminate unnecessary computations on the day of the exam.

$\frac{1}{100} = 0.01 = 1\%$

$\frac{1}{10} = 0.1 = 10\%$

$\frac{1}{5} = \frac{2}{10} = 0.2 = 0.20 = 20\%$

$\frac{3}{10} = 0.3 = 0.30 = 30\%$

$\frac{2}{5} = \frac{4}{10} = 0.4 = 0.40 = 40\%$

$\frac{1}{2} = \frac{5}{10} = 0.5 = 0.50 = 50\%$

$\frac{3}{5} = \frac{6}{10} = 0.6 = 0.60 = 60\%$

$\frac{7}{10} = 0.7 = 0.70 = 70\%$

$\frac{4}{5} = \frac{8}{10} = 0.8 = 0.80 = 80\%$

$\frac{9}{10} = 0.9 = 0.90 = 90\%$

$\frac{1}{4} = \frac{25}{100} = 0.25 = 25\%$

$\frac{3}{4} = \frac{75}{100} = 0.75 = 75\%$

$\frac{1}{3} = 0.33\frac{1}{3} = 33\frac{1}{3}\%$

$\frac{2}{3} = 0.66\frac{2}{3} = 66\frac{2}{3}\%$

$\frac{1}{8} = 0.125 = 0.12\frac{1}{2} = 12\frac{1}{2}\%$

$\frac{3}{8} = 0.375 = 0.37\frac{1}{2} = 37\frac{1}{2}\%$

$\frac{5}{8} = 0.625 = 0.62\frac{1}{2} = 62\frac{1}{2}\%$

$\frac{7}{8} = 0.875 = 0.87\frac{1}{2} = 87\frac{1}{2}\%$

$\frac{1}{6} = 0.16\frac{2}{3} = 16\frac{2}{3}\%$

$\frac{5}{6} = 0.83\frac{1}{3} = 83\frac{1}{3}\%$

$1 = 1.00 = 100\%$

$2 = 2.00 = 200\%$

$3\frac{1}{2} = 3.50 = 350\%$

Customary English and Metric System Measurements

Length	
English	**Metric**
12 inches (in) = 1 foot (ft)	10 millimeter (mm) = 1 centimeter (cm)
3 feet = 1 yard (yd)	10 centimeters = 1 decimeter (dm)
36 inches = 1 yard	10 decimeters = 1 meter (m)
5,280 feet = 1 mile (mi)	10 meters = 1 decameter (dam)
1,760 yards = 1 mile	10 decameters = 1 hectometer (hm)
	10 hectometers = 1 kilometer (km)
One meter is about 3 inches more than a yard	
One kilometer is about 0.6 mile	

Weight	
English	**Metric**
16 ounces (oz) = 1 pound (lb)	10 milligram (mg) = 1 centigram (cg)
2,000 pounds = 1 ton (T)	10 centigrams = 1 decigram (dg)
	10 decigrams = 1 gram (g)
	10 grams = 1 decagram (dag)
	10 decagrams = 1 hectogram (hg)
	10 hectograms = 1 kilogram (kg)
One kilogram is about 2.2 pounds	
1,000 kilograms is a metric ton	

Volume (capacity)	
English	**Metric**
1 cup (cp) = 8 fluid ounces (fl oz)	10 milliliter (ml or mL) = 1 centiliter (cl or cL)
2 cups = 1 pint (pt)	10 centiliters = 1 deciliter (dl or dL)
2 pints = 1 quart (qt)	10 deciliters = 1 liter (l or L)
4 quarts = 1 gallon (gal)	10 liters = 1 decaliter (dal or daL)
	10 decaliters = 1 hectoliter (hl or hL)
	10 hectoliters = 1 kiloliter (kl or kL)
One liter is a little more than 1 quart	

Arithmetic

Arithmetic Diagnostic Test

1. Which of the following are integers? $\frac{1}{2}$, -2, 0, 4, $\sqrt{25}$, $-\frac{15}{3}$, 7.5

2. Which of the following are rational numbers? 5.8, -4, $\sqrt{7}$, π, $2\frac{5}{8}$

3. List the prime numbers between 0 and 50.

4. List the perfect cubes between 1 and 100.

5. Which integers between 1 and 10 divide 2,730?

6. $3\left[3^2 + 2(4+1)\right] =$

7. $-4 + 8 =$

8. $-12 - 6 =$

9. $(-6)(-8) =$

10. $\dfrac{-48}{3} =$

11. Change $5\frac{3}{4}$ to an improper fraction.

12. Change $\frac{59}{6}$ to a mixed number in lowest terms.

13. $\frac{2}{7}+\frac{3}{5}=$

14. $1\frac{3}{8}+2\frac{5}{6}=$

15. $11-\frac{2}{3}=$

16. $6\frac{1}{8}-3\frac{3}{4}=$

17. $-\frac{7}{8}-\frac{5}{9}=$

18. $-\frac{1}{6}\times\frac{1}{3}=$

19. $2\frac{3}{8}\times1\frac{5}{6}=$

20. $-\frac{1}{4}\div\frac{9}{14}=$

21. $2\frac{3}{7}\div1\frac{1}{4}=$

22. $\dfrac{1}{3+\dfrac{2}{1+\frac{1}{3}}}=$

23. Round 4.4584 to the nearest thousandth.

24. Round –3.6 to the nearest integer.

25. $0.08 + 1.3 + 0.562 =$

26. $0.45 - 0.003 =$

27. $8.001 \times 2.4 =$

28. $0.147 \div 0.7 =$

29. Change $\frac{3}{20}$ to a decimal.

30. Change 7% to a decimal.

31. Solve the proportion for x: $\frac{4}{x}=\frac{7}{5}$

32. Change $\frac{1}{8}$ to a percent.

33. 79% of 64 =

34. 40% of what is 20?

35. What percent of 45 is 30?

36. What is the percent increase of a rise in temperature from 80° to 100°?

37. $8^3 \times 8^7 =$

38. $9^5 \div 9^{-2} =$

39. $(5^3)^2 =$

40. $\sqrt{135}$ is between what two consecutive integers and to which is it closer?

41. Simplify $\sqrt{80}$.

42. $-\sqrt{9} =$

Arithmetic Diagnostic Test Answers

The diagnostic test explanations listed below include topic headings that correspond with step-by-step learning tools and examples to help you solve specific problem types. Corresponding topic headings can be found in the Arithmetic Review section on pages 211–248.

Sets of Numbers

1. $-2, 0, 4, \sqrt{25}, -\frac{15}{3}$

2. $5.8, -4, 2\frac{5}{8}$

3. $2, 3, 5, 7, 11, 13, 17, 19, 23, 29, 31, 37, 41, 43, 47$

4. $8, 27, 64$

Divisibility Rules

5. $2, 3, 5, 6, 7$

Grouping Symbols and Order of Operations

6. 57

Integers

7. 4

8. -18

9. 48

10. -16

Fractions

11. $\frac{23}{4}$

12. $9\frac{5}{6}$

13. $\frac{31}{35}$

14. $4\frac{5}{24}$

15. $10\frac{1}{3}$

16. $2\frac{3}{8}$

17. $-\frac{103}{72} = -1\frac{31}{72}$

18. $-\frac{1}{18}$

19. $\frac{209}{48} = 4\frac{17}{48}$

20. $-\frac{7}{18}$

21. $\frac{68}{35} = 1\frac{33}{35}$

22. $\frac{2}{9}$

Decimals

23. 4.458

24. −4

25. 1.942

26. 0.447

27. 19.2024

28. 0.21

29. 0.15

30. 0.07

Ratios and Proportions

31. $x = \frac{20}{7}$ or $2\frac{6}{7}$

Percents

32. $12\frac{1}{2}\%$ or 12.5%

33. 50.56

34. 50

35. $66\frac{2}{3}\%$

36. 25%

Exponents

37. 8^{10}

38. 9^7

39. 5^6

Square Roots

40. 11 and 12, closer to 12

41. $4\sqrt{5}$

42. -3

Arithmetic Review Section

Preliminaries (Sets of Numbers)

You should already be familiar with the fundamentals of addition, subtraction, multiplication, and division of sets of numbers found under "Numbers Vocabulary" in the "Overview" section on page 206. Here are corresponding examples for your review.

Examples:

> **1.** Which of the following are integers? $\frac{1}{2}$, -2, 0, 4, $\sqrt{25}$, $-\frac{15}{3}$, 7.5

Integers are only whole numbers or their opposites. Only the numbers -2, 0, 4, $\sqrt{25} = 5$, and $-\frac{15}{3} = -5$ are integers.

> **2.** Which of the following are rational numbers? 5.8, -4, $\sqrt{7}$, π, $2\frac{5}{8}$

Any value that can be expressed as $\frac{\text{integer}}{\text{nonzero integer}}$, or as a decimal that either ends or has a repeating pattern is a rational number. Only the numbers 5.8, -4, and $2\frac{5}{8}$ are rational numbers.

> **3.** List the prime numbers between 0 and 50.

Prime numbers are integers greater than 1 that can only be divided by itself or 1. Only the numbers 2, 3, 5, 7, 11, 13, 17, 19, 23, 29, 31, 37, 41, 43, and 47 satisfy this definition for integers between 1 and 50.

> **4.** List the perfect cubes between 1 and 100.

Cubes are integers raised to the third power. The perfect cubes between 1 and 100 come from $2^3 = 8$, $3^3 = 27$, and $4^3 = 64$. The value 1 is not between 1 and 100 thus $1^3 = 1$ is not included in this list. The perfect cubes between 1 and 100 are 8, 27, and 64.

Practice: Sets of Numbers

1. Name a number less than 100 but greater than 1 that is both a perfect square and a perfect cube.

2. What is the largest sum that a composite number and a prime number can make if each is less than 97?

Answers: Sets of Numbers

1. 64

Only 64 is both a perfect square and a perfect cube and less than 100.

2. 185

The largest prime number less than 97 is 89 (90, 92, 94, 96 are divisible by 2, 91 is divisible by 7, 93 is divisible by 3, and 95 is divisible by 5) and the largest composite number less than 97 is 96. The largest sum of a prime number and a composite number each less than 97 is 89 + 96 = 185.

Divisibility Rules

The following divisibility chart will help you to quickly evaluate and rule out wrong answer choices.

If a number is divisible by	Divisibility Rule
2	it ends in 0, 2, 4, 6, or 8
3	the sum of its digits is divisible by 3
4	the number formed by the last two digits is divisible by 4
5	it ends in 0 or 5
6	it is divisible by 2 and 3 (use the rules for both)
7	N/A (no simple rule)
8	the number formed by the last three digits is divisible by 8
9	the sum of its digits is divisible by 9

Examples:

> **1.** Which integers between 1 and 10 divide 2,730?

2 – 2,730 ends in a 0

3 – the sum of the digits is 12, which is divisible by 3

5 – 2,730 ends in a 0

6 – the rules for 2 and 3 both work

7 – 2,730 ÷ 7 = 390

Even though 2,730 is divisible by 10, 10 is not between 1 and 10.

> **2.** Which integers between 1 and 10 divide 2,648?

2 – 2,648 ends in 8

4 – 48, the number formed by the last two digits, is divisible by 4

8 – 648, the number formed by the last three digits is divisible by 8

Practice: Divisibility Rules

1. Which integers between 1 and 10 divide 4,620?

2. Which integers between 1 and 10 divide 13,131?

Answers: Divisibility Rules

1. 2, 3, 4, 5, 6, and 7

   2 – 4,620 ends in a 0.

   3 – the sum of the digits is 12, which is divisible by 3.

   4 – the number formed by the last two digits, 20, is divisible by 4.

5 – 4,620 ends in 0.

6 – the number is divisible by 2 and 3.

7 – 4,620 ÷ 7 = 660.

2. 3 and 9

3 – the sum of the digits is 9 which is divisible by 3

9 – the sum of the digits is 9, which is divisible by 9

Grouping Symbols

Parentheses are used to group numbers or variables. Calculations inside parentheses take precedence and should be performed before any other operations.

$$50(2 + 6) = 50(8) = 400$$

If a parenthesis is preceded by a minus sign, the parentheses must be removed before calculations can be performed. To remove the parentheses, change the plus or minus sign of each term within the parentheses.

$$6 - (-3 + a - 2b + c) = 6 + 3 - a + 2b - c = 9 - a + 2b - c$$

Brackets and *braces* are also used to group numbers or variables. Sometimes, instead of brackets or braces, you'll see the use of larger parentheses:

$$((3+4)\cdot 5)+2$$

An expression using all three grouping symbols might look like this:

$$2\left\{1+\left[4(2+1)+3\right]\right\}$$

This expression can be simplified as follows (notice that you work from the inside out):

$$2\left\{1+\left[4(2+1)+3\right]\right\} = 2\left\{1+\left[4(3)+3\right]\right\}$$
$$= 2\left\{1+\left[12+3\right]\right\}$$
$$= 2\left\{1+\left[15\right]\right\}$$
$$= 2\left\{16\right\}$$
$$= 32$$

Order of Operations

If multiplication, division, exponents, addition, subtraction, or parentheses are all contained in one problem, the *order of operations* is as follows:

1. Parentheses
2. Exponents
3. Multiplication or Division in the order it occurs from left to right
4. Addition or Subtraction in the order it occurs from left to right

An easy way to remember the order of operations is **P**lease **E**xcuse **M**y **D**ear **A**unt **S**ally (**P**arentheses, **E**xponents, **M**ultiplication, **D**ivision, **A**ddition, **S**ubtraction).

Examples:

1. $3[3^2 + 2\underline{(4+1)}] = 3[3^2 + 2(5)]$ (most inside parentheses first)

    $3[\underline{3^2} + 2(5)] = 3[9 + 2(5)]$ (exponents next)

     $3[9 + \underline{2(5)}] = 3[9 + 10]$ (mult./div. in order from left to right next)

      $3[\underline{9+10}] = 3[19]$ (add/subtract in order from left to right)

       $3[19] = 57$

2. $10 - 3\times 6 + 10^2 + \underline{(6+1)}\times 4 = 10 - 3\times 6 + 10^2 + 7\times 4$ (parentheses first)

    $10 - 3\times 6 + \underline{10^2} + 7\times 4 = 10 - 3\times 6 + 100 + 7\times 4$ (exponents next)

    $10 - \underline{3\times 6} + 100 + \underline{7\times 4} = 10 - 18 + 100 + 28$ (mult./div. in order from left to right)

    $\underline{10-18} + 100 + 28 = -8 + 100 + 28$ (add/subtract in order from left to right)

    $\underline{-8 + 100} + 28 = 92 + 28$ (add/subtract in order from left to right)

      $92 + 28 = 120$

3. $-3^2 + (-2)^3 = -1(3)^2 + (-2)^3$ (the exponent 2 only applies to the 3, while the exponent 3 applies to the entire (-2))

      $= -1(9) + (-8)$

      $= -9 + (-8)$

      $= -17$

Remember: An easy way to remember the order of operations is **P**lease **E**xcuse **M**y **D**ear **A**unt **S**ally (**P**arentheses, **E**xponents, **M**ultiplication, **D**ivision, **A**ddition, **S**ubtraction).

Practice: Order of Operations

Simplify:

1. $6 + 4 \times 3^2$

2. $3^2 + 6(4+1)$

3. $12 - 2(8+2) + 5$

4. $8[3(3^2 - 8) + 1]$

5. $6\{4[2(3+2) - 8] - 8\}$

Answers: Order of Operations

1. 42

    $6 + 4 \times \underline{3^2} = 6 + 4 \times 9$

     $6 + \underline{4 \times 9} = 6 + 36$

      $6 + 36 = 42$

2. 39

$$3^2 + 6\underline{(4+1)} = 3^2 + 6(5)$$
$$\underline{3^2} + 6(5) = 9 + 6(5)$$
$$9 + \underline{6(5)} = 9 + 30$$
$$9 + 30 = 39$$

3. –3

$$12 - 2\underline{(8+2)} + 5 = 12 - 2(10) + 5$$
$$12 - \underline{2(10)} + 5 = 12 - 20 + 5$$
$$\underline{12 - 20} + 5 = -8 + 5$$
$$-8 + 5 = -3$$

4. 32

$$8\left[3\left(\underline{3^2 - 8}\right) + 1\right] = 8\left[3\left(\underline{3^2} - 8\right) + 1\right]$$
$$8\left[3\left(\underline{3^2} - 8\right) + 1\right] = 8\left[3(9 - 8) + 1\right]$$
$$8\left[3\left(\underline{9 - 8}\right) + 1\right] = 8\left[3(1) + 1\right]$$
$$8\left[\underline{3(1)} + 1\right] = 8\left[3 + 1\right]$$
$$8\underline{[3 + 1]} = 8[4]$$
$$8[4] = 32$$

5. 0

$$6\left\{4\left[2\underline{(3+2)} - 8\right] - 8\right\} = 6\left\{4\left[2(5) - 8\right] - 8\right\}$$
$$6\left\{4\left[\underline{2(5)} - 8\right] - 8\right\} = 6\left\{4\left[\underline{2(5)} - 8\right] - 8\right\}$$
$$6\left\{4\left[\underline{2(5)} - 8\right] - 8\right\} = 6\left\{4[10 - 8] - 8\right\}$$
$$6\left\{4\underline{[10 - 8]} - 8\right\} = 6\left\{4[2] - 8\right\}$$
$$6\left\{\underline{4[2]} - 8\right\} = 6\{8 - 8\}$$
$$6\{\underline{8 - 8}\} = 6(0)$$
$$6(0) = 0$$

Integers

Number Line

On a ***number line,*** the numbers to the right of 0 are *positive.* Numbers to the left of 0 are *negative* as follows:

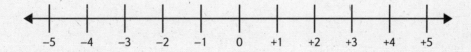

Given any two integers on a number line, the integer located furthest to the right is always larger, regardless of its sign (positive or negative). Note that fractions may also be placed on a number line and can be similarly compared.

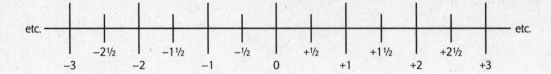

Examples:

For each pair of values, select the one with the greater value.

> **1.** −8, −3

−3 > −8 since −3 is farther to right on the number line.

> **2.** $0, -3\frac{1}{4}$

$0 > -3\frac{1}{4}$ since 0 is farther to the right on the number line.

Absolute Value

The *absolute value* of a number is its distance from 0 on a number line. It can also be interpreted as the value of the number disregarding its sign. The symbol denoting the absolute value of 5, for example is |5|. Two vertical lines are placed around the number.

The absolute value of −5 is denoted as |−5| and its value is 5.

Examples:

> **1.** |−12| = 12

> **2.** $\left|-3\frac{1}{2}\right| = 3\frac{1}{2}$

> **3.** −|−5| = −5

First find |−5|, which is 5; then find the negative of this result, which is −5.

Adding Two Integers with the Same Sign

To *add two integers with the same sign* (either both positive or both negative), add the absolute values of the integers and keep their same sign.

Examples:

> **1.**
> $$\begin{array}{r} +5 \\ +\,+7 \\ \hline +12 \end{array}$$
> |+5| = 5, |+7| = 7, 5 + 7 = 12

> **2.**
> $$\begin{array}{r} -8 \\ +\,-3 \\ \hline -11 \end{array}$$
> |−8| = 8, |−3| = 3, 3 + 8 = 11

Adding Two Integers with Different Signs

To **add two integers with different signs** (one positive and one negative), subtract their absolute values and keep the sign of the integer with the greater absolute value.

Examples:

> **1.** $-4 + 8 = 4$ $|-4| = 4, |8| = 8$ $8 - 4 = 4$ $|8| > |-4|$

> $$\begin{array}{r} +5 \\ \textbf{2.} \underline{+-7} \\ -2 \end{array}$$ $|+5| = 5, |-7| = 7$ $7 - 5 = 2$ $|-7| > |+5|$

Subtracting Positive and/or Negative Integers

To **subtract positive and/or negative integers,** just change the sign of the number being subtracted and then add.

Examples:

> **1.** $-12 - 6 = -12 + -6 = -18$

> **2.** $\begin{array}{r} +12 \\ \underline{-+4} \end{array}$ becomes $\begin{array}{r} +12 \\ \underline{+-4} \\ +8 \text{ or } 8 \end{array}$

> **3.** $\begin{array}{r} -14 \\ \underline{--4} \end{array}$ becomes $\begin{array}{r} -14 \\ \underline{++4} \\ -10 \end{array}$

When number values are positive, the "+" is dropped, $+5 = 5$.

Minus Sign Precedes a Parenthesis

If a **minus sign precedes a parenthesis,** it means everything within the parentheses is to be subtracted. Therefore, using the same rule as in subtraction of integers, simply change every sign within the parentheses to its opposite, and then add.

Examples:

> **1.** $\begin{aligned} 9 - (3 - 5 + 7 - 6) &= 9 + \left[(-3) + 5 + (-7) + 6\right] \\ &= 9 + 1 \\ &= 10 \end{aligned}$

> **2.** $\begin{aligned} 20 - (35 - 50 + 100) &= 20 + \left[(-35) + 50 + (-100)\right] \\ &= 20 + (-85) \\ &= -65 \end{aligned}$

Multiply or Divide Integers with Negative Signs

To multiply or divide integers with a negative sign use these rules:

- Multiplying or dividing with an odd number of negative signs will produce a negative answer.
- Multiplying or dividing with an even number of negative signs will produce a positive answer.

Examples:

1. $(-3)(8)(-5)(-1)(-2) = 240$

2. $(-3)(8)(-1)(-2) = -48$

3. $\dfrac{-64}{-2} = 32$

4. $\dfrac{-64}{2} = -32$

Zero Times Any Number

Zero times any number equals zero.

Examples:

1. $(0)(5) = 0$

2. $(-3)(0) = 0$

3. $(8)(9)(0)(3)(-4) = 0$

Zero Divided by a Nonzero Number

Similarly, zero divided by any *nonzero* number is zero.

Examples:

1. $0 \div 5$ also written as $\dfrac{0}{5} = 0$

2. $\dfrac{0}{-3} = 0$

Important note: Dividing by zero is "undefined" and is not permitted. $\dfrac{6}{0}$ and $\dfrac{0}{0}$ are not permitted because there are no values for these expressions. The answer is *not* zero.

Practice: Integers

1. Which is larger, $-11\frac{2}{3}$ or -12?

2. $|-4.6| =$

3. $-\left|-2\frac{1}{2}\right| =$

4. $-3 - \left[4 - 7 - (-9)\right] =$

5. $[5 - 8][4 - 9][-5 + 7] =$

6. $\dfrac{-32}{(10 - 18)} =$

7. $\dfrac{(11 - 13) + (14 - 12)}{(-3)(-2)} =$

8. $\dfrac{6(-1)(-2)}{100 - 10^2} =$

Answers: Integers

1. $-11\frac{2}{3}$

   $-11\frac{2}{3}$ is the larger value since it is farther to the right on the number line.

2. 4.6

   $|-4.6| = 4.6$ because absolute value is the value disregarding the sign.

3. $-2\frac{1}{2}$

   Find $\left|-2\frac{1}{2}\right|$, then find the negative of that: $-\left|-2\frac{1}{2}\right| = -2\frac{1}{2}$.

4. -9

   $$-3 - [4 - 7 - (-9)] = -3 - [4 + (-7) + 9]$$
   $$= -3 - [6]$$
   $$= -9$$

5. 30

   $[5 - 8][4 - 9][-5 + 7] = [-3][-5][2] = 30$

6. 4

   $\dfrac{-32}{(10 - 18)} = \dfrac{-32}{-8} = 4$

7. 0

   $\dfrac{(11 - 13) + (14 - 12)}{(-3)(-2)} = \dfrac{-2 + 2}{6} = \dfrac{0}{6} = 0$

8. no such value

   $\dfrac{6(-1)(-2)}{100 - 10^2} = \dfrac{12}{100 - 100} = \dfrac{12}{0}$

   You cannot divide by zero, so no such value exists.

Fractions

Fractions compare two values. The *numerator* is written above the fraction bar and the *denominator* is written below the fraction bar. The fraction bar indicates division.

$$\frac{1}{2} \quad \frac{1 \text{ is the numerator}}{2 \text{ is the denominator}}$$

All rules for the arithmetic operations involving integers also apply to fractions.

Fractions may be *negative* as well as *positive.* However, negative fractions are typically written $-\frac{3}{4}$, not $\frac{-3}{4}$ or $\frac{3}{-4}$ (although they are all equal): $-\frac{3}{4} = \frac{-3}{4} = \frac{3}{-4}$.

A fraction with a value less than 1, like $\frac{3}{5}$, where the numerator is smaller than the denominator, is called a ***proper fraction.*** A fraction with a value greater than or equal to 1, like $\frac{12}{7}$ or $\frac{6}{6}$, where the numerator is larger than or equal to the denominator, is called an ***improper fraction.***

Mixed Numbers

When a term contains both a whole number and a fraction, it is called *a **mixed number.*** For instance, $5\frac{1}{4}$ and $290\frac{3}{4}$ are both mixed numbers. To change an improper fraction to a mixed number, you divide the denominator into the numerator to get the whole number portion and then place the remainder over the divisor to get the fraction portion.

$$\frac{18}{7} = 2\frac{4}{7} \quad \begin{array}{l}\leftarrow \text{remainder} \\ \leftarrow \text{divisor}\end{array} \qquad \begin{array}{r}2 \\ 7\overline{)18} \\ \underline{14} \\ 4\end{array}$$

To change a mixed number to an improper fraction, you multiply the denominator of the fraction portion with the whole number, then add the numerator portion to that product, and then put that total over the original denominator.

$$4\frac{1}{2} = \frac{9}{2} \qquad \frac{2 \times 4 + 1}{2} = \frac{9}{2}$$

Examples:

1. Change $5\frac{3}{4}$ to an improper fraction.

$$5\frac{3}{4} = \frac{23}{4} \qquad 4 \times 5 + 3 = 23$$

2. Change $\frac{59}{6}$ to a mixed number.

$$\frac{59}{6} = 9\frac{5}{6} \qquad \begin{array}{r}9 \\ 6\overline{)59} \\ \underline{54} \\ 5\end{array}$$

Simplified Fractions

On the GRE, fractions should be *simplified.* This is done by dividing both the numerator and denominator by the largest number that will divide both without a remainder.

Examples:

1. $\frac{30}{50} = \frac{30 \div 10}{50 \div 10} = \frac{3}{5}$

2. $\frac{8}{40} = \frac{8 \div 8}{40 \div 8} = \frac{1}{5}$

3. $\frac{9}{15} = \frac{9 \div 3}{15 \div 3} = \frac{3}{5}$

Changing the Denominator

The *denominator* of a fraction may be changed by multiplying both the numerator and the denominator by the same number.

Examples:

> **1.** Change $\frac{1}{2}$ into tenths.

$$\frac{1}{2} = \frac{1 \times 5}{2 \times 5} = \frac{5}{10}$$

> **2.** Change $\frac{3}{4}$ into fortieths.

$$\frac{3}{4} = \frac{3 \times 10}{4 \times 10} = \frac{30}{40}$$

Factors

Factors of a number are those whole numbers that divide the number with no remainder.

Examples:

> **1.** What are the factors of 8?

$$8 = 1 \times 8 \text{ and } 8 = 2 \times 4$$

Therefore, the factors of 8 are 1, 2, 4, and 8.

> **2.** What are the factors of 24?

$$24 = 1 \times 24, \ 24 = 2 \times 12, \ 24 = 3 \times 8, \ 24 = 4 \times 6$$

Therefore, the factors of 24 are 1, 2, 3, 4, 6, 8, 12, and 24.

Common Factors

Common factors are those factors that are the same for two or more numbers.

Examples:

> **1.** What are the common factors of 6 and 8?

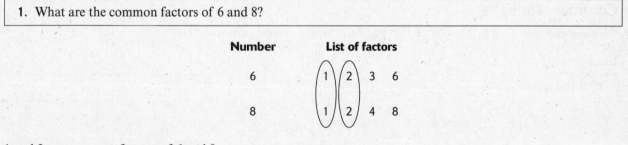

Number	List of factors
6	1 2 3 6
8	1 2 4 8

1 and 2 are common factors of 6 and 8.

Note: Some numbers may have many common factors.

2. What are the common factors of 24 and 36?

Number	List of factors
24	1 2 3 4 6 8 12 24
36	1 2 3 4 6 9 12 18 36

The common factors of 24 and 36 are 1, 2, 3, 4, 6, and 12.

Greatest Common Factor

The *greatest common factor* (GCF), also known as the greatest common divisor, is the largest factor common to two or more numbers.

Example:

1. What is the greatest common factor of 24 and 36?

Number	List of factors
24	1 2 3 4 6 8 **12** 24
36	1 2 3 4 6 9 **12** 18 36

Notice that while, 1, 2, 3, 4, 6, and 12 are all common factors of 24 and 36, 12 is the greatest common factor.

Multiples

Multiples of a number are found by multiplying that number by 1, by 2, by 3, by 4, by 5, and so on.

Examples:

1. Multiples of 3 are: 3, 6, 9, 12, 15, 18, 21, and so on.

2. Multiples of 4 are: 4, 8, 12, 16, 20, 24, 28, 32, and so on.

3. Multiples of 7 are: 7, 14, 21, 28, 35, 42, 49, 56, and so on.

Common Multiples

Common multiples are those multiples that are the same for two or more numbers.

Example:

1. What are the common multiples of 2 and 3?

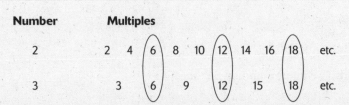

Number	Multiples
2	2 4 6 8 10 12 14 16 18 etc.
3	3 6 9 12 15 18 etc.

The common multiples of 2 and 3 are 6, 12, 18,... Notice that common multiples may go on indefinitely.

Least Common Multiple

The *least common multiple* (LCM) is the smallest multiple that is common to two or more numbers.

Example:

> **1.** What is the least common multiple of 2 and 3?

Number	Multiples
2	2 4 **6** 8 10 12 14 16 18 etc.
3	3 **6** 9 12 15 18 etc.

The least common multiple of 2 and 3 is 6.

Least Common Denominator

To add fractions, you must first change all denominators to their *least common denominator* (LCD). The LCD is also known as the least common multiple of the denominators. After all the denominators are the same, add fractions by simply adding the numerators (notice the denominator remains the same).

Examples:

> **1.** $\frac{2}{7} + \frac{3}{5} = \left(\frac{5}{5}\right)\left(\frac{2}{7}\right) + \left(\frac{7}{7}\right)\left(\frac{3}{5}\right) = \frac{10}{35} + \frac{21}{35} = \frac{31}{35}$

35 is the LCD and $\frac{2}{7} = \frac{10}{35}$, $\frac{3}{5} = \frac{21}{35}$

> **2.** $\quad \frac{3}{8} = \frac{3}{8} \quad \left\{ 8 \text{ is the LCD and } \frac{3}{8} = \frac{3}{8} \right.$
>
> $\quad +\frac{1}{2} = \frac{4}{8} \quad \left\{ 8 \text{ is the LCD and } \frac{1}{2} = \frac{4}{8} \right.$
>
> $\qquad\quad \frac{7}{8}$

> **3.** $\frac{4}{11} + \frac{9}{11} = \frac{13}{11}$ or $1\frac{2}{11}$

Since the denominators are the same, it is not necessary to find an LCD.

Adding and Subtracting Positive and Negative Fractions

The rules for integers apply to adding or subtracting positive and negative fractions.

Examples:

> **1.** $-\frac{1}{2} + \frac{1}{3} = -\frac{3}{6} + \frac{2}{6} = \frac{-3+2}{6} = -\frac{1}{6}$

> **2.** $\qquad \frac{3}{4} = \qquad \frac{9}{12}$
>
> $\quad +\left(-\frac{1}{3}\right) = +\left(-\frac{4}{12}\right)$
>
> $\qquad\qquad\quad \frac{5}{12}$

3. $-\dfrac{7}{8} - \dfrac{2}{3} = -\dfrac{7}{8} + \left(-\dfrac{2}{3}\right)$

$\qquad = \left(\dfrac{3}{3}\right)\left(-\dfrac{7}{8}\right) + \left(\dfrac{8}{8}\right)\left(-\dfrac{2}{3}\right)$

$\qquad = \dfrac{-21}{24} + \dfrac{-16}{24}$

$\qquad = \dfrac{-37}{24}$ or $-1\dfrac{13}{24}$

4. $\qquad \dfrac{9}{10} = \dfrac{9}{10} = \dfrac{9}{10}$

$\quad -\left(-\dfrac{1}{5}\right) = +\dfrac{1}{5} = +\dfrac{2}{10}$

$\qquad\qquad\qquad \dfrac{11}{10}$ or $1\dfrac{1}{10}$

Adding Mixed Numbers

The rules for adding and subtracting integers also apply to mixed numbers. To **add mixed numbers,** add the fraction portions together, add the whole numbers, then combine the two results.

Example:

1. $1\dfrac{3}{8} + 2\dfrac{5}{6} = (1 + 2) + \left(\dfrac{3}{8} + \dfrac{5}{6}\right) \qquad \dfrac{3}{8} = \dfrac{9}{24}$ and $\dfrac{5}{6} = \dfrac{20}{24}$

$\qquad\qquad = 3 + \left(\dfrac{9}{24} + \dfrac{20}{24}\right)$

$\qquad\qquad = 3 + \dfrac{29}{24}$

$\qquad\qquad = 3 + 1\dfrac{5}{24}$

$\qquad\qquad = 4\dfrac{5}{24}$

Subtracting Mixed Numbers

When you subtract mixed numbers, sometimes you may have to "borrow" from the whole number, just as you sometimes borrow from the next column when subtracting ordinary numbers.

Examples:

1. $\begin{array}{r} \overset{7}{\cancel{6}} \\ 3\,\cancel{\dfrac{\cancel{1}}{\cancel{6}}} \\ \cancel{4}\,\cancel{\dfrac{1}{6}} \end{array}\leftarrow \begin{cases} \text{borrowed 1 in the form } \dfrac{6}{6} \text{ from the 4} \\ \text{and added it to the } \dfrac{1}{6} \text{ to get } \dfrac{7}{6} \end{cases}$

$\qquad \dfrac{-2\dfrac{5}{6}}{}$

$\qquad\quad 1\dfrac{2}{6} = 1\dfrac{1}{3}$

To subtract a mixed number from a whole number, you have to "borrow" from the whole number.

2. $6 = 5\frac{5}{5} \leftarrow \left\{ \text{borrow 1 in the form of } \frac{5}{5} \text{ from the 6} \right.$

$\underline{-3\frac{1}{5}} = \underline{-3\frac{1}{5}}$

$\qquad\quad 2\frac{4}{5}$

3. $11 = 10\frac{3}{3} \leftarrow \left\{ \text{borrow 1 in the form of } \frac{3}{3} \text{ from the 11} \right.$

$\underline{-\frac{2}{3}} = \underline{-\frac{2}{3}}$

$\qquad\quad 10\frac{1}{3}$

4. $6\frac{1}{8} - 3\frac{3}{4} = 6\frac{1}{8} - 3\frac{6}{8} = \overset{5}{\cancel{6}}\overset{\frac{9}{8}}{\cancel{\frac{1}{8}}} - 3\frac{6}{8} = 2\frac{3}{8}$

5. $-\frac{7}{8} - \frac{5}{9} = -\frac{63}{72} + \left(-\frac{40}{72}\right) \qquad \frac{7}{8} = \frac{63}{72}, \frac{5}{9} = \frac{40}{72}$

$\qquad\qquad = -\frac{103}{72} \text{ or } -1\frac{31}{72}$

Multiplying Fractions

The rules for multiplying and dividing of integers also apply to multiplying and dividing of fractions. To **_multiply fractions,_** simply multiply the numerators, and then multiply the denominators. Simplify if possible.

Examples:

1. $-\frac{1}{6} \times \frac{1}{3} = -\frac{1 \times 1}{6 \times 3} = -\frac{1}{18}$

2. $\left(-\frac{3}{4}\right)\left(-\frac{5}{7}\right) = +\frac{3 \times 5}{4 \times 7} = \frac{15}{28}$

3. $\frac{2}{3} \times \frac{5}{12} = \frac{10}{36}$ Simplify $\frac{10}{36}$ to $\frac{5}{18}$.

Notice the answer was simplified because $\frac{10}{36}$ was not in lowest terms.

Whole numbers can be written as fractions: $\left(3 = \frac{3}{1}, 4 = \frac{4}{1}, \text{ and so on}\right)$.

4. $3 \times \frac{3}{8} = \frac{3}{1} \times \frac{3}{8} = \frac{9}{8} = 1\frac{1}{8}$

When multiplying fractions, it is often possible to simplify the problem by **canceling.** To cancel, find a number that divides one numerator and one denominator. In the next example, 2 in the numerator and 12 in the denominator are both divisible by 2.

5. $\dfrac{\overset{1}{\cancel{2}}}{3} \times \dfrac{5}{\underset{6}{\cancel{12}}} = \dfrac{5}{18}$

Remember: You can cancel only when *multiplying* fractions.

6. $\dfrac{1}{4} \times \dfrac{2}{7} = \dfrac{1}{\underset{2}{\cancel{4}}} \times \dfrac{\overset{1}{\cancel{2}}}{7} = \dfrac{1}{14}$

7. $\left(-\dfrac{\overset{1}{\cancel{3}}}{\underset{2}{\cancel{8}}}\right) \times \left(-\dfrac{\overset{1}{\cancel{4}}}{\underset{3}{\cancel{9}}}\right) = \dfrac{1}{6}$

Multiplying Mixed Numbers

To *multiply mixed numbers,* change any mixed numbers or whole numbers to improper fractions, then multiply as previously shown.

Examples:

1. $2\dfrac{3}{8} \times 1\dfrac{5}{6} = \dfrac{19}{8} \times \dfrac{11}{6} = \dfrac{209}{48}$ or $4\dfrac{17}{48}$

2. $\left(-3\dfrac{1}{3}\right)\left(2\dfrac{1}{4}\right) = \left(-\dfrac{\overset{5}{\cancel{10}}}{\underset{-1}{\cancel{3}}}\right)\left(\dfrac{\overset{3}{\cancel{9}}}{\underset{2}{\cancel{4}}}\right) = -\dfrac{15}{2}$ or $-7\dfrac{1}{2}$

Dividing Fractions or Mixed Numbers

To *divide fractions or mixed numbers* invert (turn upside down) the second fraction (the one "divided by") and multiply. Simplify where possible.

Examples:

1. $-\dfrac{1}{4} \div \dfrac{9}{14} = \left(-\dfrac{1}{\underset{2}{\cancel{4}}}\right)\left(\dfrac{\overset{7}{\cancel{14}}}{9}\right) = -\dfrac{7}{18}$

2. $6 \div 2\dfrac{1}{3} = \dfrac{6}{1} \div \dfrac{7}{3} = \dfrac{6}{1} \times \dfrac{3}{7} = \dfrac{18}{7}$ or $2\dfrac{4}{7}$

Complex Fractions

Sometimes a division-of-fractions problem may appear in the form below. Division problems in this form are called *complex fractions.*

$$\dfrac{\dfrac{3}{4}}{\dfrac{7}{8}}$$

The line separating the two fractions means "divided by." This problem may be rewritten as $\frac{3}{4} \div \frac{7}{8}$. Now follow the same procedure as previously shown.

$$\frac{3}{4} \div \frac{7}{8} = \frac{3}{\underset{1}{4}} \times \frac{\overset{2}{8}}{7} = \frac{6}{7}$$

Some complex fractions require applying the order of operations.

Example:

1. $\dfrac{1}{3 + \dfrac{2}{1 + \dfrac{1}{3}}}$

This problem can be rewritten using grouping symbols.

$$\frac{1}{3 + \dfrac{2}{1 + \dfrac{1}{3}}} = 1 \div \left\{ 3 + \left[2 \div \left(1 + \frac{1}{3} \right) \right] \right\} \text{ Start with the most inside grouping.}$$

$$= 1 \div \left\{ 3 + \left[2 \div \left(\frac{4}{3} \right) \right] \right\} \text{ Do the next most inside grouping.}$$

$$= 1 \div \left\{ 3 + \left[\frac{\overset{1}{2}}{1} \times \frac{3}{\underset{2}{4}} \right] \right\}$$

$$= 1 \div \left\{ 3 + \left[\frac{3}{2} \right] \right\} \text{ Do the next most inside grouping.}$$

$$= 1 \div \left\{ \frac{9}{2} \right\}$$

$$= 1 \times \frac{2}{9}$$

$$= \frac{2}{9}$$

Practice: Fractions

1. When $4\frac{5}{8}$ is made into a fraction, what will be the numerator?

2. Change $-\frac{42}{16}$ into a mixed number in simplest form.

3. What is the GCF of 36 and 60?

4. What is the LCM of 12 and 16?

5. $\frac{3}{4} + \left(-\frac{1}{2} \right) =$

6. $\left(-\frac{3}{4} \right) + \frac{1}{3} + \left(-\frac{1}{6} \right) =$

7. $\frac{1}{6} - \left(-\frac{1}{3} \right) =$

8. $-\frac{7}{12} - \frac{5}{6} =$

9. $2\frac{1}{2} \times 3\frac{1}{4} =$

10. $-5\frac{1}{4} \times 3\frac{3}{7} =$

11. $\left(-2\frac{3}{4}\right) \div (-7) =$

12. $\dfrac{2 - \frac{7}{8}}{1 + \frac{3}{4}} =$

13. $\dfrac{1 + \dfrac{1}{2 + \frac{1}{2}}}{3} =$

Answers: Fractions

1. 37

   $4\frac{5}{8} = \frac{37}{8}$. The numerator is 37.

2. $-2\frac{5}{8}$

   $-\frac{42}{16} = -\frac{21}{8} = -2\frac{5}{8}$

3. 12

   Factors of 36 are 1, 2, 3, 4, 6, 9, **12**, 18, 36. Factors of 60 are 1, 2 ,3, 4, 5, 6, 10, **12**, 15, 20, 30, 60.

   The GCF of 36 and 60 is 12.

4. 48

   Multiples of 12 are 12, 24, 36, **48**, 60,… Multiples of 16 are 16, 32, **48**, 64,…

   The LCM of 12 and 16 is 48.

5. $\frac{1}{4}$

   $\frac{3}{4} + \left(-\frac{1}{2}\right) = \frac{3}{4} + \left(-\frac{2}{4}\right) = \frac{1}{4}$

6. $-\frac{7}{12}$

   $\left(-\frac{3}{4}\right) + \frac{1}{3} + \left(-\frac{1}{6}\right) = \left(-\frac{9}{12}\right) + \frac{4}{12} + \left(-\frac{2}{12}\right) = -\frac{7}{12}$

7. $\frac{1}{2}$

   $\frac{1}{6} - \left(-\frac{1}{3}\right) = \frac{1}{6} + \frac{1}{3} = \frac{1}{6} + \frac{2}{6} = \frac{3}{6} = \frac{1}{2}$

8. $-\frac{17}{12}$ or $-1\frac{5}{12}$

   $-\frac{7}{12} - \frac{5}{6} = -\frac{7}{12} + \left(-\frac{5}{6}\right) = -\frac{7}{12} + \left(-\frac{10}{12}\right) = -\frac{17}{12}$ or $-1\frac{5}{12}$

9. $\dfrac{65}{8}$ or $8\dfrac{1}{8}$

$$2\dfrac{1}{2} \times 3\dfrac{1}{4} = \left(\dfrac{5}{2}\right)\left(\dfrac{13}{4}\right) = \dfrac{65}{8} \text{ or } 8\dfrac{1}{8}$$

10. -18

$$-5\dfrac{1}{4} \times 3\dfrac{3}{7} = \left(-\dfrac{\overset{3}{\cancel{21}}}{\underset{1}{\cancel{4}}}\right)\left(\dfrac{\overset{6}{\cancel{24}}}{\underset{1}{\cancel{7}}}\right) = -18$$

11. $\dfrac{11}{28}$

$$\left(-2\dfrac{3}{4}\right) \div (-7) = \left(-\dfrac{11}{4}\right) \div \left(-\dfrac{7}{1}\right) = \left(-\dfrac{11}{4}\right)\left(-\dfrac{1}{7}\right) = \dfrac{11}{28}$$

12. $\dfrac{9}{14}$

$$\dfrac{2-\dfrac{7}{8}}{1+\dfrac{3}{4}} = \dfrac{1\dfrac{1}{8}}{1\dfrac{3}{4}} = \dfrac{9}{8} \div \dfrac{7}{4} = \left(\dfrac{9}{\underset{2}{\cancel{8}}}\right)\left(\dfrac{\overset{1}{\cancel{4}}}{7}\right) = \dfrac{9}{14}$$

13. $\dfrac{7}{15}$

$$\dfrac{1+\dfrac{1}{2+\dfrac{1}{2}}}{3} = \dfrac{1+\dfrac{1}{\frac{5}{2}}}{3} = \dfrac{1+\left(1 \div \dfrac{5}{2}\right)}{3} = \dfrac{1+\left(1 \times \dfrac{2}{5}\right)}{3} = \dfrac{1+\dfrac{2}{5}}{3} = \dfrac{1\dfrac{2}{5}}{3} = \dfrac{\frac{7}{5}}{3} = \dfrac{7}{5} \div \dfrac{3}{1} = \dfrac{7}{5} \times \dfrac{1}{3} = \dfrac{7}{15}$$

Decimals

Each position in any decimal number has ***place value.*** For instance, in the number 485.03, the 4 is in the hundreds place, the 8 is in the tens place, the 5 is in the ones place, the 0 is in the tenths place, and the 3 is in the hundredths place. The following chart will help you identify place value.

millions	hundred thousands	ten thousands	thousands	hundreds	tens	ones	tenths	hundredths	thousandths	ten thousandths	hundred thousandths
							1/10	1/100	1/1,000	1/10,000	1/100,000
1,000,000	100,000	10,000	1,000	100	10	1	0.1	0.01	0.001	0.0001	0.00001
10^6	10^5	10^4	10^3	10^2	10^1	10^0	10^{-1}	10^{-2}	10^{-3}	10^{-4}	10^{-5}
				4	8	5	0	3			

Rounding Off

To *round off* any **positive number:**

1. Underline the place value to which you're rounding off.
2. Look to the immediate right (one place) of the underlined place value.
3. Identify the number (the one to the right). If it is 5 or higher, round off the underlined place value up 1. If the number (the one to the right) is 4 or less, leave your underlined place value as it is and change all the other numbers to the right of it to zeros, or drop them if it is to the right of the decimal point.

To *round off* any **negative number:**

1. Take the absolute value of the number.
2. Do the 3 steps as above.
3. Replace the negative sign on the number.

Examples:

> **1.** Round 4.4584 to the nearest thousandth.

The 8 is in the thousandth place. To its right is a 4. Thus, the 8 is left unchanged and to its right the digits are dropped. The rounded off answer becomes 4.458.

> **2.** Round 3456.12 to the nearest ten.

The 5 is in the tens place. To its right is a 6. Thus the 5 is increased by 1 and the digits until the decimal become zeros, then the remaining digits are dropped. The rounded off answer is 3460.

> **3.** Round –3.6 to the nearest integer.

$|-3.6| = 3.6$. Rounding to the nearest integer is the same as rounding to the nearest one. The 3 is in the one's place and to its right is a 6. Thus, 3.6 rounded to the nearest one is 4. Therefore, –3.6 rounded to the nearest integer is –4.

Fractions Written in Decimal Form

Fractions and mixed numbers can be written in decimal form (**decimal fractions**) by using a *decimal point.* All numbers to the left of the decimal point are whole numbers. All numbers to the right of the decimal point are fractions with denominators of powers of 10 (10^1, 10^2, 10^3, …).

Examples:

> **1.** $0.6 = \dfrac{6}{10} = \dfrac{3}{5}$

> **2.** $3.25 = 3\dfrac{25}{100} = 3\dfrac{1}{4}$

Adding and Subtracting Decimals

To *add or subtract decimals,* line up the decimal points and then add or subtract in the same manner you would add or subtract regular numbers. Placing zeros at the right of the number can make the problem look better.

Examples:

> **1.** $0.08 + 1.3 + 0.562 = 0.080$
> $$
> \begin{array}{r}
> 0.080 \\
> 1.300 \\
> +\,0.562 \\
> \hline
> 1.942
> \end{array}
> $$

2. $0.45 - 0.003 = 0.4\overset{4\;10}{\cancel{5}\;\cancel{0}}$

$$\underline{-0.0\,0\,3}$$
$$0.4\,4\,7$$

A whole number has an understood decimal point to its right.

3. $17 - 8.43 = 1\overset{6}{\cancel{7}}.\overset{\;9}{\cancel{1}}\overset{10}{\cancel{0}}\,\cancel{0}$

$$\underline{-8\,.\,4\,3}$$
$$8\,.\,5\,7$$

Multiplying Decimals

To *multiply decimals,* multiply as usual. Place the decimal point in the answer so that the number of digits to the right of the decimal point is equal to the sum of the number of digits to the right of the decimal point in both numbers multiplied (the multiplier and multiplicand). It is sometimes necessary to insert zeros immediately to the right of the decimal point in the answer to have the correct number of digits.

Examples:

1. $8.001 \quad \leftarrow \{$ 3 digits to the right of the decimal point

$\underline{\times 2.4} \quad \leftarrow \{$ 1 digit to the right of the decimal point

32004

$\underline{16002}$

$19.2024 \quad \begin{cases} \text{decimal point placed so there is the same number of} \\ \text{digits to the right of the decimal point } (1+3=4) \end{cases}$

2. $3.02 \quad \leftarrow \{$ 2 digits to the right of the decimal point

$\underline{\times 0.004} \quad \leftarrow \{$ 3 digits to the right of the decimal point

$0.01208 \quad \begin{cases} \text{zero inserted on the left so that there are the same number of} \\ \text{digits to the right of the decimal point } (2+3=5) \end{cases}$

Dividing Decimals

To *divide decimals,* divide as usual, except that if the *divisor* (the number you're dividing by) has a decimal, move it to the right as many places as necessary until it's a whole number. Then move the decimal point in the *dividend* (the number being divided into) to the right the same number of places. Sometimes you may have to insert zeros in the *dividend* (the number inside the division bracket).

Examples:

1. $0.147 \div 0.7$ becomes $0.7\overline{)0.147} = 7\overline{)1.47}$ with quotient 0.21

The decimal point was moved to the right 1 place in each number.

2. $0.002\overline{)26.} = 2\overline{)26000.}$ with quotient $13000.$

The decimal point was moved 3 places to the right in each number. This required inserting 3 zeros in the dividend.

Changing a Fraction to a Decimal

To *change a fraction to a decimal,* divide the numerator by the denominator. Every fraction, when changed to a decimal, either terminates (comes to and end) or has a repeating pattern in its decimal portion.

Examples:

Change each fraction into its decimal name.

1. $\frac{3}{20}$ becomes $20\overline{)3.00}\;\overset{0.15}{} = 0.15$

2. $\frac{5}{8}$ becomes $8\overline{)5.000}\;\overset{0.625}{} = 0.625$

3. $\frac{7}{12}$ becomes $12\overline{)7.00000}\;\overset{0.58333}{} = 0.58333...$ or $0.58\overline{3}$

Practice: Decimals

1. Round –123.456 to the nearest hundredth.

2. 12.005 + 6.3 =

3. –4.45 – (–3.617) =

4. (–3.5)(0.001) =

5. $\frac{-16.2}{0.81} =$

6. Change $\frac{4}{15}$ into a decimal.

Answers: Decimals

1. –123.46

   |–123.456| = 123.456. The 5 is in the hundredth place and to its right is a 6; 5 becomes 6 and to its right the digits are dropped. Replace the negative sign on the number.

2. 18.305

   $12.005 + 6.3 = 12.005$
   $+6.300$
   $\overline{18.305}$

3. –0.833

   –4.45 –(–3.617) = –4.45 + 3.617

   |–4.45| > |3.617|, therefore the result will be negative and the arithmetic is to subtract the absolute values.

   4.450
   $\underline{-3.617}$
   0.833

4. −0.0035

    −3.5 ← {total of 4 digits that are to the right of the decimal points

    <u>×0.001</u> ↙

    −0.0035 {decimal point placed so there is the same number of digits to the right
of the decimal point, which required inserting two zeros to the left of the 3

5. −20

$$0.81\overline{)16.2} = 81\overset{20}{\overline{)1620}}$$

Each number had its decimal point moved 2 places to the right, which required inserting one zero in the dividend.

6. $0.2\overline{6}$

$$15\overset{0.26....}{\overline{)4.0000}}$$
$$\underline{30}$$
$$100$$
$$\underline{90}$$
$$100$$

The "6" keeps repeating, so a bar is placed over the 6.

Ratios and Proportions

A *ratio* is a comparison of two values usually written in fraction form. The ratio of 3 to 5 can be expressed as 3:5 or $\frac{3}{5}$. A *proportion* is a statement that says that two ratios are equal. Because $\frac{5}{10}$ and $\frac{4}{8}$ both have values of $\frac{1}{2}$, it can be stated that $\frac{5}{10} = \frac{4}{8}$.

Cross-Products Fact

In a proportion, the cross products (multiplying across the equal sign) always produce equal answers. In the example of $\frac{5}{10} = \frac{4}{8}$, $5 \times 8 = 10 \times 4$.

You can use this cross-products fact to solve proportions.

Examples:

1. Solve for x: $\frac{4}{x} = \frac{7}{5}$.

Applying the cross-products fact, you get

$$7x = (4)(5)$$
$$7x = 20$$
$$x = \frac{20}{7} = 2\frac{6}{7}$$

2. Solve for x: $\frac{x}{100} = \frac{4}{25}$.

Applying the cross-products fact, you get

$$25x = (4)(100)$$
$$25x = 400$$
$$x = \frac{400}{25} = 16$$

Practice: Ratios and Proportions

1. Express the ratio of 15 to 29 in two different ways.

2. Solve for x: $\frac{x}{12} = \frac{3}{4}$.

Answers: Ratios and Proportions

1. 15:29 or $\frac{15}{29}$

2. 9

$$\frac{x}{12} = \frac{3}{4}$$
$$4x = (12)(3)$$
$$4x = 36$$
$$x = \frac{36}{4}$$
$$x = 9$$

Percents

The symbol for *percent* is %. The word percent means hundredths (per hundred). The expression 37% is read as 37 hundredths and can be expressed either as the fraction $\frac{37}{100}$ or decimal 0.37.

Changing Decimals to Percents

Decimals to Percents	Steps to change decimals to percents	Examples: Changing decimals to percents
	1. Move the decimal point two places to the right. 2. Insert a percent sign.	1. 0.75 = 75% 2. 0.005 = 0.5% 3. 1.85 = 185% 4. 20.3 = 2,030%
Percents to Decimals	**Steps to change percents to decimals:**	**Examples: Changing percents to decimals**
	1. Eliminate the percent sign. 2. Move the decimal point two places to the left. 3. Notice that sometimes inserting zeros will be necessary as in Examples 1 and 3.	1. 7% = 0.07 2. 23% = 0.23 3. 0.2% = 0.002

Changing Fractions to a Percent

There are two methods for changing a fraction to a percent.

Method 1: Changing Fractions to a Percent

1. Change the fraction to a decimal.
2. Change the decimal to a percent.

Examples:

Change each fraction into a percent.

1. $\frac{1}{8}$ $\frac{1}{8} = 0.125 = 12.5\%$ or $12\frac{1}{2}\%$

2. $\frac{2}{5}$ $\frac{2}{5} = 0.4 = 40\%$

3. $\frac{5}{2}$ $\frac{5}{2} = 2.5 = 250\%$

Method 2: Changing Fractions to a Percent

1. Create a proportion that sets the fraction equal to $\frac{x}{100}$.
2. Solve the proportion for x. Place a percent sign next to the x.

Examples:

Change each fraction into a percent.

1. $\frac{3}{8}$

$$\frac{3}{8} = \frac{x}{100}$$
$$8x = 300$$
$$x = \frac{300}{8} = 37\frac{1}{2} \text{ or } 37.5$$
$$\frac{3}{8} = 37\frac{1}{2}\% \text{ or } 37.5\%$$

2. $\frac{2}{3}$

$$\frac{2}{3} = \frac{x}{100}$$
$$3x = 200$$
$$x = \frac{200}{3} = 66\frac{2}{3}$$
$$\frac{2}{3} = 66\frac{2}{3}\%$$

Tip: To eliminate many unnecessary computations and save you time, try to make time to memorize important equivalents presented in "Fraction-Decimal-Percent Equivalents" at the beginning of this chapter (page 210).

Percentage-Type Problems

Percentage-type problems are of the form A is $B\%$ of C. If the B and C are known, the process is simply to multiply the B-percent value with the C-value.

Examples:

---
1. What is 79% of 64?

Using fractions: 79% of $64 = \dfrac{79}{100} \times \dfrac{64}{1} = \dfrac{5056}{100}$ or 50.56

Using decimals: 79% of $64 = (0.79)(64) = 50.56$

---
2. What is 15% of 50?

Using fractions: 15% of $50 = \dfrac{\overset{3}{\cancel{15}}}{\underset{\underset{2}{20}}{\cancel{100}}} \times \dfrac{\overset{5}{\cancel{50}}}{1} = \dfrac{15}{2} = 7\dfrac{1}{2}$ or 7.5

Using decimals: 15% of $50 = 0.15 \times 50 = 7.5$

---
3. What is $33\dfrac{1}{3}\%$ of 36?

The fraction method works best in this case.

$33\dfrac{1}{3}\%$ of $36 = \dfrac{1}{\underset{1}{\cancel{3}}} \times \dfrac{\overset{12}{\cancel{36}}}{1} = \dfrac{12}{1} = 12$

If the A value is known and one of the B or C values is unknown, then there are two methods that make solving the problem easier.

Equation and Proportion Methods

Method 1 - Percentage-Type Problems: Equation Method

1. Turn the question word-for-word into an equation. (Change percents to decimals or fractions, whichever you find easier.)
2. Solve the equation. (To review solving simple equations, see pages 256–257 in the Algebra section).

Method 2 - Percentage-Type Problems: Proportion Method

1. Use x to replace the unknown value.
2. Replace *is* with an *equal sign* (=) and replace *of* with *multiplication*. The proportion will look like this:

$$\dfrac{\%\text{-number}}{100} = \dfrac{\text{"is"-number}}{\text{"of "-number}}$$

Examples:

---
1. 40% of what is 20?
---

equation method | proportion method
$0.4(x) = 20$ | $\dfrac{40}{100} = \dfrac{20}{x}$
$x = \dfrac{20}{0.4}$ | $40x = 2000$
$x = 50$ | $x = 50$

Therefore, 40% of 50 is 20.

2. What percent of 45 is 30?

equation method | proportion method

$$\left(\frac{x}{100}\right)(45) = 30 \qquad\qquad \frac{x}{100} = \frac{30}{45}$$

$$\frac{45}{100}x = 30 \qquad\qquad 45x = 3000$$

$$x = \left(\frac{\overset{2}{\cancel{30}}}{1}\right)\left(\frac{100}{\underset{3}{\cancel{45}}}\right) \qquad x = \frac{3000}{45}$$

$$x = \frac{200}{3} \text{ or } 66\frac{2}{3} \qquad\qquad x = \frac{200}{3} \text{ or } 66\frac{2}{3}$$

Therefore, $66\frac{2}{3}\%$ of 45 is 30.

Percent Change

To find *percent change* (increase or decrease), use this formula:

$$\frac{\text{amount of change}}{\text{starting amount}} \times 100\% = \text{percent change}$$

Examples:

1. What is the percent increase of a rise in temperature from 80° to 100°?

The amount of change is the difference between 100 and 80 or 20.

$$\frac{\text{amount of change}}{\text{starting amount}} \times 100\% = \frac{\overset{1}{\cancel{20}}}{\underset{4}{\cancel{80}}} \times 100\% = 25\% \text{ increase}$$

2. What is the percent decrease of Jon's salary if it went from $150 per hour to $100 per hour?

$$\frac{\text{amount of change}}{\text{starting amount}} \times 100\% = \frac{\overset{1}{\cancel{50}}}{\underset{3}{\cancel{150}}} \times 100\% = \left(\frac{100}{3}\right)\% = 33\frac{1}{3}\% \text{ decrease}$$

3. What is the percent change from 2,100 to 1,890?

$$\frac{\text{amount of change}}{\text{starting amount}} \times 100\% = \frac{\overset{1}{\cancel{210}}}{\underset{10}{\cancel{2,100}}} \times 100\% = 10\% \text{ change}$$

Note: The terms percentage rise, percentage difference, and percentage change are the same as percent change.

Practice: Percents

1. Change $\frac{11}{12}$ into a percent.

2. Change 0.25% into a decimal.

3. 25% of 72 is what?

4. $16\frac{2}{3}\%$ of what is 15?

5. What percent of 60 is 45?

6. Which is greater, the percent change from 5 to 8 or the percent change from 8 to 5?

Answers: Percent

1. $91\frac{2}{3}\%$

$$\frac{11}{12} = \frac{x}{100}$$
$$12x = 1100$$

$$x = \frac{\overset{275}{\cancel{1100}}}{\underset{3}{\cancel{12}}} = 91\frac{2}{3}$$

$$\frac{11}{12} = 91\frac{2}{3}\%$$

2. 0.0025

0.25% = 0.0025 Drop the %-sign and move the decimal 2 places to the left.

3. 18

fraction method: $25\% = \frac{1}{4}$ decimal method: $25\% = 0.25$

$$\left(\frac{1}{\underset{1}{\cancel{4}}}\right)\left(\frac{\overset{18}{\cancel{72}}}{1}\right) = 18 \qquad\qquad (0.25)(72) = 18$$

4. 90

Making $16\frac{2}{3}\%$ into a fraction is the best way to begin.

$$16\frac{2}{3}\% = \left(\frac{\overset{1}{\cancel{50}}}{3}\right)\left(\frac{1}{\underset{2}{\cancel{100}}}\right) = \frac{1}{6}$$

equation method   proportion method

$$\left(\frac{1}{6}\right)x = 15 \qquad\qquad \frac{16\frac{2}{3}}{100} = \frac{15}{x}$$
$$x = \left(\frac{15}{1}\right)\left(\frac{6}{1}\right) \qquad\qquad \frac{1}{6} = \frac{15}{x}$$
$$x = 90 \qquad\qquad\qquad x = (15)(6)$$
$$x = 90$$

$16\frac{2}{3}\%$ of 90 is 15.

5. 75%

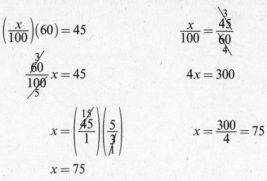

equation method   proportion method

$x = 75$

75% of 60 is 45. In this example, in the proportion method, once $\frac{45}{60}$ was simplified to $\frac{3}{4}$, you may have recognized that the percent is 75%.

6. percent change from 5 to 8

Percent change from 5 to 8: $\dfrac{\text{amount of change}}{\text{starting amount}} \times 100\% = \dfrac{3}{5} \times 100\% = 60\%$ change

Percent change from 8 to 5: $\dfrac{\text{amount of change}}{\text{starting amount}} \times 100\% = \dfrac{3}{8} \times 100\% = 37\frac{1}{2}\%$ change

The percent change from 5 to 8 is greater than the percent change from 8 to 5.

Exponents

An *exponent* is a positive, negative, or zero number placed above and to the right of a quantity. The quantity is known as the base, and the exponent expresses the power to which the base is to be raised. In 4^3, 4 is the base and 3 is the exponent. It shows that 4 is to be used as a factor three times: $4^3 = (4)(4)(4)$ and is read as *four to the third power* or *four cubed.*

Examples:

1. $2^5 = (2)(2)(2)(2)(2) = 32$

2. $(-3)^3 = (-3)(-3)(-3) = -27$

3. $\left(-\dfrac{1}{4}\right)^2 = \left(-\dfrac{1}{4}\right)\left(-\dfrac{1}{4}\right) = \dfrac{1}{16}$

More Exponents

Remember that $x^1 = x$ for all replacements of x and $x^0 = 1$ as long as $x \neq 0$.

Examples:

1. $(-5)^0 = 1$

2. $-6^0 = -1$ (in this case, the 0 exponent is only applied to the 6 since the negative sign was not in a parentheses as in example 1 above.)

3. $(2.4)^0 = 1$

4. $6^1 = 6$

Negative Exponents

If the **exponent is negative,** such as 3^{-2}, then the base and its exponent may be dropped under the number 1 in a fraction to remove the negative sign.

Examples:

1. $6^{-1} = \dfrac{1}{6^1} = \dfrac{1}{6}$

2. $3^{-2} = \dfrac{1}{3^2} = \dfrac{1}{9}$

3. $(-2)^{-3} = \dfrac{1}{(-2)^3} = \dfrac{1}{-8} = -\dfrac{1}{8}$

Multiplying Two Numbers with the Same Base

To multiply two numbers with the same base, you add their exponents and keep the same base.

Examples:

1. $8^3 \times 8^7 = 8^{3+7} = 8^{10}$

2. $(-2)^6 (-2)^{-3} = (-2)^{6+(-3)} = (-2)^3$

Dividing Two Numbers with the Same Base

To divide two numbers with the same base, you subtract the exponent on the dividing number from the exponent on the number being divided.

Examples:

1. $9^5 \div 9^{-2} = 9^{5-(-2)} = 9^{5+2} = 9^7$

2. $\dfrac{3^7}{3^4} = 3^{7-4} = 3^3$

Exponents Base and Exponent to a Power

To raise an expression involving a base and exponent to a power, keep the base and use the product of the exponent and the power as the new exponent.

Examples:

1. $\left(5^3\right)^2 = 5^{(2)(3)} = 5^6$

2. $\left[(-4)^{-4}\right]^{-2} = (-4)^{(-4)(-2)} = (-4)^8$

Practice: Exponents

Simplify each of the following into expressions without exponents.

1. $\left(-\dfrac{1}{4}\right)^3$

2. 5.6^0

3. -3^0

4. $(-7)^1$

5. 4^{-3}

6. $(-5)^{-2}$

Express each of the following with a base and one exponent.

7. $(7^6)(7^2)$

8. $\dfrac{(-3)^{12}}{(-3)^{-4}}$

9. $(6^3)^5$

Answers: Exponents

1. $-\dfrac{1}{64}$

$$\left(-\dfrac{1}{4}\right)^3 = \left(-\dfrac{1}{4}\right)\left(-\dfrac{1}{4}\right)\left(-\dfrac{1}{4}\right) = -\dfrac{1}{64}$$

2. 1

Any nonzero number to the zero power is 1.

3. -1

The zero exponent only is applied to the 3 and $3^0 = 1$.

4. -7

Any value to the 1st power is that value.

5. $\dfrac{1}{64}$

$$4^{-3} = \dfrac{1}{4^3} = \dfrac{1}{(4)(4)(4)} = \dfrac{1}{64}$$

6. $\dfrac{1}{25}$

$$(-5)^{-2} = \dfrac{1}{(-5)^2} = \dfrac{1}{(-5)(-5)} = \dfrac{1}{25}$$

7. 7^8

$$(7^6)(7^2) = 7^{6+2} = 7^8$$

8. $(-3)^{16}$

$$\frac{(-3)^{12}}{(-3)^{-4}} = (-3)^{12-(-4)} = (-3)^{12+4} = (-3)^{16}$$

9. 6^{15}

$$(6^3)^5 = 6^{(5)(3)} = 6^{15}$$

Square Roots

Square Roots of Perfect Squares

The square roots of *perfect squares* have exact answers. $\sqrt{5^2} = \sqrt{25} = 5$ and $\sqrt{(-4)^2} = \sqrt{16} = 4$. If a negative sign precedes a square root, the answer is the negative of the square root.

Example:

1. $-\sqrt{9} = -3$

2. $-\sqrt{(-4)^2} = -\sqrt{16} = -4$

Square Roots of Nonperfect Squares

To find the square root of a number that is *not a perfect square*, it is necessary to find an approximate answer by using the procedure given in the examples below.

Example:

1. Between what two consecutive integers is $\sqrt{135}$ and to which is it closer?

$$\sqrt{135} \text{ is between } \sqrt{121} \text{ and } \sqrt{144}$$

$$\sqrt{121} < \sqrt{135} < \sqrt{144}, \text{ and } \sqrt{121} = 11, \sqrt{144} = 12$$

$$11 < \sqrt{135} < 12$$

Since 135 is closer to 144 than 121, $\sqrt{135}$ is closer to 12 than to 11.

Tip: One advantage in taking the GRE by computer is that you will have access to an on-line calculator to help you easily find square roots results. After calculating the square root, use your knowledge of rounding off to determine the desired place value.

Simplifying a Square Root

Sometimes you will have to *simplify square roots,* or write them in simplest form. In fractions, $\frac{2}{4}$ can be simplified to $\frac{1}{2}$. In square roots, $\sqrt{32}$ can be simplified to $4\sqrt{2}$.

Methods to Simplify a Square Root	
Method 1	**Method 2**
Factor the number under the $\sqrt{}$ into two factors, one of which is the largest possible perfect square that divides the number. (Perfect squares are 1, 4, 9, 16, 25, 36, 49, …)	Completely factor the number under the $\sqrt{}$ into prime factors and then simplify by bringing out any factors that came in pairs.

Examples:

1. Simplify $\sqrt{32}$.

Method 1.

$\sqrt{32} = \sqrt{16 \times 2}$

$\quad = \sqrt{16} \times \sqrt{2}$

Take the square root of the perfect square number

$\quad = 4 \times \sqrt{2}$

Finally, write it as a single expression.

$\quad = 4\sqrt{2}$

Method 2.

$\sqrt{32} = \sqrt{2 \times 16}$

$\quad = \sqrt{2 \times 2 \times 8}$

$\quad = \sqrt{2 \times 2 \times 2 \times 4}$

$\quad = \sqrt{2 \times 2 \times 2 \times 2 \times 2}$

Rewrite with pairs under the radical

$\quad = \sqrt{2 \times 2} \times \sqrt{2 \times 2} \times \sqrt{2}$

$\quad = 2 \times 2 \times \sqrt{2}$

$\quad = 4\sqrt{2}$

In example 1, the largest perfect square is easy to see so Method 1 is probably the faster method to use.

2. Simplify $\sqrt{80}$.

Method 1.

$\sqrt{80} = \sqrt{16 \times 5}$

$\quad = \sqrt{16} \times \sqrt{5}$

$\quad = 4\sqrt{5}$

Method 2.

$\sqrt{80} = \sqrt{2 \times 40}$

$\quad = \sqrt{2 \times 2 \times 20}$

$\quad = \sqrt{2 \times 2 \times 2 \times 10}$

$\quad = \sqrt{2 \times 2 \times 2 \times 2 \times 5}$

$\quad = \sqrt{2 \times 2} \times \sqrt{2 \times 2} \times \sqrt{5}$

$\quad = 2 \times 2 \times \sqrt{5}$

$\quad = 4\sqrt{5}$

In Method 1, it might not be so obvious that the largest perfect square is 16, so Method 2 might be the faster method to use.

3. Simplify $\sqrt{\dfrac{384}{8}}$.

First, do the division under the square root, then proceed with the simplifying.

$$\sqrt{\frac{384}{8}} = \sqrt{48}$$

Method 1.

$\sqrt{48} = \sqrt{16 \times 3}$

$\quad = \left(\sqrt{16}\right)\left(\sqrt{3}\right)$

$\quad = 4\sqrt{3}$

Method 2.

$\sqrt{48} = \sqrt{2 \times 24}$

$\quad = \sqrt{2 \times 2 \times 12}$

$\quad = \sqrt{2 \times 2 \times 2 \times 6}$

$\quad = \sqrt{2 \times 2 \times 2 \times 2 \times 3}$

$\quad = \left(\sqrt{2 \times 2}\right)\left(\sqrt{2 \times 2}\right)\sqrt{3}$

$\quad = (2)(2)\sqrt{3}$

$\quad = 4\sqrt{3}$

Practice: Square Roots

1. $-\sqrt{(-5)^2} =$

The square roots in practice questions 2 and 3 fall between two consecutive integers. (a) Find the two integers that each square root is between, and (b) determine which of the two integers is closer to the square root.

2. $\sqrt{110}$

3. $\sqrt{26}$

4. Simplify $\sqrt{75}$

5. Simplify $\sqrt{\dfrac{156}{13}}$

Answers: Square Roots

1. -5

$$-\sqrt{(-5)^2} = -\sqrt{25} = -5$$

2. 10 and 11, closer to 10

$$\sqrt{100} < \sqrt{110} < \sqrt{121}$$
$$10 < \sqrt{110} < 11$$

$\sqrt{110}$ is closer to 10.

3. 5 and 6, closer to 5

$$\sqrt{25} < \sqrt{26} < \sqrt{36}$$
$$5 < \sqrt{26} < 6$$

$\sqrt{26}$ is closer to 5.

4. $5\sqrt{3}$

$$\sqrt{75} = \sqrt{25}\sqrt{3} = 5\sqrt{3}$$

5. $2\sqrt{3}$

$$\sqrt{\frac{156}{13}} = \sqrt{12} = \sqrt{4}\sqrt{3} = 2\sqrt{3}$$

Algebra

Algebra Diagnostic Test

1. $\{1, 3, 5\} \cap \{1, 2, 3\} =$

2. $\{2, 5\} \cup \{3, 4, 5\} =$

3. $\{1, 2, 3\} \cap \{4, 5\} =$

4. $|\{3, 5, 7, 9\}| =$

5. $|\varnothing| =$

6. Evaluate the diagram below and determine which statement is correct.

$A \cap B = C, A \cup B = C, A \cap C = B, A \cup C = B, B \cap C = A, B \cup C = A$

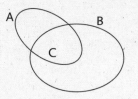

7. Express algebraically: five increased by three times x.

8. Evaluate: $-3x^2 - 4x - 6$ if $x = -5$.

9. Evaluate: $\dfrac{x}{3} - \dfrac{x + 2y}{y}$ if $x = 2$ and $y = 6$.

10. Solve for x: $2x - 9 = 21$.

11. Solve for y: $\dfrac{4}{7}y + 6 = 18$.

12. Solve for x: $3x - 5 = -2x - 25$.

13. Solve for x: $ax + by = c$.

14. Solve for y: $\dfrac{8}{y-3} = \dfrac{2}{y+3}$.

15. Solve this system for x and y: $8x + y = 4$.
$$2x - y = 6$$

16. Solve for x: $|x| = 12$.

17. Solve for x: $|x - 3| = 10$.

18. Solve for x: $-3x + 5 > 14$.

19. Solve for x: $8x + 4 \geq 6x - 10$.

20. $12x + 4x - 23x - (-3x) =$

21. $(4x - 7z) - (3x - 4z) =$

22. $6x^2y(4xy^2) =$

23. $(-2x^4y^2)^3 =$

24. $\dfrac{a^{10}b^3}{a^2b^6} =$

25. $\dfrac{-5(a^3b^2)(2a^2b^5)}{a^4b^3} =$

26. $(5^3)(2^3) =$

27. $-8(2x - y) =$

28. $(4x + 2y)(3x - y) =$

29. $\dfrac{16x^2 y + 18xy^3}{2xy} =$

30. Factor: $8x^3 - 12x^2$

31. Factor: $16a^2 - 81$

32. Factor: $x^2 - 2x - 63$

33. Factor: $3a^2 - 4a + 1$

34. Simplify: $\dfrac{x^2 - 3x + 2}{3x - 6}$

35. $\left(\dfrac{x^3}{2y}\right)\left(\dfrac{5y^2}{6x}\right) =$

36. $\left(\dfrac{x - 5}{x}\right)\left(\dfrac{x + 2}{x^2 - 2x - 15}\right) =$

37. $\dfrac{6x - 3}{2} \div \dfrac{2x - 1}{x} =$

38. $\dfrac{3x - 2}{x + 1} - \dfrac{2x - 1}{x + 1} =$

39. $\dfrac{5}{x} + \dfrac{7}{y} =$

40. $\dfrac{3}{a^3 b^5} + \dfrac{2}{a^4 b^2} =$

41. $\dfrac{2x}{x - 1} - \dfrac{x}{x + 2} =$

42. Solve for x: $3x^2 - 4x - 5 = 2x^2 + 4x - 17$

43. Solve for x: $9x^2 - 49 = 0$

44. Name the quadrant(s) in which points have positive x-coordinates.

45. Name the quadrant(s) in which points have negative x-coordinates and positive y-coordinates.

Use the graph below to answer questions 46–51.

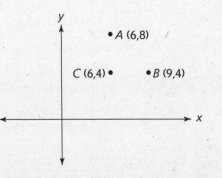

46. What is the distance between A and B?

47. What are the coordinates of the midpoint between A and B?

48. What is the slope of the line joining A and B?

49. What is the equation of the line, in slope-intercept form, joining A and B?

50. If the line joining A and B was extended, what would be its exact y-intercept?

51. Given that points A, B, and C are connected to form a triangle, what would be the area of $\triangle ABC$? What would be the perimeter of $\triangle ABC$?

52. If $f(x) = x^2 - 3x$, then $f(3) - f(1) = ?$

53. If $h(x) = |x|$, then $\dfrac{4}{h(4)} - \dfrac{-2}{h(-2)} = ?$

54. If $m(x) = 3x + 2$ and $t(x) = x^2$, then $t\big[m(-2)\big] = ?$

Algebra Diagnostic Test Answers

The diagnostic test explanations listed below include topic headings that correspond with step-by-step learning tools and examples to help you solve specific problem types. Topic headings can be found in the Algebra Review section on pages 253–288.

Set Notations

1. $\{1, 3\}$

2. $\{2, 3, 4, 5\}$

3. $\varnothing$

4. 4

5. 0

6. $A \cap B = C$

Variables and Algebraic Expressions

7. $5 + 3x$

8. -61

9. $-\dfrac{5}{3}$

Solving Linear Equations in One or Two Variables

10. $x = 15$

11. $y = 21$

12. $x = -4$

13. $x = \dfrac{c - by}{a}$

14. $y = -5$

15. $x = 1, y = -4$

16. $x = 12$ or $x = -12$

17. $x = 13$ or $x = -7$

Solving Linear Inequalities in One Variable

18. $x < -3$

19. $x \geq -7$

Polynomials

20. $-4x$

21. $x - 3z$

22. $24x^3y^3$

23. $-8x^{12}y^6$

24. $\dfrac{a^8}{b^3}$

25. $-10ab^4$

26. $\left[(5)(2)\right]^3 = 10^3 = 1{,}000$

27. $-16x + 8y$

28. $12x^2 + 2xy - 2y^2$

29. $8x + 9y^2$

30. $4x^2(2x - 3)$

31. $(4a + 9)(4a - 9)$

32. $(x - 9)(x + 7)$

33. $(3a - 1)(a - 1)$

Algebraic Fractions

34. $\dfrac{x-1}{3}$

35. $\dfrac{5x^2y}{12}$

36. $\dfrac{x+2}{x(x+3)}$

37. $\dfrac{3x}{2}$

38. $\dfrac{x-1}{x+1}$

39. $\dfrac{5y+7x}{xy}$ or $\dfrac{7x+5y}{xy}$

40. $\dfrac{3a+2b^3}{a^4b^5}$

41. $\dfrac{x^2+5x}{(x-1)(x+2)}$

Solving Quadratic Equations in One Variable

42. $x = 6$ or $x = 2$

43. $x = \dfrac{7}{3}$ or $x = -\dfrac{7}{3}$

Coordinate Geometry

44. I and IV

45. II

46. 5

47. $\left(\frac{15}{2}, 6\right)$ or (7.5,6)

48. $-\frac{4}{3}$

49. $y = -\frac{4}{3}x + 16$

50. 16 or (0,16)

51. area = 6, perimeter = 12

Functions and Function Notation

52. 2

53. 2

54. 16

Algebra Review

Set Notations

The *intersection* of two sets is a set containing only the members that are in each set at the same time. The symbol for finding the intersection of two sets is $\cap$. If two sets are *disjointed,* then they have no common members. The intersection of disjointed sets is called the *empty set* (or *null set*) and is indicated by the symbol $\varnothing$.

The *union* of two sets is a set containing all the numbers in those sets. Any duplicates are only written once. The symbol for finding the union of two sets is $\cup$.

The size or *magnitude of a set* refers to how many elements are in the set. This usually expressed by placing absolute value symbols around the set. The magnitude of the empty set is zero.

Venn diagrams (or *Euler circles*) is a method of pictorially describing sets as shown in the figure below.

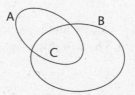

In the Venn diagram above, A represents all the elements in the smaller oval, B represents all the elements in the larger oval, and C represents all the elements that are in both ovals at the same time.

Examples:

1. $\{1, 3, 5\} \cap \{1, 2, 3\} = \{1, 3\}$

The intersection of the set with members 1, 3, 5 together with the set with members 1, 2, 3 is the set that only has the 1 and 3.

> **2.** $\{2, 5\} \cup \{3, 4, 5\} = \{2, 3, 4, 5\}$

The union of the set with members 2, 5 together with the set with members 3, 4, 5 is the set with members 2, 3, 4, 5.

> **3.** $\{1, 2, 3\} \cap \{4, 5\} = \varnothing$

The intersection of disjointed sets is the empty set.

> **4.** $|\{3, 5, 7, 9\}| = 4$

The set consisting of the elements 3, 5, 7, and 9 has 4 elements in it.

> **5.** $|\varnothing| = 0$

The empty set has no elements in it. The value zero indicates this.

> **6.** $A \cap B = C$

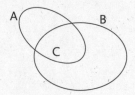

The intersection, or overlapping area, of sets A and B is C.

Practice: Set Notations

1. $\{\text{prime numbers}\} \cup \{\text{composite numbers}\} =$

2. $|\{\text{even integers}\} \cap \{\text{prime numbers}\}| =$

Answers: Set Notations

1. $\{2, 3, 4, 5, 6, \ldots\}$

   Prime numbers and composite numbers are each integers greater than 1. The union will be all integers greater than 1.

2. 1

   The correct answer is 1 since the absolute value symbols around the set notations is asking for how many values are in the set, *not* what the value is. The only prime number that is also even is the value 2. This set has only one member in it.

Variables and Algebraic Expressions

A *variable* is a symbol used to denote any element of a given set—often a letter used to stand for a number. Variables are used to change verbal expressions into *algebraic expressions.*

Important Key Words	
Addition	sum, more than, enlarge, plus
Subtraction	difference, less than, diminish, minus
Multiplication	product, times, of, twice
Division	quotient, ratio, divided by, half

Examples:

Express each of the following algebraically.

> **1.** Five increased by three times x: $5 + 3x$

> **2.** The sum of twice x and y: $2x + y$

> **3.** Twice the sum of x and y: $2(x + y)$

> **4.** The product of six and the difference between x and y: $6(x - y)$

> **5.** The ratio of x and y decreased by the quotient of s and r: $\dfrac{x}{y} - \dfrac{s}{r}$

Evaluate an Expression

To *evaluate an expression,* replace the unknowns with grouping symbols, insert the *value* for the unknowns, and then do the arithmetic, making sure to follow the rules for the order of operations.

Examples:

> **1.** Evaluate $-3x^2 - 4x - 6$ if $x = -5$.

$$
\begin{aligned}
-3x^2 - 4x - 6 &= -3(-5)^2 - 4(-5) - 6 \\
&= -3(25) + 20 - 6 \\
&= -75 + 20 - 6 \\
&= -61
\end{aligned}
$$

> **2.** Evaluate $\dfrac{x}{3} - \dfrac{x + 2y}{y}$ if $x = 2$ and $y = 6$.

$$
\begin{aligned}
\frac{x}{3} - \frac{x+2y}{y} &= \frac{(2)}{3} - \frac{(2)+2(6)}{6} \\
&= \frac{2}{3} - \frac{2+12}{6} \\
&= \frac{2}{3} - \frac{14}{6} \\
&= \frac{2}{3} - \frac{7}{3} \\
&= -\frac{5}{3}
\end{aligned}
$$

Practice: Variables and Algebraic Expressions

1. Express algebraically: 15 less than the ratio of x and y.

2. Evaluate $-3x^2 - \dfrac{4x - 3}{3}$ if $x = -6$.

Answers: Variables and Algebraic Expressions

1. $\frac{x}{y} - 15$

   "15 less than" says to subtract 15 from something.

2. -99

$$-3x^2 - \frac{4x-3}{3} = -3(-6)^2 - \frac{4(-6)-3}{3}$$
$$= -3(36) - \frac{-24-3}{3}$$
$$= -108 - \frac{-27}{3}$$
$$= -108 - (-9)$$
$$= -108 + 9$$
$$= -99$$

Solving Linear Equations in One or Two Variables

An equation is like a balance scale. In order to maintain the balance, the arithmetic operations you perform to one side of the equation must be performed to the other side of the equation. To solve a linear equation with one variable, cancel the numbers that are added or subtracted by using the opposite operation on both sides of the equation. Then divide by the number in front of the variable to get the variable by itself.

Examples:

1. Solve for x: $2x - 9 = 21$

$$2x - 9 = 21 \quad \text{(add 9 to each side)}$$
$$\underline{+9 \quad +9}$$
$$2x \quad = 30 \quad \text{(divide each side by 2)}$$
$$\frac{2x}{2} = \frac{30}{2}$$
$$x = 15$$

2. Solve for y: $\frac{4}{7}y + 6 = 18$

$$\frac{4}{7}y + 6 = 18 \qquad \left(\text{subtract 6 from each side}\right)$$
$$\underline{-6 \quad -6}$$
$$\frac{4}{7}y \quad = 12 \qquad \left(\text{divide each side by } \frac{4}{7}, \text{ which is the same as multiplying each side } \frac{7}{4}\right)$$
$$\frac{7}{4}\left(\frac{\overset{1}{\cancel{4}}}{\cancel{7}}y\right) = \frac{7}{\cancel{4}}\left(\frac{\overset{3}{\cancel{12}}}{1}\right)$$
$$y = 21$$

3. Solve for x: $3x - 5 = -2x - 25$

$$3x - 5 = -2x - 25 \qquad \text{(add } 2x \text{ to each side to get all the } x\text{'s on one side)}$$
$$\underline{+2x \qquad +2x}$$
$$5x - 5 = \qquad -25 \qquad \text{(add 5 to each side)}$$
$$\underline{+5 \qquad +5}$$
$$5x = \qquad -20 \qquad \text{(divide each side by 5)}$$
$$\frac{5x}{5} = \frac{-20}{5}$$
$$x = -4$$

4. Solve for x: $ax + by = c$

$$ax + by = c \qquad \text{(subtract } by \text{ from each side)}$$
$$\underline{-by \qquad -by}$$
$$ax \qquad = c - by \qquad \text{(divide each side by } a\text{)}$$
$$\frac{ax}{a} = \frac{c - by}{a}$$
$$x = \frac{c - by}{a}$$

5. Solve for y: $\dfrac{8}{y-3} = \dfrac{2}{y+3}$

Solve using the proportions method (refer to the proportions method discussed in the arithmetic section on page 237).

$$\frac{8}{y-3} = \frac{2}{y+3} \qquad \text{(cross multiply to clear the denominators)}$$
$$8(y+3) = 2(y-3) \qquad \text{(multiply out each side)}$$
$$8y + 24 = 2y - 6 \qquad \text{(subtract } 2y \text{ from each side to get the } y\text{'s on one side)}$$
$$\underline{-2y \qquad -2y}$$
$$6y + 24 = \qquad -6 \qquad \text{(subtract 24 from each side)}$$
$$\underline{-24 \qquad -24}$$
$$6y \qquad = -30 \qquad \text{(divide each side by 6)}$$
$$\frac{6y}{6} = \frac{-30}{6}$$
$$y = -5$$

Solving Two Equations Involving the Same Two Variables

To solve *two equations involving the same two variables,* you can use either of two algebraic methods: *elimination method* and *substitution method.*

Method 1 - The Elimination Method

1. Arrange each equation so that it has all the variables on one side.
2. Multiply each side of one equation so that the numbers to the left of the same variable in each equation are exact opposites. *(Note: Sometimes you will have to multiply each equation by different numbers to accomplish this.)*

3. Add the two equations to eliminate one variable.

4. Solve for the remaining variable.

5. Replace this value into one of the original equations to find the second variable.

Examples:

---
1. Solve for x and y: $3x + 3y = 24$

$2x + y = 13$

Both equations are already in the required form. Multiply each side of the bottom equation by –3. Now the y is preceded by exact opposites in the two equations.

$$3x + 3y = 24 \quad \rightarrow \quad 3x + 3y = 24$$
$$-3(2x + y) = -3(13) \quad \rightarrow \quad \underline{-6x - 3y = -39}$$

Add the equations, eliminating the y terms.

$$\begin{array}{r} 3x + 3y = 24 \\ \underline{-6x + -3y = -39} \\ -3x = -15 \end{array}$$

Solve for the remaining variable.

$$\frac{-3x}{-3} = \frac{-15}{-3}$$
$$x = 5$$

Replace x with 5 in one of the original equations to solve for y:

$$2x + y = 13$$
$$2(5) + y = 13$$
$$10 + y = 13$$
$$\underline{-10 -10}$$
$$y = 3$$

Answer: $x = 5$ and $y = 3$

Of course, if the numbers to the left of a variable are already opposites in each equation, you don't have to change either equation. Simply add the equations. See example 2 below.

---
2. Solve for x and y: $x + y = 7$

$x - y = 3$

$$\begin{array}{r} x + y = 7 \\ \underline{x - y = 3} \\ 2x = 10 \end{array}$$
$$\frac{2x}{2} = \frac{10}{2}$$
$$x = 5$$

Replacing x with 5 in the first equation gives:

$$5 + y = 7$$
$$\underline{-5 \qquad -5}$$
$$y = 2$$

Answer: $x = 5$ and $y = 2$

Note that this method will not work when the two equations *are the same equation* but written in two different forms. See example 3 below.

> **3.** Solve for a and b: $3a + 4b = 2$
> $ 6a + 8b = 4$

The second equation is actually the first equation multiplied by 2. In this instance, the system does not have a unique solution. Any replacements for a and b that make one of the sentences true will also make the other sentence true. In this situation, the system has an infinite number of solutions for a and b.

Sometimes each equation will have to be multiplied by different numbers to get the numbers to the left of one variable to be opposites of one another. See example 4 below.

> **4.** Solve for x: $3x + 2y = 8$
> $ 2x - 5y = 18$

The equations are already in the required form. Since it is the x value desired, find a way to eliminate the y variable. The numbers to the left of the y-terms are already of opposite sign. Multiply the upper equation with the coefficient of y from the lower equation and multiply the lower equation by the coefficient of y from the upper equation.

$$5(3x + 2y) = 5(8) \quad \rightarrow \quad 15x + 10y = 40$$
$$2(2x - 5y) = 2(18) \quad \rightarrow \quad \underline{4x - 10y = 36}$$

Add the equations.

$$15x + 10y = 40$$
$$\underline{4x - 10y = 36}$$
$$19x \qquad = 76$$
$$\frac{19x}{19} = \frac{76}{19}$$
$$x = 4$$

Answer: $x = 4$

Method 2 - The Substitution Method

1. Solve one equation for one of its variables in terms of the other variable.
2. Replace this expression for that variable in the other equation.
3. Solve the equation for that variable.
4. Replace this value into one of the original equations to find the second variable.

Examples:

> **1.** Solve for x and y: $x = y + 8$
> $ x + 3y = 48$

The first equation already has been solved for x in terms of y. Replace x with $(y + 8)$ in the second equation.

$$x + 3y = 48$$
$$(y + 8) + 3y = 48$$

Solve for y.

$$y + 3y + 8 = 48$$
$$4y + 8 = 48$$
$$\underline{-8 \quad -8}$$
$$4y \quad = 40$$
$$\frac{4y}{4} = \frac{40}{4}$$
$$y = 10$$

Replace y with 10 in one of the original equations and solve for x.

$$x = y + 8$$
$$x = 10 + 8$$
$$x = 18$$

Answer: $x = 18$ and $y = 10$

---

2. Solve for x and y: $8x + y = 4$
$\qquad\qquad\qquad\qquad 2x - y = 6$

This problem can now be solved by using *Method 1 - The Elimination Method*.

$$8x + y = 4$$
$$\underline{2x - y = 6}$$
$$10x \quad = 10$$
$$\frac{10x}{10} = \frac{10}{10}$$
$$x = 1$$

Using the top equation:

$$8x + y = 4$$
$$8(1) + y = 4$$
$$8 + y = 4$$
$$\underline{-8 \qquad -8}$$
$$y = -4$$

Answer: $x = 1$ and $y = -4$

Equations Involving Absolute Value

Recall that the numerical value when direction or sign is not considered is called the **absolute value.** The absolute value of x is written $|x|$. If $|x| = 2$, then $x = 2$ or $x = -2$ since $|2| = 2$ and $|-2| = 2$.

Examples:

1. Solve for x: $|x| = 12$

$$x = 12 \text{ or } x = -12$$

2. Solve for x: $|x - 3| = 10$

$$
\begin{array}{ccc}
x - 3 = 10 & \text{or} & x - 3 = -10 \\
\underline{+3 \quad +3} & & \underline{+3 \quad +3} \\
x \quad = 13 & \text{or} & x \quad = -7
\end{array}
$$

3. Solve for x: $|2x - 1| = 7$

$$
\begin{array}{ccc}
2x - 1 = 7 & \text{or} & 2x - 1 = -7 \\
\underline{+1 \ +1} & & \underline{+1 \quad +1} \\
2x \quad = 8 & \text{or} & 2x \quad = -6 \\
\dfrac{2x}{2} = \dfrac{8}{2} & \text{or} & \dfrac{2x}{2} = \dfrac{-6}{2} \\
 & \text{or} & \\
x = 4 & & x = -3
\end{array}
$$

4. Solve for x: $|x| = -3$

There is no solution because the absolute value of any number is never negative.

5. Solve for x: $|2x - 1| \geq 0$.

The answer is all real numbers, because the absolute value of any number is always positive or zero.

Practice: Solving Linear Equations in One or Two Variables

Solve each equation for x:

1. $3x + 5 = -16$

2. $\dfrac{3}{4}x - 5 = 19$

3. $8x - 12 = 5x - 27$

4. $wx - y = z$

5. $\dfrac{x + 2}{3} = \dfrac{3x - 4}{8}$

Solve each system of equations for x and y.

6. $3x + y = 8$
    $x - y = 4$

7. $y = 5x - 2$
    $2x + y = 19$

Solve each equation for x.

8. $|x| = 6$

9. $|3x - 5| = 10$

Answers: Solving Linear Equations in One or Two Variables

1. $x = -7$

$$3x + 5 = -16$$
$$3x = -21$$
$$x = -7$$

2. $x = 32$

$$\frac{3}{4}x - 5 = 19$$
$$\frac{3}{4}x = 24$$
$$x = 32$$

3. $x = -5$

$$8x - 12 = 5x - 27$$
$$3x - 12 = -27$$
$$3x = -15$$
$$x = -5$$

4. $x = \dfrac{y+z}{w}$ or $x = \dfrac{z+y}{w}$

$$
\begin{array}{ccc}
wx - y = z & & wx - y = z \\
wx = y + z & \text{or} & wx = z + y \\
x = \dfrac{y+z}{w} & & x = \dfrac{z+y}{w}
\end{array}
$$

5. $x = 28$

$$\frac{x+2}{3} = \frac{3x-4}{8}$$
$$8(x+2) = 3(3x-4)$$
$$8x + 16 = 9x - 12$$
$$-x + 16 = -12$$
$$-x = -28$$
$$x = 28$$

6. $x = 3, y = -1$

$$
\begin{array}{l}
3x + y = 8 \\
\underline{x - y = 4} \\
4x \quad\;\; = 12 \\
x = 3 \\
3x + y = 8 \rightarrow 3(3) + y = 8 \\
9 + y = 8 \\
y = -1
\end{array}
$$

7. $x = 3, y = 13$

$$y = 5x - 2$$
$$2x + y = 19$$
$$2x + (5x - 2) = 19$$
$$7x - 2 = 19$$
$$7x = 21$$
$$x = 3$$
$$y = 5x - 2 \rightarrow y = 5(3) - 2$$
$$y = 15 - 2$$
$$y = 13$$

8. $x = 6, x = -6$

9. $x = 5, x = -\dfrac{5}{3}$

$$|3x - 5| = 10$$
$$3x - 5 = 10 \quad \text{or} \quad 3x - 5 = -10$$
$$3x = 15 \quad \text{or} \quad 3x = -5$$
$$x = 5 \quad \text{or} \quad x = -\dfrac{5}{3}$$

Solving Linear Inequalities in One Variable

An inequality sentence is one involving ≤, <, ≥, or > separating the two sides of the sentence. Solving an inequality sentence involves the same procedures as solving an equation with one exception: When you multiply or divide each side of an inequality sentence by a negative number, the direction of the inequality switches.

Examples:

1. Solve for x: $-3x + 5 > 14$

$$-3x + 5 > 14 \qquad (\text{subtract 5 from each side})$$
$$\underline{ -5 \quad -5}$$
$$-3x \quad > \quad 9 \qquad (\text{divide each side by } -3, \text{ switch the direction of the inequality})$$
$$\dfrac{-3x}{-3} < \dfrac{9}{-3}$$
$$x < -3$$

2. Solve for x: $8x + 4 \geq 6x - 10$

$$8x + 4 \geq 6x - 10 \qquad (\text{subtract } 6x \text{ from each side to get all the } x\text{'s on one side})$$
$$\underline{-6x \qquad -6x}$$
$$2x + 4 \geq \quad -10 \qquad (\text{subtract 4 from each side})$$
$$\underline{ -4 > \qquad -4}$$
$$2x \quad \geq \quad -14 \qquad (\text{divide each side by 2})$$
$$\dfrac{2x}{2} \geq \dfrac{-14}{2}$$
$$x \geq -7$$

3. Solve for x: $-\frac{3}{8}x - 2 < 13$

$$-\frac{3}{8}x - 2 < 13 \qquad \text{(add 2 to each side)}$$

$$\underline{+2 \quad +2}$$

$$-\frac{3}{8}x \quad < 15 \qquad \left(\begin{array}{l}\text{divide each side by } -\frac{3}{8}, \text{ which is the same as multiplying each} \\ \text{side by } -\frac{8}{3}, \text{ and then switch the direction of the inequality}\end{array}\right)$$

$$\left(\cancel{\frac{8}{3}}\right)\left(\cancel{\frac{3}{8}}x\right) > \left(-\frac{8}{\cancel{3}}\right)\left(\frac{\cancel{15}^{5}}{1}\right)$$

$$x > -40$$

Practice: Solving Inequalities in One Variable

Solve for x.

1. $3x - 12 < 36$

2. $-\frac{5}{6}x - 4 < 26$

3. $6x - 11 \geq 3x - 53$

Answers: Solving Inequalities in One Variable

1. $x < 16$

$$3x - 12 < 36 \qquad \text{(add 12 to each side)}$$
$$3x < 48 \qquad \text{(divide each side by 3)}$$
$$x < 16$$

2. $x > -36$

$$-\frac{5}{6}x - 4 < 26 \qquad \text{(add 4 to each side)}$$
$$-\frac{5}{6}x < 30 \qquad \left(\text{multiply each side by } -\frac{6}{5}, \text{ switch the direction of the inequality}\right)$$
$$x > -36$$

3. $x \geq -14$

$$6x - 11 \geq 3x - 53 \qquad \text{(subtract } 3x \text{ from each side to get all the } x\text{'s on one side)}$$
$$3x - 11 \geq -53 \qquad \text{(add 11 to each side)}$$
$$3x \geq -42 \qquad \text{(divide each side by 3)}$$
$$x \geq -14$$

Polynomials

A *monomial* is an algebraic expression that consists of only one term. (A *term* is a numerical or literal expression with its own sign.) For instance, $9x$, $4a^2$, and $3mpxz^2$ are all monomials. When there are variables with exponents, the exponents must be whole numbers.

A *polynomial* consists of two or more terms. For instance, $x + y$, $y^2 - x^2$, and $x^2 + 3x + 5y^2$ are all polynomials. A *binomial* is a polynomial that consists of exactly two terms. For instance, $x + y$ is a binomial. A *trinomial* is a polynomial that consists of exactly three terms. For instance, $y^2 + 9y + 8$ is a trinomial. The number to the left of the variable is called the *numerical coefficient*. In $9y$, the 9 is the numerical coefficient.

Polynomials are usually arranged in one of two ways.

- *Ascending order* is when the power of a term increases for each succeeding term. For example, $x + x^2 + x^3$ or $5x + 2x^2 - 3x^3 + x^5$ are arranged in ascending order.

- *Descending order* is when the power of a term decreases for each succeeding term. For example, $x^3 + x^2 + x$ or $2x^4 + 3x^2 + 7x$ are arranged in descending order. Descending order is more commonly used.

Adding and Subtracting Polynomials

To **add** or **subtract polynomials**, follow the same rules as with integers introduced in the Arithmetic section (see pages 220–221), provided that the terms are alike. Notice that you add or subtract the coefficients only and leave the variables the same.

Examples:

1. $12x + 4x - 23x - (-3x) = [12 + 4 - 23 - (-3)]x = [12 + 4 - 23 + 3]x = -4x$

2. $(4x - 7z) - (3x - 4z) = 4x - 7z - 3x + 4z = (4 - 3)x + (-7 + 4)z = x - 3z$

3. $15x^2yz$
   $\underline{-18x^2yz}$
   $-3x^2yz$

Multiplying and Dividing Monomials

To **multiply** or **divide monomials**, follow the rules and definitions for powers and exponents introduced in the preceding Arithmetic section (see page 244).

Examples:

1. $6x^2y(4xy^2) = (6)(4)(x^2x)(yy^2) = 24x^{2+1}y^{1+2} = 24x^3y^3$

2. $(-2x^4y^2)^3 = (-2)^3 x^{(4)(3)} y^{(2)(3)} = -8x^{12}y^6$

3. $\dfrac{a^{10}b^3}{a^2b^6} = \left(\dfrac{a^{10}}{a^2}\right)\left(\dfrac{b^3}{b^6}\right) = a^{10-2}b^{3-6} = a^8b^{-3} = a^8\left(\dfrac{1}{b^3}\right) = \dfrac{a^8}{b^3}$

Note: You might have solved example 3 quickly by recognizing that the remaining exponent ends up where the larger exponent was originally.

4. $\dfrac{-5(a^3b^2)(2a^2b^5)}{a^4b^3} = \dfrac{-5(2)(a^3a^2)(b^2b^5)}{a^4b^3}$

   $= \dfrac{-10}{1}\left(\dfrac{a^{3+2}}{a^4}\right)\left(\dfrac{b^{2+5}}{b^3}\right)$

   $= \dfrac{-10}{1}\left(\dfrac{a^5}{a^4}\right)\left(\dfrac{b^7}{b^3}\right)$

   $= -10a^{5-4}b^{7-3}$

   $= -10ab^4$

5. $(5^3)(2^3) = [(5)(2)]^3 = 10^3$ or $1{,}000$

Multiply Polynomials

To *multiply polynomials,* multiply each term in one polynomial by each term in the other polynomial. Simplify if possible.

Examples:

1. $-8(2x - y) = -8(2x) - (-8)(y)$
$\qquad\qquad = -16x + 8y$

2. $(4x + 2y)(3x - y) = [(4x)(3x)] + [(4x)(-y)] + [(2y)(3x)] + [(2y)(-y)]$
$\qquad\qquad\qquad\quad = 12x^2 - 4xy + 6xy - 2y^2$
$\qquad\qquad\qquad\quad = 12x^2 + 2xy - 2y^2$

You may wish to use the **FOIL method** when multiplying a pair of binomials together. FOIL stands for *first terms, outside terms, inside terms, last terms.* After multiplying, simplify if possible. See the example below.

$$(3x + a)(2x - 2a)$$

Multiply *first terms* from each quantity. The first terms are the "$3x$" from the left parentheses and the "$2x$" from the right parentheses.

$$(3x + a)(2x - 2a) = \underline{6x^2}$$

Then multiply *outside terms.* The outside terms are the "$3x$" from the left parentheses and the "$-2a$" from the right parentheses.

$$(3x + a)(2x - 2a) = 6x^2 \underline{-6ax}$$

Then multiply *inside terms.* The inside terms are the "a" from the left parentheses and the "$2x$" from the right parentheses.

$$(3x + a)(2x - 2a) = 6x^2 - 6ax \underline{+ 2ax}$$

Finally, multiply *last terms.* The last terms are the "a" from the left parentheses and the "$-2a$" from the right parentheses.

$$(3x + a)(2x - 2a) = 6x^2 - 6ax + 2ax \underline{- 2a^2}$$

Now simplify.

$$(3x + a)(2x - 2a) = 6x^2 - 6ax + 2ax - 2a^2 = 6x^2 - 4ax - 2a^2$$

Divide a Polynomial by a Monomial

To **divide a polynomial by a monomial,** divide each term in the polynomial by the monomial.

Examples:

1. $\dfrac{16x^2y + 18xy^3}{2xy} = \dfrac{16x^2y}{2xy} + \dfrac{18xy^3}{2xy}$

$$= \left(\dfrac{16}{2}\right)\left(\dfrac{x^2}{x}\right)\dfrac{y}{y} + \left(\dfrac{18}{2}\right)\left(\dfrac{x}{x}\right)\left(\dfrac{y^3}{y}\right)$$

$$= \quad\quad 8x \quad + \quad\quad 9y^2$$

2. $\left(6x^2 + 2x\right) \div \left(2x\right) = \dfrac{6x^2 + 2x}{2x} = \dfrac{6x^2}{2x} + \dfrac{2x}{2x} = 3x + 1$

Factor Each Polynomial Using a Common Factor

To **factor** means to find two or more quantities whose product equals the original quantity. To **factor out a common factor:**

1. Find the largest common monomial factor of each term.
2. Divide the original polynomial by this factor to obtain the second factor. The second factor will also be a polynomial.

Examples:

1. $8x^3 - 12x^2$

The largest common factor of $8x^3$ and $12x^2$ is $4x^2$. $\dfrac{8x^3}{4x^2} = 2x$, $\dfrac{12x^2}{4x^2} = 3$. Therefore, $8x^3 - 12x^2 = 4x^2(2x - 3)$.

2. $x^5 - 4x^3 + x^2$

The largest common factor of x^5, $4x^3$, and x^2 is x^2. $\dfrac{x^5}{x^2} = x^3$, $\dfrac{4x^3}{x^2} = 4x$, $\dfrac{x^2}{x^2} = 1$.

Therefore, $x^5 - 4x^3 + x^2 = x^2(x^3 - 4x + 1)$.

Factor Each Polynomial Using Difference of Squares

The difference of two squares refers to the subtraction of two expressions that are each the results of the squares of other expressions. To **factor the difference of two squares:**

1. Find the square root of the first term and the square root of the second term.
2. Express your answer as the product of the sum of the quantities from step 1 times the difference of those quantities.

Examples:

1. $16a^2 - 81$

$$\sqrt{16a^2} = 4a, \ \sqrt{81} = 9$$

Therefore, $16a^2 - 81 = (4a + 9)(4a - 9)$.

> **2.** $9y^2 - 1$

$$\sqrt{9y^2} = 3y, \ \sqrt{1} = 1$$

Therefore, $9y^2 - 1 = (3y + 1)(3y - 1)$.

Note: $x^2 + 144$ is *not* factorable using difference of squares. Even though both x^2 and 144 are both square numbers, the expression $x^2 + 144$ is not a *difference* of squares.

Factor Polynomials Having Three Terms of the Form $ax^2 + bx + c$ when $a = 1$

To *factor polynomials having three terms of the form $ax^2 + bx + c$ when $a = 1$* (that is, the first term is simply x^2):

1. Use double parentheses and place an x at the left sides of the parentheses: $(x \quad)(x \quad)$.
2. Find two numbers that multiply to make the c value and at the same time add to make the b value.
3. Place these numbers, with their appropriate signs, in the parentheses with the x's.

Examples:

> **1.** Factor $x^2 - 2x - 63$.

This is a polynomial in the form of $ax^2 + bx + c$ with $a = 1$, $b = -2$, $c = -63$. Find two numbers that multiply to make -63 and add to make -2. Only the numbers -9 and $+7$ do that. Therefore, $x^2 - 2x - 63 = (x - 9)(x + 7)$. The two parentheses expressions could be written in reverse order as well: $(x + 7)(x - 9)$.

> **2.** Factor $x^2 - 8x + 15$.

This is a polynomial in the form of $ax^2 + bx + c$ with $a = 1$, $b = -8$, $c = 15$. Find two numbers that multiply to make $+15$ and add to make -8. Only the numbers -3 and -5 do that. Therefore, $x^2 - 8x + 15 = (x - 3)(x - 5)$. The two parentheses expressions could be written in reverse order as well: $(x - 5)(x - 3)$.

Factor Polynomials Having Three Terms of the Form $ax^2 + bx + c$ when $a \neq 1$

To *factor polynomials having three terms of the form $ax^2 + bx + c$ when $a \neq 1$* requires a trial-and-error approach. The following problems will demonstrate what type of thinking is required.

Examples:

> **1.** Factor $3a^2 - 4a + 1$.

This is a polynomial in the form of $ax^2 + bx + c$ with $a = 3$, $b = -4$, $c = 1$. Set up two parentheses expressions: $(\quad)(\quad)$. The values that will be in the *first* positions must multiply to make $3a^2$. These could be $3a$ and a. The values in the *last* position need to make $+1$. These could either be $+1$ and $+1$ or -1 and -1. The values in the inner and outer positions need to multiply and combine to make $-4a$. Consider the possibilities:

$$(3a + 1)(a + 1) \quad \text{Here, the } \textit{outer} \text{ and } \textit{inner} \text{ products combine to make } +4a$$
$$(3a - 1)(a - 1) \quad \text{Here, the } \textit{outer} \text{ and } \textit{inner} \text{ products combine to make } -4a.$$

Therefore, $3a^2 - 4a + 1 = (3a - 1)(a - 1)$.

> **2.** Factor $4x^2 + 5x + 1$.

To get $4x^2$, the *first terms* could be $2x$ and $2x$ or $4x$ and x. To get $+1$, the *last terms* could be $+1$ and $+1$ or -1 and -1. Experiment with $2x$ and $2x$ together with $+1$ and $+1$ and multiply.

$$(2x + 1)(2x + 1) = 4x^2 + 2x + 2x + 1 = 4x^2 + 4x + 1$$

This expression has $4x$ as the result of the *outer* and *inner* multiplications, but the original expression has $5x$ as the result of the *outer* and *inner* multiplications. Thus, $(2x + 1)(2x + 1)$ is not the correct factored form.

If the 1's were replaced with –1's, the only change would be that the result of the *inner* and *outer* multiplications would have the result of $-4x$. Thus, $(2x - 1)(2x - 1)$ is not the correct factored form.

Experiment with $4x$ and x together with $+1$ and $+1$ and multiply.

$$(4x + 1)(x + 1) = 4x^2 + 4x + x + 1 = 4x^2 + 5x + 1$$

Therefore, $4x^2 + 5x + 1 = (4x + 1)(x + 1)$.

Some factoring problems combine one or more of the methods described:

> **3.** Factor $4a^2 + 6a + 2$.

Notice that the expression $4a^2 + 6a + 2$ has a common factor of 2. Factoring out a 2 gives $2(2a^2 + 3a + 1)$. The expression $2a^2 + 3a + 1$ can be further factored into $(2a + 1)(a + 1)$. Therefore, $4a^2 + 6a + 2 = 2(2a + 1)(a + 1)$.

> **4.** Factor $x^4 - 81$.

$\sqrt{x^4} = x^2$ and $\sqrt{81} = 9$, therefore, $x^4 - 81 = (x^2 + 9)(x^2 - 9)$. Notice that $x^2 - 9$ is a difference of squares.

$\sqrt{x^2} = x$ and $\sqrt{9} = 3$, therefore $x^2 - 9 = (x + 3)(x - 3)$. Therefore, $x^4 - 81 = (x^2 + 9)(x + 3)(x - 3)$.

Practice: Polynomials

1. $-15x - 32x + 34x - (-4x) =$

2. $(3x^2 - 7x - 6) - (6x^2 - 4x - 5) =$

3. $-3x^4 y(-2x^2 y^7) =$

4. $(-3x^2 y^5)^3 =$

5. $\dfrac{x^{12} y^8}{x^{16} y^6} =$

6. $\dfrac{4(-3x^2 y^5)(x^4 y^3)}{x^3 y^4} =$

7. $(25^4)(4^4) =$

8. $-12(3x - 5y) =$

9. $(4x - 5y)(3x + 2y) =$

10. $\dfrac{24x^3 y^5 - 36x^2 y^3}{12xy} =$

11. Factor: $45x^3 - 60x^2$

12. Factor: $144x^2 - 49$

13. Factor: $x^2 - 5x - 36$

14. Factor: $2x^2 + x - 28$

Answers: Polynomials

1. $-9x$

   $-15x - 32x + 34x - (-4x) = -15x - 32x + 34x + 4x = -9x$

2. $-3x^2 - 3x - 1$

   $(3x^2 - 7x - 6) - (6x^2 - 4x - 5) = 3x^2 - 7x - 6 - 6x^2 + 4x + 5 = -3x^2 - 3x - 1$

3. $6x^6y^8$

   $-3x^4y(-2x^2y^7) = (-3)(-2)(x^4x^2)(yy^7) = 6x^6y^8$

4. $-27x^6y^{15}$

   $(-3x^2y^5)^3 = (-3)^3(x^2)^3(y^5)^3 = -27x^6y^{15}$

5. $\dfrac{y^2}{x^4}$

   $\dfrac{x^{12}y^8}{x^{16}y^6} = \left(\dfrac{x^{12}}{x^{16}}\right)\left(\dfrac{y^8}{y^6}\right) = \left(\dfrac{1}{x^4}\right)\left(\dfrac{y^2}{1}\right) = \dfrac{y^2}{x^4}$

6. $-12x^3y^4$

   $\dfrac{4(-3x^2y^5)(x^4y^3)}{x^3y^4} = ((4)(-3))\left(\dfrac{x^2x^4}{x^3}\right)\left(\dfrac{y^5y^3}{y^4}\right) = -12\left(\dfrac{x^6}{x^3}\right)\left(\dfrac{y^8}{y^4}\right) = -12x^3y^4$

7. 100^4 or $100,000,000$

   $(25^4)(4^4) = [(25)(4)]^4 = 100^4$ or $100,000,000$

8. $-36x + 60y$

   $-12(3x - 5y) = -12(3x) - 12(-5y) = -36x + 60y$

9. $12x^2 - 7xy - 10y^2$

   $(4x - 5y)(3x + 2y) = 12x^2 + 8xy - 15xy - 10y^2 = 12x^2 - 7xy - 10y^2$

10. $2x^2y^4 - 3xy^2$

    $\dfrac{24x^3y^5 - 36x^2y^3}{12xy} = \left(\dfrac{24x^3y^5}{12xy}\right) - \left(\dfrac{36x^2y^3}{12xy}\right) = 2x^2y^4 - 3xy^2$

11. $15x^2(3x - 4)$

    The GCF of $45x^3 - 60x^2$ is $15x^2$; $\dfrac{45x^3}{15x^2} = 3x$; $\dfrac{60x^2}{15x^2} = 4$. Therefore, $45x^3 - 60x^2 = 15x^2(3x - 4)$.

12. $(12x + 7)(12x - 7)$

    $144x^2 - 49$ is a difference of squares.

    $144x^2 - 49 = (12x + 7)(12x - 7)$

13. $(x + 4)(x - 9)$

    To factor $x^2 - 5x - 36$, find two numbers whose product is -36 and sum is -5. Only -9 and 4 satisfy the conditions.

    $x^2 - 5x - 36 = (x + 4)(x - 9)$

14. $(2x - 7)(x + 4)$

    To factor $2x^2 + x - 28$, use the trial-and-error method.

    $2x^2 + x - 28 = (2x - 7)(x + 4)$

Algebraic Fractions

Algebraic fractions are fractions using a variable in the numerator, denominator, or both numerator and denominator such as $\frac{3}{x}$, $\frac{x+1}{2}$, or $\frac{x^2-x-2}{x+1}$. Since division by 0 is impossible, variables in the denominator have certain restrictions. The denominator can *never* equal 0. Therefore in $\frac{5}{x}$, $x \neq 0$; in $\frac{2}{x-3}$, $x \neq 3$; in $\frac{3}{a-b}$, $a - b \neq 0$, which implies $a \neq b$; and in $\frac{4}{a^2b}$, $a \neq 0$ and $b \neq 0$. Be aware of these types of restrictions.

Simplify an Algebraic Fraction

To *simplify an algebraic fraction,* first factor the numerator and the denominator; then cancel (or divide out) common factors.

Examples:

1. Simplify: $\dfrac{x^2-3x+2}{3x-6}$

$$\frac{x^2-3x+2}{3x-6} = \frac{(x-1)(x-2)}{3(x-2)} = \frac{(x-1)\cancel{(x-2)}^{1}}{3\cancel{(x-2)}_{1}} = \frac{(x-1)}{3}$$

2. Simplify: $\dfrac{(3x-3)}{(4x-4)}$

$$\frac{(3x-3)}{(4x-4)} = \frac{3(x-1)}{4(x-1)} = \frac{3\cancel{(x-1)}^{1}}{4\cancel{(x-1)}_{1}} = \frac{3}{4}$$

Warning: Do *not* cancel through an addition or subtraction sign. The following is NOT allowed:

$$\frac{x+1}{x+2} \neq \frac{x+\cancel{1}}{x+\cancel{2}} \text{ or } \frac{x+6}{6} \neq \frac{x+\cancel{6}}{\cancel{6}}$$

Multiply Algebraic Fractions

To *multiply algebraic fractions,* first factor the numerators and denominators that are polynomials then cancel where possible. Multiply the remaining numerators and denominators together. *If you've canceled properly, your answer will be in simplified form.*

Examples:

1. $\left(\dfrac{x^3}{2y}\right)\left(\dfrac{5y^2}{6x}\right) = \dfrac{\cancel{x^3}^{x^2} \cdot 5\cancel{y^2}^{y}}{2\cancel{y}_{1} \cdot 6\cancel{x}_{1}} = \dfrac{5x^2y}{12}$

2. $\left(\dfrac{x-5}{x}\right)\left(\dfrac{x+2}{x^2-2x-15}\right) = \dfrac{\cancel{(x-5)}^{1}}{x} \cdot \dfrac{x+2}{\cancel{(x-5)}_{1}(x+3)} = \dfrac{x+2}{x(x+3)}$

Divide Algebraic Fractions

To *divide algebraic fractions,* invert the second fraction (the divisor) and then multiply the fractions. **Remember:** You can cancel only after you invert.

Examples:

1. $\dfrac{3x^2}{5} \div \dfrac{2x}{y} = \dfrac{3x^2}{5} \times \dfrac{y}{2x} = \dfrac{3x^{\overset{1}{2}}}{5} \times \dfrac{y}{2\underset{1}{x}} = \dfrac{3xy}{10}$

2. $\dfrac{6x-3}{2} \div \dfrac{2x-1}{x} = \dfrac{6x-3}{2} \times \dfrac{x}{2x-1} = \dfrac{3\overset{1}{(2x-1)}}{2}\dfrac{x}{\underset{1}{(2x-1)}} = \dfrac{3x}{2}$

Add or Subtract Algebraic Fractions with a Common Denominator

To *add or subtract algebraic fractions having a common denominator,* simply keep the denominator and combine (add or subtract) the numerators. Simplify if possible.

Examples:

1. $\dfrac{4}{x} + \dfrac{5}{x} = \dfrac{4+5}{x} = \dfrac{9}{x}$

2. $\dfrac{3x-2}{x+1} - \dfrac{2x-1}{x+1} = \dfrac{3x-2-(2x-1)}{x+1} = \dfrac{3x-2-2x+1}{x+1} = \dfrac{x-1}{x+1}$

Add or Subtract Algebraic Fractions with Different Denominators

To *add or subtract algebraic fractions having different denominators,* first find the lowest common denominator (LCD) and change each fraction to an equivalent fraction with the common denominator. Finally, combine the numerators and simplify if possible.

Examples:

1. $\dfrac{5}{x} + \dfrac{7}{y} =$

LCD = xy.

$$\left(\dfrac{5}{x} \times \dfrac{y}{y}\right) + \left(\dfrac{7}{y} \times \dfrac{x}{x}\right) = \dfrac{5y}{xy} + \dfrac{7x}{xy} = \dfrac{5y+7x}{xy} \text{ or } \dfrac{7x+5y}{xy}$$

2. $\dfrac{3}{a^3b^5} + \dfrac{2}{a^4b^2} =$

LCD = a^4b^5.

$$\left(\dfrac{3}{a^3b^5} \times \dfrac{a}{a}\right) + \left(\dfrac{2}{a^4b^2} \times \dfrac{b^3}{b^3}\right) = \dfrac{3a}{a^4b^5} + \dfrac{2b^3}{a^4b^5} = \dfrac{3a+2b^3}{a^4b^5}$$

3. $\dfrac{2x}{x-1} - \dfrac{x}{x+2} =$

LCD $= (x-1)(x+2)$

$$\left(\frac{2x}{x-1}\times\frac{(x+2)}{(x+2)}\right)-\left(\frac{x}{x+2}\times\frac{(x-1)}{(x-1)}\right)=\frac{2x^2+4x}{(x-1)(x+2)}-\frac{x^2-x}{(x-1)(x+2)}$$

$$=\frac{2x^2+4x-\left(x^2-x\right)}{(x-1)(x+2)}$$

$$=\frac{2x^2+4x-x^2+x}{(x-1)(x+2)}$$

$$=\frac{x^2+5x}{(x-1)(x+2)}$$

Practice: Algebraic Fractions

1. Simplify: $\dfrac{x^2+6x-27}{x^2-9}$

2. $\left(\dfrac{x^5 y}{5z^3}\right)\left(\dfrac{15z^5}{4x^3 y^4}\right)=$

3. $\dfrac{3x^2-2x-1}{x^2+x}\left(\dfrac{x+1}{x-1}\right)=$

4. $\dfrac{4x-8}{6} \div \dfrac{x-2}{3} =$

5. $\dfrac{2x+7}{x+4} - \dfrac{x-5}{x+4} =$

6. $\dfrac{1}{x} + \dfrac{3}{y} =$

7. $\dfrac{2}{x^2 y} + \dfrac{3}{xy^3} =$

8. $\dfrac{4x}{x-3} - \dfrac{x}{x+1} =$

Answers: Algebraic Fractions

1. $\dfrac{x+9}{x+3}$

$$\frac{x^2+6x-27}{x^2-9}=\frac{\cancel{(x-3)}^1(x+9)}{\cancel{(x-3)}_1(x+3)}=\frac{x+9}{x+3}$$

2. $\dfrac{3x^2 z^2}{4y^3}$

$$\left(\frac{x^5 y}{5z^3}\right)\left(\frac{15z^5}{4x^3 y^4}\right)=\left(\frac{\cancel{x^5}^{x^2}\,\cancel{y}^{1}}{\cancel{5}\,\cancel{z^3}}\right)\left(\frac{\cancel{15}^3\,\cancel{z^5}^{z^2}}{4x^3\,\cancel{y^4}}\right)=\frac{3x^2 z^2}{4y^3}$$

3. $\dfrac{3x+1}{x}$

$$\left(\dfrac{3x^2-2x-1}{x^2+x}\right)\left(\dfrac{x+1}{x-1}\right) = \dfrac{(3x+1)\overset{1}{\cancel{(x-1)}}}{x\underset{1}{\cancel{(x+1)}}} \cdot \dfrac{\overset{1}{\cancel{(x+1)}}}{\underset{1}{\cancel{(x-1)}}} = \dfrac{3x+1}{x}$$

4. 2

$$\dfrac{4x-8}{6} \div \dfrac{x-2}{3} = \dfrac{4x-8}{6} \times \dfrac{3}{x-2} = \dfrac{4\overset{1}{\cancel{(x-2)}}}{\underset{2}{\cancel{6}}} \cdot \dfrac{\overset{1}{\cancel{3}}}{\underset{1}{\cancel{(x-2)}}} = \dfrac{4}{2} = 2$$

5. $\dfrac{x+12}{x+4}$

$$\dfrac{2x+7}{x+4} - \dfrac{x-5}{x+4} = \dfrac{2x+7-(x-5)}{x+4} = \dfrac{2x+7-x+5}{x+4} = \dfrac{x+12}{x+4}$$

6. $\dfrac{y+3x}{xy}$ or $\dfrac{3x+y}{xy}$

$$\dfrac{1}{x} + \dfrac{3}{y} = \left(\dfrac{1}{x} \times \dfrac{y}{y}\right) + \left(\dfrac{3}{y} \times \dfrac{x}{x}\right) = \dfrac{y}{xy} + \dfrac{3x}{xy} = \dfrac{y+3x}{xy} \text{ or } \dfrac{3x+y}{xy}$$

7. $\dfrac{2y^2+3x}{x^2y^3}$ or $\dfrac{3x+2y^2}{x^2y^3}$

$$\dfrac{2}{x^2y} + \dfrac{3}{xy^3} = \left(\dfrac{2}{x^2y} \times \dfrac{y^2}{y^2}\right) + \left(\dfrac{3}{xy^3} \times \dfrac{x}{x}\right) = \dfrac{2y^2}{x^2y^3} + \dfrac{3x}{x^2y^3} = \dfrac{2y^2+3x}{x^2y^3} \text{ or } \dfrac{3x+2y^2}{x^2y^3}$$

8. $\dfrac{3x^2+7x}{(x-3)(x+1)}$

$$\dfrac{4x}{x-3} - \dfrac{x}{x+1} = \left(\dfrac{4x}{x-3} \times \dfrac{(x+1)}{(x+1)}\right) - \left(\dfrac{x}{x+1} \times \dfrac{(x-3)}{(x-3)}\right)$$

$$= \dfrac{4x^2+4x}{(x-3)(x+1)} - \dfrac{x^2-3x}{(x-3)(x+1)}$$

$$= \dfrac{4x^2+4x-x^2+3x}{(x-3)(x+1)}$$

$$= \dfrac{3x^2+7x}{(x-3)(x+1)}$$

Solving Quadratic Equations in One Variable

A *quadratic equation* is an equation that can be written as $ax^2 + bx + c$ with $a \neq 0$. Some quadratic equations can be solved quickly by *factoring*, but factoring is not always possible. Quadratic equations can also be solved by using the *quadratic formula*.

Steps to Solve a Quadratic Equation Using Factoring

1. Place all terms on one side of the equal sign, leaving zero on the other side.
2. Factor the quadratic expression.
3. Set each factor equal to zero.
4. Solve each of these equations.

Examples:

1. Solve for x by factoring: $x^2 - 6x = 16$

Following the steps above:

$x^2 - 6x = 16$ becomes $x^2 - 6x - 16 = 0$

$x^2 - 6x - 16 = 0$ becomes $(x - 8)(x + 2) = 0$

$$x - 8 = 0 \quad \text{or} \quad x + 2 = 0$$
$$x = 8 \quad \text{or} \quad x = -2$$

2. Solve for x by factoring: $3x^2 - 4x - 5 = 2x^2 + 4x - 17$

$3x^2 - 4x - 5 = 2x^2 + 4x - 17$ becomes $x^2 - 8x + 12 = 0$

$x^2 - 8x + 12 = 0$ becomes $(x - 6)(x - 2) = 0$

$$x - 6 = 0 \quad \text{or} \quad x - 2 = 0$$
$$x = 6 \quad \text{or} \quad x = 2$$

3. Solve for x by factoring: $9x^2 - 49 = 0$

The quadratic is already in the "= 0" form.

$9x^2 - 49 = 0$ becomes $(3x + 7)(3x - 7) = 0$

$$3x + 7 = 0 \quad \text{or} \quad 3x - 7 = 0$$
$$3x = -7 \quad \text{or} \quad 3x = 7$$
$$x = -\frac{7}{3} \quad \text{or} \quad x = \frac{7}{3}$$

4. Solve for x by factoring: $x^2 = 6x$

$x^2 = 6x$ becomes $x^2 - 6x = 0$

$x^2 - 6x = 0$ becomes $x(x - 6) = 0$

$$x = 0 \quad \text{or} \quad x - 6 = 0$$
$$x = 0 \quad \text{or} \quad x = 6$$

The Quadratic Formula

Frequently, even when a quadratic equation can be factored, finding the appropriate factors is difficult. When finding the appropriate factors becomes difficult, use the quadratic formula.

The *quadratic formula* is a rule that allows you to solve all quadratic problems, even the quadratic equations that are not factorable. The general quadratic equation is $ax^2 + bx + c = 0$.

The quadratic formula says $x = \dfrac{-b \pm \sqrt{b^2 - 4ac}}{2a}$. In order to use the formula, all terms must be on one side of the equation set equal to zero.

The following examples are taken from the previous original four examples. Each problem begins with the original problem rewritten in the "= 0" form. Notice that the answers are the same as when the problems were solved by factoring.

Examples:

---

1. Solve for x using the quadratic formula: $x^2 - 6x - 16 = 0$

$a = 1, b = -6, c = -16$

$$x = \frac{-(-6) \pm \sqrt{(-6)^2 - 4(1)(-16)}}{2(1)}$$

$$= \frac{6 \pm \sqrt{36 + 64}}{2}$$

$$= \frac{6 \pm \sqrt{100}}{2}$$

$$= \frac{6 \pm 10}{2}$$

$$= \frac{6 + 10}{2} = \frac{16}{2} = 8 \text{ or } \frac{6 - 10}{2} = \frac{-4}{2} = -2$$

---

2. Solve for x using the quadratic formula: $x^2 - 8x + 12 = 0$

$a = 1, b = -8, c = 12$

$$x = \frac{-(-8)) \pm \sqrt{(-8)^2 - 4(1)(12)}}{2(1)}$$

$$= \frac{8 \pm \sqrt{64 - 48}}{2}$$

$$= \frac{8 \pm \sqrt{16}}{2}$$

$$= \frac{8 \pm 4}{2}$$

$$= \frac{8 + 4}{2} = \frac{12}{2} = 6 \text{ or } \frac{8 - 4}{2} = \frac{4}{2} = 2$$

---

3. Solve for x using the quadratic formula: $9x^2 - 49 = 0$

$a = 9, b = 0, c = -49$

$$x = \frac{-(0) \pm \sqrt{(0)^2 - 4(9)(-49)}}{2(9)}$$

$$= \frac{\pm\sqrt{4(9)(49)}}{18}$$

$$= \frac{\pm(2)(3)(7)}{18}$$

$$= \frac{\pm 42}{18}$$

$$= \frac{42}{18} = \frac{7}{3} \text{ or } \frac{-42}{18} = -\frac{7}{3}$$

4. Solve for x using the quadratic formula: $x^2 - 6x = 0$

$a = 1, b = -6, c = 0$

$$x = \frac{-(-6) \pm \sqrt{(-6)^2 - 4(1)(0)}}{2(1)}$$

$$= \frac{6 \pm \sqrt{36 - 0}}{2}$$

$$= \frac{6 \pm \sqrt{36}}{2}$$

$$= \frac{6 \pm 6}{2}$$

$$= \frac{6 + 6}{2} = \frac{12}{2} = 6 \text{ or } \frac{6 - 6}{2} = \frac{0}{2} = 0$$

Practice: Solving Quadratic Equations in One Variable

Solve for x in the following quadratic equations using either factoring or the quadratic formula.

1. $x^2 = -7x + 8$

2. $4x^2 - 81 = 0$

3. $3x^2 + 9x = 0$

Answers: Solving Quadratic Equations in One Variable

1. -8 or 1

Using factoring

$x^2 + 7x - 8 = 0$

$(x + 8)(x - 1) = 0$

$x + 8 = 0 \quad$ or $\quad x - 1 = 0$

$x = -8 \quad$ or $\quad x = 1$

Using the quadratic formula

$x^2 + 7x - 8 = 0, \ a = 1, b = 7, c = -8$

$$x = \frac{-(7) \pm \sqrt{(7)^2 - 4(1)(-8)}}{2(1)}$$

$$= \frac{-7 \pm \sqrt{49 + 32}}{2}$$

$$= \frac{-7 \pm \sqrt{81}}{2}$$

$$= \frac{-7 \pm 9}{2}$$

$$= \frac{-7 + 9}{2} = \frac{2}{2} = 1 \text{ or } \frac{-7 - 9}{2} = \frac{-16}{2} = -8$$

2. $-\frac{9}{2}$ or $\frac{9}{2}$

Using factoring

$4x^2 - 81 = 0$

$(2x + 9)(2x - 9) = 0$

$2x + 9 = 0 \quad$ or $\quad 2x - 9 = 0$

$2x = -9 \quad$ or $\quad 2x = 9$

$x = -\frac{9}{2} \quad$ or $\quad x = \frac{9}{2}$

Using the quadratic formula

$4x^2 - 81 = 0, \ a = 4, b = 0, c = -81$

$$x = \frac{-(0) \pm \sqrt{(0)^2 - 4(4)(-81)}}{2(4)}$$

$$= \frac{0 \pm \sqrt{1296}}{8}$$

$$= \frac{\pm 36}{8}$$

$$= \frac{\pm 9}{2}$$

3. 0 or –3

Using factoring

$$3x^2 + 9x = 0$$

$$3x(x+3) = 0$$

$$3x = 0 \quad \text{or} \quad x + 3 = 0$$

$$x = 0 \quad \text{or} \quad x = -3$$

Using the quadratic formula

$$3x^2 + 9x = 0, \ a = 3, \ b = 9, \ c = 0$$

$$x = \frac{-(9) \pm \sqrt{(9)^2 - 4(3)(0)}}{2(3)}$$

$$= \frac{-9 \pm \sqrt{81}}{6}$$

$$= \frac{-9 \pm 9}{6}$$

$$= \frac{-9 + 9}{6} = \frac{0}{6} = 0$$

$$= \frac{-9 - 9}{6} = \frac{-18}{6} = -3$$

Coordinate Geometry

Each point on a number line is assigned a number. In the same way, each point in a plane is assigned a pair of numbers. These numbers represent the placement of the point relative to two intersecting lines. In ***coordinate graphs,*** two perpendicular number lines are used and are called the *coordinate axes.* One axis is horizontal and is called the *x-axis.* The other is vertical and is called the *y-axis.* The point of intersection of the two number lines is called the *origin* and is represented by the coordinates (0,0).

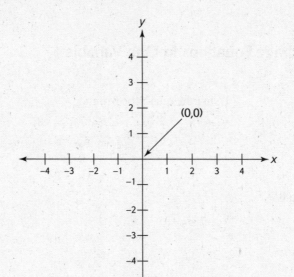

Each point on a plane is located by a unique pair of ordered numbers called the *coordinates.* Some coordinates are noted below.

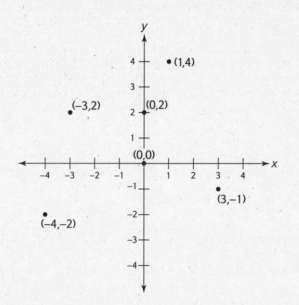

Notice that on the x-axis, numbers to the right of 0 are positive and to the left of 0 are negative. On the y-axis, numbers above 0 are positive and below 0 are negative. The first number in the ordered pair is called the ***x-coordinate,*** or *abscissa,* while the second number is the ***y-coordinate,*** or *ordinate.* The x-coordinate shows the right or left direction, and the y-coordinate shows the up or down direction. The coordinate graph is divided into four regions (quarters) called *quadrants.* These quadrants are labeled below.

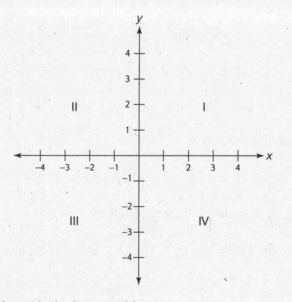

In quadrant I, x is always positive and y is always positive.

In quadrant II, x is always negative and y is always positive.

In quadrant III, x and y are both always negative.

In quadrant IV, x is always positive and y is always negative.

Examples:

> **1.** In which quadrant(s) do points have positive *x*-coordinates?

Points have positive *x*-coordinates in quadrants I and IV.

> **2.** In which quadrant(s) do points have negative *x*-coordinates and positive *y*-coordinates?

Only in quadrant II do points have negative *x*-coordinates and positive *y*-coordinates.

Distance and Midpoint

Given the coordinates of any two points, you can find the *distance* between them, the *length* of the segment, and the *midpoint* (the point that is located halfway between them) by using appropriate formulas.

Given that A (x_1, y_1) and B (x_2, y_2) are any two points then:

$$\text{Distance between A and B} = \sqrt{(x_2 - x_1)^2 + (y_2 - y_1)^2} \text{ or } \sqrt{(x_1 - x_2)^2 + (y_1 - y_2)^2}$$

$$\text{Midpoint between A and B} = \left(\frac{x_1 + x_2}{2}, \frac{y_1 + y_2}{2}\right) \text{ or } \left(\frac{x_2 + x_1}{2}, \frac{y_2 + y_1}{2}\right)$$

Examples:

Use the following graph for example questions 1 and 2.

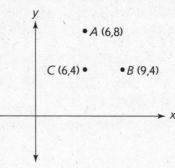

> **1.** What is the distance between *A* and *B*?

$$AB = \sqrt{(6-9)^2 + (8-4)^2} = \sqrt{(-3)^2 + (4)^2} = \sqrt{9+16} = \sqrt{25} = 5$$

> **2.** What are the coordinates of the midpoint between *A* and *B*?

$$\text{Midpoint } (AB) = \left(\frac{6+9}{2}, \frac{8+4}{2}\right) = \left(\frac{15}{2}, \frac{12}{2}\right) = \left(\frac{15}{2}, 6\right) \text{ or } (7.5, 6)$$

Constructing a Graph

Given the equation of a line, you can **construct the graph** of this line by finding ordered pairs that make the equation true. One method for finding the solutions begins with giving a value to one variable and solving the resulting equation for the other value. Repeat this process to find other solutions. (Note: When giving a value for one variable, start with 0, then try 1, and so on.) Then graph the solutions.

Example:

1. Graph the equation $x + y = 6$.

If x is 0, then y is 6: $(0) + y = 6$; $y = 6$.

If x is 1, then y is 5: $(1) + y = 6$; $y = 5$.

If x is 2, then y is 4: $(2) + y = 6$; $y = 4$.

Using a simple chart is helpful.

x	y
0	6
1	5
2	4

Now plot these coordinates and connect them.

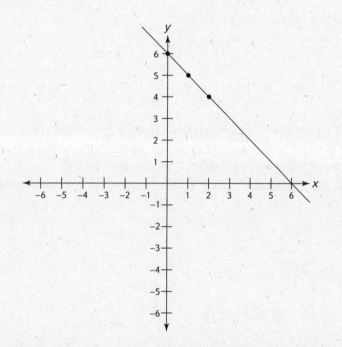

Notice that these solutions form a straight line when plotted. Equations whose solution sets form a straight line are called *linear equations*. Equations that have a variable raised to a power, show division by a variable, involve variables with square roots, or have variables multiplied together will not form straight lines when their solutions are graphed. These are called *nonlinear equations.*

Slope and *y*-intercept

There are two relationships between the graph of a linear equation and the equation itself. One involves the *slope of the line,* and the other involves the point of intersection of the line with the y-axis, known as the *y-intercept.* When a linear equation is written in the $y = mx + b$ form, the m value becomes the slope of the line, and the b value is the location on the y-axis where the line intercepts the y-axis. Thus, the $y = mx + b$ form is called the *slope-intercept form* for the equation of a line.

Example:

> **1.** Find the slope and y-intercept of the line with equation $3x - 4y = 12$.

$$3x - 4y = 12 \qquad \text{(Solve for } y \text{ by first subtracting } 3x \text{ from each side.)}$$

$$\underline{-3x \qquad -3x}$$

$$-4y = -3x + 12 \qquad \text{(Divide each term on each side by } -4.)$$

$$\frac{-4y}{-4} = \frac{-3x}{-4} + \frac{12}{-4}$$

$$y = \frac{3}{4}x - 3$$

Therefore, the slope of the line is $\frac{3}{4}$, and its y-intercept is at -3.

Slope-Intercept

Given any two points on a line, you can locate the equation of the line that passes through these points. This will require finding the slope of the line and the y-intercept.

Given that A (x_1, y_1) and B (x_2, y_2) are any two points then:

$$m = \frac{y_2 - y_1}{x_2 - x_1} \text{ or } \frac{y_1 - y_2}{x_1 - x_2}$$

To find an equation of a line given either two of its points (or the slope and one of its points), use the following step-by-step approach.

1. Find the slope, m (either it is given or you need to calculate it from two given points).
2. Find the y-intercept, b (either it is given or you need to use the equation $y = mx + b$ and substitute the slope value found in Step 1 and the x- and y-coordinates of any given point).
3. Write the equation of the line in the $y = mx + b$ form using the values found in steps 1 and 2.

Examples:

Use the graph below for questions 1–3.

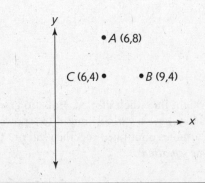

> **1.** What is the slope of the line joining A and B?

$$m = \frac{4 - 8}{9 - 6} = -\frac{4}{3} \left(\text{or } \frac{8 - 4}{6 - 9} = -\frac{4}{3} \right)$$

2. What is the equation of the line, in slope-intercept form, joining A and B?

$$y = mx + b \qquad \left(\text{Replace } m \text{ with } -\frac{4}{3}.\right)$$

$$y = -\frac{4}{3}x + b \qquad \left(\begin{array}{l}\text{Use the point } (6,8) \text{ and replace } x \text{ with 6 and } y \text{ with 8}\\ \text{then solve the resulting equation for } b.\end{array}\right)$$

$$8 = -\frac{4}{\cancel{3}_1}\left(\frac{\cancel{6}^2}{1}\right) + b$$

$$8 = -8 + b$$

$$16 = b$$

Therefore, the equation is $y = -\frac{4}{3}x + 16$.

3. If the line joining A and B were extended, what would be its exact y-intercept?

The b-value represents the y-intercept, thus the exact y-intercept is 16.

Finding Perimeter and Area

Once the coordinates of a figure are known, certain measurements regarding the figure can be calculated. That is, you can find its *perimeter* (distance around), and its **area.**

Examples:

Use the graph below for questions 1 and 2.

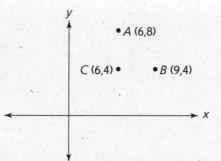

Points A, B, and C, when connected, form a triangle.

1. What is the perimeter of $\triangle ABC$?

To find the perimeter of a triangle, simply add the lengths of its sides.

$$AB = \sqrt{(6-9)^2 + (8-4)^2} = \sqrt{(-3)^2 + (4)^2} = \sqrt{9+16} = \sqrt{25} = 5$$

$$AC = \sqrt{(6-6)^2 + (8-4)^2} = \sqrt{(0)^2 + (4)^2} = \sqrt{16} = 4$$

$$BC = \sqrt{(9-6)^2 + (4-4)^2} = \sqrt{(3)^2 + (0)^2} = \sqrt{9} = 3$$

Therefore, the perimeter of $\triangle ABC = 5 + 4 + 3 = 12$.

> **2.** What is the area of △*ABC*?

Since point *A* is directly above point *C* and point *B* is directly to the right of point *C*, then △*ABC* is a right triangle. Now use *BC* as a base and *AC* as a height, and find the area of △*ABC* using the formula $A = \frac{1}{2}bh$, where *b* is the length of the base and *h* is the length of the height.

Area of $\triangle ABC = \frac{1}{2}(3)(4) = \frac{1}{2}(12) = 6$.

Practice: Coordinate Geometry

1. In which quadrant is (−4,−2) located?

Use the graph below for questions 2–8.

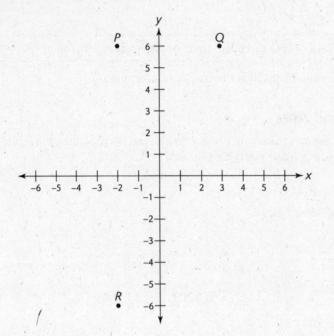

2. What is the distance from *Q* to *R*?

3. What are the coordinates of the midpoint between *Q* and *R*?

4. What is the slope of the line joining *Q* and *R*?

5. What is the equation of the line, in slope-intercept form, joining *Q* and *R*?

6. What is the exact *y*-intercept of the line joining *Q* and *R*?

7. What is the perimeter of △*PQR*?

8. What is the area of △*PQR*?

Answers: Coordinate Geometry

1. III

(−4,−2) is located in quadrant III.

2. 13

Point Q is at (3,6) and point R is at (−2,−6).

$$QR = \sqrt{(-2-3)^2 + (-6-6)^2}$$
$$= \sqrt{(-5)^2 + (-12)^2}$$
$$= \sqrt{25 + 144}$$
$$= \sqrt{169}$$
$$= 13$$

3. $\left(\frac{1}{2}, 0\right)$

$$\text{Midpoint } QR = \left(\frac{-2+3}{2}, \frac{-6+6}{2}\right)$$
$$= \left(\frac{1}{2}, \frac{0}{2}\right)$$
$$= \left(\frac{1}{2}, 0\right)$$

4. $\frac{12}{5}$

$$m = \frac{-6-6}{-2-3} = \frac{-12}{-5} = \frac{12}{5} \text{ or } m = \frac{6-(-6)}{3-(-2)} = \frac{12}{5}$$

5. $y = \frac{12}{5}x - \frac{6}{5}$

From question 4, slope of line $QR = \frac{12}{5}$. Use point Q (3,6) and the slope value to substitute into $y = mx + b$.

$$y = mx + b$$
$$6 = \frac{12}{5}\left(\frac{3}{1}\right) + b$$
$$6 = \frac{36}{5} + b \qquad \left(\frac{6}{1} - \frac{36}{5} = \frac{30}{5} - \frac{36}{5} = -\frac{6}{5}\right)$$
$$-\frac{6}{5} = b$$

The equation of the line passing through Q and R is $y = \frac{12}{5}x - \frac{6}{5}$.

6. $-\frac{6}{5}$ or $-1\frac{1}{5}$

The y-intercept is the b-value from the slope-intercept form of the equation of the line joining Q and R, which is $-\frac{6}{5}$ or $-1\frac{1}{5}$.

7. 30

$$\text{Perimeter } \Delta PQR = \qquad PR \qquad + \qquad PQ \qquad +QR$$

$$= \sqrt{\left(-2-(-2)\right)^2+(-6-6)^2} + \sqrt{(-2-3)^2+(6-6)^2} +13$$

$$= \sqrt{(0)^2+(-12)^2} \qquad + \sqrt{(-5)^2+(0)^2} \qquad +13$$

$$= \sqrt{144} \qquad\qquad\quad + \sqrt{25} \qquad\qquad +13$$

$$= 12 \qquad\qquad\qquad + 5 \qquad\qquad\quad +13$$

$$\text{Perimeter } \Delta PQR = 30$$

8. 30

Since P and Q are directly across from one another and P and R are directly one above the other, ΔPQR is a right triangle. Use PQ as a base and PR as a height.

$$\text{Area } \Delta PQR = \frac{1}{2}(PQ)(PR)$$

$$= \frac{1}{2}(5)(12)$$

$$= 30$$

Functions and Function Notation

A *function* is an equation that expresses an output for any acceptable input. Often the letters f, g, or h are used to denote functions. Consider the function $f(x) = x^2 - 2x$. The English phrase "find the value of the function when x is 6" is expressed as $f(6) = ?$

The function is then evaluated by replacing each x with the value 6.

$$f(x) = x^2 - 2x$$

$$f(6) = (6)^2 - 2(6)$$

$$f(6) = 36 - 12$$

$$f(6) = 24$$

Examples:

1. If $f(x) = x^2 - 3x$, then $f(3) - f(1) = ?$

First find $f(3)$ and $f(1)$. Then solve the subtractions of these results.

$$f(x) = x^2 - 3x \qquad\qquad f(x) = x^2 - 3x$$

$$f(3) = (3)^2 - 3(3) \qquad f(1) = (1)^2 - 3(1)$$

$$f(3) = 9 - 9 \qquad\qquad f(1) = 1 - 3$$

$$f(3) = 0 \qquad\qquad\quad f(1) = -2$$

$$f(3) - f(1) = 0 - (-2) = 2$$

2. If $h(x) = |x|$ then $\dfrac{4}{h(4)} - \dfrac{-2}{h(-2)} = ?$

First find $h(4)$ and $h(-2)$. Then make the appropriate replacements and evaluate the results.

$$h(x) = |x| \qquad h(4) = |4| \qquad h(-2) = |-2|$$
$$h(4) = 4 \qquad h(-2) = 2$$
$$\frac{4}{h(4)} = \frac{4}{4} = 1 \qquad \frac{-2}{h(-2)} = \frac{-2}{2} = -1$$
$$\frac{4}{h(4)} - \frac{-2}{h(-2)} = 1 - (-1) = 2$$

3. If $m(x) = 3x + 2$ and $t(x) = x^2$, then $t[m(-2)] = ?$

First find $m(-2)$, then use its value to replace the x and $t(x)$ function.

$$m(x) = 3x + 2 \qquad t(x) = x^2$$
$$m(-2) = 3(-2) + 2 \qquad t[m(-2)] = [m(-2)]^2$$
$$m(-2) = -6 + 2 \qquad t[m(-2)] = [-4]^2$$
$$m(-2) = -4 \qquad t[m(-2)] = 16$$

Practice: Functions and Function Notation

1. If $f(x) = 5x + 3$, then $f(4) - f(-2) = ?$

2. If $f(x) = x^2 - 3x + 7$ and $g(x) = |-2x - 5|$, then $f(-2) - g(-2) = ?$

3. If $g(x) = x - 2$ and $h(x) = x^2 + 1$, then $g[h(0)] = ?$ and $h[g(0)] = ?$

Answers: Functions and Function Notation

1. 30

$$f(x) = 5x + 3,$$
$$f(4) = 5(4) + 3 \qquad f(-2) = 5(-2) + 3$$
$$f(4) = 20 + 3 \qquad f(-2) = -10 + 3$$
$$f(4) = 23 \qquad f(-2) = -7$$
$$f(4) - f(-2) = 23 - (-7) = 30$$

2. 16

$$f(x) = x^2 - 3x + 7 \text{ and } g(x) = |-2x - 5|$$
$$f(-2) = (-2)^2 - 3(-2) + 7 \qquad g(-2) = |-2(-2) - 5|$$
$$f(-2) = 4 + 6 + 7 \qquad g(-2) = |4 - 5|$$
$$f(-2) = 17 \qquad g(-2) = |-1| = 1$$
$$f(-2) - g(-2) = 17 - 1 = 16$$

3. $g[h(0)] = -1, \ h[g(0)] = 5$

$$g(x) = x - 2 \qquad\qquad h(x) = x^2 + 1$$
$$g(0) = 0 - 2 = -2 \qquad\quad h(0) = (0)^2 + 1 = 1$$
$$g[h(0)] = \qquad\qquad\qquad h[g(0)] =$$
$$g(1) = 1 - 2 = -1 \qquad\quad h(-2) = (-2)^2 + 1 = 5$$

Geometry

Geometry Diagnostic Test

1. Lines that stay the same distance apart and never meet are called _____ lines.

2. Lines that meet to form right angles are called _____ lines.

3. A(n) _____ angle measures less than 90 degrees.

4. A(n) _____ angle measures 90 degrees.

5. A(n) _____ angle measures more than 90 degrees but less than 180 degrees.

6. A(n) _____ angle measures 180 degrees.

7. Find the smaller angle of a pair of complementary angles such that the larger one is 30 degrees greater than twice the smaller one.

8. Find the larger of two supplementary angles such that the smaller one is half the larger one.

9. In the diagram below, find the measure of $\angle 1$, $\angle 2$, and $\angle 3$.

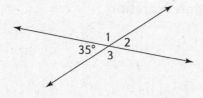

10. In the diagram below, find the value of x, then find the measure of all the numbered angles.

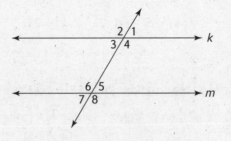

$k \| m; \angle 1 = 2x + 6$ and $\angle 6 = 10x + 30$

Questions 11 and 12 refer to the figure below.

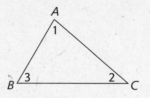

11. Name ∠*A* of this triangle in three different ways.

12. ∠1 + ∠2 + ∠3 = _____°.

13. What are the generic names of polygons with 4, 5, 6, 7, 8, 9, and 10 sides?

14. What are the interior angle sums of convex polygons having 4, 5, 6, 7, 8, 9, or 10 sides?

15. What is the sum of all the exterior angles, one at each vertex, for any convex polygon?

16. What is the measure of one interior angle and one exterior angle of a regular dodecagon (12-sided polygon)?

17. In △*ABC* below,

   segment *BD* is a(n) _____

   segment *BE* is a(n) _____

   segment *BF* is a(n) _____

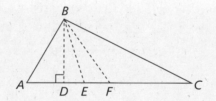

BD⊥*AC, AF = FC, ∠ABE = ∠CBE*

18. A(n) _____ triangle has three equal sides. Therefore, each interior angle measures _____°.

19. In the diagram below, *ABC* is an isosceles triangle with base *BC* and ∠*B* = 38°. Find ∠*A* and ∠*C*.

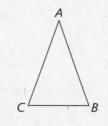

Questions 20 and 21 refer to the diagram below.

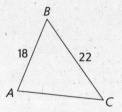

20. In $\triangle ABC$, what is the range of possible values for AC?

21. In $\triangle ABC$, which angle is smaller, $\angle A$ or $\angle C$?

22. In the diagram below, what is the measure of $\angle RST$ if it is an exterior angle of $\triangle QRS$ and $\angle Q = 4x - 3$, $\angle R = 6x - 7$, and $\angle RST = 9x + 5$?

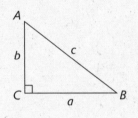

Questions 23–26 refer to the diagram below.

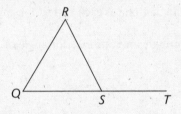

23. If $b = 8$ and $a = 15$, find c.

24. If $b = 10$ and $c = 26$, find a.

25. If $\angle A = 45°$ and $a = 9$, find $\angle B$, b, and c.

26. If $\angle B = 60°$ and $a = 12$, find $\angle A$, b, and c.

27. If in trapezoid $ABCD$ below, $\angle A = 45°$, $\angle B = 30°$, $CD = 10$, and $BC = 12$, find the exact length of AB.

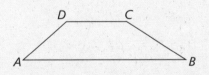

28. Examine the table of quadrilaterals below and place a check mark (✓) next to the statements that *must* be true?

Property Statements	Square	Rectangle	Rhombus	Parallelogram	Trapezoid
Diagonals are equal					
Diagonals bisect each other					
Diagonals are perpendicular					
Diagonals bisect the angles					
All sides are equal in length					
All angles are equal in measure					
Opposite angles are equal in measure					
Opposite sides are equal in length					
At least one pair of opposite sides are parallel					
At least two pairs of consecutive angles are supplementary					

Questions 29–36 relate to the circle with diameter at AC, center at O; points A, B, C, and D lie on the circle, and segment EF is tangent to the circle at point C.

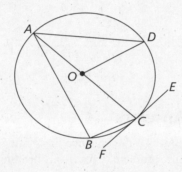

29. Name all the radii.

30. Name all the chords. What is the longest chord in a circle called?

31. Name all the central angles.

32. Name all the inscribed angles.

33. Name all the angles that *must* have a measure of 90°.

34. If $\overset{\frown}{CD} = 80°$ and $\overset{\frown}{BC} = 50°$, find $\angle DOC$ and $\angle DAB$.

35. If $AC = 12$ inches, find the exact area and circumference of the circle.

36. If $\angle DOC = 40°$ and $DO = 10$ inches, find the exact length of $\overset{\frown}{CD}$ and the exact area of sector DOC.

37. Find the perimeter and area of the trapezoid below.

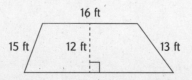

38. Find the area and perimeter of a rhombus if its diagonals have lengths of 24 inches and 10 inches.

39. The area of a triangle with a base of 20 inches is 32 square inches. What is the height associated with this base?

40. Find the exact volume and surface area of a right circular cylinder with a base radius of 12 inches and a height of 10 inches.

41. Find the volume of a cube whose surface area is 24 square inches.

42. A rectangular prism has a diagonal length of $\sqrt{61}$ feet. It has a length of 4 feet and a height of 3 feet. What is its width?

43. If $\triangle ABC \cong \triangle EFG$ and $\angle A = 35°$, $\angle B = 75°$, then $\angle G = ?$

44. Use the diagram below to find x and y.

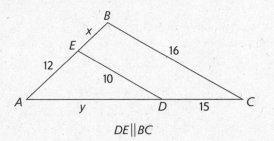

$DE \parallel BC$

Geometry Diagnostic Test Answers

The diagnostic test explanations listed below include topic headings that correspond with step-by-step learning tools and examples to help you solve specific problem types. Topic headings can be found in the Geometry Review section on pages 294–326.

Lines, Segments, Rays, and Angles

1. parallel

2. perpendicular

3. acute

4. right

5. obtuse

6. straight

7. 20 degrees

8. 120 degrees

9. $\angle 1 = \angle 3 = 145°$, $\angle 2 = 35°$

10. $x = 12$, $\angle 1 = \angle 3 = \angle 5 = \angle 7 = 30°$, $\angle 2 = \angle 4 = \angle 6 = \angle 8 = 150°$

Polygons and their Angles

11. $\angle BAC$, $\angle CAB$, $\angle 1$

12. 180

13. 4 sides – quadrilateral, 5 sides – pentagon, 6 sides – hexagon, 7 sides – septagon or heptagon, 8 sides – octagon, 9 sides – nonagon, 10 sides – decagon

14. 4 sides – 360°, 5 sides – 540°, 6 sides – 720°, 7 sides – 900°, 8 sides – 1080°, 9 sides – 1260°, 10 sides – 1440°

15. 360°

16. each exterior angle is 30°, each interior angle is 150°

Triangles

17. BD is an altitude, BE is an angle bisector, BF is a median

18. equilateral, 60

19. $\angle A = 104°$, $\angle C = 38°$

20. AC can be any value between 4 and 40

21. $\angle C$

22. $\angle RST = 140°$

23. 17

24. 24

25. $\angle B = 45°$, $b = 9$, $c = 9\sqrt{2}$

26. $\angle A = 30°$, $b = 12\sqrt{3}$, $c = 24$

27. $16 + 6\sqrt{3}$

Quadrilaterals

28.

Property	Square	Rectangle	Rhombus	Parallelogram	Trapezoid
Diagonals are equal	✓	✓			
Diagonals bisect each other	✓	✓	✓	✓	
Diagonals are perpendicular	✓		✓		
Diagonals bisect the angles	✓		✓		
All sides are equal in length	✓		✓		
All angles are equal in measure	✓	✓			
Opposite angles are equal in measure	✓	✓	✓	✓	
Opposite sides are equal in length	✓	✓	✓	✓	
At least one pair of opposite sides are parallel	✓	✓	✓	✓	✓
At least two pairs of consecutive angles are supplementary	✓	✓	✓	✓	✓

Circles

29. *OA, OC, OD*

30. *AB, AC, AD, BC;* diameter

31. $\angle AOD, \angle DOC$

32. $\angle DAC, \angle DAB, \angle CAB, \angle ABC, \angle ACB$

33. $\angle ABC, \angle ACE, \angle ACF$

34. $\angle DOC = 80°, \angle DAB = 65°$

Perimeter, Circumference, and Area of Plane Figures

35. area = 36π sq. in., circumference = 12π in.

36. $\widehat{CD} = \dfrac{20}{9}\pi$ in., area of sector $DOC = \dfrac{100}{9}\pi$ sq. in.

37. perimeter = 74 ft., area = 276 sq. ft.

38. perimeter = 52 in., area = 120 sq. in.

39. height = 3.2 in. or $3\dfrac{1}{5}$ in.

Surface Area, Volume, and Diagonal Lengths

40. volume = 1440π cu. in., surface area = 528π sq. in.

41. volume = 8 cu. in.

42. width = 6 ft.

Congruence and Similarity

43. $\angle G = 70°$

44. $x = 7.2$ or $7\dfrac{1}{5}, y = 25$

Geometry Review

Lines, Segments, Rays, and Angles

A *line* will always be considered to be straight. It continues forever in opposite directions. A line consists of an infinite number of points and is named by any two points on it. A line may also be named by one lowercase letter.

The above line can be referred to as line *AB*, line *BA*, or line *k*.

A *line segment* is a portion of a line that contains two endpoints and all the points that are in between them. A line segment is named by its two endpoints. A segment has a length and is expressed by stating the two endpoints next to one another. On the GRE, a line segment, and its length will be expressed using the same expression. It is important to recognize the context of the expression that is being referenced.

The segment that has endpoints at *A* and *B* is referred to as *AB* or segment *AB*. The distance between *A* and *B*, or the length of segment *AB* is also referred to as *AB*.

A *midpoint* of a line segment is the halfway point, or the point equidistant from the endpoints.

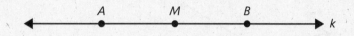

If *AM* = *MB*, then *M* is the midpoint of *AB*. In the previous sentence, the *AM* and *MB* are considered to be lengths, and the *AB* is considered to be the segment itself.

A *ray* is a portion of a line with one endpoint and continues forever in only one direction. Referring to figure above, ray *AB* would be the portion of the line starting at *A*, its endpoint, passing through *B* and continuing on in that direction. Ray *BA* would start at *B*, its endpoint, pass through *A* and continue forever in that direction. Notice that ray *AB* and ray *BA* are not the same ray, yet ray *AB* and ray *AM* represent the same ray.

An *angle* is formed by two rays that have the same endpoint (or two lines that intersect at a point). The endpoint of intersection of an angle is called the *vertex of the angle* and the rays are called the *sides* of the angle. An angle is measured in degrees from 0 to 360. The number of degrees indicates the size of the angle. The angle symbol ∠ is often used instead of the word "angle."

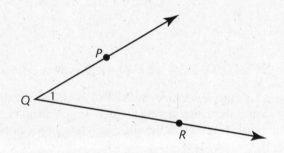

In the figure above, there are several common ways to name the angle:

- by the letter of the vertex, ∠*Q*
- by the number in its interior, ∠1.
- by three letters with the middle letter the vertex of the angle, ∠*PQR* or ∠*RQP*.

A *right angle* has a measure of 90°. In the figure below, the small square symbol in the interior of angle means a right angle. Angle *T* is a right angle.

Any angle whose measure is less than 90° is called an *acute angle.* Any angle whose measure is larger than 90° but smaller than 180° is called an *obtuse angle.* A *straight angle* has a measure of 180°.

In the figure below, ∠*PQR* is an acute angle, ∠*PQS* is an obtuse angle, and ∠*RQS* is a straight angle.

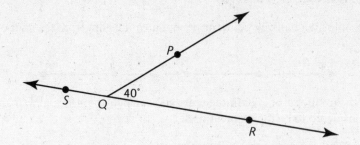

When lines intersect, four angles are formed. The angles opposite each other are called ***vertical angles.*** The angles sharing a common side and a common vertex are ***adjacent angles.*** Vertical angles are always equal in measure and adjacent angles formed by intersecting lines will always have a sum of 180°.

In the figure below, line *n* and line *m* intersect.

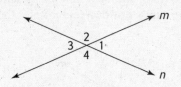

$$\angle 1 = \angle 3, \angle 2 = \angle 4, \angle 1 + \angle 2 = \angle 2 + \angle 3 = \angle 3 + \angle 4 = \angle 4 + \angle 1 = 180°$$

Two angles whose sum is 90° are called ***complementary angles.*** Two angles whose sum is 180° are called ***supplementary angles.*** Adjacent angles formed from intersecting lines are supplementary. An ***angle bisector*** is a ray, segment, or line from the vertex of an angle that divides the angle into two angles of equal measure.

Two lines that meet to form right angles are called ***perpendicular lines.*** The symbol ⊥ is used to denote perpendicular lines. Two or more lines that remain the same distance apart at all times are called ***parallel lines.*** Parallel lines never meet. The symbol ∥ is used to denote parallel lines.

In the figure below, ray *m* is an angle bisector. *k* ⊥ *n* and *l* ⊥ *n*. *k* ∥ *l*.

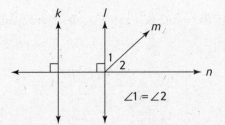

When two parallel lines are both intersected by a third line, eight angles, none of which are straight angles, are formed. Angles in the same relative positions will have equal measures. With this, knowing any one angle, or how any two angles are related, the measures of all 8 angles can be determined.

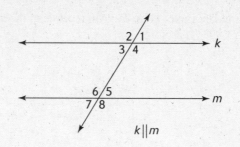

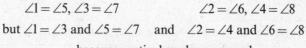

$$\angle 1 = \angle 5, \angle 3 = \angle 7 \qquad \angle 2 = \angle 6, \angle 4 = \angle 8$$

$$\text{but } \angle 1 = \angle 3 \text{ and } \angle 5 = \angle 7 \quad \text{and} \quad \angle 2 = \angle 4 \text{ and } \angle 6 = \angle 8$$

because vertical angles are equal

therefore,

$$\angle 1 = \angle 3 = \angle 5 = \angle 7 \quad \text{and} \quad \angle 2 = \angle 4 = 6 = \angle 8$$

When two parallel lines are intersected by a third line, any two angles will either have equal measures or be supplementary.

Examples:

1. Lines that stay the same distance apart and never meet are called _____ lines.

This is a definition of parallel lines.

2. Lines that meet to form right angles are called _____ lines.

This is the definition of perpendicular lines.

3. A(n) _____ angle measures less than 90 degrees.

This is the definition of an acute angle.

4. A(n) _____ angle measures 90 degrees.

This is the definition of a right angle.

5. A(n) _____ angle measures more than 90 degrees but less than 180 degrees.

This is the definition of an obtuse angle.

6. A(n) _____ angle measures 180 degrees.

This is the definition of a straight angle.

7. Find the smaller angle of a pair of complementary angles such that the larger one is 30 degrees greater than twice the smaller one.

Let x represent the measure of the smaller angle. Then $2x + 30$ represents the measure of the larger angle. Complementary angles have a sum of 90°. Therefore,

$$x + (2x + 30) = 90$$
$$3x + 30 = 90$$
$$3x = 60$$
$$x = 20$$

The smaller angle has a measure of 20 degrees.

8. Find the larger of two supplementary angles such that the smaller one is half the larger one.

Let x represent the measure of the larger angle. Then $\frac{1}{2}x$ represents the measure of the smaller angle. Supplementary angles have a sum of 180°. Therefore,

$$x + \frac{1}{2}x = 180$$
$$\frac{3}{2}x = 180$$
$$x = 120$$

The larger angle has a measure of 120 degrees.

9. In the diagram below, find the measure of $\angle 1$, $\angle 2$, and $\angle 3$.

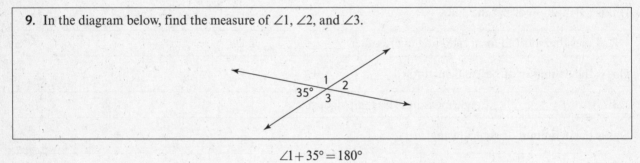

$$\angle 1 + 35° = 180°$$
$$\angle 1 = 145°$$

And since vertical angles have equal measure, $\angle 2 = 35°$, $\angle 3 = 145°$.

10. In the diagram below, find the value of x, then find the measure of all the numbered angles.

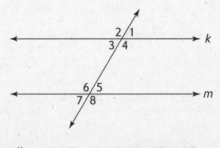

$k \parallel m$; $\angle 1 = 2x + 6$ and $\angle 6 = 10x + 30$

Lines k and m are parallel. Since $\angle 1$ and $\angle 6$ are not equal, then they must be supplementary. Therefore,

$$\angle 1 + \angle 6 = 180$$
$$(2x+6)+(10x+30)=180$$
$$12x+36=180$$
$$12x=144$$
$$x=12$$

$\angle 1 = 2x+6 = 2(12)+6 = 24+6 = 30,\quad \angle 6 = 10x+30 = 10(12)+30 = 120+30 = 150$

$\angle 1 = \angle 3 = \angle 5 = \angle 7 = 30°\qquad\qquad \angle 2 = \angle 4 = \angle 6 = \angle 8 = 150°$

Practice: Lines, Segments, Rays, and Angles

1. Find the value of $x + y$. All measures are in degrees.

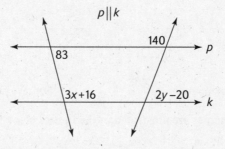

2. If in the figure below, the measure of angle 2 is twice that of angle 1, how big is angle ABC and what type of angle is it?

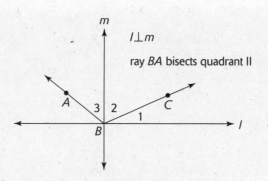

Answers: Lines, Segments, Rays, and Angles

1. 57

   Since $p \parallel k$, then

$$2y-20+140=180 \quad \text{and} \quad (3x+16)+83=180$$
$$(2y-20 \neq 140)\qquad\qquad 3x+99=180$$
$$\text{Then, } 2y-20+140=180 \qquad 3x=81$$
$$2y+120=180 \qquad\qquad x=27$$
$$2y=60$$
$$y=30$$

   Therefore, $x + y = 27 + 30 = 57$.

2. 105°, obtuse

Since $l \perp m$, then $\angle 1 + \angle 2 = 90°$.

Since $\angle 2$ is twice as large as $\angle 1$, then $\angle 2$ is 60° and $\angle 1$ is 30°. Since ray BA bisects quadrant II, then $\angle 3 = 45°$. $\angle ABC = \angle 3 + \angle 2 = 45 + 60 = 105$.

Since $\angle ABC$ is between 90 and 180, $\angle ABC$ is obtuse.

Polygons and their Angles

Closed shapes, or figures in a plane, with three or more sides are called *polygons*. *Poly* means "many," and *gon* means "sides." Thus, polygon means "many sides."

Convex polygons are polygons such that regardless of what side is extended, the polygon always remains on one side of the extension. *Concave polygons* have at least one side, and when extended there is a polygon on each side of the extension. The GRE examination only deals with convex polygons. Examples of convex and concave polygons are provided below.

Convex polygon   Concave polygon

Convex polygons, and their generic names are illustrated in the figures below.

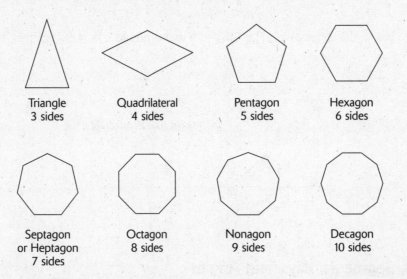

Triangle
3 sides

Quadrilateral
4 sides

Pentagon
5 sides

Hexagon
6 sides

Septagon
or Heptagon
7 sides

Octagon
8 sides

Nonagon
9 sides

Decagon
10 sides

Regular polygons are polygons that have all sides the same length and all angles the same measure. A regular three-sided polygon is the *equilateral triangle*. A regular four-sided polygon is the *square*. A regular five-sided polygon is called a *regular pentagon*. A regular six-sided polygon is called a *regular hexagon*.

A *diagonal of a polygon* is a line segment that connects one vertex with another vertex and is not itself a side.

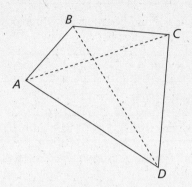

In quadrilateral *ABCD, AC,* and *BD* are both diagonals. If all the diagonals from one vertex of a polygon were drawn, it would divide the polygon into nonoverlapping triangles. The figure below illustrates nonoverlapping triangles in a quadrilateral, pentagon, and hexagon.

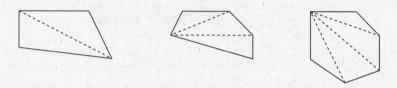

In each case, the number of triangles created is 2 less than the number of sides of the polygon. Since the sum of the angles of any triangle is 180°, you can now find the sum of the angles of any convex polygon by taking 2 less than the number of sides times 180°. That is, if *n* is how many sides a polygon has, then 180(*n* – 2) is the sum of all its interior angles.

Another interesting fact about the angles of any convex polygon is that if each side was extended in one direction, and the exterior angles at the vertices were measured, then the sum of all the exterior angles, one at each vertex would equal 360°.

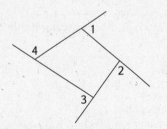

In the case of the quadrilateral above, ∠1 + ∠2 + ∠3 + ∠4 = 360°.

A 15-sided polygon would have 15 exterior angles, one at each vertex, and the sum of those 15 angles would also be 360°.

Examples:

Questions 1 and 2 refer to the figure below.

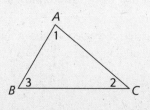

> **1.** Name $\angle A$ of this triangle in three different ways.

If three letters are used, the vertex must be the middle letter. The three possible answers are $\angle BAC$, $\angle CAB$, and $\angle 1$.

> **2.** $\angle 1 + \angle 2 + \angle 3 = $ ____°.

The sum of the angles of a triangle is always 180°.

> **3.** What are the generic names of polygons with 4, 5, 6, 7, 8, 9, and 10 sides?

4 sides – quadrilateral, 5 sides – pentagon, 6 sides – hexagon, 7 sides – septagon or heptagon, 8 sides – octagon, 9 sides – nonagon, 10 sides – decagon

> **4.** What are the interior angle sums of convex polygons having 4, 5, 6, 7, 8, 9, or 10 sides?

The formula for the sum of the interior angle sums is $180(n-2)$, where n is the number of sides of the polygon.

n	$180(n-2)$	Total (in degrees)
4	180(2)	360
5	180(3)	540
6	180(4)	720
7	180(5)	900
8	180(6)	1080
9	180(7)	1260
10	180(8)	1440

> **5.** What is the sum of all the exterior angles, one at each vertex, for any convex polygon?

The sum is always 360°.

> **6.** What is the measure of one interior angle and one exterior angle of a regular dodecagon (12-sided polygon)?

There are two methods to do this problem.

Method 1:

Find the interior angle, then subtract that from 180 to find the exterior angle. The sum of the interior angles is $180(12-2) = 180(10) = 1800°$.

Since there are 12 angles in a 12-sided figure, and a regular polygon has each of its interior angles equal to one another, each angle will have a measure of $\frac{1800°}{12} = 150°$.

Then each exterior angle has a measure of $180° - 150° = 30°$.

Method 2:

Find each exterior angle, then subtract that from 180 to find the interior angle. The sum of all the exterior angles is 360°.

Since the figure is regular, each of its exterior angles will have the same measure. There are 12 exterior angles, therefore each exterior angle has the measure $\frac{360°}{12} = 30°$, which means each interior angle has the measure $180° - 30° = 150°$.

Practice: Polygons and their Angles

1. How many sides does a polygon have if the interior angle sum of a polygon is 1980°?

2. How many sides does a regular polygon have if each exterior angle measures 18°?

Answers: Polygons and their Angles

1. 13

   The sum of the angles of any convex polygon with n sides is $180(n-2)$.

   $$180(n-2) = 1980 \quad \text{(divide each side by 180)}$$
   $$n - 2 = 11$$
   $$n = 13$$

   The polygon has 13 sides.

2. 20

   The sum of the exterior angles of any polygon is 360°. A regular polygon has each of its exterior angles equal in measure. Let n be the number of sides, then

   $$\frac{360°}{n} = 18°$$
   $$18n = 360$$
   $$n = 20$$

   The polygon has 20 sides.

Triangles

Triangles can be classified by the lengths of their sides.

- A triangle having all three sides equal in measure is called an *equilateral triangle.*
- A triangle having at least two equal sides is called an *isosceles triangle.*
- A triangle having no equal sides is called a *scalene triangle.*

Triangles can also be classified by their angles.

- A triangle having all three angles equal in measure is called an *equiangular triangle.*
- A triangle having a right angle in its interior is called a *right triangle.*
- A triangle having an obtuse angle in its interior is called an *obtuse triangle.*
- A triangle having all acute angles in its interior is called an *acute triangle.*

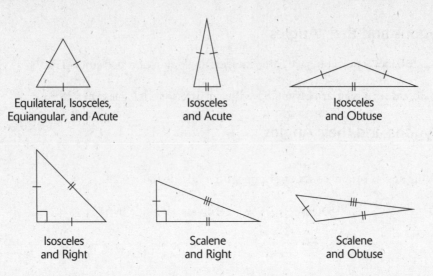

In any triangle, if two of its sides have equal length, the angles opposite those sides have equal measure, and if any two angles in a triangle have equal measure, then the sides opposite those angles have equal length. If all three sides in a triangle are equal, then all three angles in the triangle are equal and vice-versa. In any triangle, if one side is longer than another side, then the angle opposite the longer side will be greater than the angle opposite the shorter side and vice-versa.

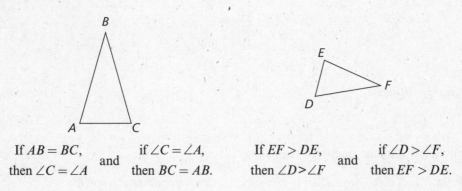

| If $AB = BC$, | | if $\angle C = \angle A$, | If $EF > DE$, | | if $\angle D > \angle F$, |
| then $\angle C = \angle A$ | and | then $BC = AB$. | then $\angle D > \angle F$ | and | then $EF > DE$. |

Any side of a triangle can be called a **base.** With each base, there is an associated **height** (or *altitude*). Each height segment is the perpendicular segment from a vertex to its opposite side or the extension of the opposite side. The height, **h,** can go inside the triangle to its associated base, **b,** it can be one of the sides of the triangle, or it can go outside the triangle as shown in the diagram below.

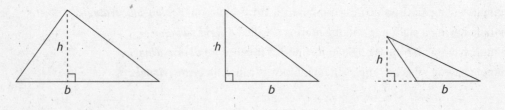

Every triangle has three medians. A **_median_** is a line segment drawn from a vertex to the midpoint of the opposite side. In the figure below, *BD* is a median to side *AC*.

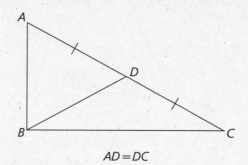

$$AD = DC$$

Every triangle has three **_angle bisectors._** The angle bisector divides an angle into two smaller angles that are equal in measure. In the figure below, *GI* is the angle bisector from vertex *G*.

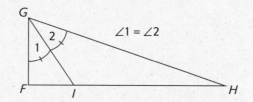

An interesting fact: In any triangle, if one segment is any two of the three special segments in a triangle (altitude, median, angle bisector), then it is automatically the third one, and the triangle is isosceles. The vertex from which the segments are drawn becomes the vertex of the isosceles triangle, and it is at the vertex of the isosceles triangle where the equal sides meet. See figure below.

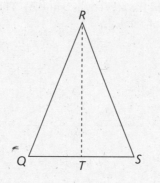

- If *RT* is an altitude <u>and</u> an angle bisector or
- If *RT* is an altitude <u>and</u> a median or
- If *RT* is an angle bisector <u>and</u> a median
- Then *RT* is all three, △*QRS* is isosceles, and *QR* = *RS*.

The sum of the lengths of any two sides of a triangle must be larger than the length of the third side. This statement can be interpreted as, "given any two sides of a triangle, the remaining side must be greater than the difference of the two lengths, but less than the sum of the two lengths." For example:

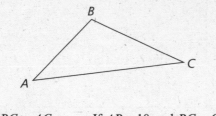

$$AB + BC > AC,$$
$$AB + AC > BC,$$
$$AC + BC > AB$$

If $AB = 10$ and $BC = 6$, then
$$(10 - 6) < AC < (10 + 6)$$
$$4 < AC < 16$$

If one side of a triangle is extended, the exterior angle formed by that extension is equal to the sum of the remote interior angles. For example:

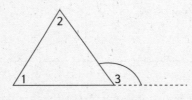

$$\angle 3 = \angle 1 + \angle 2$$

In any right triangle, the relationship between the lengths of the sides is stated by the **_Pythagorean theorem._** The side opposite the right angle is called the **_hypotenuse_** (side c). The hypotenuse will always be the longest side in a right triangle. The other two sides are called the **_legs_** (sides a and b). The theorem states that the square of the hypotenuse equals the sum of the squares of the legs.

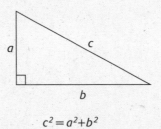

$$c^2 = a^2 + b^2$$

An extension of this theorem can be used to determine the type of triangle based on knowing its angle measures or the lengths of its three sides. If a, b, and c are the lengths of the sides of any triangle with c being the longest side, then the following is true:

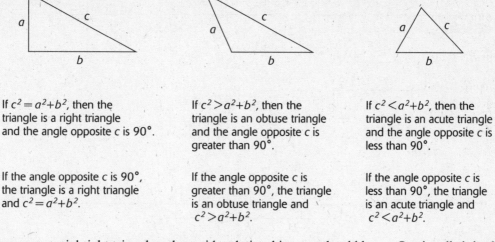

If $c^2 = a^2 + b^2$, then the triangle is a right triangle and the angle opposite c is 90°.

If $c^2 > a^2 + b^2$, then the triangle is an obtuse triangle and the angle opposite c is greater than 90°.

If $c^2 < a^2 + b^2$, then the triangle is an acute triangle and the angle opposite c is less than 90°.

If the angle opposite c is 90°, the triangle is a right triangle and $c^2 = a^2 + b^2$.

If the angle opposite c is greater than 90°, the triangle is an obtuse triangle and $c^2 > a^2 + b^2$.

If the angle opposite c is less than 90°, the triangle is an acute triangle and $c^2 < a^2 + b^2$.

There are two very special right triangles whose side relationships you should know. One is called the **30-60-90 right triangle** and the other is the **45-45-90 right triangle.**

In the 30-60-90 right triangle, the side opposite the 30 degrees is the shortest side, the hypotenuse is twice as long as the shortest side, and the side opposite the 60 degrees is the shortest side times $\sqrt{3}$. This is shown in the figure below.

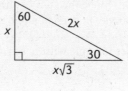

In the 45-45-90 right triangle, the legs have equal lengths and the length of the hypotenuse is a leg times $\sqrt{2}$. This is shown in the figure below.

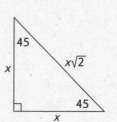

Besides these two special right triangles, right triangles with sides 3-4-5, 5-12-13, 7-24-25, and 8-15-17 are often used on tests.

Examples:

1. In △*ABC* below,

   segment *BD* is a(n) _____.

   segment *BE* is a(n) _____.

   segment *BF* is a(n) _____.

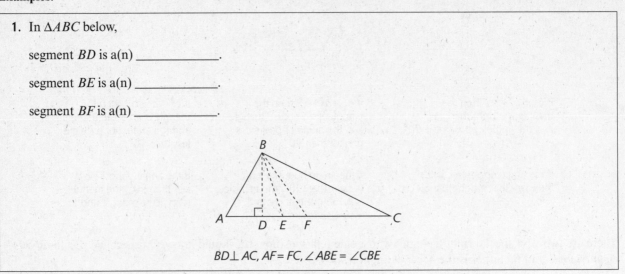

$BD \perp AC,\ AF = FC,\ \angle ABE = \angle CBE$

Since $BD \perp AC$, BD is an altitude. Since $\angle ABE = \angle CBE$, BE is an angle bisector. Since $AF = FC$, BF is a median.

2. A(n) _____ triangle has three equal sides. Therefore, each interior angle measures ____°.

An equilateral triangle has all three sides equal. Since the sum of the angles of any triangle is 180°, and equal sides means opposite angles are equal in a triangle, then each angle measures 60°.

3. In the diagram below, *ABC* is an isosceles triangle with base *BC* and $\angle B = 38°$. Find $\angle A$ and $\angle C$.

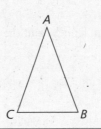

Since *BC* is the base of the isosceles triangle, that means that $AC = AB$, which in turn means $\angle B = \angle C$. Hence, $\angle C = 38°$. The sum of the angles of a triangle is 180°, thus $\angle A + 38° + 38° = 180°$, then $\angle A = 104°$.

Questions 4 and 5 refer to the figure below.

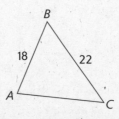

4. In △*ABC* above, what is the range of possible values for *AC*?

AC is greater than the difference of the two given lengths and less than their sum, thus $4 < AC < 40$.

5. In $\triangle ABC$ above, which angle is smaller, $\angle A$ or $\angle C$?

Since $BC > AB$, then $\angle A > \angle C$, which means $\angle C$ is the smaller angle.

6. In the diagram below, what is the measure of $\angle RST$ if it is an exterior angle of $\triangle QRS$ and $\angle Q = 4x - 3$, $\angle R = 6x - 7$, and $\angle RST = 9x + 5$?

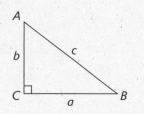

The exterior angle of a triangle equals the sum of its remote interior angles, thus

$$\angle RST = \quad \angle Q \quad + \quad \angle R$$
$$9x + 5 = (4x - 3) + (6x - 7)$$
$$9x + 5 = 10x - 10$$
$$5 = x - 10$$
$$15 = x$$
$$\angle RST = 9x + 5$$
$$= 9(15) + 5$$
$$= 135 + 5$$
$$= 140°$$

Questions 7–10 refer to the figure below.

7. If $b = 8$ and $a = 15$, find c.

$$c^2 = a^2 + b^2$$
$$c^2 = (15)^2 + (8)^2$$
$$c^2 = 225 + 64$$
$$c^2 = 289$$
$$c = \sqrt{289}$$
$$c = 17$$

This is an example of the special 8-15-17 right triangle.

8. If $b = 10$ and $c = 26$, find a.

$$c^2 = a^2 + b^2$$
$$26^2 = a^2 + (10)^2$$
$$676 = a^2 + 100$$
$$576 = a^2$$
$$\sqrt{576} = a$$
$$24 = a$$

This is an example of the special 5-12-13 right triangle with each side doubled.

9. If $\angle A = 45°$ and $a = 9$, find $\angle B$, b, and c.

Since the angle at C is 90° and the sum of the angles of a triangle is always 180°, then $\angle B = 45°$. In the 45-45-90 right triangle, the legs are equal and the hypotenuse is a leg times $\sqrt{2}$. Therefore, $b = 9$ and $c = 9\sqrt{2}$.

10. If $\angle B = 60°$ and $a = 12$, find $\angle A$, b, and c.

Since the angle at C is 90° and the sum of the angles of a triangle is always 180°, then $\angle A = 30°$. In the 30-60-90 right triangle, the side opposite the 30 degree angle is the short leg, the hypotenuse is twice that value, and the long leg is the short leg times $\sqrt{3}$. Therefore, $b = 12\sqrt{3}$ and $c = 2(12) = 24$.

Practice: Triangles

Use the figure below for questions 1–3.

The angles of a triangle are given by $\angle Q = 3x + 12$, $\angle R = 4x - 3$, $\angle S = 2x + 18$.

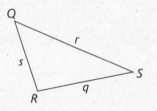

1. Find the value of x.

2. Classify the triangle.

3. Find the relationship between q^2, r^2, and s^2.

4. Which of the following could be the third side of a triangle with sides of 2 and 3?

    Ⓐ 1

    Ⓑ 3

    Ⓒ 5

Answer: Triangles

1. 17

$$\angle Q \quad + \quad \angle R \quad + \quad \angle S \quad = 180°$$
$$(3x+12) \quad + \quad (4x-3) \quad + \quad (2x+18) = 180$$
$$9x+27 = 180$$
$$9x = 153$$
$$x = 17$$

2. acute and scalene

$$\angle Q = 3x+12 \qquad \angle R = 4x-3 \qquad \angle S = 2x+18$$
$$= 3(17)+12 \qquad = 4(17)-3 \qquad = 2(17)+18$$
$$= 51+12 \qquad = 68-3 \qquad = 34+18$$
$$= 63 \qquad = 65 \qquad = 52$$

Since the angles are each different, then the opposite sides are all of different lengths. Therefore the triangle is a scalene triangle. Since each of the angles is less than 90°, the triangle is also an acute triangle.

3. $r^2 < q^2 + s^2$

Since the triangle is an acute triangle, then the square of the longest side is less than the sum of the squares of the other two sides. $\angle R$ is the largest angle, thus its opposite side, r, is the longest side. Therefore, $r^2 < q^2 + s^2$.

4. B

The third side of the triangle must be greater than the difference of 3 and 2 but less than the sum of 3 and 2. The only value that satisfies both conditions is 3.

Quadrilaterals

A polygon having four sides is called a ***quadrilateral.*** There are four angles in its interior. The sum of the measures of these interior angles will always be 360°. A quadrilateral is named by using the four letters of its vertices named in order either clockwise or counterclockwise.

A *square* is a quadrilateral with four equal sides and four right angles. Both pairs of opposite sides are parallel. Diagonals of a square are equal, bisect each other, are perpendicular to each other, and bisect the angles through which they pass. Figure *ABCD* below is a square.

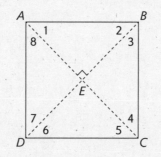

$$AB \parallel CD,\ AD \parallel BC,\ AB = BC = CD = AD$$
$$\angle ABC = \angle BCD = \angle CDA = \angle DAB = 90°$$
$$AC = BD,\ AC \perp BD,\ AE = EC = BE = DE$$
$$\angle 1 = \angle 2 = \angle 3 = \angle 4 = \angle 5 = \angle 6 = \angle 7 = \angle 8 = 45°$$

A ***rectangle*** has opposite sides equal and parallel and four right angles. Diagonals of a rectangle are equal and bisect each other. Figure *ABCD* below is a rectangle.

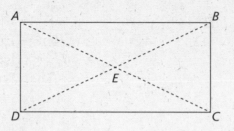

$$AB \parallel CD, \ AD \parallel BC, \ AB = CD, \ AD = BC$$
$$AC = BD, \ AE = EC = BE = DE$$
$$\angle ABC = \angle BCD = \angle CDA = \angle DAB = 90°$$

A ***parallelogram*** has opposite sides equal and parallel, opposite angles equal, and consecutive angles supplementary. Diagonals of a parallelogram are not necessarily equal, but they do bisect each other. Figure *ABCD* below is a parallelogram.

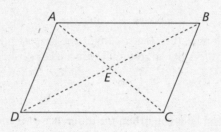

$$AB \parallel CD, \ AD \parallel BC, \ AB = CD, \ AD = BC$$
$$AE = EC, \ BE = DE$$
$$\angle ABC + \angle BCD = 180°, \ \angle BCD + \angle CDA = 180°,$$
$$\angle CDA + \angle DAB = 180°, \ \angle DAB + \angle ABC = 180°,$$
$$\angle ABC = \angle CDA, \ \angle DAB = \angle BCD$$

A ***rhombus*** *is* a parallelogram with four equal sides but not necessarily four equal angles. Diagonals of a rhombus are not necessarily equal, but they do bisect each other, are perpendicular to each other, and bisect the angles through which they pass. Figure *ABCD* below is a rhombus.

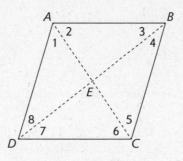

$$AB \parallel CD,\ AD \parallel BC,\ AB = CD = AD = BC$$
$$AE = EC,\ BE = DE,\ AC \perp BD$$
$$\angle ABC + \angle BCD = 180°,\ \angle BCD + \angle CDA = 180°$$
$$\angle CDA + \angle DAB = 180°,\ \angle DAB + \angle ABC = 180°$$
$$\angle ABC = \angle CDA,\ \angle DAB = \angle BCD$$
$$\angle 1 = \angle 2 = \angle 5 = \angle 6,\ \angle 3 = \angle 4 = \angle 7 = \angle 8$$

A ***trapezoid*** has only one pair of parallel sides. The parallel sides are called the ***bases.*** The nonparallel sides are called the ***legs***. The ***median*** of a trapezoid is a line segment that is parallel to the bases and bisects the legs (connects the midpoints of the legs). An ***isosceles trapezoid*** is a trapezoid whose legs are equal in length. Only in the isosceles trapezoid are the diagonals equal in length but do not bisect each other. In an isosceles trapezoid, each pair of angles on the same base are equal in measure. Figure *ABCD* below is a trapezoid with median *EF*.

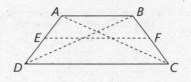

$$AB \parallel CD \text{ (the bases)}$$
$$AE = ED,\ BF = FC,\ FE \parallel AB \text{ and } FE \parallel CD,\ (FE \text{ is a median})$$
$$\angle ABC + \angle BCD = 180°,\ \angle BAD + \angle CDA = 180°$$

If *AD* = *BC* (an isosceles trapezoid), then *AC* = *BD*, ∠*DAB* = ∠*CBA*, ∠*ADC* = ∠*BCD*.

Examples:

1. If in trapezoid $ABCD$ below, $\angle A = 45°$, $\angle B = 30°$, $CD = 10$, and $BC = 12$, find the exact length of AB.

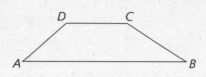

Begin by drawing a perpendicular segment to AB from D and from C creating two special right triangles.

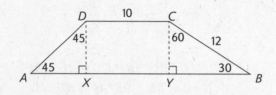

In the 30-60-90 right triangle BCY, CY will be half as long as BC, therefore $CY = 6$. BY will then be $6\sqrt{3}$. The figure $DCYX$ is a rectangle, therefore $DC = XY$ and $DX = CY$. So $XY = 10$ and $DX = 6$. In the 45-45-90 right triangle DXA, the legs are equal in length, therefore, $AX = 6$. The length of AB is the sum of the lengths of AX, XY, and BY.

$$AB = AX + XY + BY$$
$$= 6 + 10 + 6\sqrt{3}$$
$$= 16 + 6\sqrt{3}$$

2. In chart form, summarize the properties of quadrilaterals.

Property	Square	Rectangle	Rhombus	Parallelogram	Trapezoid
Diagonals are equal	✓	✓			
Diagonals bisect each other	✓	✓	✓	✓	
Diagonals are perpendicular	✓		✓		
Diagonals bisect the angles	✓		✓		
All sides are equal in length	✓		✓		
All angles are equal in measure	✓	✓			
Opposite angles are equal in measure	✓	✓	✓	✓	
Opposite sides are equal in length	✓	✓	✓	✓	
At least one pair of opposite sides are parallel	✓	✓	✓	✓	✓
At least two pairs of consecutive angles are supplementary	✓	✓	✓	✓	✓

Practice: Quadrilaterals

1. A rhombus has a side of length 5 and the longer of its two diagonals has a length of 8. Find the length of the shorter diagonal.

2. The opposite angles of a parallelogram have measures of $12x + 18$ and $4x + 58$. Find the measure of the largest angle in this parallelogram.

Answers: Quadrilaterals

1. 6

The sides of a rhombus are all equal. The diagonals of a rhombus bisect each other and are perpendicular to one another. If the longer diagonal is 8, half of it will be 4. Since there is a right triangle, use the Pythagorean theorem. Refer to the diagram below.

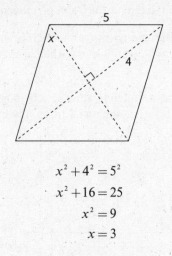

$$x^2 + 4^2 = 5^2$$
$$x^2 + 16 = 25$$
$$x^2 = 9$$
$$x = 3$$

Since half the shorter diagonal is 3, the entire diagonal will be 6.

2. 102°

Opposite angles in a parallelogram have equal measure. Therefore,

$$12x + 18 = 4x + 58$$
$$8x + 18 = 58$$
$$8x = 40$$
$$x = 5$$
$$12x + 18 = 12(5) + 18$$
$$= 60 + 18$$
$$= 78$$

Therefore, one set of opposite angles are each 78° and the other pair of opposite angles are each 102° since consecutive angles in a parallelogram have a sum of 180°. The largest angle in this parallelogram has a measure of 102°.

Circles

A *radius* of a circle can either be the segment that joins the center to any point on the circle or the length of that segment. All radii of the same circle have the same length.

A *diameter* of a circle can either be the segment that joins any two points on a circle and passes through the center of the circle or the length of that segment. In any circle, all diameters have the same length and a diameter equals two radii in length. A *chord* of a circle is a line segment whose endpoints lie on the circle. The *diameter* is the longest chord in any circle.

An *arc* is the portion of a circle between any two points on the circle. Arcs are measured in degree units or in length units. In degrees, it is a portion of the 360° that is a full rotation. In length, it is a portion of the circumference, which is the distance around the circle.

A ***central angle*** in a circle has the center as its vertex and two radii as its sides. The measure of a central angle in degrees is the same as the number of degrees in the arc it intercepts.

An ***inscribed angle*** in a circle has its vertex on the circle and two chords as its sides. The measure of an inscribed angle in degrees is half the number of degrees of the arc it intercepts.

A ***tangent*** to a circle is a line that intersects a circle at only one point. That point is referred to as *the point of tangency*. When a diameter or a radius meet a tangent at the point of tangency, they form a 90° angle.

The symbol $\overset{\frown}{AB}$ is used to denote the arc between points *A* and *B*. It is written on top of the two endpoints that form the arc. It is in the context of use that you would know whether the measure is intended to be a degree measure or a length measure.

When an arc involves half or more than half of a circle, three letters must be used with the first and third indicating the ends of the arc and the middle letter indicating an additional point through which the arc passes.

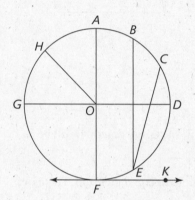

The diagram above is of circle *O*. (A circle is named by its center.) Points *A, B, C, D, E, F, G,* and *H* lie on the circle. The radii shown are *OA, OD, OF, OG,* and *OH*. The diameters shown are *AF* and *DG*. *DG* = 2(*OH*). Chords shown that are not diameters are *BE* and *CE*.

The shortest path along the circle from point *A* to point *E* is $\overset{\frown}{AE}$. The longest path along the circle from point *A* to point *E* can be shown by $\overset{\frown}{AFE}$. The central angles shown are ∠*AOD*, ∠*DOF*, ∠*FOG*, ∠*FOH*, ∠*GOH*, ∠*GOA*, and ∠*HOA*. In degrees, $\overset{\frown}{AH}$ = ∠*AOH*, $\overset{\frown}{ADH}$ = 360° − ∠*AOH*.

The inscribed angle shown is ∠*BEC*. In degrees, $\frac{1}{2}\overset{\frown}{BC}$ = ∠*BEC*. Line *FK* is tangent to circle *O*. The point of tangency is *F*. ∠*AFK* = 90°.

Examples:

Questions 1–7 relate to the circle with diameter at AC, center at O, points A, B, C, and D lie on the circle, and segment EF is tangent to the circle at point C.

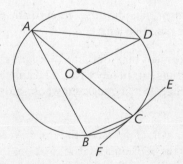

1. Name all the radii.

OA, OC, OD

2. Name all the chords.

AB, AC, AD, BC

3. What is the longest chord in a circle called?

diameter

4. Name all the central angles.

∠*AOD*, ∠*DOC*

5. Name all the inscribed angles.

∠*ABC*, ∠*ACB*, ∠*BAD*, ∠*CAD*

6. Name all the angles that *must* have a measure of 90°.

∠*ACE*, ∠*ACF* (where a tangent and diameter meet, they form a 90° angle).

∠*ABC* (it is an inscribed angle that intercepts a half circle, so it is $\frac{1}{2}$ of 180°).

7. If $\overarc{CD} = 80°$ and $\overarc{BC} = 50°$, find ∠*DOC* and ∠*DAB*.

$\overarc{CD} = ∠DOC$ therefore, ∠*DOC* = 80°.

∠$DAB = \frac{1}{2}\overarc{DB}$ and $\overarc{DB} = \overarc{DC} + \overarc{CB}$, therefore, ∠$DAB = \frac{1}{2}(80° + 50°) = 65°$.

Practice: Circles

Questions 1–3 relate to the circle with diameter at AC, center at O, points A, B, C, and D lie on the circle, and segment EF is tangent to the circle at point C.

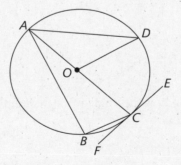

1. If ∠*BCA* = 37°, then ∠*CAB* = ?

2. If ∠*CAB* = 30°, how does *BC* compare to *OD*?

Answers: Circles

1. 53°

   Since AC is a diameter, then inscribed angle ABC intercepts a semicircle, which makes its measure $\frac{1}{2}(180°) = 90°$. The sum of angles of a triangle is always 180°.

   $$\angle CAB + \angle BCA + \angle ABC = 180$$
   $$\angle CAB + \quad 37 \quad + \quad 90 \quad = 180$$
   $$\angle CAB + \qquad 127 \qquad = 180$$
   $$\angle CAB = 53$$

2. $BC = OD$

   As discussed above, $\angle ABC = 90°$. With $\angle CAB = 30°$, triangle ABC is a 30-60-90 right triangle, which makes $BC = \frac{1}{2}(AC)$. Since OD is a radius and AC is a diameter, $OD = \frac{1}{2}(AC)$. Therefore $BC = OD$.

Perimeter, Circumference, and Area of Plane Figures

Perimeter is the distance around the outside of a polygon. *Circumference* is the distance around a circle. *Area* is the number of square units that fill the interior of a plane figure.

For the circle, the **circumference** and **area** formulas use the symbol π. This is a value that is approximately 3.14 in decimal form or about $\frac{22}{7}$ in fraction form. See "Important Geometric Formulas" on pages 208–209 for *perimeter*, *circumference*, and *area* formulas of the most common geometric figures.

In addition to these fundamental formulas, there are the formulas for the length of an arc of a circle and the area of a sector of a circle. The length of an arc is a portion of the circumference. The sector of a circle is a portion of the area of a circle between two radii. In order to calculate either of these quantities, you need to know a central angle and the length of a radius.

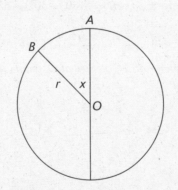

If x is the measure of the central angle and r is the length of the radius, then the length of $\overset{\frown}{AB}$ is $\overset{\frown}{AB} = \frac{x}{360}(2\pi r)$ and area of sector $AOB = \frac{x}{360}(\pi r^2)$.

Examples:

1. Find the perimeter and area of the trapezoid below.

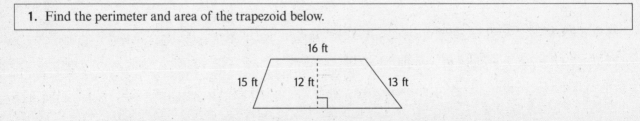

In order to make this easier to solve, draw the perpendicular segments from the ends of the upper base to the lower base, creating two right triangles. Then use the Pythagorean theorem to find missing lengths.

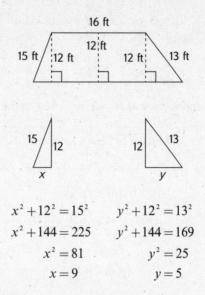

$$x^2 + 12^2 = 15^2 \qquad y^2 + 12^2 = 13^2$$
$$x^2 + 144 = 225 \qquad y^2 + 144 = 169$$
$$x^2 = 81 \qquad\qquad y^2 = 25$$
$$x = 9 \qquad\qquad y = 5$$

Now the figure can be redrawn with all the measurements indicated.

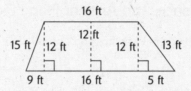

The trapezoid now can be seen as having base lengths of 16 ft. and 30 ft., (9 + 15 + 5 = 30), and a height of 12 ft.

$$\text{perimeter} = \text{ sum of all the sides} = (15 + 16 + 13 + 30)\,\text{ft} = 74 \text{ ft}$$

$$\text{area} = \frac{h(b_1 + b_2)}{2} = \frac{(12)(16 + 30)}{2}\,\text{sq. ft.} = 276 \text{ sq. ft.}$$

---

2. Find the area and perimeter of a rhombus if its diagonals have lengths of 24 inches and 10 inches.

A rhombus is a quadrilateral with all sides equal in length. The diagonals of a rhombus are perpendicular to one another and bisect each other. If one diagonal has length of 24 inches, then each half would be 12 inches. If the other diagonal has length of 10 inches, then each half would be 5 inches. Now you have a right triangle with legs of 5 and 12. Use the Pythagorean theorem to find the hypotenuse, which is the length of one side of the rhombus.

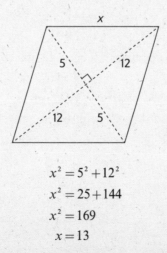

$$x^2 = 5^2 + 12^2$$
$$x^2 = 25 + 144$$
$$x^2 = 169$$
$$x = 13$$

Each side of the rhombus is 13 inches, therefore its perimeter is 4(13) or 52 inches.

To find the area of the rhombus, find the area of each of the identical four triangles created with the intersecting diagonals. Each is a right triangle with legs of 5 and 12. Use one of these as the height and the other as the base.

$$\text{Area triangle} = \frac{bh}{2} = \frac{(5)(12)}{2} \text{ sq. in.} = 30 \text{ sq. in.}$$
$$\text{Area rhombus} = 4(30) \text{ sq. in.} = 120 \text{ sq. in.}$$

---

3. The area of a triangle with a base of 20 inches is 32 square inches. What is the height associated with this base?

$$\text{Area triangle} = \frac{bh}{2}$$
$$32 = \frac{(20)(h)}{2}$$
$$64 = 20h$$
$$3.2 = h$$

The height is 3.2 inches or $3\frac{1}{5}$ inches.

Practice: Perimeter, Circumference, and Area of Plane Figures

1. The length of a diagonal in a rectangle is 13 inches and one side has a length of 5 inches. Find the perimeter and area of this rectangle.

2. An arc of a circle has a central angle of 30 degrees. The arc length is 12π inches. Find the area of this circle.

Answers: Perimeter, Circumference, and Area of Plane Figures

1. perimeter = 34 in., area = 60 sq. in.

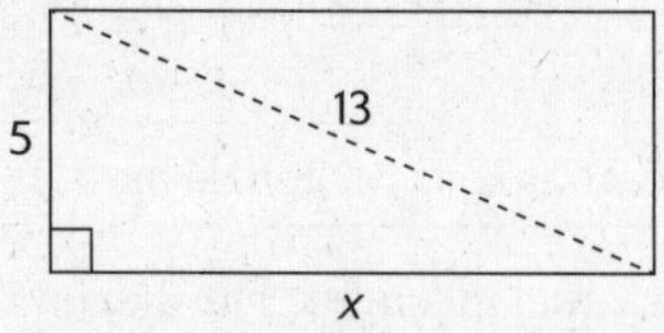

$$x^2 + 5^2 = 13^2$$
$$x^2 + 25 = 169$$
$$x^2 = 144$$
$$x = 12$$
$$\text{perimeter} = 2(5+12)\text{in.}$$
$$= 34 \text{ in.}$$
$$\text{area} = (5)(12)\text{sq. in.}$$
$$= 60 \text{ sq. in.}$$

2. 5184π sq. in.

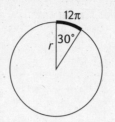

Arc length $= \dfrac{x}{360}(2\pi r)$, where x is the measure of the central angle.

$$12\pi = \dfrac{\overset{1}{\cancel{30}}}{\underset{12}{\cancel{360}}}(2\pi r)$$

$$12\pi = \dfrac{2\pi r}{12}$$

$$144\pi = 2\pi r$$

$$72 = r$$

$$\text{Area} = \pi r^2$$

$$= \pi(72)^2$$

$$= 5184\pi \text{ sq. in.}$$

Surface Area, Volume, and Diagonal Lengths of 3-Dimensional Figures

Surface area is the sum of all the areas of the surfaces of a 3-dimensional figure. *Volume* is the number of cubic units that fill the interior of a 3-dimensional figure. See "Important Geometric Formulas" on pages 208–209 for the surface area and volume formulas of the most common 3-dimensional geometric figures.

In a rectangular prism, besides the length, width, and height, there is a diagonal that goes from one corner to the extreme opposite corner. Refer to the figure below.

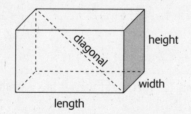

The relationship between the length (*l*), width (*w*), height (*h*), and the diagonal (*d*) of a rectangular prism is illustrated with the following formula:

$$d = \sqrt{l^2 + w^2 + h^2}$$

Examples:

1. Find the exact volume and surface area of a right circular cylinder with a base radius of 12 inches and a height of 10 inches.

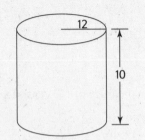

$$\begin{aligned}
\text{Surface area} &= 2\pi r^2 + 2\pi rh \\
&= 2\pi(12)^2 + 2\pi(12)(10) \\
&= 2\pi(144) + 2\pi(120) \\
&= 288\pi + 240\pi \\
&= 528\pi \text{ sq. in.}
\end{aligned}$$

$$\begin{aligned}
\text{Volume} &= \pi r^2 h \\
&= \pi(12)^2(10) \\
&= \pi(144)(10) \\
&= 1440\pi \text{ cu. in.}
\end{aligned}$$

2. Find the volume of a cube whose surface area is 24 square inches.

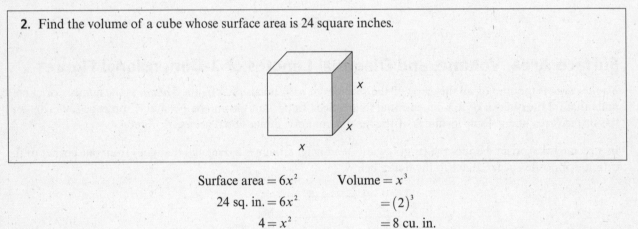

$$\begin{aligned}
\text{Surface area} &= 6x^2 \\
24 \text{ sq. in.} &= 6x^2 \\
4 &= x^2 \\
2 \text{ in.} &= x
\end{aligned}$$

$$\begin{aligned}
\text{Volume} &= x^3 \\
&= (2)^3 \\
&= 8 \text{ cu. in.}
\end{aligned}$$

3. A rectangular prism has a diagonal length of $\sqrt{61}$ feet. It has a length of 4 feet and a height of 3 feet. What is its width?

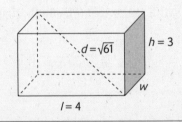

$$d = \sqrt{l^2 + w^2 + h^2}$$
$$\sqrt{61} = \sqrt{4^2 + w^2 + 3^2}$$
$$\sqrt{61} = \sqrt{16 + w^2 + 9} \quad \text{(square both sides)}$$
$$61 = w^2 + 25$$
$$36 = w^2$$
$$6 = w$$

The width is 6 feet.

Practice: Surface Area, Volume, and Diagonal Lengths of 3-Dimensional Figures

1. Find the surface area and diagonal length of a cube whose volume is 343 cubic feet.

2. A cylinder has a height of 3 feet and a volume of 147π cubic feet. Find the surface area of this cylinder.

Answers: Surface Area, Volume, and Diagonal Lengths of 3-Dimensional Figures

1. surface area $= 294$ cu. ft., diagonal $= 7\sqrt{3}$ ft.

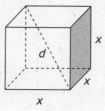

$$\text{Volume} = x^3 \qquad \text{Surface area} = 6x^2 \qquad \text{diagonal} = \sqrt{x^2 + x^2 + x^2}$$
$$343 \text{ cu. ft.} = x^3 \qquad\qquad = 6(7)^2 \qquad\qquad = \sqrt{3x^2}$$
$$7 \text{ ft.} = x \qquad\qquad = 6(49) \qquad\qquad = x\sqrt{3}$$
$$\qquad\qquad = 294 \text{ cu. ft.} \qquad\qquad = 7\sqrt{3} \text{ ft.}$$

2. 140π sq. ft.

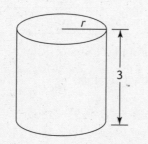

$$\text{Volume} = \pi r^2 h \qquad \text{Surface area} = 2\pi r^2 + 2\pi rh$$
$$147\pi \text{ cu. ft.} = \pi r^2 (3) \qquad\qquad = 2\pi (7)^2 + 2\pi (7)(3)$$
$$49 = r^2 \qquad\qquad = 2\pi (49) + 2\pi (21)$$
$$7 \text{ ft.} = r \qquad\qquad = 98\pi + 42\pi$$
$$\qquad\qquad = 140\pi$$

Congruence and Similarity

Two figures are said to be *congruent* if they have the same shape and have exactly the same size. The symbol for "is congruent to" is ≅. When congruent figures are named, the order in which their vertices are named indicates which angles and sides have the same measure. If $\triangle ABC \cong \triangle DEF$, then $\angle A = \angle D$, $\angle B = \angle E$, $\angle C = \angle F$ and $AB = DE$, $AC = DF$, $BC = EF$.

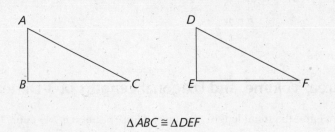

$$\triangle ABC \cong \triangle DEF$$

If two figures are *similar,* they have exactly the same shape but are not necessarily the same size. When similar figures are named, the order in which their vertices are named also indicates which angles are equal in measure and which sides are proportional in measure. The symbol for "is similar to" is ~. If $\triangle ABC \sim \triangle DEF$, then $\angle A = \angle D$, $\angle B = \angle E$, $\angle C = \angle F$ and $\dfrac{AB}{DE} = \dfrac{AC}{DF} = \dfrac{BC}{EF}$.

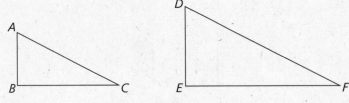

$$\triangle ABC \sim \triangle DEF$$

Triangles that Are Similar

The easiest way to show that two triangles are similar is to show that two angles in one of them have the same measure as two angles in the other.

Examples:

1. If $\triangle ABC \cong \triangle EFG$ and $\angle A = 35°$, $\angle B = 75°$, then $\angle G = ?$

If $\triangle ABC \cong \triangle EFG$, then $\angle A = \angle E$, $\angle B = \angle F$, and $\angle C = \angle G$.

In any triangle, the sum of its angles is 180°. Therefore,

$$\angle A + \angle B + \angle C = 180°$$
$$35° + 75° + \angle C = 180°$$
$$110° + \angle C = 180°$$
$$\angle C = 70°$$
$$\text{but } \angle C = \angle G, \text{ therefore}$$
$$\angle G = 70°$$

2. Use the diagram below to find x and y.

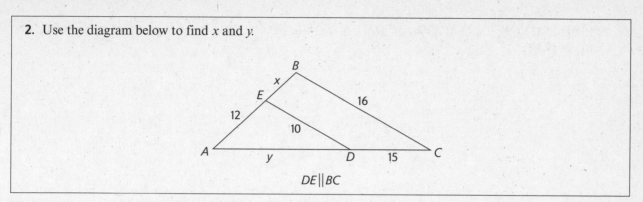

$DE \parallel BC$

There are two triangles in the figure above: $\triangle ADE$ and $\triangle ACB$. Angle A is the same measure in each triangle. Since $DE \parallel BC$, then $\angle ADE$ and $\angle C$ have the same measure. This makes $\triangle ADE \sim \triangle ACB$. Redraw the triangles separately with their corresponding measures.

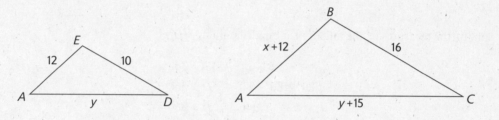

Therefore,

$$\frac{AD}{AC} = \frac{DE}{BC} \qquad \text{and} \qquad \frac{AE}{AB} = \frac{DE}{BC}$$

$$\frac{y}{y+15} = \frac{\overset{5}{\cancel{10}}}{\underset{8}{\cancel{16}}} \qquad\qquad \frac{12}{x+12} = \frac{\overset{5}{\cancel{10}}}{\underset{8}{\cancel{16}}}$$

$$8y = 5(y+15) \qquad 5(x+12) = 8(12)$$
$$8y = 5y + 75 \qquad\quad 5x + 60 = 96$$
$$3y = 75 \qquad\qquad\quad 5x = 36$$
$$y = 25 \qquad\qquad\quad x = \frac{36}{5} \text{ or } 7\frac{1}{5} \text{ or } 7.2$$

Practice: Congruence and Similarity

1. If figure $ABCD \cong$ figure $GHIJ$ and $\angle A = \angle B = \angle C = 80°$, find $\angle I + \angle J$.

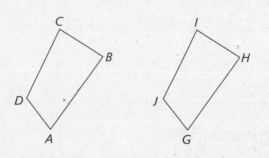

2. If figure $MNOP \sim$ figure $WXYZ$ and $MN = 6$, $NO = 8$, $OP = 10$, $PM = 4$, $WX = 9$, find the perimeter of figure $WXYZ$.

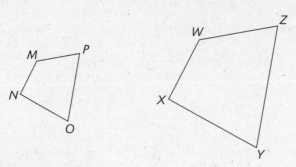

Answers: Congruence and Similarity

1. 200°

   The sum of the measures of the angles of a quadrilateral is 360°.

   $$\angle A + \angle B + \angle C + \angle D = 360°$$
   $$80° + 80° + 80° + \angle D = 360°$$
   $$240° + \angle D = 360°$$
   $$\angle D = 120°$$

   Since figure $ABCD \cong$ figure $GHIJ$, $\angle C = \angle I$ and $\angle D = \angle J$ so $\angle I = 80°$ and $\angle J = 120°$.

   $\angle I + \angle J = 80° + 120° = 200°$

2. 42

   Since figure $MNOP \sim$ figure $WXYZ$, then

   $$\frac{MN}{WX} = \frac{NO}{XY} = \frac{OP}{YZ} = \frac{PM}{ZW}$$

   $$\frac{MN}{WX} = \frac{NO}{XY} \qquad \frac{MN}{WX} = \frac{OP}{YZ} \qquad \frac{MN}{WX} = \frac{PM}{ZW}$$

   $$\overset{2}{\underset{3}{\frac{\cancel{6}}{\cancel{9}}}} = \frac{8}{XY}, \qquad \overset{2}{\underset{3}{\frac{\cancel{6}}{\cancel{9}}}} = \frac{10}{YZ}, \qquad \overset{2}{\underset{3}{\frac{\cancel{6}}{\cancel{9}}}} = \frac{4}{ZW}$$

   $$2XY = 24 \qquad 2YZ = 30 \qquad 2ZW = 12$$
   $$XY = 12 \qquad\; YZ = 15 \qquad\;\; ZW = 6$$

   The perimeter of figure $WXYZ = WX + XY + YZ + ZW$
   $$= 9 + 12 + 15 + 6$$
   $$= 42$$

Data Analysis

Data Analysis Diagnostic Test

1. How many different arrangements of shirts and ties are there if there are 5 shirts and 3 ties?

2. In how many different ways can 5 people sit in a row of 5 chairs if all 5 have to be seated?

3. In how many different ways can 3 of out 7 horses finish 1st, 2nd, 3rd if all 7 horses finish the race?

4. How many committees of 4 can be made from a group of 7 people?

5. Pizza Joe's offers customers a choice of five different toppings from column A and four different toppings from column B. You are to select two toppings from each column to make a four-item pizza. How many different possibilities are there?

6. The positive integers 4 through 20 are individually written on index cards and placed in a bowl. What is the probability of randomly selecting a prime number?

Use the spinner with 12 equally divided sections pictured below for questions 7–9.

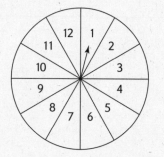

7. What is the probability of spinning a number that is both a multiple of 2 and a multiple of 3 in one spin?

8. What is the probability of *not* spinning a factor of 8 in one spin?

9. If the spinner is spun twice, what is the probability that the spinner will stop on the number 6 the first time and the number 2 the second time?

Use the frequency table below for question 10.

x	f
1	2
2	2
3	1
5	2
7	3

10. Use the frequency table above to find each of the following:

   a) mean

   b) median

   c) mode

   d) range

   e) 1st quartile

   f) 75th percentile

   g) interquartile range

   h) standard deviation

Data Analysis Diagnostic Test Answers

The diagnostic test explanations listed below include topic headings that correspond with step-by-step learning tools and examples to help you solve specific problem types. Topic headings can be found in the Data Analysis Review section on pages 328–336.

Methods for Counting

1. 15

2. 5! or 120 different ways

3. 210

4. 35

5. 60

Probability

6. $\frac{6}{17}$

7. $\frac{1}{6}$

8. $\frac{2}{3}$

9. $\frac{1}{144}$

Basic Statistics

10. a) mean = 4

    b) median = 4

    c) mode = 7

    d) range = 6

    e) 1st quartile = 2

    f) 75th percentile = 7

    g) interquartile range = 5

    h) standard deviation = $\sqrt{5.6}$

Data Analysis Review

Methods for Counting

The *counting principle*, or *multiplying principle* states that if there are a number of successive choices to be made, and the choices are independent of each other (order makes no difference), the total number of possible choices is the product of each of the choices at each stage.

Example:

1. How many different arrangements of shirts and ties are there if there are 5 shirts and 3 ties?

There are 5 choices for shirts and 3 choices for ties, therefore there are $5 \times 3 = 15$ possible choices. The 15 choices can be illustrated. Let the 5 choices for shirts be called S1, S2, S3, S4, and S5. Let the 3 choices for ties be called T1, T2, and T3.

The 15 possible pairings are as follows:

S1-T1, S1-T2, S1-T3
S2-T1, S2-T2, S2-T3
S3-T1, S3-T2, S3-T3
S4-T1, S4-T2, S4-T3
S5-T1, S5-T2, S5-T3

Permutations

If there are a number of successive choices to make and the choices are affected by the previous choice or choices (dependent upon order), then *permutations* are involved.

Example:

2. In how many different ways can 5 people sit in a row of 5 chairs if all 5 have to be seated?

$$\underbrace{\begin{array}{c}\text{\# of choices}\\\text{for 1st chair}\end{array}}_{5} \times \underbrace{\begin{array}{c}\text{\# of choices}\\\text{for 2nd chair}\end{array}}_{4} \times \underbrace{\begin{array}{c}\text{\# of choices}\\\text{for 3rd chair}\end{array}}_{3} \times \underbrace{\begin{array}{c}\text{\# of choices}\\\text{for 4th chair}\end{array}}_{2} \times \underbrace{\begin{array}{c}\text{\# of choices}\\\text{for 5th chair}\end{array}}_{1}$$

The product $5 \times 4 \times 3 \times 2 \times 1$ can be written as 5! (read **5 factorial** or **factorial 5**). Thus, there are 5! or 120 different ways to arrange 5 people in 5 chairs in a row.

Sometimes permutation problems do not use all the choices available. In these situations, the use of a *permutations formula* can simplify matters. The symbol to denote this is $P(n, r)$ or $_nP_r$, which is read as "the permutations of n things taken r at a time."

The formula used is $P(n,r) = {_nP_r} = \dfrac{n!}{(n-r)!}$.

Permutations Formula

Example:

3. In how many different ways can 3 of out 7 horses finish 1st, 2nd, and 3rd if all 7 horses finish the race?

The order in which the horses finish the race makes a difference. That is why this situation is referred to as a permutation. In this case, we are taking 7 things 3 at a time.

Since $n = 7$ and $r = 3$, (7 taken 3 at a time) the equation becomes

$$P(7, 3) = {_7P_3} = \frac{7!}{(7-3)!} = \frac{7!}{4!} = \frac{7 \times 6 \times 5 \times \overset{1}{\cancel{(4 \times 3 \times 2 \times 1)}}}{\underset{1}{\cancel{(4 \times 3 \times 2 \times 1)}}} = 7 \times 6 \times 5 = 210$$

This problem could also have been solved using the counting principle.

$$\underbrace{\begin{array}{c}\text{\# of choices}\\\text{for 1st place}\end{array}}_{7} \times \underbrace{\begin{array}{c}\text{\# of choices}\\\text{for 2nd place}\end{array}}_{6} \times \underbrace{\begin{array}{c}\text{\# of choices}\\\text{for 3rd place}\end{array}}_{5} \qquad 7 \times 6 \times 5 = 210$$

329

Combinations

There are situations in which the order that items are selected does not matter. Those situations are referred to as *combinations*. The symbol used to denote this situation is $C(n, r)$ or $_nC_r$, which is read as "the number of combinations of n things taken r at a time." The formula used is $C(n,r) = {}_nC_r = \dfrac{n!}{r!(n-r)!}$.

Example:

> 4. How many committees of 4 can be made from a group of 7 people?

Notice that the order of selection makes no difference. Since $n = 7$ and $r = 4$ (7 people taken 4 at a time), the equation is as follows:

$$C(7, 4) = {}_7C_4 = \frac{7!}{4!(7-4)!} = \frac{7 \times 6 \times 5 \times 4 \times 3 \times 2 \times 1}{4 \times 3 \times 2 \times 1 \times (3)!} = \frac{7 \times \overset{1}{\cancel{6}} \times 5 \times \overset{1}{\cancel{(4 \times 3 \times 2 \times 1)}}}{\underset{1}{\cancel{(4 \times 3 \times 2 \times 1)}} \; \underset{1}{3 \times 2 \times 1}} = 35$$

Therefore, 35 committees of 4 can be made from a group of 7 people.

Counting Principle and Combinations Formula

Sometimes you might see a problem on the GRE that involves both the counting principle and the combinations formula.

Example:

> 5. Pizza Joe's offers customers a choice of five different toppings from column A and four different toppings from column B. You are to select two toppings from each column to make a four-item pizza. How many different possibilities are there?

Here we have two key choices: which two toppings from column A and which two toppings from column B. The number of possibilities for each will be multiplied together by the counting principle. To find how many topping choices there are from each column, you will need to use the combinations formula.

$$\underbrace{\begin{array}{c} \#\,\text{ways to select} \\ 2 \text{ out of 5 from} \\ \text{column A} \end{array}}_{C(5, 2)} \times \underbrace{\begin{array}{c} \#\,\text{ways to select} \\ 2 \text{ out of 4 from} \\ \text{column B} \end{array}}_{C(4, 2)}$$

$$\left(\frac{5!}{2!(5-2)!}\right) \times \left(\frac{4!}{2!(2-2)!}\right)$$

$$\left(\frac{5 \times 4 \times 3 \times 2 \times 1}{(2 \times 1)(3 \times 2 \times 1)}\right) \times \left(\frac{4 \times 3 \times 2 \times 1}{(2 \times 1)(2 \times 1)}\right)$$

$$10 \quad \times \quad 6$$

$$60$$

Therefore, there are 60 different possibilities.

Probability

Probability is the numerical measure of the chance of an outcome or event occurring. When all outcomes are equally likely to occur, the probability of the occurrence of a given outcome can be found by using the following formula:

$$\text{probability} = \frac{\text{number of favorable outcomes}}{\text{number of possible outcomes}}$$

The probability of an event not occurring is 1 – (probability that it does occur).

Examples:

1. The positive integers 4 through 20 are individually written on index cards and placed in a bowl. What is the probability of randomly selecting a prime number?

The integers 4 through 20 are 4, 5, 6, 7, 8, 9, 10, 11, 12, 13, 14, 15, 16, 17, 18, 19, and 20.

There are 17 integers from 4 to 20. The integers that are prime numbers are 5, 7, 11, 13, 17, and 19. There are 6 prime integers from 4 to 20.

$$\text{probability} = \frac{\text{\# favorable}}{\text{\# total}} = \frac{6}{17}$$

Use the spinner with 12 equally divided sections pictured below for questions 2–4.

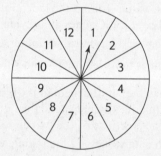

2. What is the probability of spinning a number that is both a multiple of 2 and a multiple of 3 in one spin?

To be a multiple of 2 and 3 means to be a multiple of 6. Of the 12 numbers, only 6 and 12 are multiples of 6.

$$\text{probability} = \frac{\text{\# favorable}}{\text{\# total}} = \frac{2}{12} = \frac{1}{6}$$

3. What is the probability of *not* spinning a factor of 8 in one spin?

The factors of 8 are 1, 2, 4, and 8. The probability of spinning a factor of 8 becomes
$\text{probability} = \frac{\text{\# favorable}}{\text{\# total}} = \frac{4}{12} = \frac{1}{3}$. Therefore, the probability of not spinning a factor of 8 is $1 - \frac{1}{3} = \frac{2}{3}$.
You could also have found the numbers that were not factors of 8, namely 3, 5, 6, 7, 9, 10, 11, and 12 (there are 8 of them), and then said the probability of not spinning a factor of 12 is $\frac{8}{12} = \frac{2}{3}$.

> **4.** If the spinner is spun twice, what is the probability that the spinner will stop on the number 6 the first time and the number 2 the second time?

This problem can be solved in two ways. One way is to first find the individual probabilities and multiply them together. The probability of spinning a 6 the first time is $\frac{1}{12}$. There is only one 6 and there are 12 numbers. Similarly, the probability of spinning a 2 on the second spin is also $\frac{1}{12}$. Therefore, the probability of spinning a 6 on the first spin followed by spinning a 2 on the second spin is $\frac{1}{12} \times \frac{1}{12} = \frac{1}{144}$.

The second method is to use the counting principle to find the total number of ways of spinning a first number followed by a second number. There are 12 numbers possible for each spin, therefore there are $12 \times 12 = 144$ possibilities. Of these, only one is a 6 followed by a 2. Therefore, the probability is $\frac{1}{144}$.

Basic Statistics

Any measure indicating a center of a distribution is called a ***measure of central tendency.*** The three basic measures of central tendency are mean (or arithmetic mean), median, and mode.

The ***mean*** (arithmetic mean) is what is usually called the average. To determine the arithmetic mean, find the sum of the data values and then divide by the number of data values.

The ***median*** of a set of numbers arranged in ascending or descending order is the middle number. If there is an odd number of data values in the set, then one of the data values is the median and there will be an equal number of data values on either side of this middle value. To find the location of the median value when there is an odd number of data values, add 1 to the number of data values and divide that number by 2. This then is the position of the median value. For example, if there were 15 data values in the set, then $\frac{15+1}{2} = \frac{16}{2} = 8$, the 8th data value would be the median value with 7 data values to its left and 7 data values to its right.

If there is an even number of data values in the set, the median is the arithmetic mean of the middle two numbers. To find the position of the two middle numbers, take the number of data values in the set and divide by 2. That number and the next integer are the positions of the two middle values. For example, if the data set has 20 values, then $\frac{20}{2} = 10$, the 10th and 11th data values are the middle values and the median would be the average of these two values. The median is easy to calculate and is not influenced by extreme measurements.

The ***mode*** is the data value that appears most, or whose frequency is the greatest. In order to have a mode, there must be a repetition of a data value.

The ***range*** for a set of data values is the difference between the largest and the smallest values.

When a set of data values is listed from least to greatest, the median value is sometimes referred to as the *2nd quartile* or the *50th percentile* value. To the left of the median are a set of data values called the lower values and to the right of the median are a set of data values called the upper values. The median of the lower values is called the *1st quartile* or *25th percentile* value, and the median of the upper values is called the *3rd quartile* or the *75th percentile* value.

The difference between the 3rd quartile and the 1st quartile, (or the 75th percentile and the 25th percentile) is called the ***interquartile range.***

The *standard deviation* of a set of data is a measure of how far data values of a population are from the mean value of the population. A small standard deviation indicates that the data values tend to be very close to the mean value. A large standard deviation indicates that the data values are "spread out" from the mean value.

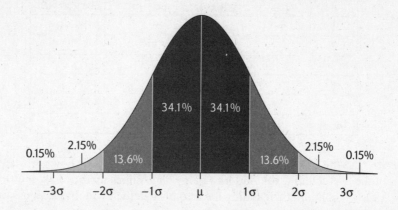

The figure above represents a set of data that has a normal distribution. In it, μ represents the mean value of the set of data. Each shaded band has a width of one standard deviation. For normally distributed data, you will find approximately 68% of all the data values within one standard deviation from the mean. You will find approximately 95.5% of all the data values within two standard deviations from the mean. At three standard deviations from the mean, approximately 99.8% of all the data values are found.

The basic method for calculating the standard deviation for a population is lengthy and time consuming. It involves five steps:

1. Find the mean value for the set of data.
2. For each data value, find the difference between it and the mean value; then square that difference.
3. Find the sum of the squares found in Step 2.
4. Divide the sum found in Step 3 by how many data values there are.
5. Find the square root of the value found in Step 4.

The result found in Step 4 is referred to as the *variance.* The square root of the variance is the standard deviation. This form of the standard deviation assumes all the data values are used, not merely a sample of all the data.

Frequency Table and Measure of Central Tendency

A *frequency table* or a *frequency chart* is often used to summarize the data information. Generally there is a column on the left, the data values, and a column on the right, the frequency, which indicates how many of each data value are in the data set.

By adding the values in the frequency column, you find the total number of data values. By multiplying each data value with its frequency, then adding these totals together, you can quickly find the sum of all the data values.

Example:

1. Use the frequency table at the right to find each of the following:
   a) mean
   b) median
   c) mode
   d) range
   e) 1st quartile
   f) 75th percentile
   g) interquartile range
   h) standard deviation

x	f
1	2
2	2
3	1
5	2
7	3

In order to make all the calculations, add three more columns and one more row to the table. The "*m*" will be the mean value.

x	*f*	(*x*)(*f*)	(*x* – *m*)²	(*x* – *m*)²(*f*)
1	2			
2	2			
3	1			
5	2			
7	3			
Totals				

a) To *calculate the mean,* find the sum of all the data values and divide that by how many data values there are. By adding the values in the "*f*" column, you find how many data values there are. By multiplying each data value by its frequency, the "(*x*)(*f*)" column, then adding these totals together, you find a quick way to get the sum of all the data values.

x	*f*	(*x*)(*f*)	(*x* – *m*)²	(*x* – *m*)²(*f*)
1	2	2		
2	2	4		
3	1	3		
5	2	10		
7	3	21		
Totals	10	40		

Therefore, $m = \dfrac{40}{10} = 4$, the mean has a value of 4.

b) To find the *median value,* notice that there are 10 data values. The median will be the average of the data values in the 5th and 6th positions. Based on the frequency table, the 1st and 2nd values are each 1 and the 3rd and 4th values are each 2. The 5th value is 3 and the 6th value is 5. The average of 3 and 5 is 4. The median value is 4. If the data values were all listed in order, it would look like this:

$$\underset{\text{1st}}{1}, \underset{\text{2nd}}{1}, \underset{\text{3rd}}{2}, \underset{\text{4th}}{2}, \underset{\text{5th}}{3}, \underset{\text{6th}}{5}, \underset{\text{7th}}{5}, \underset{\text{8th}}{7}, \underset{\text{9th}}{7}, \underset{\text{10th}}{7}$$

$$\underset{\text{median}}{\uparrow}$$

c) The *mode* is the value repeated most often. Based on the frequency table, the value 7 occurs 3 times, which is more than any other value occurred. The mode is the value 7.

d) The *range* is the difference between the greatest value, 7, and the least value, 1. Since 7 – 1 = 6, the range is 6.

e) The *1st quartile,* or the *25th percentile,* is the median of the lower values. The median of the original data set was the average between the 5th and 6th values. Therefore there are 5 values in the lower portion. The 1st quartile then is the median of these 5 values. Since $\dfrac{5+1}{2} = \dfrac{6}{2} = 3$, the 1st quartile will be the 3rd value. The 3rd value is 2, therefore the 1st quartile is 2.

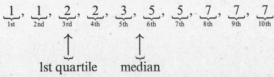

334

f) The **75th percentile,** or the **3rd quartile,** is the median of the upper values. There are 5 data values in the upper portion, so the 7th percentile will also be the 3rd value of the upper values. This would make it the 8th data value. The 75th percentile is 7.

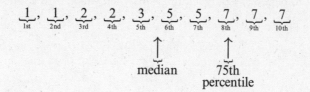

g) The **interquartile range** is the difference between the 3rd quartile and the 1st quartile values. The 3rd quartile value was 7, the 1st quartile value was 2, $7 - 2 = 5$. The interquartile range is 5.

Five Steps to Calculate the Standard Deviation

The additional columns in the frequency table are now used.

1. Calculate the mean. For this data set the mean, *m,* was 4.

2. For each data value, find (data value – mean)^2:

x	*f*	*(x)(f)*	*(x − m)*^{2}	*(x − m)*^{2}*(f)*
1	2	2	$(1 - 4)^2 = 9$	
2	2	4	$(2 - 4)^2 = 4$	
3	1	3	$(3 - 4)^2 = 1$	
5	2	10	$(5 - 4)^2 = 1$	
7	3	21	$(7 - 4)^2 = 9$	
Totals	10	40		

3. Find the sum of the squares found in Step 2. This is done by taking each (data value – mean)^2 result and multiplying it by the frequency of the data value, then adding these results together.

x	*f*	*(x)(f)*	*(x − m)*^{2}	*(x − m)*^{2}*(f)*
1	2	2	$(1 - 4)^2 = 9$	$(9)(2) = 18$
2	2	4	$(2 - 4)^2 = 4$	$(4)(2) = 8$
3	1	3	$(3 - 4)^2 = 1$	$(1)(1) = 1$
5	2	10	$(5 - 4)^2 = 1$	$(1)(2) = 2$
7	3	21	$(7 - 4)^2 = 9$	$(9)(3) = 27$
Totals	10	40		56

4. Divide the results of Step 4 by the number of data values:

$$\frac{56}{10} = 5.6$$

5. Find the square root of the answer to Step 4. This is then the standard deviation. Standard deviation is $\sqrt{5.6}$.

Practice: Data Analysis

1. A scientist discovered that the instrument used for an experiment was off by 2 milligrams. If each weight in his experiment needed to be increased by 2 milligrams, then which of the following statistical measures would not be affected?

   Ⓐ mean
   Ⓑ median
   Ⓒ mode
   Ⓓ range
   Ⓔ standard deviation

2. Three green marbles, two blue marbles, and five yellow marbles are placed in a jar. What is the probability of selecting at random a yellow marble followed by a green marble if the first marble is not replaced before drawing the second marble?

3. There are 9 players on a basketball team. Only 5 of them can play at any one time. How many different teams of 5 are possible?

Answers: Data Analysis

1. range and standard deviation

   The values of the mean, median, and mode will each increase by 2. The range and standard deviation values will remain unaffected.

2. $\frac{1}{6}$

   There are $3 + 2 + 5 = 10$ total marbles. The probability that the first draw will be yellow is $\frac{5}{10} = \frac{1}{2}$. Without replacing a marble, there will only be 9 marbles remaining, 3 of which are green. The probability of now selecting a green marble is $\frac{3}{9} = \frac{1}{3}$. The probability of both events is $\frac{1}{2} \times \frac{1}{3} = \frac{1}{6}$.

   Another approach is to first find the number of ways to select a yellow marble followed by a green marble. Using the counting principle: $5 \times 3 = 15$. Then use the counting principle to find the number of ways to select one marble followed by another one: $10 \times 9 = 90$. Then the probability becomes $\frac{15}{90} = \frac{1}{6}$.

3. 126

   The order in which the players are selected does not matter, therefore use the combinations formula. Since $n = 9$ and $r = 5$ (9 players taken 5 at a time), the equation is as follows:

   $$C(9, 5) = \frac{9!}{(9-5)!(5!)} = \frac{\overset{3}{\cancel{9}} \times \overset{2}{\cancel{8}} \times 7 \times \overset{3}{\cancel{6}} \times \overset{1}{\cancel{(5!)}}}{\underset{1}{\cancel{4}} \times \underset{1}{\cancel{3}} \times \underset{1}{\cancel{2}} \times 1 \times \underset{1}{\cancel{(5!)}}} = 126$$

Word Problems

Word Problems Diagnostic Test

1. Traveling from point A to point B, John averages 30 miles per hour. The return trip is along the same route and he averages 40 miles per hour. Find John's average speed for the entire trip, to the nearest tenth of a mile per hour.

2. Jim can do a job in 8 hours by himself that would take Tom 12 hours to do by himself. Working together, how long should it take to do the job?

3. A chemist wants to dilute 50 ml of a 40% acid solution into a 30% acid solution. How much pure water must be added?

4. Carlos is 5 years older than three times his daughter's age. Two years ago, he was 4 years older than four times her age. How many years from today will he be twice her age?

5. Find the product of three consecutive odd integers such that twice the smallest increased by the largest is thirteen less than four times the middle integer.

Word Problems Diagnostic Test Answers

The diagnostic test explanations listed below include topic headings that correspond with step-by-step learning tools and examples to help you solve specific problem types. Topic headings can be found in the Word Problems Review section on pages 338–346.

Motion Problem

1. 34.3 miles/hour

Work Problem

2. $4\frac{4}{5}$ hours or 4.8 hours

Mixture Problem

3. $16\frac{2}{3}$ ml

Age Problem

4. 12 years

Integer Problems

5. 1,287

Word Problems Review

Motion Problems

Motion problems all use the basic formula of (average rate)(total time) = (total distance) or more simply $r \times t = d$.

Usually a chart that organizes the given information is helpful in creating an equation to be solved that can answer the question. Such a chart could look like this:

	Average Rate	Total Time	Total Distance
A			
B			

Examples:

1. Traveling from point A to point B, John averages 30 miles per hour. On the return trip along the same route, he averages 40 miles per hour. Find, to the nearest tenth of a mile per hour, his average speed for the entire trip.

The most common error made on this type of problem is to add the rates together and divide by 2. Average speed is found by taking the total distance traveled and dividing by the total time it took to travel that distance. To make the problem more simple, assume the distance traveled was 120 miles, a number that is easily divided by both 30 and 40.

	Average Rate	Total Time	Total Distance
A to B	30 mi/hr	x	120 mi
B to A	40 mi/hr	y	120 mi

Then $30x = 120$ and $40y = 120$, which means that the entire trip of 240 miles took 7 hours. Thus the average

$x = 4 \qquad\qquad y = 3$

speed becomes $\dfrac{240 \text{ miles}}{7 \text{ hours}} \approx 34.29$ mi/hr, which rounded off to the nearest tenth of a mile per hour is 34.3 mi/hr.

The problem can also be solved algebraically:

Let d be the one-way distance, then $\dfrac{d \text{ mi}}{30 \text{ mi/hr}} = \dfrac{d}{30}$ hr is the time used going from A to B and $\dfrac{d \text{ mi}}{40 \text{ mi/hr}} = \dfrac{d}{40}$ hr is the time used going from B to A.

$$\begin{aligned}
\text{average speed} &= \frac{\text{total distance}}{\text{total time}} \\[2mm]
&= \frac{2d}{\dfrac{d}{30} + \dfrac{d}{40}} \\[2mm]
&= \frac{2d}{\dfrac{70d}{1200}} \\[2mm]
&= \frac{2\cancel{d}}{1} \times \frac{\overset{}{1200}}{\underset{35}{\cancel{70d}}} \\[2mm]
&\approx 34.29
\end{aligned}$$

You should also be able to get an estimate before starting the problem. To travel a certain distance going 30 miles per hour will take longer than going that distance at 40 miles per hour, which means that the average speed will be closer to 30 mi/hr than to 40 mi/hr. Had this been a multiple-choice question and only one answer was between 30 and 35, it is the one, and calculations would have been unnecessary.

2. If a girl can run m miles in h hours, how fast will she run k miles at the same rate?

Let x be the rate for each direction and t the time for the second run.

	Average Rate	Total Time	Total Distance
A	x mi/hr	h hr	m mi
B	x mi/hr	t hr	k mi

$$xh = m \quad \text{and} \quad xt = k$$
$$x = \frac{m}{h} \qquad\qquad x = \frac{k}{t}$$

$$\text{Therefore, } \frac{m}{h} = \frac{k}{t}$$
$$tm = hk$$
$$t = \frac{hk}{m}$$

It will take $\frac{hk}{m}$ hours to run k miles.

3. A boat travels 30 miles against a current in 3 hours. It travels the same 30 miles with the current in 1 hour. How fast is the current and what is the boat's speed in still water?

Let b be the boat's speed in still water, and let c be the current's speed. Going with the current, the boat's speed will be $b + c$ mi/hr. Going against the current, the boat's speed will be $b - c$ mi/hr. Use a chart to organize the information.

	Average Rate	Total Time	Total Distance
With the current	$b + c$ mi/hr	1 hr	30 mi
Against the current	$b - c$ mi/hr	3 hr	30 mi

This now translates into the following system of equations:

$$(b+c)(1) = 30 \qquad \rightarrow \qquad b+c = 30$$
$$(b-c)(3) = 30 \quad \text{(divide each side by 3)} \qquad \underline{b-c = 10} \quad \text{(add the equations)}$$
$$2b \;\;\;\; = 40$$
$$b = 20$$

Since $b + c = 30$ and $b = 20$, then $c = 10$. The current's speed is 10 mi/hr, and the boat's speed in still water is 20 mi/hr.

Work Problems

Work problems, which usually involve how much time it takes each of two ways to complete a job or one way to complete a job and the other to undo a job, can be quickly calculated. If two methods of completing a job are given, to find the time it would take working together, take the product of the two times and divide by the sum of the two times. If one method undoes the job, then take the product of the two times and divide by the difference of the two times.

If the work problem involves more than two methods of either completing or undoing the job, then an algebraic approach to get the answer would look like this:

$$\frac{1}{\text{first's person's time}} + \frac{1}{\text{second's person's time}} + \frac{1}{\text{third's person's time}} + \cdots = \frac{1}{\text{time together}}$$

Examples:

1. Jim can do a job in 8 hours by himself that would take Tom 12 hours to do himself. Working together, how long should it take to do the job?

Using the fast method: $\frac{(8)(12)}{8+12} = \frac{96}{20} = 4\frac{4}{5}$ or 4.8.

Using the algebraic method, let x be the amount of time it takes together:

$$\frac{1}{8} + \frac{1}{12} = \frac{1}{x} \qquad \text{(multiply each side by the LCD of } 24x)$$
$$24x\left(\frac{1}{8} + \frac{1}{12}\right) = 24x\left(\frac{1}{x}\right)$$
$$3x + 2x = 24$$
$$5x = 24$$
$$x = \frac{24}{5} = 4\frac{4}{5} \text{ or } 4.8$$

It will take them $4\frac{4}{5}$ or 4.8 hours together.

2. If it takes 6 hours to fill a tank with water and 15 hours to drain it, how long would it take to fill the tank if the drain was accidently left open?

Using the fast method: $\frac{(15)(6)}{15-6} = \frac{90}{9} = 10$.

Using the algebraic method, let x be the amount of time it takes together:

$$\frac{1}{6} - \frac{1}{15} = \frac{1}{x} \qquad \text{(multiply each side by the LCD of } 30x)$$
$$30x\left(\frac{1}{6} - \frac{1}{15}\right) = 30x\left(\frac{1}{x}\right)$$
$$5x - 2x = 30$$
$$3x = 30$$
$$x = 10$$

With the drain open, it will take 10 hours to fill the tank.

3. Working alone, Bill can do a job in 4 hours. With Fred's help, it takes only $2\frac{2}{9}$ hours. How long should it take Fred working alone to do the job?

Using the fast method: First change $2\frac{2}{9}$ to $\frac{20}{9}$. Let x be how long it would take Fred alone: $\frac{4x}{4+x} = \frac{20}{9}$. You can quickly see that x is 5.

Using the algebraic method:

$$\frac{1}{4} + \frac{1}{x} = \frac{1}{2\frac{2}{9}} \qquad \left(\frac{1}{2\frac{2}{9}} = \frac{1}{\frac{20}{9}} = \frac{9}{20}\right)$$

$$\frac{1}{4} + \frac{1}{x} = \frac{9}{20} \qquad \text{(multiply each side by the LCD of } 20x)$$

$$20x\left(\frac{1}{4} + \frac{1}{x}\right) = 20x\left(\frac{9}{20}\right)$$

$$5x + 20 = 9x$$

$$20 = 4x$$

$$5 = x$$

It would take Fred 5 hours to do the job alone.

Mixture Problems

Mixture problems, like motion problems, are more easily solved using a chart to organize the given information. Depending on the type of mixture problem, different organizing charts can be used.

Examples:

1. A chemist wants to dilute 50 ml of a 40% acid solution into a 30% acid solution. How much pure water must be added?

This problem involves acid and water. We begin with 50 ml of a solution of which 40% is acid and 60% is not acid. Pure water is being added and then the new mixture will only be 30% acid and 70% not acid.

Let x be how many ml of water is being added.

	Start	Add	Totals
Mixture	50 ml	x ml	x + 50 ml
Acid	(0.40)(50) ml	0 ml	(0.30)(x + 50) ml
Not acid	(0.60)(50) ml	x ml	(0.70)(x + 50) ml

There are now two different equations that can be used to find x.

$$(0.40)(50) + 0 = (0.30)(x + 50) \text{ or } (0.60)(50) + x = (0.70)(x + 50)$$

The easier one is the one on the left since the x only appears on one side of the equation.

$$(0.40)(50) + 0 = (0.30)(x + 50)$$

$$20 = 0.3x + 15$$

$$5 = 0.3x$$

$$\frac{50}{3} = x \text{ or } x = 16\frac{2}{3}$$

The chemist must add $16\frac{2}{3}$ ml of pure water.

2. One solution is 75% saltwater and another solution is 50% saltwater. How many gallons of each should be used to make 10 gallons of a solution that is 60% saltwater?

Let x be the number of gallons of the 75% saltwater solution. Then $10 - x$ will be the number of gallons of the 50% solution since there will be a total of 10 gallons in the final mixture.

	Start	Add	Totals
Mixture	x gal	$10 - x$ gal	10 gal
Salt	(0.75)(x) gal	(0.50)(10 − x) gal	(0.60)(10)
Water	(0.25)(x) gal	(0.50)(10 − x) gal	(0.40)(10)

There are now two different equations that can be used to find x.

$$(0.75)(x) + (0.50)(10 - x) = (0.60)(10) \text{ or } (0.25)(x) + (0.50)(10 - x) = (0.40)(10)$$

Selecting the first equation:

$$(0.75)(x) + (0.50)(10 - x) = (0.60)(10)$$
$$0.75x + 5 - 0.50x = 6$$
$$0.25x + 5 = 6$$
$$0.25x = 1$$
$$x = \frac{1}{0.25}$$
$$x = 4 \text{ and } 10 - x = 6$$

Therefore, 4 gallons of 75% and 6 gallons of 50% solutions are used.

3. Nuts worth $1.50 per pound are mixed with nuts worth $1.75 per pound to make 20 pounds of nuts worth $1.65 per pound. How many pounds of each type is used?

Let x be the number of pounds of $1.75/lb nuts. Then $20 - x$ would be the number of pounds of $1.50/lb nuts since there will be 20 pounds in the final mixture.

A slightly different chart will be used to organize the information.

	Cost/lb	# Pounds	Total Cost
Mixture	$1.65	20	($1.65)(20)
$1.75/lb	$1.75	x	($1.75)($x$)
$1.50/lb	$1.50	$20 - x$	($1.50)(20 − x)

The total cost of the individual type of nuts should equal the total cost of the mixture:

$$1.75x + 1.50(20 - x) = 1.65(20)$$
$$1.75x + 30 - 1.50x = 33$$
$$0.25x + 30 = 33$$
$$0.25x = 3$$
$$x = \frac{3}{0.25}$$
$$x = 12 \text{ and } 20 - x = 8$$

Therefore, 12 pounds of the $1.75/lb and 8 pounds of the $1.50/lb nuts are used.

Age Problems

Age problems usually require a representation of ages now, ages in the past, and/or ages in the future. Use a chart to keep the information organized.

Examples:

1. Currently, Carlos is 5 years older than three times his daughter, Juanita's, age. Two years ago, he was 4 years older than four times her age. How many years from now will he be twice her age?

Let j represent Juanita's current age. Then $3j + 5$ is Carlos' current age.

Person	Current Age	Age 2 Years Ago
Juanita	j	$j - 2$
Carlos	$3j + 5$	$(3j + 5) - 2$

Translating the sentence "Two years ago, he was 4 years older than four times her age" algebraically, you get

$$
\begin{array}{cc}
\text{Carlos' age} & \text{Juanita's age} \\
\text{2 years ago} & \text{2 years ago} \\
\overbrace{(3j+5)-2} = 4 & \overbrace{(j-2)} + 4 \\
\end{array}
$$

$$3j + 5 - 2 = 4j - 8 + 4$$
$$3j + 3 = 4j - 4$$
$$3 = j - 4$$
$$7 = j$$

Therefore, currently, Juanita is 7 years old and Carlos is $3(7) + 5$ or 26 years old. The question asks when in the future he will be twice as old as his daughter.

Let t be how many years into the future this takes place and set up a new chart.

Person	Current Age	Age t Years from Now
Juanita	7	$7 + t$
Carlos	26	$26 + t$

"Carlos will be twice his daughter's age" translates into

$$26 + t = 2(7 + t)$$
$$26 + t = 14 + 2t$$
$$26 = 14 + t$$
$$12 = t$$

Therefore, in 12 years, Carlos will be twice his daughter's age. In 12 years he will be 38 and his daughter will be 19, hence his age will be twice hers.

2. Ed is 12 years older than Jim. Five years ago, the sum of their ages was 42. What will be the product of their ages in 5 years?

Let x be Jim's age now and $12 + x$ Ed's age now.

Person	Current Age	Age 5 Years Ago
Jim	x	$x - 5$
Ed	$12 + x$	$12 + x - 5$ or $x + 7$

Translate "Five years ago, the sum of their ages was 42" into an algebraic equation.

$$(x-5)+(12+x-5)=42$$
$$2x+2=42$$
$$2x=40$$
$$x=20 \quad \text{and} \quad 12+x=32$$

Therefore, Jim is currently 20 years old and Ed is 32 years old. In 5 years, Jim will be 25 and Ed will be 37 years old and the product of their ages will be $(25)(37) = 925$.

Integer Problems

Integer problems usually involve consecutive integers, consecutive even integers, or consecutive odd integers. If you let x represent any integer, then $x + 1$ would represent the next larger integer, $x + 2$ would be the next larger after that, then $x + 3$, and so on.

If you let x represent either an odd or an even integer, then the next odd or even integer would be 2 more than that, or $x + 2$, and the one after that would be $x + 4$ and so on.

Examples:

1. Find the product of three consecutive odd integers such that twice the smallest increased by the largest is thirteen less than four times the middle integer.

Let x be the smallest of the 3 consecutive odd integers. Then $x + 2$ and $x + 4$ would be the next two consecutive odd integers.

Translate "twice the smallest increased by the largest is thirteen less than four times the middle integer" into

$$2x+(x+4)=4(x+2)-13$$
$$3x+4=4x+8-13$$
$$3x+4=4x-5$$
$$4=x-5$$
$$9=x \quad \text{and} \quad x+2=11, x+4=13$$

The integers are 9, 11, and 13 and their product is $(9)(11)(13) = 1{,}287$.

2. The sum of four consecutive even integers is 60. What is the largest integer?

Let x, $x + 2$, $x + 4$, and $x + 6$ represent the 4 consecutive even integers.

$$x + (x + 2) + (x + 4) + (x + 6) = 60$$
$$4x + 12 = 60$$
$$4x = 48$$
$$x = 12 \text{ and } x + 2 = 14, x + 4 = 16, x + 4 = 18$$

Therefore the largest integer is 18.

Practice: Word Problems

1. Part one of a trip was a distance of 1,120 miles at 280 miles per hour. Part two of that trip was the same distance at 70 miles per hour. What was the average speed for the two parts combined?

2. Roberto and Julio do a whole job in $2\frac{1}{10}$ days. Had Roberto worked alone, he would have needed 7 days. How long would it have taken Julio to do the job alone?

3. Two quarts of a 25% acid solution are mixed with one quart of 40% acid solution. What percent acid is the mixture?

4. Kobe is 12 years younger than his brother Caleb. Last year, the sum of their ages was 30. What will be the product of their ages in 5 years?

5. The product of two consecutive positive even integers is 168. What is their sum?

Answers: Word Problems

1. 112 miles per hour.

   Average speed is found by taking total distance and dividing it by total time. The total distance is 1,120 + 1,120 or 2,240 miles.

   To find the total time, find the individual times by taking distance and dividing it by rate. The time for part one of the trip is $\frac{1,120 \text{ mi}}{280 \text{ mi/hr}} = 4 \text{ hr}$. The time for part two of the trip is $\frac{1,120 \text{ mi}}{70 \text{ mi/hr}} = 16 \text{ hr}$.

   The total time for the trip is 20 hours. The average speed is $\frac{2,240 \text{ mi}}{20 \text{ hr}} = 112 \text{ mi/hr}$.

2. 3 days

   Fast method: Let x represent the amount of time Julio needs:

   $$\frac{\text{product of their times}}{\text{sum of their times}} = \text{total time together}$$

   $$\frac{7x}{x + 7} = \frac{21}{10} \quad \left(2\frac{1}{10} = \frac{21}{10}\right)$$

   Visually, it can be seen that if x is 3, the above equation is true. Therefore, Julio would need 3 days.

Algebraic method: Let x represent the amount of time Julio needs.

$$\frac{1}{x}+\frac{1}{7}=\frac{1}{2\frac{1}{10}}$$

$$\frac{1}{x}+\frac{1}{7}=\frac{1}{\frac{21}{10}}$$

$$\frac{1}{x}+\frac{1}{7}=\frac{10}{21} \qquad \text{(multiply each side by the LCD of } 21x)$$

$$21x\left(\frac{1}{x}+\frac{1}{7}\right)=21x\left(\frac{10}{21}\right)$$

$$21+3x=10x$$

$$21=7x$$

$$3=x$$

3. 30%

Since the question only involves acid, find the amount of total acid there is and divide that by the three quarts that the final mixture contains.

Two quarts that are 25% acid have 2(0.25) or 0.5 quarts of acid. One quart that is 40% acid has 1(0.4) quarts of acid. Therefore, the final solution has $\frac{0.5+0.4}{3}=\frac{0.9}{3}=0.3=30\%$ acid.

4. 405

Let x represent Caleb's age now. Then $x-12$ represents Kobe's age now.

Person	Current Age	Age 1 Year Ago
Caleb	x	$x-1$
Kobe	$x-12$	$(x-12)-1$

"Last year the sum of their ages was 30" translates into $x-1+(x-12)-1=30$.

$$x-1+(x-12)-1=30$$

$$2x-14=30$$

$$2x=44$$

$$x=22 \quad \text{then } x-12=10$$

Caleb is currently 22 years old, and Kobe is currently 10 years old. In 5 years, Caleb will be 27 and Kobe will be 15. The product of their ages will be $(27)(15)=405$.

5. 26

Let x be the smaller of the two positive even integers. Then $x+2$ will be the larger integer. "The product of two consecutive positive even integers is 168" translates into

$$x(x+2)=168$$

$$x^2+2x=168$$

$$x^2+2x-168=0 \qquad \text{(solve by factoring)}$$

$$(x-12)(x+14)=0$$

$$x-12=0 \quad \text{or} \quad x+14=0$$

$$x=12 \quad \text{or} \qquad x=-14$$

The smaller integer is 12 or –14, but the problem said the integers were positive. Therefore, the smaller integer is 12 and the larger one is 14 and their sum is 26.

Data Interpretation

Data Interpretation Diagnostic Test

Questions 1–4 refer to the following circle graphs.

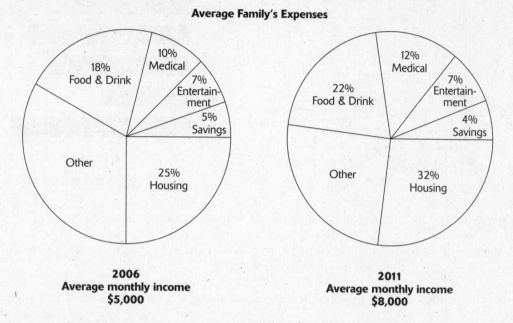

Average Family's Expenses

2006
Average monthly income
$5,000

2011
Average monthly income
$8,000

1. For the year in which the average family's monthly medical expenses were $500, what was the family's average monthly expense on savings?

2. What is the ratio of average monthly medical expenses in 2006 to the average monthly medical expenses in 2011?

3. To the nearest tenth of a percent, what was the percent increase from 2006 to 2011 in the percentage spent on food and drink?

4. How much more did the average family spend monthly on "other" in 2011 than they did in 2006?

Questions 5 and 6 refer to the following bar graph.

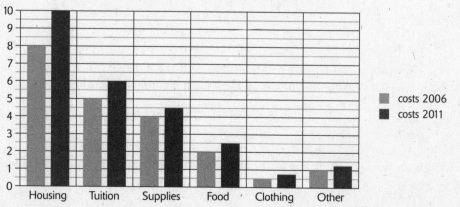

Glendale College: Costs in thousands of dollars

5. Which category of expenses had the greatest percent increase in costs from 2006 to 2011?

6. To the nearest whole percent, by what percent did the total expenses increase from 2006 to 2011?

Questions 7–9 refer to the following graphs.

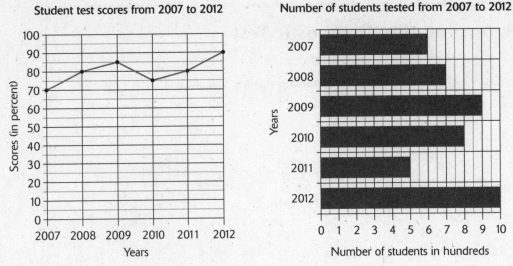

Student test scores from 2007 to 2012

Number of students tested from 2007 to 2012

7. For the years 2007 to 2012, how many students who were tested scored above 80%?

8. For which consecutive years was the percent change in the number of students tested the least? To the nearest whole percent, what was that percent change?

9. For the odd-numbered years, what was the approximate lowest score that any student tested achieved on the test?

Questions 10–12 refer to the following Venn diagram.

**Percent of all students at
Hollywood High enrolled in classes**

A → Spanish
B → Algebra
C → History

10. What percent of all the students at Hollywood High are not enrolled in history?

11. If there are 2,000 students enrolled at Hollywood High, how many are taking exactly two of the three courses indicated?

12. If 300 students are not enrolled in any of the indicated courses, how many students are enrolled at Hollywood High?

Questions 13–15 refer to the following table.

Profile of the Neighborhood		
# People Living at Even-numbered Addresses	Favorite Baseball League	# People Living at Odd-numbered Addresses
30	American	42
25	National	27
16	Neither	20
	Sex	
42	Male	54
29	Female	35

13. To the nearest percent, what percent of the neighborhood prefers the National league?

14. In this neighborhood, how many people living in odd-numbered addresses are younger than 36 years?

15. What would be the ratio of females to males in the even-numbered addresses if 5 of the males were replaced with females?

Data Interpretation Diagnostic Test Answers

The diagnostic test explanations listed below include topic headings that correspond with step-by-step learning tools and examples to help you solve specific problem types. Topic headings can be found in the Data Interpretation Review section on pages 350–359.

Circle or Pie Graphs

1. $250

2. $\frac{25}{48}$

3. 22.2%

4. $90

Bar Graphs

5. Clothing, 50%

6. 22%

Line Graphs

7. 1,665

8. 2009–2010, 11%

9. cannot be determined from the given information

Venn Diagrams

10. 65%

11. 420

12. 3,000

Charts and Tables

13. 33%

14. cannot be determined from the given information

15. $\frac{34}{37}$

Data Interpretation Review

Circle or Pie Graphs

A *circle* or *pie graph* shows the relationship between the whole circle (100%) and the various slices that represent portions of that 100%. The larger the slice, the greater the percentage it represents.

Examples:

Questions 1–4 refer to the following circle graphs.

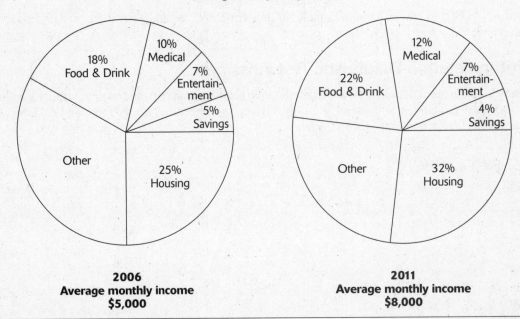

Average Family's Expenses

2006
Average monthly income
$5,000

2011
Average monthly income
$8,000

> **1.** For the year in which the average family's monthly medical expenses were $500, what was the family's average monthly expense on savings?

In 2011, the medical expenses were 12% of $8,000, which is $960. In 2006, the medical expenses were 10% of $5,000, which is $500. Therefore, the question is referring to the 2006 graph. In that year, savings were 5% of the total monthly income, and 5% of $5,000 is $250. You could also have said that since 5% is half of 10%, the savings amount would be half the medical amount and arrived at the same answer.

> **2.** What is the ratio of average monthly medical expenses in 2006 to the average monthly medical expenses in 2011?

The average monthly medical expenses in 2006 was 10% of $5,000 or $500. The average monthly medical expenses in 2011 was 12% of $8,000 or $960. The ratio becomes $\frac{500}{960} = \frac{25}{48}$.

3. To the nearest tenth of a percent, what was the percent increase from 2006 to 2011 in the percentage spent on food and drink?

Note that the question is not referring to money, but to the change in the percentage values. The 2006 average monthly percentage spent on food and drink was 18% and in 2011 it was 22%.

Percent change $= \dfrac{\text{amount of change}}{\text{starting amount}} \times 100\% = \dfrac{4\%}{18\%} \times 100\% = 22.2\bar{2}\%$, which is 22.2% when rounded to the nearest tenth of a percent.

4. How much more did the average family spend monthly on "other" in 2011 than they in 2006?

In the 2006 graph, the sum of the given percentages is 65% (18% + 10% + 7% + 5% + 25% = 65%), leaving 35% (100% − 65% = 35%) for the "other" category. The average monthly amount of money spent on "other" in 2006 was 35% of $5,000 or $1,750. In the 2011 graph, the sum of the given percentages is 77%, (22% + 12% + 7% + 4% + 32% = 77%), leaving 23% (100% − 77% = 23%) for the "other" category. The average monthly amount spent on "other" in 2011 was 23% of $8,000 or $1,840. The family spent, on average, $90 more per month in 2011 on "other" than in 2006 ($1,840 − $1,750 = $90).

Bar Graphs

Bar graphs convert information into separate bars or columns. The bars can either be vertical or horizontal. You must be able to determine the relationship between the bars in the graph.

Examples:

Questions 1 and 2 refer to the following bar graph.

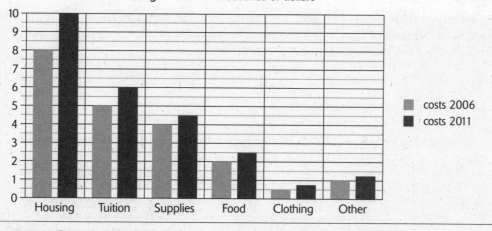

Glendale College: Costs in thousands of dollars

1. Which category of expenses had the greatest percent increase in costs from 2006 to 2011?

In this bar graph, different categories of expenditures are listed horizontally, and cost, in thousands of dollars, are shown vertically. The light gray bar above the "housing" category indicates that housing in 2006 cost $8,000.

Recall that percent change $= \dfrac{\text{amount of change}}{\text{starting amount}} \times 100\%$.

Category	2006	2011	Percent Change
Housing	8,000	10,000	$\frac{2,000}{8,000} \times 100\% = 25\%$
Tuition	5,000	6,000	$\frac{1,000}{5,000} \times 100\% = 20\%$
Supplies	4,000	4,500	$\frac{500}{4,000} \times 100\% = 12.5\%$
Food	2,000	2,500	$\frac{500}{2,000} \times 100\% = 25\%$
Clothing	500	750	$\frac{250}{500} \times 100\% = 50\%$
Other	1,000	1,250	$\frac{250}{1,000} \times 100\% = 25\%$

Clothing had the greatest percentage increase in costs from 2006 to 2011. Its costs increased by 50%.

2. To the nearest whole percent, by what percent did the total expenses increase from 2006 to 2011?

Total expenses in 2006 were $8,000 + $5,000 + $4,000 + $2,000 + $500 + $1,000 = $20,500.

Total expenses in 2011 were $10,000 + $6,000 + $4,500 + $2,500 + $750 + $1,250 = $25,000.

percent change $= \dfrac{\text{amount of change}}{\text{starting amount}} \times 100\% = \dfrac{4,500}{20,500} \times 100\% \approx 21.95\%$, which is 22% when rounded to the nearest whole percent.

Line Graphs

Line graphs convert data into points on a grid. These points are then connected to show a relationship between items, dates, times, etc. Slopes of lines indicate trends. The larger the absolute value of the slope value, the greater the change will be from one piece of information to another.

Examples:

Questions 1–3 refer to the following graphs.

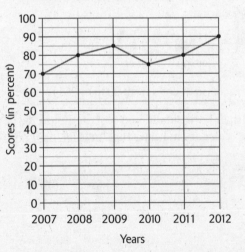

Student test scores from 2007 to 2012

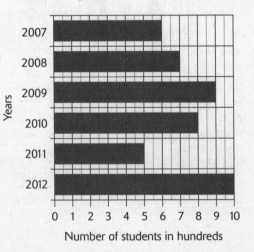

Number of students tested from 2007 to 2012

1. For the years 2007 to 2012, how many students who were tested scored above 80%?

This question requires the use of both the line graph on the left and the bar graph on the right. Note that the bar graph measures the number of students in hundreds. In 2009, the test average was 85% and in 2009, 900 students were tested. Thus, in 2009, 85% of 900 or 765 students tested above 80%. In 2012, the test average was 90% and in 2012, 1,000 students were tested. Thus, in 2012, 90% of 1,000 or 900 students tested above 80%. The years 2009 and 2012 were the only years in which students tested above 80%. Therefore, for the years 2007 to 2012, 765 + 900 = 1,665 students tested above 80%.

2. For which consecutive years was the percent change in the number of students tested the least? To the nearest whole percent, what was that percent change?

Recall that percent change $= \dfrac{\text{amount of change}}{\text{starting amount}} \times 100\%$.

Consecutive Years	Number of Students Tested	Percent Change
2007 2008	600 700	$\dfrac{100}{600} \times 100\% = 16\frac{2}{3}\%$ or $16.\overline{6}\%$
2008 2009	700 900	$\dfrac{200}{700} \times 100\% = 28\frac{4}{7}\%$ or $28.\overline{571428}\%$
2009 2010	900 800	$\dfrac{100}{900} \times 100\% = 11\frac{1}{9}\%$ or $11.\overline{1}\%$
2010 2011	800 500	$\dfrac{300}{800} \times 100\% = 37\frac{1}{2}\%$ or 37.5%
2011 2012	500 1,000	$\dfrac{500}{500} \times 100\% = 100\%$

For the years 2009 to 2010 the percent change was the least. Rounded to the nearest whole percent it is 11%.

3. For the odd-numbered years, what was the approximate lowest score that any student tested achieved on the test?

The information given cannot provide an answer. The line graph indicates the average percent scores, not what any single test score could have been.

Venn Diagrams

Venn diagrams show sets of objects with certain characteristics using geometric figures, usually ovals or circular regions. Numbers placed within a region indicate the number of objects, or percent of the total number of objects, that have that particular characteristic. When a number is placed in an area of overlapping regions, then that is how many objects, or the percent of objects, that share the characteristics of the overlapping regions.

Examples:

Questions 1–3 refer to the following Venn diagram.

**Percent of all students at
Hollywood High enrolled in classes**

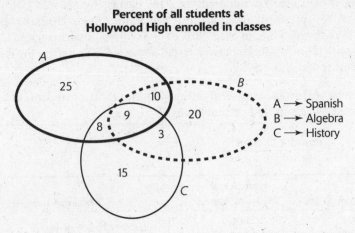

In this Venn diagram, region A represents the percent of the students at Hollywood High that are taking Spanish, region B represents the percent of students at Hollywood High taking algebra, and region C represents the percent of students at Hollywood High taking history.

Only looking at region A and the regions it overlaps, we can make the following conclusions from the diagram:

a) 25% of the students at Hollywood High take Spanish but do not take either algebra nor history

b) 10% of the students at Hollywood High take Spanish and algebra, but not history

c) 9% of the students at Hollywood High take Spanish, algebra, and history

d) 8% of the students at Hollywood High take Spanish and history, but not algebra

If all the percentage numbers are added together, you get 90%. Thus, 10% of the students at Hollywood High do not take any of the three listed classes.

---

1. What percent of all the students at Hollywood High are not enrolled in history?

One approach is to take the percentage of students that are enrolled in history, then subtract that from 100%. Another approach is to add the percentages indicated outside of history, and be sure to add in the 10% that are not taking any of the three classes.

According to the diagram, there are 8% + 9% + 3% + 15% = 35% of the students taking history, thus there are 100% − 35% = 65% of the students not taking history.

---

2. If there are 2,000 students enrolled at Hollywood High, how many are taking exactly two of the three courses indicated?

The overlap of regions A and B, but not including region C, only has 10% in it. The overlap of regions A and C, but not including region B, only has 8% in it. The overlap of regions B and C, but not including region A, only has 3% in it. Thus, there are 10% + 8% + 3% = 21% of the 2,000 students, or 420 students taking exactly 2 of the 3 courses indicated.

3. If 300 students are not enrolled in any of the indicated courses, how many students are enrolled at Hollywood High?

Since 10% of the students are not enrolled in any of the indicated courses, then 10% of the enrollment is 300. This can be solved as an equation or as a proportion.

$$0.10x = 300$$
$$x = \frac{300}{0.10} = 3,000$$

$$\frac{\text{part}}{\text{whole}} : \quad \frac{10}{100} = \frac{300}{x}$$
$$10x = 30,000$$
$$x = 3,000$$

There are 3,000 students enrolled at Hollywood High.

Charts and Tables

Charts and tables are often used to give an organized picture of data. You must pay close attention to column or row headings for important information.

Examples:

Questions 1–3 refer to the following table.

# People Living at Even-numbered Addresses	Favorite Baseball League	# People Living at Odd-numbered Addresses
30	American	42
25	National	27
16	Neither	20
	Sex	
42	Male	54
29	Female	35

1. To the nearest percent, what percent of the neighborhood prefers the National league?

First, find the total number of people in the neighborhood, then find how many prefer the National league.

Total: $(30 + 25 + 16) + (42 + 27 + 20) = 160$

Prefer National league: $25 + 27 = 52$

$$\frac{52}{160} = \frac{x}{100}$$
$$160x = 5200$$
$$x = 32.5$$

Therefore, to the nearest percent, 33% prefer the National league.

> **2.** In this neighborhood, how many people living in odd-numbered addresses are younger than 36 years?

The answer cannot be determined from the given information. There are 89 people living in odd-numbered addresses. Therefore, the median age is the number in the 45th position when the ages are listed from least to greatest. This means that there are 44 people whose ages would be to the left of the 36, but this does not guarantee that all of them are less than 36. The age in the 44th position could be 36 as well as the age in the 45th position.

> **3.** What would be the ratio of females to males in the even-numbered addresses if 5 of the males were replaced with females?

Prior to making the replacement, there are 42 males and 29 females in the even-numbered addresses. After the replacement, there will be 37 males and 34 females. The ratio of *females* to *males* will then become $\frac{34}{37}$.

Practice: Data Interpretation

Use the following graph for questions 1 and 2.

Rainfall—Portland—Dec. 5–11, 2011

1. What was the median rainfall for the week shown?

2. Between which two consecutive days was the change the greatest?

Use the following graph for questions 3 and 4.

Railroad Track in Use 1875–1915 (in thousands of miles)

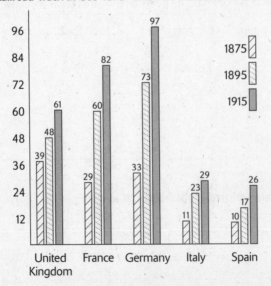

3. How many countries showed a larger increase in miles from 1875 to 1895 than from 1895 to 1915?

4. In hundreds of miles of track, how much more was in use in France in 1895 than in Spain in 1915?

Use the following graphs for questions 5 and 6.

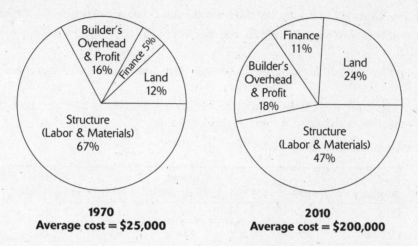

1970
Average cost = $25,000

2010
Average cost = $200,000

5. Based on the average cost at the time, by what percent did the cost of financing the building of a house increase from 1970 to 2010?

6. Based on the average cost at the time, how much more went into structure in 2010 than in 1970?

Use the following graph for questions 7 and 8.

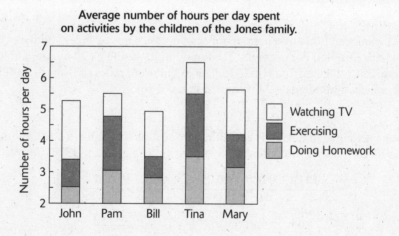

Average number of hours per day spent on activities by the children of the Jones family.

7. For which activity was the average daily hours the least?

8. What is the average amount of television, in hours and minutes, that all 5 children watch per day?

Answers: Data Interpretation

1. 2.1

The median of the 7 values will be the 4th when listed from least to greatest. Even though most of the values can only be approximated, the 4th value is exactly 2.1. The values when written from least to greatest are as follows:

approximately 0.4, approximately 1.0, exactly 1.4, **<u>exactly 2.1</u>**,
approximately 2.4, approximately 2.7, approximately 2.9

2. Tuesday to Wednesday

From Monday to Tuesday, the change was from approximately 1.0 to 2.1 or about +1.1

From Tuesday to Wednesday, the change was from 2.1 to approximately 0.4 or about –1.7

From Wednesday to Thursday, the change was from approximately 0.4 to 1.4 or about +1

From Thursday to Friday, the change was from 1.4 to approximately 2.9 or about +1.5

From Friday to Saturday, the change was from approximately 2.9 to approximately 2.4 or about –0.5

From Saturday to Sunday, the change was from approximately 2.4 to approximately 2.7 or about +0.3.

The greatest change took place from Tuesday to Wednesday. This could also have been done visually by finding the segment with the greatest slope in absolute value.

3. three (France, Germany, and Italy)

Country	1875	1895	Change 1875 to 1895	1915	Change 1895 to 1915
U.K	39	48	+9	61	+13
France	29	60	**+31**	82	+22
Germany	33	73	**+40**	97	+26
Italy	11	23	**+12**	29	+6
Spain	10	17	+7	26	+9

Three countries, France, Germany, and Italy, showed a larger increase in miles from 1875 to 1895 than from 1895 to 1915.

4. 340 hundreds

Be aware that the information given in track miles is in thousands of miles and the question asked for an answer in hundreds of miles. For example, 2 thousand miles would be 20 hundred miles. France in 1895 had 60 thousand miles of track and Spain in 1915 had 26 thousand miles of track. The difference is 34 thousand miles of track, which in hundreds is 340 hundred miles of track.

5. 1,660%

To find the percent change in financing costs, find the cost of financing in 2010, subtract the cost of financing in 1970, then divide this difference by the cost of financing in 1970. Convert this to a percentage.

$$\frac{(0.11)(200,000)-(0.05)(25,000)}{(0.05)(25,000)} = \frac{22,000-1,250}{1,250}$$

$$= \frac{20,750}{1,250}$$

$$= 16.6$$

$$= 1,660\%$$

6. $77,250

Structure costs for 2010 minus structure costs in 1970: $(0.47)(\$200,000) - (0.67)(\$25,000) = \$77,250$

7. Television watching

This graph is an example of an accumulation bar graph. Be careful when looking at it. Consider the information for John. The first bar ends at 2.5 hours meaning that John spends, on average, 2.5 hours per day doing homework. The bar above this goes from 2.5 hours to 3.5 hours, meaning John spends about 1 hour per day (3.5 − 2.5 = 1) exercising. The last bar goes from about 3.5 hours to about 5.25 hours, meaning John spends about 1.75 hours per day (5.25 − 3.5 = 1.75) watching television.

The chart below is a summary for the children and their average hours spent doing the activities.

Child	Homework	Exercise	TV
John	2.5	3.5 − 2.5 = 1	5.25 − 3.5 = 1.75
Pam	3	4.75 − 3 = 1.75	5.5 − 4.75 = 0.75
Bill	2.75	3.5 − 2.75 = 0.75	5 − 3.5 = 1.5
Tina	3.75	5.5 − 3.75 = 1.75	6.5 − 5.5 = 1
Mary	3.25	4.75 − 3.25 = 1.5	5.75 − 4.75 = 1
TOTALS	15.25	6.75	6

8. 1 hour and 12 minutes

Using the chart above, all 5 children combined watch 6 hours of television per day.

Therefore, on average they watch $\frac{6}{5} = 1.2$ hours of TV per day. The question wanted the answer in hours and minutes. 0.2 hours means $0.2 \, \text{hr} \times \frac{60 \, \text{min}}{\text{hr}} = 12$ minutes.

PART IV

FULL-LENGTH PRACTICE TEST

Chapter 6

Practice Test 1

This section contains one full-length GRE designed to give you extra practice and insight (Practice Tests 2–4 can be found on the accompanying CD-ROM). While this practice test does not adapt by section based upon your previous sections' right or wrong answers (as the computer-adaptive test does), you will gain valuable test-taking skills and insight into your strengths and weaknesses. The practice test is followed by completed answers, explanations, and analysis techniques.

The format, level of difficulty, question structures, and number of questions are similar to those on the actual GRE General Test. The actual GRE is copyrighted and may not be duplicated, and these questions are not taken directly from actual tests.

When taking this practice test, try to simulate the test conditions. Remember the total testing time when you take the computer-base GRE is about 3 hours and 45 minutes, but this allows for a short 10-minute break and for an experimental unscored section. Budget your time effectively when you take this written practice test. If you need a break, stop the clock and take a 10-minute break after the third section. Try to spend no more than $1\frac{1}{2}$ minutes on each multiple-choice question and 30 minutes on each writing task.

The total testing time for this practice test is 3 hours and 10 minutes.

  Section 1: Analytical Writing – Analyze an Issue
  Section 2: Analytical Writing – Analyze an Argument
  Section 3: Verbal Reasoning
  Section 4: Quantitative Reasoning
  Section 5: Verbal Reasoning
  Section 6: Quantitative Reasoning

REMEMBER: The answer choices for multiple-choice questions on the actual computer version of the GRE are not labeled with letters. Answer choices in this study guide have lettered choices A, B, C, D, E, etc. for clarity. On the actual exam, you will be required to click on ovals or squares to select your answer.

HELPFUL HINT:
○ oval – answer will be a single choice
□ square – answer will be one or more choices

Section 1: Analytical Writing – Analyze an Issue

Time: 30 minutes

Directions: In this section, you will have 30 minutes to plan and write an essay. The topic will appear as a brief quotation about an issue of general interest. You will be required to analyze and explain your views on the issue. A response to any other issue will receive a score of zero.

Take a few minutes to read the topic and instructions before you write your essay. Make sure that you respond according to the specific instructions and support your position on the issue with reasons and examples drawn from such areas as your reading, experience, observations, and/or academic studies. Use the last five minutes to read over your essay and revise as necessary.

Your response will be evaluated for its overall quality, based on how well you:

- Respond to the specific instructions
- Address the complexities and implications of the issue
- Organize and develop your essay
- Express your ideas with reasons and examples that are relevant
- Use standard written English

Issue Topic

> Pharmaceutical companies should be encouraged to pursue treatments and cures for conditions that affect the greatest number of people.

Write a response expressing to what degree you agree or disagree with the recommendation. Provide explanations for the reasoning behind your stance. Be sure to consider and discuss the most persuasive reasons and evidence that could pose a challenge to your position.

IF YOU FINISH BEFORE TIME IS CALLED, CHECK YOUR WORK ON THIS SECTION ONLY. DO NOT WORK ON ANY OTHER SECTION IN THE TEST.

Section 2: Analytical Writing – Analyze an Argument

Time: 30 minutes

Directions: In this section, you will have 30 minutes to plan and write a critique of an argument given in the form of a short passage. A response to any other issue will receive a score of zero.

Take a few minutes to analyze the argument and plan your response before you write your essay. Note that you are NOT being asked to present your own views on the subject. Make sure that you respond according to the specific instructions and support your line of reasoning with relevant examples. Use the last five minutes to read over your essay and revise as necessary.

Your response will be evaluated for its overall quality, based on how well you:

- Respond to the specific instructions
- Identify and analyze the components of the argument
- Organize and develop your critique
- Support your ideas with reasons and examples that are relevant
- Use standard written English

Argument Topic

The following appeared in the meeting minutes of a local chamber of commerce:

> Last year Hernville's Back to School Tax Holiday promotion proved very popular. The one-day event allowed parents to purchase clothes and school supplies without sales tax as they prepared for the first day of school. The retailers who responded to the survey reported a large increase in sales that day. The Hernville Chamber of Commerce recommends that the one-day promotion be expanded to a once-monthly event to stimulate the local economy and promote job growth.

Write a response that considers which questions would need to be answered about the proposal to determine if it will result in the outcome predicted. Be sure to discuss how answering these questions will help evaluate the recommended proposal.

IF YOU FINISH BEFORE TIME IS CALLED, CHECK YOUR WORK ON THIS SECTION ONLY. DO NOT WORK ON ANY OTHER SECTION IN THE TEST.

365

Section 3: Verbal Reasoning

Time: 30 minutes
20 Questions

General Directions: For each question, indicate the best answer using the directions given. Read the directions for each question carefully.

Directions: For each blank in questions 1 to 6, select the word or phrase from the corresponding columns that best completes the text. Your answer will consist of one, two, or three letters, depending on the number of blanks in each question.

1. It has long been said that all of the world's literature is based on just seven basic story lines and now this principle seems to be applied to automobiles, whose similarities in styling, performance, and appointments are all becoming more _____ with each new model year.

   Ⓐ homogenized
   Ⓑ heterogeneous
   Ⓒ diverse
   Ⓓ divergent
   Ⓔ disparate

2. Geoffrey Chaucer, regarded as one of the greatest of all English poets, is so often _____ for his literary masterpiece *The Canterbury Tales* that his remarkable career as a public servant in the court of Edward III is frequently forgotten.

   Ⓐ lionized
   Ⓑ reproached
   Ⓒ vilified
   Ⓓ censured
   Ⓔ caviled

3. With the world's population topping seven billion, it is natural for modern man to worry about humanity's long-term impact on the planet; however, over 300 years ago scientific papers exploring (i) _____ had already been written, expressing alarm over man's repercussions on the earth. Apparently we are still (ii) _____ this issue.

Blank (i)	**Blank (ii)**
Ⓐ demography	Ⓓ agreeing with
Ⓑ statistics	Ⓔ resisting
Ⓒ anthropology	Ⓕ grappling with

4. Ever since Aristotle _____ that the spectacle itself, including all of the visual components that we now associate with the theater, is actually an essential aspect of theater, playwrights and producers have had to agree. However, in some modern theatrical productions, it seems that spectacle has completely taken over as the major aspect of theater. Nowadays theatergoers are presented with helicopters landing on stage, chandeliers falling from the ceiling, and cast members flying 35 miles per hour over the heads of the audience as they do battle with the forces of evil.

   Ⓐ pretended
   Ⓑ admonished
   Ⓒ opined
   Ⓓ preached
   Ⓔ extolled

5. Arid areas such as Southern California rarely receive a large amount of rain in a short period and, consequently, residents are inexperienced in handling much rainfall. However, over the course of one memorable winter, rainfall records weren't merely broken, they were (i) _____. For example, in one Los Angeles community, an astonishing 3.45 inches of rain fell in just a single afternoon, shattering the old daily record of 1.5 inches. Residents along the foothills kept a wary eye on the rain, fearful of mudslides after a recent wildfire had (ii) _____ towering slopes above their communities.

Blank (i)	Blank (ii)
Ⓐ validated	Ⓓ denuded
Ⓑ obliterated	Ⓔ deprecated
Ⓒ surrendered	Ⓕ denigrated

6. Cave pearls are so rare that most people have never even heard of them, but they do exist. Taking thousands of years of (i) _____to develop, cave pearls are formed as drops of water fall from the ceiling of a cave and hit the limestone floor, throwing up a speck of rock. This grain is (ii) _____ in its little stone cup every time a drop from the ceiling hits it, and eventually it builds up a solid, almost perfectly-round calcite pearl. Most cave pearls are usually the size of a marble, but some immense specimens as large as baseballs have been discovered in Vietnamese caves. Scientists speculate that their (iii) _____ size can be attributed to the enormous distance between the ceiling and floor of these unusual caves.

Blank (i)	Blank (ii)	Blank (iii)
Ⓐ accretion	Ⓓ bulldozed	Ⓖ prodigious
Ⓑ accreditation	Ⓔ pounded	Ⓗ customary
Ⓒ acculturation	Ⓕ jostled	Ⓘ natural

Directions: For each of questions 7 to 13, select one answer choice unless otherwise instructed.

Questions 7 to 9 are based on the following reading passage.

(1) European philosophical thinking has gone through many stages throughout history and one of the major shifts gradually occurred as the Renaissance ceded to the Enlightenment in the late seventeenth and early eighteenth centuries. (2) During the Renaissance, Europeans had a propensity to view God as the center of the universe, a supreme being who individually dictated and oversaw every event. (3) Consequently, people believed that God played a direct role in their lives. (4) For example, when the plague hit a village particularly hard, they believed it was obviously a punishment for the villagers' many faults; when a family's home was destroyed in a fire, it was obviously because that family had sinned and they deserved it; when a comet streaked across the sky, it obviously foreboded evil to come. (5) During the Renaissance, man's dominant question regarding events like these was always "Why?" (6) However, as the ideals of the new Age of Enlightenment become more prevalent, mankind's essential question evolved into "How?" (7) Instead of accepting that all bad events were sent by God, enlightened people, applying their increased faith in scientific knowledge and rational explanation, pondered *how* things worked: what causes earthquakes; when to expect the next comet; how dirty water might trigger disease.

(8) The effect of this shift in mankind's thinking cannot be underestimated. (9) It marked a significant change in outlook, making mankind central and placing him at the helm of a smoothly-running ship that he can control. (10) The still-powerful God was left to his heavens, smiling benevolently as he watched his creations working through their own problems, coming up with their own solutions.

7. Based on the author's point about the change in mankind's thinking during the Enlightenment, which of the following can reasonably be inferred?

Ⓐ Mankind lost faith in religion after the Renaissance.
Ⓑ During the Renaissance, many natural disasters occurred.
Ⓒ The Enlightenment caused man to believe that he completely understood the world.
Ⓓ Philosophical changes in thought are likely to occur in mankind's future.
Ⓔ Only minor changes in thought occurred between the late seventeenth and early eighteenth centuries.

Directions: For question 8, consider each of the three choices separately and select <u>all</u> that apply.

8. The author's primary point(s) could include which of the following?

    A   Mankind adopted philosophical thinking only during the Enlightenment.
    B   Mankind began to understand the causes of natural phenomenon during the Enlightenment.
    C   Mankind began to move beyond earlier Renaissance comprehension, wherein God openly castigated mankind for his sins.

9. Select the sentence in the passage that metaphorically pictures the change in philosophical thought in the Age of Reason.

Question 10 is based on the following reading passage.

Colonies of various species of bats are found throughout North America, but the populations of bats that are indigenous to the northeastern United States have been sharply depleted; the crisis is due to extremely high mortality from a new bio-threat, a fungus that attacks the tiny creatures while they are hibernating. This newly-recognized epidemic has been termed "white-nose syndrome," due to the appearance of the bats who are afflicted by the fungal invasion. Although the specific mechanism of death has not yet been identified, this fungus is spreading rapidly and, if left unchecked, it could decimate the entire native bat population of the northeastern United States.

10. If all of the information in this passage is true, which of the following statements is NOT true about the decline in the bat populations?

    Ⓐ   Bats throughout North America have been affected by this rapidly-spreading fungal plague.
    Ⓑ   Bats often display the telltale "white-nose syndrome," indicating they are affected.
    Ⓒ   Bats are attacked by the fungus while they are hibernating.
    Ⓓ   Bats have a very high mortality rate due to the new fungus.
    Ⓔ   Bats are dying from the fungus by the thousands, but the actual cause of death is unknown.

Question 11 is based on the following reading passage.

Each individual diamond has its own unique molecular formula, determined by the precise pattern in which its atoms bonded in the extreme heat and pressure of the Earth's crust, but those diamonds with a deep ocean-blue color are exceedingly rare. The immense stone now known as the Hope Diamond, which was discovered in seventeenth-century India, weighs in at 45.52 carats, making it the largest and most spectacular deep blue diamond ever seen by man.

11. All of the following statements are supported by information in this passage EXCEPT:

    Ⓐ   Every diamond has its own unique molecular "signature" by which it can be identified.
    Ⓑ   The Hope Diamond is huge, unique, and spectacular, but some people claim that it is cursed.
    Ⓒ   Diamonds with a deep ocean-blue color are extremely rare.
    Ⓓ   The stone, now known as the Hope Diamond, was discovered in India centuries ago.
    Ⓔ   The Hope Diamond is the largest blue diamond ever seen.

Questions 12 and 13 are based on the following reading passage.

Most Americans are familiar with John F. Kennedy's political career: They know he dedicated his life to public service and eventually became the 35th President of the United States; they have seen photographs of the dashing, youthful President accompanied by his beautiful and stylish wife, Jackie; and they are all-too-aware that this "Camelot" era was brought to a shocking and abrupt end by his tragic assassination. However, few people still recall the heroic exploits of John Kennedy as a young man in World War II, when he was just a young Navy Lieutenant commanding a high-speed PT boat on high-risk missions against superior forces, the amazing heroism he displayed after his ship was rammed and sunk, and the inspiring tale of his physical recovery and eventual triumph.

12. Which of the following statements is most likely to be the author's purpose in writing this passage?

   Ⓐ   To bring additional attention to Kennedy's many political victories.
   Ⓑ   To illustrate all of the phases of Kennedy's life.
   Ⓒ   To illustrate how many Americans are perceived to have short memories.
   Ⓓ   To increase people's knowledge by describing a little-known chapter of Kennedy's life.
   Ⓔ   To imply that Kennedy was a dilettante and a "Jack of all trades."

13. Choose the best description of the author's tone in his description of Kennedy.

   Ⓐ   veneration
   Ⓑ   enmity
   Ⓒ   antipathy
   Ⓓ   animus
   Ⓔ   affliction

Directions: For questions 14 to 17, indicate the <u>two</u> answer choices that, when used to complete the sentence, fit the meaning of the sentence as a whole and produce completed sentences that are alike in meaning.

14. Lou Gehrig, who famously proclaimed he was "the luckiest man on the face of the earth" when disease forced him to _____ his baseball career, set an astonishing record by playing in 2,130 consecutive games, a streak that was unbeatable for 56 years until finally bested by Cal Ripken, Jr. in 1995.

   Ⓐ   relinquish
   Ⓑ   condone
   Ⓒ   assert
   Ⓓ   defend
   Ⓔ   abandon
   Ⓕ   champion

15. Architect Antoni Gaudí wanted the interior space of his famous *Sagrada Família* Church in Barcelona to feel like one was walking in a forest, with an intricate _____ canopy soaring above tall columns representing tree trunks.

   Ⓐ   sylvan
   Ⓑ   homey
   Ⓒ   godlike
   Ⓓ   fanciful
   Ⓔ   honeycombed
   Ⓕ   woodsy

16. Some readers enjoy the epic length of Victorian novels, many of which run over 800 pages; other readers much prefer more _____ twentieth century novels, which average fewer than 300 pages.

   Ⓐ   verbose
   Ⓑ   turbid
   Ⓒ   tacit
   Ⓓ   laconic
   Ⓔ   succinct
   Ⓕ   descriptive

17. Kepler's first law of planetary motion posits that the orbit of every planet is an ellipse; this was a startling new idea, which _____ the then-accepted belief that every planet, in fact, every heavenly body, must travel in a perfect circle at a perfectly constant speed.

  A corroborated
  B confirmed
  C contravened
  D repudiated
  E recapitulated
  F reconfirmed

Directions: For each of questions 18 to 20, select one answer choice unless otherwise instructed.

Questions 18 and 19 are based on the following reading passage.

Vietnam's intricate system of caves has long been a mystery, an enigma that was left unexplored. During decades of war, it was well-known that Vietnamese fighters hid in caves that were all but invisible to the untrained eye. But the recent discovery of one of the longest river caves in the world, the amazing 12-mile-long Hang Khe Ry, has helped foster the creation of Phong Nha-ke Bang National Park, which already attracts hundreds of thousands of visitors a year. In the same vicinity, cave explorers were helped by a local villager who remembered hiding in caves when he was a child during the war, and they found Hang Son Doong, a colossal limestone passage over 2.5 miles long and estimated to be 600 to 800 feet high. The immensity of this cave is mind-boggling.

Inside this capacious space you could not just park a 747 jetliner; you could fit in an entire block of 40-story modern skyscrapers. Midway through the passage, two sinkholes let in shafts of daylight that allow 100-foot-tall trees to sprout from the cave floor. The scale of everything in the cave appears unearthly; one of the sinkholes is an amazing 300 feet across, a calcite column towers more than 200 feet above the floor of the cave, and clouds form near the ceiling. While explorers have discovered longer caves (the Mammoth Cave system in Kentucky) and have discovered deeper caves (Krubera-Voronja in the Caucasus Mountains of Georgia) the explorers of Hang Son Doong may very well have found the largest cave in the world.

18. Which of the following most clearly describes the relationship between the first and second paragraphs?

  Ⓐ The first paragraph mentions other caves, while the second does not.
  Ⓑ The second paragraph provides evidence to support a claim in the first paragraph.
  Ⓒ The first paragraph sets up the dimensions of the massive cave.
  Ⓓ The first paragraph presents information about other big caves in the world, but the second paragraph does not.
  Ⓔ The second paragraph provides a logical conclusion to the first.

Directions: For question 19, consider each of the choices separately and select <u>all</u> that apply.

19. Based on the information in this passage, which of the following can be logically inferred about the discovery of the Hang Son Doong cave?

  A More unexplored caves possibly exist in the area of the Phong Nha-ke Bang National Park.
  B Plant life thrives inside the cave.
  C No larger cave exists in the world.

Directions: For the question 20, consider each of the choices separately and then select <u>all</u> that apply.

Question 20 is based on the following reading passage.

For hundreds of years, oral tradition has been the major vehicle by which ideas and stories were passed from generation to generation within the African-American community. Interestingly, there are vast differences between the two major forms of oral communication that helped develop the voice of African-American society. The pulpit, with its venerable respect for religious tradition, became the place for uplifting sermons designed to elevate and to educate. Meanwhile, the argot of the streets, with its gritty realism, gave birth to rap, an art form designed to speak directly to people about their daily lives and daily problems. They may be called different means to the same end, but both oral traditions serve a valuable purpose in the African-American community.

20. Which of the following can be inferred about the African-American community?

    Ⓐ Written language has not played as strong a role in the African-American community as spoken language has.

    Ⓑ Written language will likely gain more influence as rap lyrics and famous sermons are published.

    Ⓒ Oral tradition has been a dominant force in the African-American community.

IF YOU FINISH BEFORE TIME IS CALLED, CHECK YOUR WORK ON THIS SECTION ONLY. DO NOT WORK ON ANY OTHER SECTION IN THE TEST.

Section 4: Quantitative Reasoning

Time: 35 minutes

20 Questions

General Directions: For each question, indicate the best answer, using the directions given.

- All numerical values used are real numbers.
- Figures or diagrams are not necessarily drawn to scale and should not be used to estimate sizes by measurement unless they are data displays (graphs and charts) or coordinates on a coordinate axes. These will always be drawn to scale.
- Lines that appear straight can be assumed to be straight.
- A symbol that appears in repeated quantities represents the same value or object for each quantity.
- On a number line, positive numbers are to the right of zero and increase to the right and negative numbers are to the left of zero and decrease to the left.
- Distances are always either zero or a positive value.

Directions: For questions 1 to 7, compare Quantity A and Quantity B, using additional information centered above the two quantities if such information is given. Select one of the following four answer choices below each question.

Ⓐ   Quantity A is greater.
Ⓑ   Quantity B is greater.
Ⓒ   The two quantities are equal.
Ⓓ   The relationship cannot be determined from the information given.

Question 1 refers to the following information.

x and y are positive integers

$$xy = 24$$

	Quantity A	**Quantity B**
1.	the square root of the greatest sum of x and y	the square of the least absolute value difference of x and y

	Quantity A	**Quantity B**
2.	the 23rd digit in the decimal expansion of $\frac{6}{7}$	4

Question 3 refers to the following information.

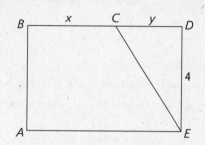

Note: Figure not drawn to scale.

Area of rectangle *ABDE* = 36
Area of trapezoid *ABCE* = 24

Quantity A	**Quantity B**
3. $\dfrac{y^2}{x^3}$	$\dfrac{4}{3}$

Question 4 refers to the following information.

$$A = \{a, b, c, d, e\} \text{ where } a, b, c, d, \text{ and } e$$
$$\text{are positive integers between 0 and 6}$$

Quantity A	**Quantity B**
4. Mean of *A*	Median of *A*

Question 5 refers to the following information.

$$|x - 5| = x$$
$$|y - 3| = y$$

Quantity A	**Quantity B**
5. $(x - y)^5$	$\sqrt{x + y}$

Quantity A	**Quantity B**
6. the probability of randomly selecting a prime number from the integers between –6 and 7	0.25

Quantity A	**Quantity B**
7. the number of arrangements of the letters A, B, C, D, and E using each letter only once	the number of different committees of two that can be formed from a group of 15 people

Directions: Questions 8 to 20 have several different formats. Unless otherwise directed, indicate a single answer choice. For Numeric Entry questions, follow the instructions below.

Numeric Entry Questions

- Write out your answer choice with numerals.
- Your answer may be an integer, a decimal, or a fraction, and it may be negative.
- If a question asks for a fraction, there will be two boxes—one for the numerator and one for the denominator.
- Equivalent forms of the correct answer, such as 4.5 and 4.50, are all correct. Fractions do not need to be reduced to lowest terms.
- Enter the exact answer unless the question asks you to round your answer.

8. A box contains eight identical red marbles and four identical blue marbles. Four marbles are to be selected from the box. How many different ways can the selections be made if two of the marbles need to be red and two of the marbles need to be blue?

   Ⓐ 42
   Ⓑ 168
   Ⓒ 224
   Ⓓ 336
   Ⓔ 672

9. A bag contains 12 ping-pong balls, equally divided among the colors of red, blue, yellow, and green. If 2 of these ping-pong balls are randomly selected, what is the probability that neither is blue? Write the probability as a ratio.

   $$\frac{\Box}{\Box}$$

10. A large corporation offers its employees one of two different pension plans, Plan A and Plan B. Records show that 70% of the employees choose Plan A and the rest of the employees choose Plan B. Also, 60% of those employees who choose Plan A are married and 70% of those who choose Plan B are married. If a married employee is selected at random, what is the probability the employee is in Plan A?

   Ⓐ $\frac{1}{3}$

   Ⓑ $\frac{4}{7}$

   Ⓒ $\frac{3}{5}$

   Ⓓ $\frac{2}{3}$

   Ⓔ $\frac{3}{4}$

11. If 2, 3, 6, w, x, y, z, 14, and 19 are the integer ages of a group of campers and $6 < w \le x < y < z < 14$, then which of the following could be the median age of the campers? Indicate all that apply.

   Ⓐ 7
   Ⓑ 8
   Ⓒ 9
   Ⓓ 11
   Ⓔ 12

12. Set A contains the unique factors of 640 that are not multiples of 4. Set B contains the unique factors of 750 that are not multiples of 5. What is the difference between the sum of the values in set A and the sum of the values in set B?

   Ⓐ 3
   Ⓑ 4
   Ⓒ 5
   Ⓓ 6
   Ⓔ 10

13. Machine A can do a certain job alone in 10 hours. Machine B can do the same job alone in 12 hours. Both machines start working on the job at 9:00 a.m. Machine A stops working at 1:00 p.m., and Machine B continues working on the job until it is complete. To the nearest minute, at what time will Machine B finish the job?

   Ⓐ 4:04 p.m.
   Ⓑ 4:10 p.m.
   Ⓒ 4:12 p.m.
   Ⓓ 4:20 p.m.
   Ⓔ 4:40 p.m.

Questions 14 to 16 are based on the following data.

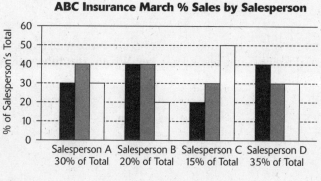

14. If Salesperson D's total sales for Auto, Home, and Life were $28,000, then what were the total Auto sales for the four salespersons?

   Ⓐ $20,000–$24,000
   Ⓑ $24,000–$28,000
   Ⓒ $28,000–$32,000
   Ⓓ $32,000–$36,000
   Ⓔ $36,000–$40,000

15. If Salesperson B sold $4,000 of Life, then what was Salesperson A's Auto sales?

16. Life amounted to what percent of the total March sales for ABC Insurance?

    - Ⓐ 27%
    - Ⓑ 29%
    - Ⓒ 31%
    - Ⓓ 33%
    - Ⓔ 35%

17. Four people, A, B, R, and T, are each given marbles from a box of 60 marbles. The marbles are distributed such that T gets seven more than R, B gets twice as many as A, and R gets three more than B. If the maximum number of marbles are distributed under the above rules, how many of the 60 marbles will be left over after the distribution?

    □

18. If the average of two numbers is y, and one of the numbers is equal to z, then the other number is equal to which of the following?

    - Ⓐ $2z - y$
    - Ⓑ $\dfrac{y + z}{2}$
    - Ⓒ $z - y$
    - Ⓓ $2y - z$
    - Ⓔ $y + 2z$

19. The mean of three numbers is 57. The second number is one more than twice the first number. The third number is four less than three times the second number. What is the difference between the mean and the median of these three numbers?

    - Ⓐ 16
    - Ⓑ 17
    - Ⓒ 18
    - Ⓓ 19
    - Ⓔ 20

20. If $f(x) = 2x - 3$ and $g(x) = x^2 + 2$ and $g(f(a)) = 51$, then which of the following could be values of a? Indicate all that apply.

    - Ⓐ −4
    - Ⓑ −2
    - Ⓒ 1
    - Ⓓ 2
    - Ⓔ 5
    - Ⓕ 6

IF YOU FINISH BEFORE TIME IS CALLED, CHECK YOUR WORK ON THIS SECTION ONLY. DO NOT WORK ON ANY OTHER SECTION IN THE TEST.

Section 5: Verbal Reasoning

Time: 30 minutes
20 Questions

General Directions: For each question, indicate the best answer using the directions given. Read the directions for each question carefully.

Directions: For each blank in questions 1 to 6, select the word or phrase from the corresponding columns that best completes the text. Your answer will consist of one, two, or three letters, depending on the number of blanks in each question.

1. The relationship between John Adams and his wife Abigail is probably the best-known and most-studied marriage of any of the original American statesmen. Because the Adamses were apart for so much of their 54-year marriage, they communicated voluminously by letter, and it is this _____ record that has provided a treasure-trove for historians.

   Ⓐ electronic
   Ⓑ evanescent
   Ⓒ ephemeral
   Ⓓ explicable
   Ⓔ epistolary

2. In the annals of manned spaceflight, one name is (i) _____; that name is Yuri Gagarin, the first human who ever rode a rocket into space. Yet, in spite of his great fame, very little is known about the terrible airplane crash that took his life, a crash that experts have long (ii) _____ to explain.

Blank (i)	Blank (ii)
Ⓐ consigned to oblivion	Ⓓ deigned
Ⓑ considered as abstruse	Ⓔ condescended
Ⓒ acknowledged as preeminent	Ⓕ struggled

3. In a seeming paradox, the Los Angeles metropolitan area has both (i) _____ choices of fresh, locally-grown food but also (ii) _____ in the city's childhood obesity rate.

Blank (i)	Blank (ii)
Ⓐ uneven	Ⓓ a troubling increase
Ⓑ profuse	Ⓔ an unhealthy decrease
Ⓒ scant	Ⓕ no change

4. When Pan Am Flight 103 was blown out of the sky by a terrorist bomb on December 21, 1988, its blazing debris rained down on the Scottish village of Lockerbie. Immediately thereafter, thousands of reporters and other media people (i) _____, stalking and hounding residents for weeks in a relentless hunt for (ii) _____.

Blank (i)	Blank (ii)
Ⓐ joined the village	Ⓓ a rational explanation of the event
Ⓑ descended on the hamlet	Ⓔ residents who had known someone on the plane
Ⓒ submerged into the streets	Ⓕ any new reaction to the tragedy

5. The preflight briefing took place in a barren and (i) _____ 1950s-era Air Force staging room, where every general in attendance was already (ii) _____ that the next-generation air-to-air missile was going to be the radar-guided *Falcon*, built by the giant defense contractor Hughes Aircraft. The only dissenting opinion was held by a quietly-confident, some might say (iii) _____, young pilot who would fly the jet carrying the last competitor, the heat-seeking *Sidewinder*, which was offered by an underfinanced, virtually unknown small company.

Blank (i)	Blank (ii)	Blank (iii)
Ⓐ austere	Ⓓ equivocal	Ⓖ jocular
Ⓑ baroque	Ⓔ ambivalent	Ⓗ verbose
Ⓒ resplendent	Ⓕ sanguine	Ⓘ taciturn

6. XYZ Aerospace Corporation of Mojave, California, is pleased to announce they have (i) _____ an agreement for a joint venture with the Caribbean nation of Trinidad, thus completing XYZ's extensive search for a location that is remote, yet tourist-friendly, to build a world-class private spaceport and resort featuring their new (ii) _____ space plane, the second generation *Aries II*. The Trinidad Minister of Commerce issued a statement saying his government has such great confidence in the success of the *Aries II*, and in the (iii) _____ economic boom, that they will undertake major investments in local infrastructure before the new spacecraft has even completed her maiden test flight.

Blank (i)	Blank (ii)	Blank (iii)
Ⓐ constituted	Ⓓ military-industrial	Ⓖ antecedent
Ⓑ circumscribed	Ⓔ commercial	Ⓗ precedent
Ⓒ consummated	Ⓕ noncommercial	Ⓘ consequent

Directions: For each of questions 7 to 12, select one answer choice unless otherwise instructed.

Questions 7 and 8 are based on the following reading passage.

In the bone-dry desert of southern California stands a solitary body of water called the Salton Sea which has a curious history. Because the area has no natural outlet, water first accumulated here approximately 1,500 years ago; the Salton Trough covered an approximate 130-mile-long, 70-mile-wide basin in the desert, just north of the Gulf of California. This lake and wetlands once covered much of the Imperial Valley, but the basin experienced several fill/recession episodes, resulting in Lake Cahuilla, which dried up completely about 300 years ago. In the most recent episode, the failure of a man-made aqueduct diverted the entire Colorado River into the low-lying area and the Salton Basin was flooded once again, resulting in the present-day Salton Sea.

7. Which of the following best summarizes the information about the history of the lake?

   Ⓐ The Salton Sea is an entirely natural phenomenon, unaffected by works of man.
   Ⓑ The Salton Sea has been a water reservoir continuously for at least 1,500 years.
   Ⓒ The Salton Sea is the current name of a lake that has come and gone for hundreds of years.
   Ⓓ The Salton Sea is a man-made lake, deliberately placed where an earlier lake had been.
   Ⓔ The Salton Sea is a reservoir for water diverted from the Colorado River.

8. All of the following statements are supported by the passage above, EXCEPT:

   Ⓐ This body of water has sometimes been caused entirely by natural forces.
   Ⓑ This body of water has sometimes been caused entirely by the work of man.
   Ⓒ This body of water is surrounded by the bone-dry California desert.
   Ⓓ This body of water was once called Lake Cahuilla.
   Ⓔ This body of water drains into the present-day Gulf of California.

Question 9 is based on the following reading passage.

(1) Raphael's famous painting, *The School of Athens,* depicts a large group of ancient philosophers, including such notables as Socrates, Plato, Aristotle, and Diogenes. (2) But a figure representing Heraclitus sits apart from the others, appearing aloof and surly. (3) Even more interesting, though, is the fact that it is now generally accepted that Raphael used Michelangelo as the basis for his depiction of this figure. (4) This gives the viewer an insight into the mixture of admiration and condescension Raphael felt for his contemporary, his artistic competitor.

9. Which of the following clarifies the author's main purpose in the second sentence?

   Ⓐ   It introduces the feeling of disdain, which is part of Raphael's mixed feelings for Michelangelo.
   Ⓑ   It explains how Heraclitus did not like his contemporary philosophers.
   Ⓒ   It serves to complete the list of philosophers depicted in the famous painting.
   Ⓓ   It separates Michelangelo from other contemporary painters.
   Ⓔ   Its visualization illustrates Raphael's respect for Michelangelo.

Question 10 is based on the following reading passage.

(1) Many decry the vast numbers of lives lost in natural disasters. (2) For instance, in the year 2010 alone more than a quarter million people died as a result of droughts, earthquakes, blizzards, volcanoes, super typhoons, and landslides; this one-year death toll exceeds the number of people killed by terrorism in the previous 40 years combined. (3) However, social scientists now refer to some of these deaths from natural disasters as a form of suicide. (4) Of course, these scientists don't mean to imply that victims intentionally jump into the mouth of a volcano; rather, they put the blame on population growth, on mankind's lifestyle, and on shoddy building practices. (5) They note that, while natural disasters have been fairly regular throughout earth's recent eons, today there are so many more people, especially those living in poverty, who now build poorly-constructed houses in less-desirable locations, such as near earthquake faults, at the base of volcanoes, and in the direct line of flood zones. (6) Perhaps the earth alone is not entirely to blame for the increased loss of life in natural disasters.

10. Select the single sentence in the passage that provides the strongest evidence for the passage's conclusion.

Questions 11 and 12 are based on the following reading passage.

Over the centuries since Europeans first settled in America, the process of removing Native American tribes from their ancestral homelands has assumed a variety of mechanisms. It began as a series of small-scale "voluntary" relocations, aided and abetted by coercion and bribery, but it finally became a government-run, countrywide genocidal enterprise. A clear example of this process is the treatment of the Cherokee Nation. This tribe tried to coexist with settlers; they became one of the "Five Civilized Tribes"; they argued their case for sovereignty in the U.S. Supreme Court and eventually won a victory when the Court ruled that the state of Georgia had no jurisdiction over Native American lands. But their repeated relocations continued and finally culminated in the notorious "Trail of Tears," an Army-enforced march to Oklahoma in which at least four thousand Cherokees died. In the end, the tribe was cheated out of its land and denied the compensation that had been promised by the government.

11. Which of the following is an assumption underlying the argument in this passage?

   Ⓐ   Most Native American tribes have been removed from their ancestral lands.
   Ⓑ   European settlers were the lucky recipients of prime land when tribes voluntarily relocated.
   Ⓒ   The Cherokee Nation lives in the present-day state of Oklahoma.
   Ⓓ   The loss of their ancestral lands has been devastating to both the culture and the population of Native American tribes.
   Ⓔ   The tribes' loss of their native lands has been an ongoing process over several centuries.

12. The writer's main point is best encapsulated in which of the following statements?

 Ⓐ The process whereby Native American tribes have been forcibly removed from their ancestral lands amounts to cultural and physical genocide.

 Ⓑ European settlers began the removal process, using coercion or bribery to get prime lands, so they are to blame for the outcome.

 Ⓒ By refusing to intervene, the U.S. Federal government has been at least complicit in the taking of Native American lands.

 Ⓓ The Cherokee Nation was one of the "Five Civilized Tribes" and, by cooperating with the settlers and the government, they received better treatment.

 Ⓔ The Cherokee Nation decided to fight for their lands in court, rather than on the battlefield, and that made all the difference in the outcome.

Directions: For questions 13 to 16, indicate the <u>two</u> answer choices that, when used to complete the sentence, fit the meaning of the sentence as a whole and produce completed sentences that are alike in meaning.

13. A community activist says the city's failure to comply fully with his public records requests should cause people to become _____ about what other information the city is keeping secret.

 Ⓐ serene

 Ⓑ phlegmatic

 Ⓒ apprehensive

 Ⓓ philosophical

 Ⓔ perturbed

 Ⓕ disinterested

14. Scribbling in his notebook, the NFL representative kept his eyes peeled for untucked jerseys, bare midriffs, and unauthorized footwear, among other _____ the strict League dress code.

 Ⓐ conformity to

 Ⓑ breaches of

 Ⓒ adherence to

 Ⓓ transgressions against

 Ⓔ compliance with

 Ⓕ imitation of

15. On August 27, 1859, a man named Edwin Drake drilled the first successful oil well in Pennsylvania, striking oil at a depth less than 70 feet underground; this event marked the birth of the modern oil industry in America, and we have been dealing with the _____ of our petroleum-fueled lifestyle ever since.

 Ⓐ causes

 Ⓑ consequences

 Ⓒ beginnings

 Ⓓ ramifications

 Ⓔ origins

 Ⓕ moribundity

16. The magazine article clearly showed the daunting _____ to agriculture in Greenland; however, it was a bit unfair in condemning Greenland's farms for importing fodder, when, in fact, the entire European Union is highly dependent on imports for feeding its livestock.

   A benefits
   B promise
   C challenges
   D emergence
   E obstructions
   F decline

Directions: For each of questions 17 to 20, select one answer choice unless otherwise instructed.

Questions 17 and 18 are based on the following reading passage.

Thomas Edward Lawrence, who rose to worldwide fame as Lawrence of Arabia, was the most visible military figure, and certainly the most dashing romantic hero, to emerge from the fire and chaos of World War I. Lawrence's daring exploits on desert battlefields of the Eastern Front, leading local Arab tribes to victory over the Ottoman Turks, helped to turn the tide of the war, and they earned him the respect and admiration of his peers and commanding officers. Lawrence was trumpeted in the popular press of the day, always photographed in the dashing robes of a desert prince, and he received the overwhelming adulation of a battered public that was all-too-eager to embrace a wartime hero, a solace that had been denied them by the war's near-complete lack of publicly-celebrated individuals.

17. Which of the following best summarizes the author's main point in this passage?

   Ⓐ Lawrence of Arabia was a noble warrior-poet.
   Ⓑ Lawrence of Arabia was the only notable hero of World War I.
   Ⓒ Lawrence of Arabia dressed in flowing native robes in battle.
   Ⓓ Lawrence of Arabia was a successful warrior and the media superstar of his day.
   Ⓔ Lawrence of Arabia was a mediocre soldier, but he knew how to work the press.

Directions: For question 18, consider each of the choices separately and then select <u>all</u> that apply.

18. According to the passage, Lawrence of Arabia is notable for which of the following reasons

   A He won a series of unlikely victories in the desert and, thus, turned the tide of battle in World War I.
   B He cashed in on his media exposure after the war ended and became well-known and wealthy.
   C He worked tirelessly after the war to promote the sovereignty of the various Arab tribes.

Questions 19 and 20 are based on the following reading passage.

In order to conduct a census of endangered African mountain gorillas, researchers must travel to remote, high-altitude jungles in the Virunga Mountains. When they arrive, however, they do everything possible to avoid making actual contact with the animals themselves. "We do not want to encounter unhabituated gorillas," explained one researcher, "because it is stressful for them." So, rather than tracking and recording individual gorillas, researchers conducting the census sought out clues to the gorillas' numbers, clues such as gorilla dung, nests, and trails. The fresh data from this latest gorilla census will be compared to numbers collected several years ago to see if the population and health of the gorilla community is holding steady, or if their numbers are in decline.

19. Which of the following is an inference that can be properly drawn from the information in the passage?

   Ⓐ The gorilla population is in decline.
   Ⓑ The gorilla population is holding steady.
   Ⓒ The gorilla population is stable, but their health is in decline.
   Ⓓ The gorillas react negatively to stressful encounters with humans.
   Ⓔ The gorilla population cannot be properly measured by such indirect census methods.

20. All of the following statements concur with the facts in the passage above EXCEPT:

    Ⓐ Researchers try to avoid making direct contact with the gorillas themselves.

    Ⓑ Researchers utilize indirect evidence to estimate the gorilla population.

    Ⓒ Researchers are concerned about the long-term sustainability of the gorilla community.

    Ⓓ Researchers will use data from the new census to draw conclusions, based on data from an earlier census.

    Ⓔ Researchers will attempt to count gorillas by visually sighting individuals.

IF YOU FINISH BEFORE TIME IS CALLED, CHECK YOUR WORK ON THIS SECTION ONLY. DO NOT WORK ON ANY OTHER SECTION IN THE TEST.

STOP

Section 6: Quantitative Reasoning

35 minutes

20 Questions

General Directions: For each question, indicate the best answer, using the directions given.

- All numerical values used are real numbers.
- Figures or diagrams are not necessarily drawn to scale and should not be used to estimate sizes by measurement unless they are data displays (graphs and charts) or coordinates on a coordinate axes. These will always be drawn to scale.
- Lines that appear straight can be assumed to be straight.
- A symbol that appears in repeated quantities represents the same value or object for each quantity.
- On a number line, positive numbers are to the right of zero and increase to the right and negative numbers are to the left of zero and decrease to the left.
- Distances are always either zero or a positive value.

Directions: For questions 1 to 7, compare Quantity A and Quantity B, using additional information centered above the two quantities if such information is given. Select one of the following four answer choices below each question.

- Ⓐ Quantity A is greater.
- Ⓑ Quantity B is greater.
- Ⓒ The two quantities are equal.
- Ⓓ The relationship cannot be determined from the information given.

Question 1 refers to the following information.

x is 25% of y

y is 75% of z

Quantity A	**Quantity B**
1. $\dfrac{z-x}{y}$	1

Question 2 refers to the following information.

The radius of Circle A is less than the diameter of Circle B

Quantity A	**Quantity B**
2. Area of Circle A	Area of Circle B

Question 3 refers to the following information.

$$12x - 96y = 8$$

Quantity A	**Quantity B**
3. $\dfrac{1}{2}x - 4y$	$\dfrac{1}{3}$

	Quantity A	**Quantity B**
4.	the number of integers x so that $-3 < 2x - 1 < 13$	the greatest integer n so that $2^n < 200$

Question 5 refers to the following information.

Machine A produces 300 screws every 75 seconds

Machine B produces 540 screws every $1\frac{1}{2}$ minutes

	Quantity A	**Quantity B**
5.	the number of hours needed to produce 100,000 screws if the two machines run simultaneously	3

Question 6 refers to the following information.

n is a positive integer

Set D = $\{n, n + 1, n + 6, n - 3, n + 2, n - 5, n + 3\}$

	Quantity A	**Quantity B**
6.	mean of Set D	median of Set D

Question 7 refers to the following information.

The operator $\otimes$ is defined by $x \otimes y = \sqrt{\dfrac{x+y}{(x-y)^2}}$ for all positive numbers x and y.

	Quantity A	**Quantity B**
7.	$12 \otimes 4$	$2 \otimes 8$

Directions: Questions 8 to 20 have several different formats. Unless otherwise directed, indicate a single answer choice. For Numeric Entry questions, follow the instructions below.

Numeric Entry Questions

- Write out your answer choice with numerals.
- Your answer may be an integer, a decimal, or a fraction, and it may be negative.
- If a question asks for a fraction, there will be two boxes—one for the numerator and one for the denominator.
- Equivalent forms of the correct answer, such as 4.5 and 4.50, are all correct. Fractions do not need to be reduced to lowest terms.
- Enter the exact answer unless the question asks you to round your answer.

8. Let *A* be the area of the following figure:

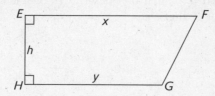

If *x* is decreased by 25% and *y* is increased by 50%, the area of the resulting figure is *B*. If *A = B*, then which of the following statements BEST describes the relationship between *x* and *y*?

Ⓐ $4x - 6y = 4$
Ⓑ $x + y = 12$
Ⓒ $y = 2x$
Ⓓ $x = 2y$
Ⓔ $x - y = 2$

9. The net weight of a certain type of boxed cereal is approximately normally distributed with a mean of 15.8 ounces and a standard deviation of 0.15 ounces. What is the probability that a randomly selected box of this cereal will have a net weight between 15.5 ounces and 15.95 ounces?

Ⓐ 70%–75%
Ⓑ 75%–80%
Ⓒ 80%–85%
Ⓓ 85%–90%
Ⓔ 90%–95%

10. Let *x* equal the sum of all of the integers from 100 to 200, inclusive. What is the sum of the digits of the value of *x*?

☐

11. When integer J is divided by 5, the remainder is 1. When integer J is divided by 3 the remainder is 2. Which of the following could be the value of J? Indicate <u>all</u> that apply.

Ⓐ 81
Ⓑ 116
Ⓒ 127
Ⓓ 176
Ⓔ 311
Ⓕ 486

12. Tali has budgeted for her cruise vacation. She plans to spend 60% of her budget for the cruise fare, 10% for air travel, 20% for on-board expenses, and 10% on gifts. When she returned home, she found that she spent 20% more than the budgeted amount on air travel, 10% less than the budgeted amount on the cruise fare, 20% more than the budgeted amount on on-board expenses, and 20% less than the budgeted amount on gifts. Her overall actual cruise vacation expenses amounted to what percent of her budgeted amount?

Ⓐ 97%
Ⓑ 98%
Ⓒ 99%
Ⓓ 100%
Ⓔ 101%

13. A student started working at a salary of *x* dollars per hour. Over the course of one year, the student's salary was raised 10%, then later lowered 15%, then later raised 20%, then later lowered 15%. What was the student's salary after this series of changes?

   Ⓐ 0.95*x*

   Ⓑ 0.98*x*

   Ⓒ *x*, unchanged

   Ⓓ 1.02*x*

   Ⓔ 1.05*x*

Questions 14 to 16 are based on the following data.

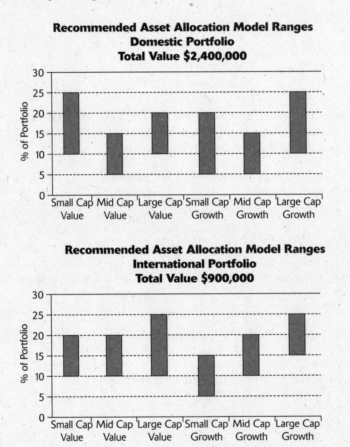

14. If the minimum recommended amount was invested in large cap stocks, by how much would the domestic large cap investments exceed the international large cap investments?

   Ⓐ $135,000

   Ⓑ $255,000

   Ⓒ $300,000

   Ⓓ $375,000

   Ⓔ $630,000

15. What is the total difference between the maximum recommended and minimum recommended amounts for all mid cap investments?

$

16. If the minimum recommended amounts were invested in small cap international, the maximum recommended amounts were invested in large cap international, and equal amounts were invested in mid cap international value and mid cap international growth, what percent of the international portfolio consisted of growth stocks?

   Ⓐ 17.5%
   Ⓑ 30%
   Ⓒ 42.5%
   Ⓓ 47.5%
   Ⓔ 50%

17. If the ratio of w to x is 4 to 5, the ratio of x to y is 7 to 8, and the ratio of y to z is 3 to 2, then what is the ratio of w to z?

   Ⓐ Between $\frac{1}{4}$ and $\frac{1}{2}$

   Ⓑ Between $\frac{1}{2}$ and $\frac{3}{4}$

   Ⓒ Between $\frac{3}{4}$ and $\frac{1}{1}$

   Ⓓ Between $\frac{1}{1}$ and $\frac{5}{4}$

   Ⓔ Between $\frac{5}{4}$ and $\frac{3}{2}$

18. Under Plan A, if Amber starts receiving her Social Security payments on her March 1 birthday when she is 66, she will receive $466 per month. Under Plan B, if Amber waits till her March 1 birthday when she is 70 years old, she will receive $589 per month. If these payments remain constant (no cost of living increases or other expenses), how old will Amber be when the total amount received under Plan B equals the total amount received under Plan A?

   Ⓐ 84 years 8 months
   Ⓑ 84 years 10 months
   Ⓒ 85 years 0 months
   Ⓓ 85 years 2 months
   Ⓔ 85 years 4 months

19. If $ax + by + c = 0$ is the equation of a line in the x-y coordinate plane, then for which of the following values of a, b, and c would the line intercept the positive x-axis and the negative y-axis? Indicate <u>all</u> that apply.

   Ⓐ $a = 7, b = 3, c = -4$
   Ⓑ $a = -6, b = 2, c = 8$
   Ⓒ $a = 2, b = -3, c = 8$
   Ⓓ $a = -4, b = -6, c = -2$
   Ⓔ $a = 6, b = -4, c = -5$

20. If $2x^3 + 4 = -5$, then what is the value of $6x^3 + 15$?

IF YOU FINISH BEFORE TIME IS CALLED, CHECK YOUR WORK ON THIS SECTION ONLY. DO NOT WORK ON ANY OTHER SECTION IN THE TEST.

Answer Key for Practice Test 1

Section 3: Verbal Reasoning

1. A
2. A
3. A and F
4. C
5. B and D
6. A, F, and G
7. D
8. B and C
9. Sentence 9
10. A
11. B
12. D
13. A
14. A and E
15. A and F
16. D and E
17. C and D
18. B
19. A and B
20. A and C

Section 4: Quantitative Reasoning

1. A
2. C
3. C
4. D
5. B
6. C
7. A
8. B
9. $\frac{6}{11}\left(\frac{72}{132}, \frac{36}{66}, \frac{18}{33}, \frac{12}{22}$ are also acceptable answers$\right)$
10. D
11. A, B, C, and D
12. D
13. C
14. B
15. 9,000
16. C
17. 5
18. D
19. C
20. B and E

Section 5:
Verbal Reasoning

1. E
2. C and F
3. B and D
4. B and F
5. A, F, and I
6. C, E, and I
7. C
8. E
9. A
10. Sentence 5
11. D
12. A
13. C and E
14. B and D
15. B and D
16. C and E
17. D
18. A
19. D
20. E

Section 6:
Quantitative Reasoning

1. A
2. D
3. C
4. C
5. B
6. B
7. B
8. D
9. C
10. 12
11. B, D, and E
12. B
13. A
14. B
15. 660,000
16. D
17. D
18. D
19. B and E
20. −12

Charting and Analyzing Your Test Results

The first step in analyzing your results is to chart your answers. Use the following charts to identify your strengths and areas of improvement. Complete the process of evaluating your essays and analyzing problems in each area for Practice Test 1. Reevaluate your results as you look for:

- Trends
- Types of errors (frequently repeated errors)
- Low scores in the results of *specific* topic areas

This reexamination and analysis is a tremendous asset to help you maximize your best possible score. The answers and explanations following these charts will provide you clarification to help you solve these types of questions in the future.

Analytical Writing Assessment Worksheets

Analyze your responses using the following charts, and compare your responses to the sample "high-scoring strong responses" on page 393 and 395 as a reference guide. Then estimate your score using the Analytical Writing Scoring Guide on pages 3–4 for characteristics of a strong high-scoring essay to rate your essay. Remember that when you take the actual GRE, scores are averaged from two separate readers.

Analysis of an Issue			
Ask Yourself These Questions	**Strong Response Score 5 or 6**	**Moderate Response Score 3 or 4**	**Weak Response Score 1 or 2**
1. Does the essay focus on the assigned topic and respond to the specific task?			
2. Does the essay show an understanding of the complexity of the issue?			
3. Does the essay provide well-developed reasons and/or examples?			
4. Does the essay show relevant supporting details?			
5. Is the essay organized and does it use transitions to connect ideas?			
6. Does the essay show a command of standard written English?			

Analysis of an Argument			
Questions	**Strong Response Score 5 or 6**	**Moderate Response Score 3 or 4**	**Weak Response Score 1 or 2**
1. Does the essay focus on the specific topic and cover all of the tasks?			
2. Does the essay identify and analyze important features of the passage?			
3. Does the essay develop and express your evaluation?			
4. Does the essay support your evaluation with relevant reasons and/or examples?			
5. Is the essay well-organized?			
6. Does the essay show a command of standard written English?			

Multiple-Choice Questions

Verbal Reasoning Worksheet

Types of Questions Missed					
Question Type	**Total Possible**	**Number Correct**	**Number Incorrect**		
			(A) Simple Mistake	**(B) Misread Problem(s)**	**(C) Lack of Knowledge**
Reading Comprehension Section 3: Questions 7–13 and 18–20 Section 5: 7–12 and 17–20	20				
Text Completion Section 3: Questions 1–6 Section 5: Questions 1–6	12				
Sentence Equivalence Section 3: Questions 14–17 Section 5: Questions 13–16	8				
Total Possible Explanations for Incorrect Answers: Columns A, B, and C					
Total Number of Answers Correct and Incorrect	40	Add the total number of correct answers here: _____	Add columns A, B, and C: _____ Total number of incorrect answers		

Quantitative Reasoning Worksheet

Types of Questions Missed					
Content Style Topic	**Total Possible**	**Number Correct**	**Number Incorrect**		
			(A) Simple Mistake	**(B) Misread Problem**	**(C) Lack of Knowledge**
Arithmetic Section 4: Question 2 Section 6: Questions 7, 12	3				
Algebra Section 4: Questions 1, 5, 18, 20 Section 6: Questions 3, 6, 17, 19, 20	9				
Geometry Section 4: Question 3 Section 6: Questions 1, 2, 8, 18	5				
Data Analysis Section 4: Questions 4, 6, 9, 11, 19 Section 6: Questions 4, 11	7				
Word Problems Section 4: Questions 7, 8, 10, 12, 13, 17 Section 6: Questions 5, 9, 10, 13	10				
Data Interpretation Section 4: Questions 14, 15, 16 Section 6: Question 14, 15, 16	6				
Total Possible Explanations for Incorrect Answers: Columns A, B, and C					
Total Number of Answers Correct and Incorrect	40	Add the total number of correct answers here: _____	Add columns A, B, and C: _____ Total number of incorrect answers		

Practice Test 1 Answers and Explanations

Section 1: Analytical Writing – Analyze an Issue

Sample student responses are provided below to help you evaluate your essay. Author comments at the end of this section will further help you identify your areas of improvement.

Issue Topic

Pharmaceutical companies should be encouraged to pursue treatments and cures for conditions that affect the greatest number of people.

Write a response expressing to what degree you agree or disagree with the recommendation. Provide explanations for the reasoning behind your stance. Be sure to consider and discuss the most persuasive reasons and evidence that could pose a challenge to your position.

High-scoring Strong Response

The utilitarian philosophy says that the best path is the one that leads to the greatest good for the greatest number. Generally people accept this concept, especially when it comes to political or economic decisions. The idea that pharmaceutical companies should be encouraged to develop treatments that will benefit the greatest number of people sounds good on the surface although there are circumstances where I would take issue with that philosophy.

Encouraging pharmaceutical companies to pursue treatments for the diseases that affect large numbers of people is a good idea because it will alleviate a greater part of human suffering. For example, many people around the world suffer from difficult to combat diseases like malaria or cholera. The problem is that the countries where people most need help fighting these problems are also the countries with the least amount of money. A big drug company might make more profit on an exotic cancer-fighting drug that will help only 5,000 people rather than a cheap treatment that could help five million. Perhaps pharmaceutical companies that develop inexpensive drugs for diseases that affect many people—but that aren't very lucrative—could be rewarded with longer patents for their treatments that make more money but help far fewer people. This would encourage companies to help a wider range of people while still promoting their research efforts.

Another consideration is that leaving aside diseases that predominate in poor countries, pharmaceutical companies already have encouragement to develop treatments for conditions that affect the largest number of people. Drugs that treat the largest number of people will also be purchased by larger numbers of people who suffer from that condition. Drugs that treat pain, indigestion, and lifestyle diseases are the most popular and financially rewarding because so many people need them. As the Baby Boomers enter senior citizenship they will represent the largest chunk of the U.S. population, and it makes sense for pharmaceutical companies to pursue treatments for conditions related to aging. Little outside encouragement will be needed in this regard.

Although it is valuable to alleviate the largest degree of human suffering, in the end I cannot completely agree with the utilitarian approach. A main problem with just focusing on drugs that treat the greatest number of people is that it limits research opportunities. Many breakthroughs in science and medicine occur when researchers are tackling a specific disease or condition but then find another, wider application for their findings. A pharmaceutical researcher may be trying to develop a drug to treat a specific form of cancer that afflicts just 3,000 people in the U.S. There may not be very much financial reward to the drug company, but the development of that treatment may have implications for other kinds of cancers which affect a far greater number of people. It is difficult to predict what will be successful in treating disease. After all, the discovery of penicillin was largely an accident. In the end, the recommendation is a sound one with just a few caveats.

Average-scoring Moderate Response

This recommendation makes sense in many circumstances yet has a serious limit. If drug companies are encouraged to develop treatments for diseases that affect the greatest number of people that will be of greater benefit to society. This is a good outcome. However, there are cases where drug companies should also be rewarded for pursuing cures that may help only a few individuals.

The pharmaceutical companies will want to make drugs that help the most people since those treatments will make the most money. This is a good, natural encouragement because in this case more sick people will be helped. For example, some estimate that diabetes will affect about one in four people by the year 2050. Even though that figure is in the future drug companies should be encouraged now to find ways to treat this disease before it gets too serious.

This recommendation should be followed when the people who most need help live somewhere outside the company's home country, maybe there are not many people in the United States who suffer from a disease that people in poor countries get all the time. If pharmaceutical companies were encouraged to think about other places then it would help more people.

The one situation where drug companies should be encouraged to find treatments for conditions that don't affect as many people is with orphan drugs. This is when there are only a small number of patients who need a treatment. Often the pharmaceutical company won't want to spend the money to research a drug that will not make them very much money. In these cases maybe companies could be encouraged to pursue treatments by getting incentives. In most cases the encouragement is not needed, but in this one lives could be saved by some incentives.

Low-scoring Weak Response

Every year people find out they have an illness and there is no treatment for it. They pretty much get a death notice from their doctor because there is no drug to cure their condition. This could be fixed if pharmaceutical companies had to make drugs for everybody.

If they did this then the companies would make more money because more people would buy their drugs. This would make them more successful. So they could in turn create more new treatments and it would help even more people.

Finding cures for more people would make the population healthier on the hole and might prevent more disease. If the companies treat the greatest number of people then fewer people will end up getting infected and spreading their disease.

Lastly, if pharmaceutical companies make drugs for a large number of people it will mean a better situation for their families too since disease affects not just the sick person but their families and friends as well. This would make the impact even bigger and the company more successful.

Author Comments

The **strong response** provides a clear position that responds specifically to the task. The examples are persuasive because they are developed in detail. Even the hypothetical situation of the pharmaceutical researcher demonstrates logical consideration of the recommendation through a sustained argument. Transition words guide the reader from point to point and the use of effective vocabulary (utilitarian, alleviate, lucrative) conveys ideas fluently.

The **moderate response** presents a clear position and provides examples of circumstances where the recommendation would apply. The examples (diabetes, orphan drugs) are logically sound but are not developed in depth or detail. Although the organization is clear, the response lacks transitions. Minor errors include a run-on sentence and a few misspellings.

The **weak response** is limited in addressing the specific directions for the prompt. It fails to provide a clear position, instead outlining arguments both for and against the recommendation. The generally adequate organization doesn't quite compensate for the lack of developed examples and informal tone.

Section 2: Analytical Writing – Analyze an Argument

Sample student responses are provided below to help you evaluate your essay. Author comments at the end of this section will further help you identify your areas of improvement.

Argument Topic

The following appeared in the meeting minutes of a local chamber of commerce:

> Last year Hernville's Back to School Tax Holiday promotion proved very popular. The one-day event allowed parents to purchase clothes and school supplies without sales tax as they prepared for the first day of school. The retailers who responded to the survey reported a large increase in sales that day. The Hernville Chamber of Commerce recommends that the one-day promotion be expanded to a once-monthly event to stimulate the local economy and promote job growth.

Write a response that considers which questions would need to be answered about the proposal to determine if it will result in the outcome predicted. Be sure to discuss how answering these questions will help evaluate the recommended proposal.

High-scoring Strong Response

While a tax holiday may hold strong appeal for consumers and the Hernville Chamber of Commerce there are serious considerations and questions to be addressed before the proposal could move forward.

A primary question is to what degree a monthly tax-free shopping day for clothes and school supplies would stimulate job growth and economic activity in Hernville. For an event that happens only twelve times a year it seems unlikely that retailers would hire additional employees. It is more probable that existing employees might work a few hours of overtime to cover anticipated customer demand. While this might put a few more dollars in the pockets of existing employees it's not likely to have a wider impact on hiring of new employees. The argument would need to answer the question of how many new employees businesses would plan to hire due to the proposed tax holiday expansion.

The argument also claims that the tax holiday would stimulate economic activity. However the tax holiday appears to be limited to school supplies and clothing. Would adult as well as children's clothing be included? Would the tax holiday be extended to other types of consumer goods as well? If the holiday remains limited to just a few categories it seems questionable that it would spur greater consumer spending and the resultant economic growth. Even though children do grow throughout the school year, increased business in this one sector seems unlikely to have a wide impact on economic growth throughout Hernville.

Even if there were increased spending and growth the size of its impact is unclear. The argument states that retailers reported a "large increase" in sales on that day. How much is that in relative numbers? Did it represent a significant increase over normal sales? When retailers compared their monthly numbers did they see actual growth, or did purchases spike on this one day and then average out to regular levels? If the tax holiday resulted in overall larger sales that would support the idea of extending the program, but if the actual monthly sales did not increase then the idea loses merit. Maybe people just chose to do their normal back to school shopping on this one day but did not make additional purchases.

The Hernville Chamber of Commerce makes an interesting proposal but fails to address many important questions about the program's impact. Questions about employee hiring, types of goods exempt from tax, and the actual impact on sales need to be answered before the proposal can be seriously considered.

Average-scoring Moderate Response

The Hernville Chamber of Commerce is suggesting that a tax-free day once a month will help the economy and aid in job growth. Although the recommendation has some good ideas, there are some tough questions to be answered.

One practical issue is what would be tax-free on the one day. If the tax holiday is just for school supplies and children's clothes it is unlikely to have much of an impact. Parents might buy school supplies only twice a year, once in August and once in January to restock, which would not create much of a boost. If the tax holiday was extended to other items it could create other problems.

For example, how much money the city of Hernville would stand to lose if people shifted their spending to the one day a month to avoid taxes? How much money did it lose with the tax holiday last year? This would be important to know to see if the plan is worth it to the city.

The other question about the recommendation is how it will promote job growth. Stores might anticipate higher sales for that one day a month but might be unlikely to add staff just for something that happens a dozen times a year.

Low-scoring Weak Response

Taxes are too high and this recommendation could help the consumer. There are some questions to be asked first before the Chamber of Commerce continues with the plan.

First, what day of the month will be the tax-free day? A weekday when many people and their kids are working or in school or on a weekend when they have more free time? It would be better to have it happen on a Saturday or Sunday when more people can participate.

Another question is what will be tax-free. Will it just be clothes for kids, or can adults buy clothes as well? Anyone can use school supplies like pencils and tape, but the big issue would be whether people can buy clothes and other items for themselves.

The last question is how the registers would work on the tax holiday. Would they have to all be reprogrammed to take off the tax?

This is a good idea with just a few questions to answer.

Author Comments

The **strong response** presents a cogent examination of the argument by identifying relevant questions and then examining the implications of potential responses. By establishing cause-and-effect relationships and anticipating possible outcomes, the writer develops an insightful analysis of the proposal. Logical transitions, such as the one between the third and fourth paragraph, make the flow of ideas easy to follow. Effective vocabulary use (sector, questionable, exempt) and a variety of sentence types convey confidence.

The **moderate response** does a more complete job of identifying relevant questions. Its main flaw is in the uneven development of the analysis and limited development of its main points. While the writer does pose questions that help assess the recommendation, more explanation of why these are relevant questions would make the response more thoughtful. The few minor flaws in sentence structure and mechanics do not interfere with comprehension.

The **weak response** is limited in its examination of the argument because it only identifies a few of the relevant issues and only in sketchy detail. The writer also discusses the less relevant question of reprogramming the registers rather than focusing on more central concerns. Although the writer poses questions about the Chamber's plan, the analysis of why these are important questions to ask is minimal. Problems with sentence structure result in a lack of clarity.

Section 3: Verbal Reasoning

Text Completion

1. **A.** This sentence constructs parallel ideas by comparing well-known similarities in literature with the increasing similar patterns in automobile design. Since the overall focus seems to be on repeating similar patterns, the correct answer must likewise indicate a minimum of differences. Thus, choice A is the correct answer; a collection of cars that displays little or no differences can properly be called *homogenized.* The other answer choices all lead us away from this uniformity; each of these inaccurate words indicates diversity or dissimilarity.

2. **A.** The connotation of this sentence calls for a positive word, one that means someone who is celebrated and revered; among the possible choices, the only word that fits is *lionized.* The other choices carry negative connotations or meanings. Choice B, *reproached,* means to criticize someone for a fault. To be *vilified* (C) is to be maligned or verbally abused. *Censured* (D) means to be formally and officially condemned or criticized. Finally, choice E, *caviled,* means to criticize something using picky, trivial objections.

3. **A and F.** The entire passage deals with the ever-increasing human population and how this unrestrained growth will affect the world. The word *demography* (A), which specifically explores the relationship between population and the surrounding environment, is the best choice for the first blank. Choice B, *statistics,* does not fit as well because it does not include the connection between population and the environment that *demography* has. Choice C, *anthropology,* may at first seem like a viable choice, but it, too, is not specific enough. *Anthropology* deals with the study of human culture and human development, but it does not have the specific focus on population growth that *demography* has. The second blank requires a word that acknowledges the "alarm" and "worry" that have concerned mankind for centuries; *grappling with* (F) fits the idea that mankind has, indeed, wrestled with these concepts for centuries. Choice D, *agreeing with,* makes little sense in this context. Mankind may be in agreement that his impact on the environment is worrisome, but this sentence requires a word that clarifies how mankind is dealing with this issue. The word *resisting* (E) may at first seem synonymous with *grappling,* but it refers more to the aspect of opposing something, whereas *grappling* implies that this issue is something mankind must wrestle or struggle with, either mentally or physically.

4. **C.** The main idea in this passage is that "playwrights and producers have had to agree" with Aristotle's opinion that spectacle is "an essential aspect of theater." The word *opined* (C) means to proffer an opinion, to explain one's idea. Choice A, *pretended,* does not logically agree with the connotation of this sentence; neither Aristotle, nor the playwrights, producers, and theatergoers are merely pretending that spectacle is important. Choice B, *admonished,* means to berate or criticize, which also makes little sense in the context of this sentence. Choice D, *preached,* is too strong and value-laden a word to pinpoint what Aristotle actually meant. Finally, choice E is inaccurate because it is too positive; to *extol* means to praise highly.

5. **B and D.** The first blank needs a word that fits the context of rainfall records that "weren't merely broken," but which were exceeded by a large amount. The word *obliterated* (B) correctly matches this context. Neither of the other words makes sense in the first blank; choice A, *validated,* means to confirm or substantiate, and choice C, *surrendered,* means to give up or to yield something. Next, the second blank needs a word that clarifies damage done by a previous wildfire, and such a wildfire is likely to have *denuded* (D) the landscape by stripping the hills of their trees. Under these conditions, it is natural for local residents to fear that mudslides might result from such strong rains. The other choices, *deprecated* (E) and *denigrated* (F), are synonymous words that mean to belittle or disparage.

6. **A, F, and G.** One must consider the overall context of the passage to decipher the first blank; when you know the pearls are built-up over thousands of years you can select the correct answer, *accretion* (A), which means something that grows slowly and gradually. The other answer choices do not make logical sense in this context. For the second blank, a word is needed to fit with the idea that the tiny speck of rock is knocked around in its little stone cup every time a drop of water hits it; the word *jostled* (F) fits this meaning. Choices D and E, *bulldozed* and *pounded,* each refer to actions that are too strong. The third blank can be answered by elimination, even if one does not know the meaning of the accurate word, *prodigious,* which refers to something unusual and immense. Choices H, *customary,* and I, *natural,* both mean the opposite, something that is not out of the ordinary.

Reading Comprehension

7. **D.** Since European philosophical thinking has gone through many stages throughout history and one of the major shifts occurred between the Renaissance and the Enlightenment, it is reasonable to infer that mankind does periodically shift the way he views the world and, thus, mankind's philosophy will probably continue to evolve over time. Choice A is too strong; the passage does state that man gained more faith in scientific knowledge and rational explanation, but that does not necessarily mean he *lost* faith in religion. Choice B also takes the ideas in the passage too far; the passage includes a mention of the plague and of a family losing a home because of fire, but it does not logically follow that *many* natural disasters occurred. Choice C represents a misreading of the passage; mankind's shift in philosophical thinking does not imply he believed he completely understood his world. Choice E is directly contradicted by the first sentence, which states that a "major shift" in mankind's thinking did, indeed, occur during this period.

8. **B and C.** The author makes several points, include the idea that mankind changed during the late seventeenth and early eighteenth centuries, shifting from a Renaissance mindset that believed God directly punished mankind for evil deeds, to the more enlightened belief that mankind could scientifically understand the causes of such human suffering. These ideas are encompassed in choices B and C. Choice A, however, is too limited; the author never implies that mankind had not thought philosophically before the Enlightenment, only that his thinking changed.

9. **Sentence 9: It marked a significant change in outlook, making mankind central and placing him at the helm of a smoothly-running ship that he can control.** This sentence, the second sentence in the final paragraph, metaphorically establishes mankind at the helm of a ship, an image which is a metaphor for mankind's increased control over his own life, especially as he gained improved scientific knowledge of earthly affairs.

10. **A.** Choice A is the correct answer, because it directly contradicts a fact stated in the passage; thus far, the fungus has affected only bats in the northeastern United States, not "throughout North America." The statements in all of the other answer choices do, in fact, concur with the information in this passage.

11. **B.** The statement in choice B begins with some facts about the Hope Diamond that are correctly drawn from the passage, but then it veers off-topic by including the idea that the diamond is supposedly "cursed"; this point may very well be true, but it is not included in this passage, so choice B is the correct exception. Meanwhile, all of the statements in the other answer choices are, indeed, supported by the information in the passage.

12. **D.** This author prefaces his points about Kennedy's World War II service by reminding the reader that "few people still recall" these exploits; thus, it is safe to conclude that the best answer is choice D, *to increase people's knowledge* of Kennedy. Most of the other answer choices include an element of misdirection about the author's purpose; for example, he was not writing to bring attention to Kennedy's *political* victories, so choice A can be eliminated. And, while this author does mention two episodes of Kennedy's life, it is not his purpose to write about *all* phases of his life, so choice B can be eliminated. Choices C and E both clearly misidentify this author's purpose.

13. **A.** This writer focuses almost exclusively on the positive aspects of Kennedy's life, so the correct description must be a word with positive connotations. The best answer for this question is choice A, *veneration,* which indicates great respect or admiration. The other answer choices all indicate the contrary: Choice B, *enmity,* means animosity or hatred; choice C, *antipathy,* and choice D, *animus,* both indicate a strong dislike; and choice E, *affliction,* refers to a condition of adversity.

Sentence Equivalence

14. **A and E.** The key phrase to focus on when filling in the blank in this sentence is that "disease forced" Lou Gehrig to retire early from baseball. The two verbs that fit best are *relinquish* (A) and *abandon* (E), both of which connote giving up or surrendering something. Choice B, *condone,* means to tolerate or allow something without criticizing it. Choice C, *assert,* means to claim something is true or insist upon it. Choices D and F, *defend* and *champion,* do not fit the context of the sentence.

15. **A and F.** According to the sentence, the interior of the *Sagrada Família* Church should duplicate the feeling of walking in a forest. It has tall columns that represent tree trunks, and the ceiling high above imitates a canopy of trees. The correct answers are choice A, *sylvan,* which means forest-like and shaded by trees, and its synonym, choice F, *woodsy,* which both provide the intended visual effect. The remaining choices do not have the necessary connection to tree-covered forests or woods. Choice B, *homey,* means simple, unassuming, and comfortable; choice C, *godlike,* may seem appropriate for a church, but it does not include the connotation of a forest that this sentence requires. Choices D, *fanciful,* and E, *honeycombed,* each provide a visually complex image, but not one that suggests a forest.

16. **D and E.** This sentence contrasts the unusual length of Victorian novels with more contemporary short-length twentieth century novels. Since Victorian novels usually "run over 800 pages" and twentieth century novels "average fewer than 300 pages," the words needed to complete the sentence need to reflect the shorter length of twentieth century novels. Choice D, *laconic,* and choice E, *succinct,* both fit this context, since each means using few words, or being concise. Choice A is the opposite of what you need for this sentence; *verbose* means to be overly-verbal, using too many words. Choice F makes no sense; a *descriptive* novel could be either a long or a short work. The other options are off-topic; *turbid* (B) refers to things that are unclear or muddy, and *tacit* (C) refers to something that is understood without being said openly, like an unstated agreement.

17. **C and D.** Since the sentence identifies Kepler's first law as a "startling new idea," one can make the connection that it must have overturned, or at least disagreed with, the accepted doctrine of the day. Next, if you look for answer choices that contain this element of contradiction, you will find two excellent candidates: choice C, *contravened,* meaning to contradict, and choice D, *repudiated,* meaning to reject or abandon. The words in all of the other answer choices actually indicate the opposite; their meaning is to substantiate (choice A), or to confirm (choices B and F), or to reiterate and summarize (choice E).

Reading Comprehension

18. **B.** The first paragraph ends with the claim that "the immensity of this cave is mind-boggling." The second paragraph provides evidence to bolster that claim (B); each sentence lists new information supporting the "mind-boggling" assertion. Choice A is inaccurate because it reverses the information in the paragraphs. The *second* paragraph mentions other caves and the *first* does not. Additionally, choice A does not address the *relationship* between the two paragraphs; it merely relates what each paragraph "mentions." Choice C is incorrect for the same reason; it does not specifically address the relationship between the paragraphs. D is factually wrong; the second paragraph does offer information about other caves in the world. Choice E is incorrect because it states that the second paragraph provides a conclusion to the first, a claim which is simply not accurate.

19. **A and B.** One can reasonably infer the statement in answer choice A. Since two huge caves have been recently discovered in the area of the Phong Nha-ke Bang National Park, the Hang Khe Ry River cave and enormous Hang Son Doong cave, it is quite possible that there are more as-yet unexplored caves awaiting discovery. Choice B is supported by the fact that 100-foot tall trees grow in sunlight falling through a huge sinkhole. Since trees of such large size can exist in the cave, it is logical to conclude that other plants must also thrive. Choice C, however, is not supported by the passage. While the passage states that the Hang Son Doong cave "may very well [be] the largest cave in the world," this phrase is not definite enough for us to assume that it is *certainly* the largest cave.

20. **A and C.** One can infer that spoken language in the African-American community has played a stronger role than has written language (choice A) because the passage states that "oral tradition has been *the major vehicle* by which ideas and stories were passed from generation to generation in the African-American community." One can also easily infer that if oral tradition has been the "major vehicle" for ideas, it can also be called a "dominant force" in the community (C). The passage offers no solid support for the idea that written language will gain more influence with the publication of sermons and rap lyrics (B); indeed, the passage makes no mention of any publications at all.

Section 4: Quantitative Reasoning

1. **A.** The possible values for x and y are 1 and 24, 2 and 12, 3 and 8, or 4 and 6.

    The greatest sum of x and y is 25, $(1 + 24)$. The least absolute value difference of x and y is 2, $(|6 - 4| = |4 - 6| = 2)$.

    Quantity A $= \sqrt{25} = 5$. Quantity $= (2)^2 = 4$. Quantity A is greater.

2. **C.** The decimal name for $\frac{6}{7}$ is found by dividing 7 into 6. This creates a repeating decimal with 6 digits in the repeating pattern. Every 6th digit is 2 and the digit preceding it is 4. Thus, the 24th digit is 2. The 23rd digit is the one that precedes the 24th digit, so it is 4.

$$\frac{0.857142857142...}{7\overline{)6.000000000000...}}$$

    The two quantities have equal value.

3. **C.** Since the area of rectangle $ABDE$ is 36 and $DE = 4$, then $AE = 9$, thus $x + y = 9$. Since the area of trapezoid $ABCE$ is 24, the area of triangle CDE is 12.

    The area of $\triangle CDE = \frac{1}{2}(DE)(CD)$; $12 = \frac{1}{2}(4)(y) \Rightarrow y = 6$. With $x + y = 9$ and $y = 6$, then $x = 3$. $x^3 = 3^3 = 27$ and $y^2 = 6^2 = 36$. $\frac{y^2}{x^3} = \frac{36}{27} = \frac{4}{3}$.

    The two quantities are equal.

4. **D.** The false assumption made here is to assume that the integers are all different and that they are 1, 2, 3, 4, 5. In that case, the mean and the median would both be 3. But set A could have had the integers 1, 1, 1, 2, 5. In this case, the median is 1 and the mean is 2.

    The relationship cannot be determined from the information given.

5. **B.**

$$|x - 5| = x \Rightarrow x - 5 = x \quad \text{or} \quad x - 5 = -x \Rightarrow x = 2.5$$
$$-5 = 0 \quad \text{or} \quad 2x = 5$$
$$\text{not possible} \quad \text{or} \quad x = 2.5$$

$$|y - 3| = y \Rightarrow y - 3 = y \quad \text{or} \quad y - 3 = -y \Rightarrow y = 1.5$$
$$-3 = 0 \quad \text{or} \quad 2y = 3$$
$$\text{not possible} \quad \text{or} \quad y = 1.5$$

$$(x - y)^5 = (2.5 - 1.5)^5 = 1^5 = 1, \quad \sqrt{x + y} = \sqrt{2.5 + 1.5} = \sqrt{4} = 2$$

    Quantity B is greater.

6. **C.** There are 12 integers between –6 and 7, (–5, –4, –3, –2, –1, 0, 1, 2, 3, 4, 5, 6). Of these, only 2, 3, and 5 are prime numbers. The probability of selecting a prime number at random is then $\frac{3}{12} = \frac{1}{4} = 0.25$. The two quantities are equal in value.

7. **A.** The number of arrangements of the 5 different letters, A, B, C, D, E, is a permutation of 5 things taken 5 at a time which is 5! or $(5)(4)(3)(2)(1) = 120$. The number of committees of two that can be formed from a group of 15 is a combination of 15 things taken two at a time.

$$_{15}C_2 = \frac{15!}{2!(15-2)!} = \frac{(15)(14)(13!)}{2!\,13!} = \frac{(15)(14)}{2} = 105$$

Quantity A is greater.

8. **B.** This problem involves finding the number of possible selections for the red marbles and then the number of selections for the blue marbles and then, since these selections are independent, multiplying those two quantities together. Each computation is a combinations problem. The formula for combinations is

$_nC_r = \dfrac{n!}{r!(n-r)!}$. For the red marbles, you are selecting 2 from 8. The number of ways this can be done is

$_8C_2 = \dfrac{8!}{2!(8-2)!} = \dfrac{8!}{2!(6)!} = \dfrac{8 \times 7 \times 6!}{2!(6)!} = \dfrac{8 \times 7}{2 \times 1} = 28$. For the blue marbles, you are selecting 2 from 4. The

number of ways this can be done is $_4C_2 = \dfrac{4!}{2!(4-2)!} = \dfrac{4!}{2!(2)!} = \dfrac{4 \times 3 \times 2!}{2!(2)!} = \dfrac{4 \times 3}{2 \times 1} = 6$. Multiplying the two results gives $28 \times 6 = 168$.

If you forget the formula, then for the red marbles there are 8 ways of choosing the first red marble and then 7 ways of choosing the second one (since one is already selected). Multiplying gives 56. But this total involves duplicates (for example, choose the first and then the third or choose the third then the first), we must divide by the number of ways we can order the choices, in this case, 2. So dividing 56 by two gives the result of 28. The same technique could be used for the blue marbles. For the blue marbles, there are 4 ways of choosing the first blue marble and then 3 ways of choosing the second one. Multiplying gives 12. But this total again involves duplicates. Divide by the number of ways we can order the choices, in this case, 2. So, dividing by two gives the result of 6.

(Note: If you were selecting 3 out of 8, then you would multiply $8 \times 7 \times 6$ and divide by the number of ways of arranging three selections, which is 6. In this case the total would be 56.)

9. $\dfrac{6}{11}$ This problem involves finding the ratio between the number of possible selections where neither ball is blue and the total ways of selecting 2 from the bag of 12. Each computation is a combinations problem. The formula for combinations is $_nC_r = \dfrac{n!}{r!(n-r)!}$. Since the bag contains 12 ping-pong balls and 3 are blue, 9 are not blue. So first find the number of ways of selecting 2 ping-pong balls from 9 nonblue ping-pong balls. $_9C_2 = \dfrac{9!}{2!(9-2)!} = \dfrac{9!}{2!\,7!} = \dfrac{9 \times 8 \times 7!}{2!\,7!} = \dfrac{9 \times 8}{2 \times 1} = 36$. Next, find the number of ways of selecting 2 ping-pong balls from the total of 12 ping-pong balls. $_{12}C_2 = \dfrac{12!}{2!(12-2)!} = \dfrac{12!}{2!\,10!} = \dfrac{12 \times 11 \times 10!}{2!\,10!} = \dfrac{12 \times 11}{2 \times 1} = 66$.

Dividing gives $\dfrac{36}{66}$. For fill-in type questions you do not have to reduce, so $\dfrac{36}{66}$ would be an acceptable answer. You could reduce giving $\dfrac{18}{33}$ or $\dfrac{12}{22}$ or the full reduced ratio of $\dfrac{6}{11}$.

If you have forgotten the combinations formula, you could use the following logic. Find the probability that the first ball is not blue and multiply that with the probability that the second is not blue given that the first was not blue. The probability that the first is not blue is $\dfrac{9}{12}$. Since a blue was not selected, there will be 8 balls of the remaining 11 balls that are not blue. The probability of selecting a second ball that is not blue is $\dfrac{8}{11}$. Then the probability of selecting two balls that are not blue becomes $\left(\dfrac{9}{12}\right)\left(\dfrac{8}{11}\right) = \dfrac{72}{132}$. Since this is a fill-in question, the ratio could be left this way, or simplified to $\dfrac{12}{22}$ or $\dfrac{6}{11}$.

This problem asked for the probability to be written as a ratio. If a decimal response or percentage response was required, then dividing would give approximately 0.545 or about 54.5%.

10. **D.** One method to solve this kind of problem is to use a tree-diagram.

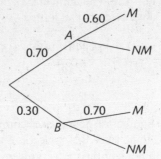

Married and Plan A: $(0.70)(0.60) = 0.42$

Married and Plan B: $(0.30)(0.70) = 0.21$

Total Married: $0.42 + 0.21 = 0.63$

Divide the Plan A Married by the total Married: $\frac{0.42}{0.63} = \frac{2}{3}$

Another method is to use a table of values. Note: It is not necessary to complete the table or the diagram to find the right answer.

	Plan A	Plan B	Total
Married	$(0.70)(0.60) = 0.42$	$(0.30)(0.70) = 0.21$	$0.42 + 0.21 = 0.63$
Not Married			
Total	0.70	0.30	1.00

Divide the Plan A Married by the total Married: $\frac{0.42}{0.63} = \frac{2}{3}$

11. **A, B, C, and D.** There are nine ages in the list. The median age, the middle age of the ordered list, would be the fifth one, or x. Since both w and x can be the same age, they could both be 7. Therefore, 7 is the smallest possible value for the median age. If z is 13 and y is 12, then x could be 11. Therefore, 11 is the largest possible value for the median age. Thus, the values from 7 through 11 are possible answers.

12. **D.** For Set A, 640 is factored as $2^7 \times 5$. The unique factors that are not multiples of 4 are 1, 2, 5, and 10.

    For Set B, 750 is factored as $2 \times 3 \times 5^3$. The unique factors that are not multiples of 5 are 1, 2, 3, and 6.

    The sum of the numbers in Set A is 18. The sum of the numbers in Set B is 12. The difference is 6.

13. **C.** To solve this kind of problem, consider the fractional part of the job done by each machine. Since Machine A could do the job alone in 10 hours and actually worked for 4 hours, Machine A did $\frac{4}{10}$ of the job. To complete the job, Machine B must do the remaining portion of the job, or $\frac{6}{10}$ of the job. Since Machine B can do the job alone in 12 hours, $\frac{x}{12} = \frac{6}{10}$. Solving for x gives you the amount of time Machine B actually worked. The complete solution is as follows:

$$\frac{\text{actually worked (A)}}{\text{alone (A)}} + \frac{\text{actually worked (B)}}{\text{alone (B)}} = 1$$

$$\frac{4}{10} + \frac{x}{12} = 1$$

$$\frac{x}{12} = \frac{6}{10}$$

$$10x = 72$$

$$x = 7.2$$

Therefore, Machine B worked 7.2 hours. Since there are 60 minutes in one hour, 0.1 hours is 6 minutes. So 7.2 hours is the same as 7 hours 12 minutes. Since Machine B started working at 9:00 a.m., it will finish at 4:12 p.m.

14. **B.** Salesperson D accounted for 35% of the March sales for ABC Insurance. To determine the total March sales for ABC Insurance, divide Salesperson D's sales by 35%: $\frac{\$28,000}{0.35} = \$80,000$. Using this total March amount, the total sales for each of the other salespersons can be determined.

> Salesperson A: (0.30)($80,000) = $24,000
> Salesperson B: (0.20)($80,000) = $16,000
> Salesperson C: (0.15)($80,000) = $12,000
> Salesperson D: (0.35)($80,000) = $28,000

Multiply each salespersons sales total by their respective percentages for Auto:

> Salesperson A: (0.30)($24,000) = $7,200
> Salesperson B: (0.40)($16,000) = $6,400
> Salesperson C: (0.20)($12,000) = $2,400
> Salesperson D: (0.40)($28,000) = $11,200

Add to find the total: $7,200 + $6,400 + $2,400 + $11,200 = $27,200

Once the total March sales of $80,000 is known, the computation could be shortened by simply dealing with the percentages:

$$(0.30)(0.30) + (0.40)(0.20) + (0.20)(0.15) + (0.40)(0.35) = 0.34$$

Then multiply this total percentage for auto by the gross March sales total:

$$(0.34)(\$80,000) = \$27,200$$

15. **9,000** Life amounted to 20% of Salesperson B's total March sales. To get Salesperson B's total March sales, divide $4,000 for Life by 20%: $\frac{\$4,000}{0.20} = \$20,000$. Since this $20,000 is 20% of the company's total, the total March sales for ABC Insurance is $100,000. Salesperson A represents 30% of ABC Insurance's March sales, or 30% of $100,000 is $30,000. Salesperson A's Auto sales is 30% of this amount, or (0.30)($30,000) = $9,000.

16. **C.** Multiply each salesperson's Life percentage by that salesperson's company percentage and add them up:

$$(0.30)(0.30) + (0.20)(0.20) + (0.50)(0.15) + (0.30)(0.35) = 0.31$$

This technique would work with any company total. You could pick a value for the March total for ABC Insurance, compute each salesperson's March Life sales, take the sum and then divide to find the overall percentage. This clearly would be an alternative approach requiring a great deal of computation.

17. **5** The relationships can be summarized as: $T = R + 7$, $B = 2A$, $R = B + 3$. The value of A is only represented in one relationship. So, assign a value to A and then calculate the rest of the values. Keep increasing the value of A until the sum gets as close to 60 as possible. The following table illustrates the results:

A	B	R	T	Total
1	2	5	12	20
2	4	7	14	27
3	6	9	16	34
4	8	11	18	41
5	10	13	20	48
6	12	15	22	55

The difference between the largest sum and 60 is 5. As you start filling in the table, some patterns should become clear. For example as A increases by one, the other three values increase by 2. Therefore, the total increases by 7. As soon as you determine the pattern, the sequence of totals can be determined without additional computation.

An algebraic solution can be constructed as follows. Write each variable in terms of A. Then, add up the four variables. $B = 2A$, $R = B + 3 = 2A + 3$, $T = R + 7 = (2A + 3 + 7 = 2A + 10)$. Adding gives $(A) + (2A) + (2A + 3) + (2A + 10) = 7A + 13$. Therefore, $7A + 13 < 60$, or $7A < 47$. The largest value of A that satisfies this inequality, is 6, and $(7)(6) + 13 = 55$. Now subtract from 60 to get the required answer of 5.

18. D. Let y be the average of x and z. Then $y = \dfrac{x+z}{2}$.

Solve for x as follows:
$$y = \frac{x+z}{2}$$
$$2y = x + z$$
$$2y - z = x$$

19. C. First, construct relationships for the three numbers in terms of the first number.

Let the first number $= x$

Then the second number $= 2x + 1$

Then the third number $= (3)(2x + 1) - 4 = 6x + 3 - 4 = 6x - 1$

Then set up an equation and solve:

$$\frac{(x) + (2x+1) + (6x-1)}{3} = 57$$
$$(x) + (2x+1) + (6x-1) = (57)(3)$$
$$9x = 171$$
$$x = 19$$

The values of the three numbers are:

First number $= x = 19$

Second number $= 2x + 1 = (2)(19) + 1 = 39$

Third number $= 6x - 1 = (6)(19) - 1 = 113$

The value of the second number is in the middle of the ordered numbers, and is median. To find the difference between the mean and median, subtract:

$$\text{mean} - \text{median} = 57 - 39 = 18$$

20. B and E Write an equation using the relationships defined in the functions:

$$g(f(a)) = g(2a - 3) = (2a - 3)^2 + 2 = 51$$
$$(2a - 3)^2 + 2 = 51$$
$$4a^2 - 12a + 9 + 2 = 51$$
$$4a^2 - 12a + 11 = 51$$
$$4a^2 - 12a - 40 = 0$$
$$a^2 - 3a - 10 = 0$$
$$(a - 5)(a + 2) = 0$$
$$a = 5 \text{ and } a = -2$$

Section 5: Verbal Reasoning

Text Completion

1. **E.** Choice E is the correct word to complete this sentence. The word *epistolary* literally means "conducted by epistles," or communication by letters. On the other hand, since these events took place over two centuries ago, the word *electronic* (A) cannot be appropriate. The words *evanescent* (B) and *ephemeral* (C) both refer to something that does not last very long, which is the opposite of the Adams's pen-and-paper letters. Finally, the word *explicable* (D) means something that can be explained; the Adams's relationship *was* explained, but it was through the study of the epistolary record, the many letters exchanged by the couple.

2. **C and F.** The passage indicates that Yuri Gagarin had "great fame;" thus the correct answer for first blank cannot be *consigned to oblivion* (A) and, likewise, it cannot be *considered as abstruse* (B), which means hidden away. So, knowing that *acknowledged as preeminent* (C) fits in the first blank (whether or not you agree with the statement's veracity), you can then evaluate the choices for the second blank. The word *deigned* means to condescend, so you can eliminate choice D. Choice E is also incorrect; since Gagarin is preeminent, experts would never *condescend* to explain his death in a mysterious crash. Thus, *struggled* (F) is the correct choice for the second blank. Gagarin *was* famous and his name *is* still preeminent, so experts will continue struggling to solve the mysterious crash in which he perished.

3. **B and D.** The most efficient way to answer this particular question may be to start by filling in the second blank first. When the subject is something like "childhood obesity," it is obvious that a decrease in the rate would be seen as good and an increase in the rate seen as bad; this will eliminate choice E, which states that a decrease is *unhealthy.* It also eliminates choice F, *no change,* which does not cohere with the rest of the sentence, leaving choice D, *a troubling increase,* as the correct answer. Now that you know the answer for the second blank, you can look for its paradox to fill the first blank. The correct choice is B; in spite of the *profuse* choices of fresh food that are available, paradoxically, Los Angeles still suffers from *a troubling increase* in childhood obesity.

4. **B and F.** When such a monumental event happens, the normal pattern is for the media to arrive en masse to gather and report news; therefore, the idea of the media *descending on the hamlet* (B) is apropos. The media were not seen as *joining the village* (A) because the passage states that they were "stalking and hounding the residents." For the second blank, choice F makes the most sense, as it restates typical media behavior in any tragedy: They badger the locals to get *any new reaction to the tragedy.* Knowing that the plane was simply flying over the hamlet, residents are sufficiently unlikely to know anyone on the plane (E) or have any information regarding the cause of the crash (D), making motives along these lines by the media illogical.

5. **A, F, and I.** For the first blank, the word "barren" leads us directly to the best choice, the word *austere,* which means very plain, (A). For the second blank, you need to find a word that reflects the optimistic confidence of the generals, who were convinced that the *Falcon* would be chosen as the next air-to-air missile; *sanguine* (F), which means confident, fits this meaning. The quiet young pilot, who held the "only dissenting opinion," may be best described by the word *taciturn* (I), which means reserved and unpretentious. Choices G and H are both wrong for the same reason; they each refer to a talkative and lighthearted person, quite the opposite of this quiet young pilot.

6. **C, E, and I.** One meaning of the word *consummate* (C) is to complete a business deal; this idea is exactly what is needed to fill the first blank, a word meaning to finalize the agreement between the XYZ Aerospace Corporation and the nation of Trinidad. Only the word *commercial* (E) fits the context of the second blank; both of the other choices contradict the concept of "tourist-friendly" that this sentence includes. The third blank needs a word that indicates one effect will follow a previous cause. The nation of Trinidad, confident in the success of the project, predicts that a *consequent* (I) "economic boom" will follow. Both *antecedent* (G) and *precedent* (H) are the opposite of what is needed, meaning that "economic boom" would come before the space program.

Reading Comprehension

7. **C.** Choice C is the most accurate summary; this body of water has "come and gone" for centuries. Choices A and D are each too limited in scope; the Salton Sea has been *both* a natural and a man-made phenomena. Both choices B and E contradict facts in the passage, which states this body of water "dried up completely about 300 years ago" and that the current lake was created by the "failure of a man-made aqueduct."

8. **E.** All of these statements agree with the information in the passage, except for choice E, which incorrectly states that the Salton Sea drains into the Gulf of California. In fact, the passage indicates that "the area has no natural outlet."

9. **A.** In the second sentence, the phrase "appearing aloof and surly" intimates that Raphael had mixed feelings; he did not entirely admire his competitor. In the fourth sentence, the phrase "condescension Raphael felt for his contemporary" reinforces the idea that Raphael felt disdain for Michelangelo. Choices B, C, and D do not accurately answer this question; they do not clarify the author's purpose. Choice E contradicts the passage, which describes the figure in the painting as "aloof and surly," terms that do not indicate respect.

10. **Sentence 5: They note that, while natural disasters have been fairly regular throughout earth's recent eons, today there are so many more people, especially those living in poverty, who now build poorly-constructed houses in less-desirable locations, such as near earthquake faults, at the base of volcanoes, and in the direct line of flood zones.** To choose the accurate answer for this question, you must first pinpoint the author's conclusion. It is located in the 6th (last) sentence: "Perhaps the earth alone is not entirely to blame for the increased loss of life in natural disasters." The preceding sentence (the 5th) sets up this conclusion by providing specific evidence through listing the ways in which man has placed himself directly in the path of potential natural disasters: building poorly-constructed houses on earthquake faults, at the base of volcanoes, or in the line of flood zones. Sentence 4 does contain some evidence for the passage's conclusion by mentioning "population growth…mankind's lifestyle, and…shoddy building practices," but these considerations alone are not specific enough to be considered the "strongest evidence" for the conclusion. None of the other sentences provides specific evidence for this conclusion.

11. **D.** This question requires the reader to identify an *assumption* underlying the dispute, and an assumption is never stated explicitly, so you can quickly eliminate any answer choice that merely parrots facts from the passage. In this case, both choices A and E are correct factually, but neither statement is an assumption, so neither one can be the correct answer to this question. Likewise, choice C is probably correct in stating that many Cherokees live in Oklahoma today, but that is a fact, not an underlying assumption. Choice B is not supported by the passage; the relocation of most tribes was not, in fact, voluntary. On the other hand, the correct idea is presented in choice D, tribal life was entirely devastated, which is not a quote from the passage; rather, it is an implicit assumption that underlies the argument without actually being stated.

12. **A.** Any accurate restatement of a writer's main point must both agree with the facts he or she cites in the passage and it must somehow include "the big picture." Of these answer choices, choice A is the best statement of this writer's main point, namely that he or she feels that Native American tribes have been treated deplorably by both the settlers and the government and this process has, indeed, amounted to an undesignated genocide. The other answer choices either restate facts from the passage (B) or they contradict facts from the passage (C, D, and E).

Sentence Equivalence

13. **C and E.** A community activist who feels that he or she is not getting answers to requests for public records would be upset (*perturbed*, choice E) over the lack of response. He or she would therefore want others to share this frustration and worry (*apprehension*, choice C) about what else the city is "hiding." Choice A (*serene*) means calm, the opposite of the intent in this sentence. *Phlegmatic* (B) means unemotional or difficult to arouse. Neither choice D (*philosophical*) nor F (*disinterested*) fits the context of the sentence.

14. **B and D.** The NFL official is searching for any violations of the dress code. The only answers that fit this concept are *breaches of* (B) and *transgressions against* (D). All of the other answer choices contradict the meaning of the sentence.

15. **B and D.** The best words to complete this sentence are *consequences* (B) and *ramifications* (D), both of which correctly note the author's concern for the long-term effects of the oil industry. Choices A, C, and E all misidentify the author's point as explicating the inception of the oil industry, rather than its long-term effects. Choice F, *moribundity,* actually means "near death" or "in decline."

16. **C and E.** The key word in the sentence is "daunting," which means intimidating or discouraging, so the correct word choices must reflect this negative tone. This eliminates choice A, *benefits,* and choice B, *promise,* because these words are too positive-sounding to fit the tone of the sentence. Also, choices D and F, which refer to the beginning or end of such agriculture, do not fit the sentence correctly. Thus, choices C, *challenges,* and E, *obstructions,* are correct, because they both continue the concept of "daunting" that immediately precedes the blank.

Reading Comprehension

17. **D.** Choice D provides the best summary of this author's overall point, that Lawrence not only created improbable victories on the battlefield, but also that the public adulation and the media spotlight were thrust upon him, for better or for worse. On the other hand, the passage never mentions the idea of a *warrior-poet* (A), nor does it state that Lawrence was the *only notable hero* of the war (B), nor does it imply that he was only a *mediocre* soldier (E). The passage does indicate that Lawrence wore native robes to good effect (C), but that is merely a single explicit fact; it is not the author's main point of the passage.

18. **A.** Choice A is the only answer that correctly restates facts from this passage. There is no evidence that he *cashed in* on his celebrity, so choice B is eliminated. Also, even though choice C presents a statement that is almost certainly true, Lawrence *did* work for the benefit of the tribes, this information is not mentioned in the passage, so it cannot be a correct answer for this question.

19. **D.** Choice D is an inference that can be logically drawn from this passage. The researcher described techniques to avoid direct contact with the wild gorillas, and he or she mentioned the goal was to avoid stressing the gorillas; thus it is logical to conclude that the gorillas will react negatively to such encounters. Choices A, B, and C are not supported by the information in the passage. Choice E contradicts the passage; apparently, the researchers *can* accurately estimate the gorilla population through these indirect methods.

20. **E.** All of these statements agree with the information in the passage, except for choice E, which incorrectly states that the researchers will try to make actual visual sightings of specific individual gorillas to conduct their census.

Section 6: Quantitative Reasoning

1. **A.** In order to simplify the expression in Quantity A, rewrite both x and z in terms of y. Using fractions, x is 25% of y becomes $x = \frac{1}{4}y$ and y is 75% of z becomes $y = \frac{3}{4}z$ or $z = \frac{4}{3}y$. Then

$$\frac{z-x}{y} = \frac{\frac{4}{3}y - \frac{1}{4}y}{y} = \frac{\frac{16}{12}y - \frac{3}{12}y}{y} = \frac{\frac{13}{12}y}{y} = \frac{13}{12},$$ which is greater than 1. Quantity A is greater.

2. **D.** The area of a circle $= \pi r^2$, where r is its radius.

Suppose that the radius of Circle A is 6 and the diameter of Circle B is 8.

Then the area of Circle A is then 36π and the area of circle B is $16\pi \left(\pi \left(4^2 \right) \right)$, which would make Quantity A greater. But suppose the radius of Circle A is again 6 and the diameter of Circle B is now 12. Then the two circles would have the same area of 36π.

The relationship cannot be determined from the information given.

3. **C.** First look to see if there is a relationship between the given equation and the one being used in the comparison.

If you were to divide each side of the given equation by 24, you get the following: $\dfrac{12x - 96y}{24} = \dfrac{8}{24}$.

Simplifying the left side of the equation gives $\dfrac{1}{2}x - 4y$, which is Quantity A, and simplifying the right side of the equation gives $\dfrac{1}{3}$, which is Quantity B. The two quantities are equal.

4. **C.**

$$-3 \ < \ 2x - 1 \ < \ 13 \quad \text{(add 1 to each side of each inequality statement)}$$
$$-2 \ < \ 2x \ < \ 14 \quad \text{(divide each side of each inequality statement by 2)}$$
$$-1 \ < \ x \ < \ 7$$

There are 7 integers that satisfy these conditions, namely 0, 1, 2, 3, 4, 5, and 6. Quantity A has the value 7.

$2^7 = 128$ and $2^8 = 256$, therefore Quantity B has the value 7.

The two quantities are equal.

5. **B.** Machine A produces 300 screws every 75 seconds is equivalent to saying it produces 4 screws every second $\left(\dfrac{300 \text{ screws}}{75 \text{ seconds}} = 4 \text{ screws/sec} \right)$.

Machine B produces 540 screws every $1\dfrac{1}{2}$ minutes is the same as saying it produces 540 screws every 90 seconds, which is equivalent to saying it produces 6 screws every second. If the machines run simultaneously, they produce 10 screws every second.

At this rate, it will take $\dfrac{100{,}000 \text{ screws}}{10 \text{ screws/second}} = 10{,}000$ seconds to produce 100,000 screws. To convert 10,000 seconds to hours, you must divide by (60)(60) or 3,600. $\dfrac{10{,}000 \text{ seconds}}{3{,}600 \text{ seconds/hour}} \approx 2.8$ hours. Quantity B is greater.

6. **B.** The median value is the middle value when the values are listed from smallest to largest.

$n - 5, n - 3, n, \underline{n + 1}, n + 2, n + 3, n + 6$, thus $n + 1$ is the median of Set D.

The mean value is the sum of all the values divided by how many values there are.

$$\frac{(n-5)+(n-3)+n+(n+1)+(n+2)+(n+3)+(n+6)}{7} = \frac{7n+4}{7} = n + \frac{4}{7}$$

Since $1 > \dfrac{4}{7}$, then $n + 1 > n + \dfrac{4}{7}$, thus Quantity B is greater.

7. **B.** Apply the definition to both quantities.

$$12 \otimes 4 = \sqrt{\frac{(12+4)}{(12-4)^2}} = \sqrt{\frac{16}{64}} = \frac{4}{8} = \frac{1}{2} \ (\text{or } 0.5), \ 2 \otimes 8 = \sqrt{\frac{(2+8)}{(2-8)^2}} = \sqrt{\frac{10}{36}} = \frac{\sqrt{10}}{6} \approx 0.53$$

Quantity B is greater.

8. **D.** This figure is a trapezoid and the area of a trapezoid is Area = average of the bases × height = $\left(\dfrac{x+y}{2} \right) h$.

In order for the areas to remain the same both before and after x and y are changed, the sum of x and y must remain the same before and after the change. If x is reduced by 25%, then x becomes $0.75x$. If y is increased by 50%, then y becomes $1.5y$. For the sums to remain the same, $x + y = 0.75x + 1.5y$. Multiplying both sides of the equation by 4 gives $4x + 4y = 3x + 6y$. Subtracting $3x$ and $4y$ from both sides gives $x = 2y$, choice D. This is the best answer since it does not rely on specific values for either x or y. If we let $x = 4$ and $y = 2$, then choice A would also be correct, but not the best answer since it relies on specific values. If we let $x = 8$ and $y = 4$, then answer choice B would also be correct, but not the best answer since it too relies on specific values.

9. **C.** This problem involves probabilities using the normal distribution. Recall that the normal distribution looks like this:

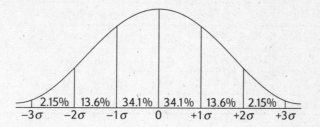

This figure shows the approximate probabilities for each one-standard deviation interval from three standard deviations below the mean to three standard deviations above the mean. In this problem, the mean is 15.8 and the standard deviation is 0.15. The weight of 15.5 ounces is two standard deviations below the mean ($15.8 - 2 \times 0.15 = 15.8 - 0.30 = 15.5$) and the weight of 15.95 ounces is one standard deviation above the mean ($15.8 + 1 \times 0.15 = 15.95$). The sum of the probabilities from two standard deviations below the mean through one standard deviation above the mean is $13.6\% + 34.1\% + 34.1\% = 81.8\%$. These figures are approximate, but clearly 81.8% is in the range from 80%–85%.

10. **12** Clearly, it is too time consuming to actually add all of the integers, even with the supplied online calculator. A logical approach must be found. One such approach is to add the numbers, twice, as follows:

$$100 \ + \ 101 \ + \ 102 \ + \ \ldots \ + \ 198 \ + \ 199 \ + \ 200$$
$$200 \ + \ 199 \ + \ 198 \ + \ \ldots \ + \ 102 \ + \ 101 \ + \ 100$$

Now add the terms vertically. All 101 terms add up to 300. So, simply multiply 300 times 101 giving a product of 30,300. This, of course, is twice what you are actually looking for. Therefore, divide by 2 giving 15,150. The sum of the digits in 15,150 is 12.

11. **B, D, and E.** There are six numbers to test to see if the conditions are met. If the remainder is 1 when the number is divided by 5, then the number must end in 1 or 6. The number 127, choice C, is eliminated. We know that if the sum of the digits of a number is divisible by 3 then the number is too. So, to test for divisibility by 3, subtract the remainder of 2 from each of the remaining numbers and add the digits and see if that sum is divisible by 3.

Test 81: Subtract 2 from 81 and get 79. The sum of 7 and 9 is 16, which is not divisible by 3. Eliminate 81.

Test 116: Subtract 2 from 116 and get 114. The sum of 1, 1, and 4 is 6, which is divisible by 3. Good. This is one of the numbers that satisfies the conditions of the problem.

Continuing this process eliminates 486, leaving 116, 176, and 311 as the numbers that satisfy the conditions of the problem (choices B, D, and E, respectively).

Looking at the problem algebraically, the smallest number that satisfies the conditions is 11. Since we need multiples of 3 and 5, add multiples of 15 to 11. We get a formula of $11 + 15x$, where x is any whole number. In our problem, $11 + 15(7) = 116$, $11 + 15(11) = 176$, and $11 + 15(20) = 311$.

The following approach would make use of the on-screen calculator:

If there is a remainder of 1 when dividing by 5, the decimal remainder must be 0.2. If there is a remainder of 2 when dividing by 3, the decimal remainder must be $0.66\overline{6}$. So merely do the dividing and check on the decimal remainders.

Choice	Divide by 5	Divide by 3	Conditions met?
(A) 81	$81 \div 5 = 16.2$	$81 \div 3 = 27.0$	no
(B) 116	$116 \div 5 = 23.2$	$116 \div 3 = 38.6\overline{66}$	yes
(C) 127	$127 \div 5 = 25.4$	$127 \div 3 = 42.3\overline{33}$	no
(D) 176	$176 \div 5 = 35.2$	$176 \div 3 = 58.6\overline{66}$	yes
(E) 311	$311 \div 5 = 62.2$	$311 \div 3 = 103.6\overline{66}$	yes
(F) 486	$486 \div 5 = 97.2$	$486 \div 3 = 162.0$	no

Only choices B, D, and E meet the conditions.

12. **B.** Tali budgeted 10% for air travel. She spent 20% more, or another 2%, bringing the amount for air travel to 12%. She budgeted 60% for the cruise fare. She spent 10% less than this amount, or 6%, bringing the amount for cruise fare down to 54%. She budgeted 20% for on-board expenses. She spent 20% more than budgeted, or another 4%, bringing the amount for on-board expenses to 24%. She budgeted 10% for gifts. She spent 20% less than budgeted, or 2%, bringing the amount she spent on gifts to 8%. Adding the actual percentages, gives 12% + 54% + 24% + 8% = 98%. She spent approximately 98% of her budgeted amount on her cruise vacation.

13. **A.** First, multiply x by 1.1, since x is being increased by 10%. Then multiply that new salary by 0.85, since this new salary is being reduced by 15%, and so on. One series of products will yield the correct answer as follows: $(1.10)(0.85)(1.20)(0.85)(x) \approx 0.95x$.

14. **B.** Determine the minimum recommended amount for domestic large cap.

Add the percentages for both value and growth domestic large cap investments and multiply by domestic total:

$$(0.10 + 0.10)(\$2,400,000) = \$480,000$$

Determine the minimum recommended amount for international large cap.

Add the percentages for both value and growth international large cap investments and multiply the international total:

$$(0.10 + 0.15)(\$900,000) = \$225,000$$

Find the difference:

$$\$480,000 - \$225,000 = \$255,000$$

15. **660,000** Determine the maximum recommended domestic mid cap investments:

$$(0.15 + 0.15)(\$2,400,000) = \$720,000$$

Determine the minimum recommended domestic mid cap investments:

$$(0.05 + 0.05)(\$2,400,000) = \$240,000$$

Determine the maximum recommended international mid cap investments:

$$(0.20 + 0.20)(\$900,000) = \$360,000$$

Determine the minimum recommended international mid cap investments:

$$(0.10 + 0.10)(\$900{,}000) = \$180{,}000$$

Finally add the maximums and subtract the minimums:

$$\$720{,}000 + \$360{,}000 - \$240{,}000 - \$180{,}000 = \$660{,}000$$

The computation could be shortened by combining all the steps into one:

$$(0.15 + 0.15 - 0.05 - 0.05)(\$2{,}400{,}000) + (0.20 + 0.20 - 0.10 - 0.10)(\$900{,}000)$$
$$= (0.20)(\$2{,}400{,}000) + (0.20)(\$900{,}000)$$
$$= \$660{,}000$$

16. **D.** This problem deals only with percentages of the international portfolio, and ultimately uses only the percentages of the *growth stocks*. From the International Portfolio chart, the minimum recommended percentage for small cap value stocks is 10%, and the minimum recommended percentage for small cap growth stocks is 5%. From the International Portfolio chart, the maximum recommended percentage for large cap value is 25%, and the maximum recommended percentage for large cap growth is also 25%. This now accounts for 65% (10% + 5% + 25% + 25% = 65%) of the portfolio, leaving 35% to be equally divided among the mid-cap stocks. Since $\frac{0.35}{2} = 0.175$, 17.5% of the International portfolio will go to mid-cap value stocks and 17.5% of the portfolio will go to mid-cap growth stocks. Therefore, the percentage of the portfolio that went to growth stocks is 5% + 25% + 17.5%, or 47.5%.

17. **D.** Write each ratio as a fraction and then cross-multiply:

$$\frac{w}{x} = \frac{4}{5} \qquad \frac{x}{y} = \frac{7}{8} \qquad \frac{y}{z} = \frac{3}{2}$$
$$5w = 4x \qquad 8x = 7y \qquad 2y = 3z$$

We want to create a relationship between w and z. We want the x-terms and the y-terms equal in value. Multiply the first equation by 4, the second by 2, and the third by 7 to get the following three equations.

$$4(5w) = 4(4x) \qquad 2(8x) = 2(7y) \qquad 7(2y) = 7(3z)$$
$$20w = 16x \qquad 16x = 14y \qquad 14y = 21z$$

The relationship between w and z is now clear. $20w = 21z$ or $\frac{w}{z} = \frac{21}{20}$. This value is between $\frac{1}{1}$ and $\frac{5}{4}$.

18. **D.** Let x represent the number of months past her 70th birthday until the two plans produce equal amounts. She will have been receiving \$466 per month for the 4 years (48 months) until she was 70 and then will continue to receive this amount for the additional x months.

Under Plan B, Amber waits 4 years, or 48 months to start receiving her payments. To find the break even point, set up an equation and solve:

$$589x = 466(x + 48)$$
$$589x = 466x + (466)(48)$$
$$589x = 466x + 22{,}368$$
$$123x = 22{,}368$$
$$x \approx 182 \text{ months}$$
$$x \approx 15 \text{ years } 2 \text{ months}$$

Therefore, since x represents month from when the \$589 payments start, which is age 70, Amber will be 70 years + 15 years 2 months, which is 85 years 2 months.

19. B and E. Rewriting the equation in slope-intercept form gives $y = \frac{-a}{b}x + \frac{-c}{b}$, where $\frac{-a}{b}$ represents the slope of the line and $\frac{-c}{b}$ represents the y-intercept. If the line passes through the negative y-axis and the positive x-axis, it must have a positive slope and a negative y-intercept. To have a positive slope, both a and b must be of opposite sign. This eliminates choices A and D. Also, to have a negative y-intercept, b and c must have the same sign. This eliminates choice A (again) and choice C. Choices B and E meet both criteria and therefore produce an acceptable line.

Another approach to the problem: Use the given values for a, b, and c and write each equation. Then for each equation find the x- and y-intercepts and see if they make the required conditions true. You find the x-intercept by setting y equal to zero and solving for x, and you find the y-intercept by setting x equal to zero and solving for y.

Answer Choice	a	b	c	Equation	x-intercept	y-intercept	$x > 0$ and $y < 0$
(A)	7	3	−4	$7x + 3y - 4 = 0$	$7x + 3(0) - 4 = 0$ $7x = 4$ $x = \frac{4}{7}$	$7(0) + 3y - 4 = 0$ $3y = 4$ $y = \frac{4}{3}$	No
(B)	−6	2	8	$-6x + 2y + 8 = 0$	$-6x + 2(0) + 8 = 0$ $-6x = -8$ $x = \frac{-8}{-6}$ $x = \frac{4}{3}$	$-6(0) + 2y + 8 = 0$ $2y = -8$ $y = -4$	Yes
(C)	2	−3	8	$2x - 3y + 8 = 0$	$2x - 3(0) + 8 = 0$ $2x = -8$ $x = -4$	$2(0) - 3y + 8 = 0$ $-3y = -8$ $y = \frac{-8}{-3}$ $y = \frac{8}{3}$	No
(D)	−4	−6	−2	$-4x - 6y - 2 = 0$	$-4x - 6(0) - 2 = 0$ $-4x = 2$ $x = -\frac{2}{4}$ $x = -\frac{1}{2}$	$-4(0) - 6y - 2 = 0$ $-6y = 2$ $y = -\frac{2}{6}$ $y = -\frac{1}{3}$	No
(E)	6	−4	−5	$6x - 4y - 5 = 0$	$6x - 4(0) - 5 = 0$ $6x = 5$ $x = \frac{5}{6}$	$6(0) - 4y - 5 = 0$ $-4y = 5$ $y = -\frac{5}{4}$	Yes

Answer choices B and E produce an acceptable line.

20. −12 Solving for x in the first equation and substituting that value into the second expression certainly would work, but involves time-consuming calculations. If you adjust the first equation by adding 1 to both sides, you get $2x^3 + 5 = -4$. The second expression can be written as $3(2x^3 + 5)$. Since $2x^3 + 5 = -4$, $6x^3 + 15 = 3(2x^3 + 5) = 3(-4) = -12$.

Or alternatively, if $2x^3 + 4 = -5$, then $2x^3 = -9$. Multiplying each side of the equation by 3 gives $6x^3 = -27$. Now substitute this for the $6x^3$ in the expression $6x^3 + 15$: $6x^3 + 15 = -27 + 15 = -12$.

Final Preparation

One Week Before the Exam

1. **Clear your schedule** one week before the exam. Try to avoid scheduling appointments or events during this week so that you can focus on your preparation.

2. **GRE website.** Review the GRE website at www.ets.org/gre for updated exam information.

3. **Review your notes** from this study guide and make sure that you know the question types, basic skills, strategies, and directions for each section of the test.

4. **Practice tests.** Allow yourself enough time to review the practice problems you have already completed from this study guide and accompanying CD-ROM. If you haven't yet taken all of the practice tests, take the practice tests during this week. Be sure to time yourself as you practice.

5. **Computer skills development.** Computer-based simulated practice is critical at this time so that the necessary computer skills are fresh in your mind. Taking the practice tests on the accompanying CD-ROM is a good starting point, but for a true computer-based test simulation, go to www.ets.org/gre and take the GRE PowerPrep II practice test. Even if you have already worked these online problems, rework them so that you are at ease with skipping questions, marking questions, moving forward and backward, and using the on-screen calculator.

6. **Testing center.** Make sure that you are familiar with the driving directions to the test center and the parking facilities.

7. **Relax the night before the exam.** The evening before the exam, try to get a good night's sleep. Trying to cram a year's worth of reading and studying into one night can cause you to feel emotionally and physically exhausted. Save your energy for exam day.

Exam Day

1. **Arrive early.** Arrive at the exam location in plenty of time (at least 30 minutes early).

2. **Dress appropriately** to adapt to any room temperature. If you dress in layers, you can always take off clothing to adjust to warmer temperatures.

3. **Identification.** Remember to bring the required identification documents: valid photo-bearing ID and your authorization voucher (if you requested one from ETS).

4. **Electronic devices.** Leave all electronic devices at home or in your car (cell phone, smartphone, PDA, calculator, etc.). You may also be asked to remove your watch during the exam.

5. **Answer easy questions first.** Start off crisply, working the questions you know first (within each section of 20 questions), then going back and trying to answer the others. Use the elimination strategy to determine if a problem is possibly solvable or too difficult to solve.

6. **Don't get stuck on any one question.** Never spend more than $1\frac{1}{2}$ minutes on a multiple-choice question.

7. **Guess** if a problem is too difficult or takes too much time.

8. **Scratch paper** is a test-taking advantage. Use scratch paper to perform calculations, redraw diagrams, note eliminated choices, or simply make helpful notes to jog your memory.

John Wiley & Sons, Inc.
End-User License Agreement

READ THIS. You should carefully read these terms and conditions before opening the software packet(s) included with this book "Book." This is a license agreement "Agreement" between you and John Wiley & Sons, Inc. "Wiley." By opening the accompanying software packet(s), you acknowledge that you have read and accept the following terms and conditions. If you do not agree and do not want to be bound by such terms and conditions, promptly return the Book and the unopened software packet(s) to the place you obtained them for a full refund.

1. **License Grant.** Wiley grants to you (either an individual or entity) a nonexclusive license to use one copy of the enclosed software program(s) (collectively, the "Software") solely for your own personal or business purposes on a single computer (whether a standard computer or a workstation component of a multiuser network). The Software is in use on a computer when it is loaded into temporary memory (RAM) or installed into permanent memory (hard disk, CD-ROM, or other storage device). Wiley reserves all rights not expressly granted herein.

2. **Ownership.** Wiley is the owner of all right, title, and interest, including copyright, in and to the compilation of the Software recorded on the physical packet included with this Book "Software Media." Copyright to the individual programs recorded on the Software Media is owned by the author or other authorized copyright owner of each program. Ownership of the Software and all proprietary rights relating thereto remain with Wiley and its licensers.

3. **Restrictions on Use and Transfer.**

   (a) You may only (i) make one copy of the Software for backup or archival purposes, or (ii) transfer the Software to a single hard disk, provided that you keep the original for backup or archival purposes. You may not (i) rent or lease the Software, (ii) copy or reproduce the Software through a LAN or other network system or through any computer subscriber system or bulletin-board system, or (iii) modify, adapt, or create derivative works based on the Software.

   (b) You may not reverse engineer, decompile, or disassemble the Software. You may transfer the Software and user documentation on a permanent basis, provided that the transferee agrees to accept the terms and conditions of this Agreement and you retain no copies. If the Software is an update or has been updated, any transfer must include the most recent update and all prior versions.

4. **Restrictions on Use of Individual Programs.** You must follow the individual requirements and restrictions detailed for each individual program on the Software Media. These limitations are also contained in the individual license agreements recorded on the Software Media. These limitations may include a requirement that after using the program for a specified period of time, the user must pay a registration fee or discontinue use. By opening the Software packet(s), you agree to abide by the licenses and restrictions for these individual programs that are detailed on the Software Media. None of the material on this Software Media or listed in this Book may ever be redistributed, in original or modified form, for commercial purposes.

5. **Limited Warranty.**

   (a) Wiley warrants that the Software and Software Media are free from defects in materials and workmanship under normal use for a period of sixty (60) days from the date of purchase of this Book. If Wiley receives notification within the warranty period of defects in materials or workmanship, Wiley will replace the defective Software Media.

   (b) WILEY AND THE AUTHOR(S) OF THE BOOK DISCLAIM ALL OTHER WARRANTIES, EXPRESS OR IMPLIED, INCLUDING WITHOUT LIMITATION IMPLIED WARRANTIES OF MERCHANTABILITY AND FITNESS FOR A PARTICULAR PURPOSE, WITH RESPECT TO THE SOFTWARE, THE PROGRAMS, THE SOURCE CODE CONTAINED THEREIN, AND/OR THE TECHNIQUES DESCRIBED IN THIS BOOK. WILEY DOES NOT WARRANT THAT THE FUNCTIONS CONTAINED IN THE SOFTWARE WILL MEET YOUR REQUIREMENTS OR THAT THE OPERATION OF THE SOFTWARE WILL BE ERROR FREE.

   (c) This limited warranty gives you specific legal rights, and you may have other rights that vary from jurisdiction to jurisdiction.